1-2-3 For Dummies

Cheat Sheet

W9-ARP-439

Common Tasks in 1-2-3

To do this:	Type this:
To erase data	/**R**ange **E**rase
To clear screen to start new worksheet	/**W**orksheet **E**rase **Y**es
To change column width	/**W**orksheet **C**olumn **S**et-Width
To choose a new number format	/**R**ange **F**ormat
To choose a new label alignment	/**R**ange **L**abel
To protect the worksheet from further changes	/**W**orksheet **G**lobal **P**rot **E**nable
To designate what cells in the worksheet to print	/**P**rint **P**rinter **R**ange
To print the worksheet	/**P**rint **P**rinter **A**lign **G**o **P**age
To freeze columns and rows on the screen	/**W**orksheet **T**itles **B**oth, **H**orizontal, or **V**ertical
To save a worksheet	/**F**ile **S**ave
To open a worksheet	/**F**ile **R**etrieve

Common Tasks in Wysiwyg

To do This:	Type this:
To choose a new font	:**F**ormat **F**ont
To bold, italicize, or underline text	:**F**ormat **B**old, **I**talics, or **U**nderline
To display worksheets gridlines	:**D**isplay **O**ptions **G**rid **Y**es
To add a border around a cell range	:**F**ormat **L**ines
To shade a cell range	:**F**ormat **S**hade
To center a title across columns	:**T**ext **A**lign **C**enter
To add a graph to your worksheet	:**G**raph **A**dd
To zoom in and out on the worksheet	:**D**isplay **Z**oom
To print entire report on a single paper	:**P**rint **L**ayout **C**ompression **A**utomatic
To print report with the long edge of the paper	:**P**rint **C**onfiguration **O**rientation **L**andscape
To preview the printed report on screen	:**P**rint **P**review

. . . For Dummies: #1 Computer Book Series for Beginners

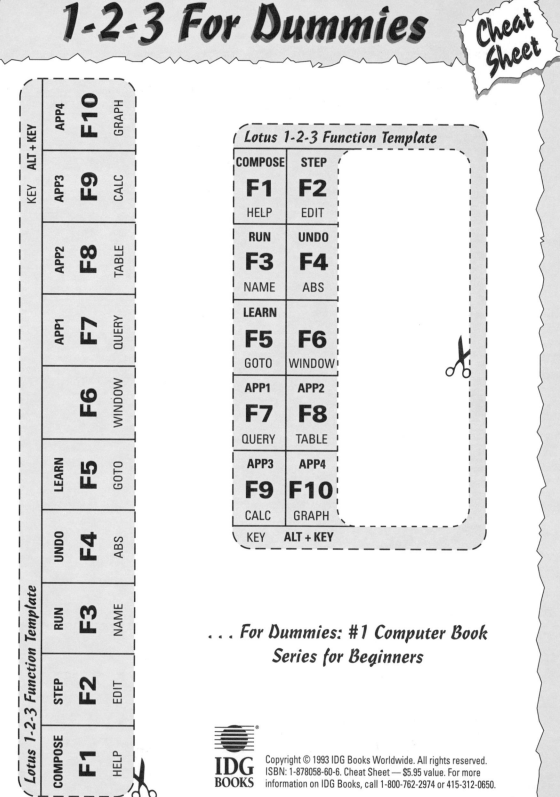

 TM

References for the Rest of Us

COMPUTER BOOK SERIES FROM IDG

Are you intimidated and confused by computers? Do you find that traditional manuals are overloaded with technical details you'll never use? Do your friends and family always call you to fix simple problems on their PCs? Then the *"... For Dummies"*™ computer book series from IDG is for you.

"... For Dummies" books are written for those frustrated computer users who know they aren't really dumb but find that PC hardware, software, and indeed the unique vocabulary of computing make them feel helpless. *"... For Dummies"* books use a lighthearted approach, a down-to-earth style, and even cartoons and humorous icons to diffuse computer novices' fears and build their confidence. Lighthearted but not lightweight, these books are a perfect survival guide to anyone forced to use a computer.

> *"I like my copy so much I told friends; now they bought copies."*
>
> **Irene C., Orwell, Ohio**

> *"Quick, concise, nontechnical, and humorous."*
>
> **Jay A., Elburn, IL**

> *"Thanks, I needed this book. Now I can sleep at night."*
>
> **Robin F., British Columbia, Canada**

Already, hundreds of thousands of satisfied readers agree. They have made *"... For Dummies"* books the #1 introductory level computer book series and have written asking for more. So if you're looking for the most fun and easy way to learn about computers look to *"... For Dummies"* books to give you a helping hand.

IDG BOOKS

1-2-3 FOR DUMMIES™

by Greg Harvey

Foreword by Larry Roshfeld,
Lotus Development Corporation

IDG BOOKS

IDG Books Worldwide, Inc.
An International Data Group Company

San Mateo, California ✦ Indianapolis, Indiana ✦ Boston, Massachusetts

1-2-3 For Dummies

Published by
IDG Books Worldwide, Inc.
An International Data Group Company
155 Bovet Road, Suite 310
San Mateo, CA 94402

Library of Congress Catalog Card No.: 92-75796

ISBN 1-878058-60-6

Printed in the United States of America

10 9 8 7

1B/QV/QS/ZU

Distributed in the United States by IDG Books Worldwide, Inc.

Distributed in Canada by Macmillan of Canada, a Division of Canada Publishing Corporation; by Woodslane Pty. Ltd. in Australia and New Zealand; and by Computer Bookshops in the U.K and Ireland.

For general information on IDG Books in the U.S., including information on discounts and premiums, contact IDG Books at 800-762-2974 or 415-312-0650.

For information on where to purchase IDG Books outside the U.S., contact Christina Turner at 415-312-0633.

For information on translations, contact Marc Jeffrey Mikulich, Foreign Rights Manager, at IDG Books Worldwide; FAX NUMBER 415-358-1260.

For sales inquiries and special prices for bulk quantities, write to the address above or call IDG Books Worldwide at 415-312-0650.

is a registered trademark of
IDG IDG Books Worldwide, Inc.
BOOKS

About the Author

Greg Harvey, the author of over 30 computer books, has been training business people in the use of IBM PC, DOS, and software application programs such as WordPerfect, Lotus 1-2-3, and dBASE since 1983. He has written numerous training manuals, user guides, and books for business users of software. He currently teaches Lotus 1-2-3 and dBASE courses in the Department of Information Systems at Golden Gate University in San Francisco.

About IDG Books Worldwide

Welcome to the world of IDG Books Worldwide.

IDG Books Worldwide, Inc., is a subsidiary of International Data Group, the world's largest publisher of computer-related information and the leading global provider of information services on information technology. International Data Group publishes over 195 computer publications in 62 countries. Forty million people read one or more International Data Group publications each month.

If you use personal computers, IDG Books is committed to publishing quality books that meet your needs. We rely on our extensive network of publications, including such leading periodicals as *Macworld, InfoWorld, PC World, Computerworld, Publish, Network World*, and *SunWorld*, to help us make informed and timely decisions in creating useful computer books that meet your needs.

Every IDG book strives to bring extra value and skill-building instructions to the reader. Our books are written by experts, with the backing of IDG periodicals, and with careful thought devoted to issues such as audience, interior design, use of icons, and illustrations. Our editorial staff is a careful mix of high-tech journalists and experienced book people. Our close contact with the makers of computer products helps ensure accuracy and thorough coverage. Our heavy use of personal computers at every step in production means we can deliver books in the most timely manner.

We are delivering books of high quality at competitive prices on topics customers want. At IDG, we believe in quality, and we have been delivering quality for over 25 years. You'll find no better book on a subject than an IDG book.

John Kilcullen
President and CEO
IDG Books Worldwide, Inc.

IDG Books Worldwide, Inc. is a subsidiary of International Data Group. The officers are Patrick J. McGovern, Founder and Board Chairman; Walter Boyd, President. International Data Group's publications include: **ARGENTINA'S** Computerworld Argentina, Infoworld Argentina; **ASIA'S** Computerworld Hong Kong, PC World Hong Kong, Computerworld Southeast Asia, PC World Singapore, Computerworld Malaysia, PC World Malaysia; **AUSTRALIA'S** Computerworld Australia, Australian PC World, Australian Macworld, Network World, Mobile Business Australia, Reseller, IDG Sources; **AUSTRIA'S** Computerwelt Oesterreich, PC Test; **BRAZIL'S** Computerworld, Gamepro, Game Power, Mundo IBM, Mundo Unix, PC World, Super Game; **BELGIUM'S** Data News (CW) **BULGARIA'S** Computerworld Bulgaria, Ediworld, PC & Mac World Bulgaria, Network World Bulgaria; **CANADA'S** CIO Canada, Computerworld Canada, Graduate Computerworld, InfoCanada, Network World Canada; **CHILE'S** Computerworld Chile, Informatica; **COLOMBIA'S** Computerworld Colombia; **CZECH REPUBLIC'S** Computerworld, Elektronika, PC World; **DENMARK'S** CAD/CAM WORLD, Communications World, Computerworld Danmark, LOTUS World, Macintosh Produktkatalog, Macworld Danmark, PC World Danmark, PC World Produktguide, Windows World; **ECUADOR'S** PC World Ecuador; **EGYPT'S** Computerworld (CW) Middle East, PC World Middle East; **FINLAND'S** MikroPC, Tietoviikko, Tietoverkko; **FRANCE'S** Distributique, GOLDEN MAC, InfoPC, Languages & Systems, Le Guide du Monde Informatique, Le Monde Informatique, Telecoms & Reseaux; **GERMANY'S** Computerwoche, Computerwoche Focus, Computerwoche Extra, Computerwoche Karriere, Information Management, Macwelt, Netzwelt, PC Welt, PC Woche, Publish, Unit; **GREECE'S** Infoworld, PC Games; **HUNGARY'S** Computerworld SZT, PC World; **INDIA'S** Computers & Communications; **IRELAND'S** Computerscope; **ISRAEL'S** Computerworld Israel, PC World Israel; **ITALY'S** Computerworld Italia, Lotus Magazine, Macworld Italia, Networking Italia, PC Shopping Italy, PC World Italia; **JAPAN'S** Computerworld Today, Information Systems World, Macworld Japan, Nikkei Personal Computing, SunWorld Japan, Windows World; **KENYA'S** East African Computer News; **KOREA'S** Computerworld Korea, Macworld Korea, PC World Korea; **MEXICO'S** Compu Edicion, Compu Manufactura, Computacion/ Punto de Venta, Computerworld Mexico, MacWorld, Mundo Unix, PC World, Windows; **THE NETHERLANDS'** Computer! Totaal, Computable (CW), LAN Magazine, MacWorld, Totaal "Windows"; **NEW ZEALAND'S** Computer Listings, Computerworld New Zealand, New Zealand PC World; **NIGERIA'S** PC World Africa; **NORWAY'S** Computerworld Norge, C/World, Lotusworld Norge, Macworld Norge, Networld, PC World Ekspress, PC World Norge, PC World's Produktguide, Publish& Multimedia World, Student Data, Unix World, Windowsworld; IDG Direct Response; **PANAMA'S** PC World Panama; **PERU'S** Computerworld Peru, PC World; **PEOPLE'S REPUBLIC OF CHINA'S** China Computerworld, China Infoworld, PC World China, Electronics International, Electronic Product World, China Network World; IDG HIGH TECH BEIJING'S New Product World; IDG SHENZHEN'S Computer News Digest; **PHILIPPINES'** Computerworld Philippines, PC Digest (PCW); **POLAND'S** Computerworld Poland, PC World/Komputer; **PORTUGAL'S** Cerebro/PC World, Correio Informatico/ Computerworld, MacIn; **ROMANIA'S** Computerworld, PC World; **RUSSIA'S** Computerworld-Moscow, Mir - PC, Sety; **SLOVENIA'S** Monitor Magazine; **SOUTH AFRICA'S** Computer Mail (CIO), Computing S.A., Network World S.A.; **SPAIN'S** Amiga World, Computerworld Espana, Communicaciones World, Macworld Espana, NeXTWORLD, Super Juegos Magazine (GamePro), PC World Espana, Publish, Sunworld; **SWEDEN'S** Attack, ComputerSweden, Corporate Computing, Lokala Natverk/LAN, Lotus World, MAC&PC, Macworld, Mikrodatorn, PC World, Publishing & Design (CAP), Datalngenjoren, Maxi Data, Windows World; **SWITZERLAND'S** Computerworld Schweiz, Macworld Schweiz, PC Katalog, PC & Workstation; **TAIWAN'S** Computerworld Taiwan, Global Computer Express, PC World Taiwan; **THAILAND'S** Thai Computerworld; **TURKEY'S** Computerworld Monitor, Macworld Turkiye, PC World Turkiye; **UKRAINE'S** Computerworld; **UNITED KINGDOM'S** Computing /Computerworld, Connexion/Network World, Lotus Magazine, Macworld, Open Computing/Sunworld; **UNITED STATES'** AmigaWorld, Cable in the Classroom, CD Review, CIO, Computerworld, Desktop Video World, DOS Resource Guide, Electronic Entertainment Magazine, Federal Computer Week, Federal Integrator, GamePro, IDG Books, Infoworld, Infoworld Direct, Laser Event, Macworld, Multimedia World, Network World, NeXTWORLD, PC Letter, PC World, PlayRight, Power PC World, Publish, SunWorld, SWATPro, Video Event; **VENEZUELA'S** Computerworld Venezuela, MicroComputerworld Venezuela; **VIETNAM'S** PC World Vietnam.

Acknowledgments

Let me take this opportunity to thank all of the people whose dedication and talent combined to make this book so much fun to write.

At IDG Books, I want to thank John Kilcullen, Terrie and David Solomon, Diane Steele (whose penetrating insights and good humor made working together such fun and helped keep me on schedule), Pat Seiler, Bob Garza, Mary Ann Cordova, Dana Sadoff, Chuck Hutchinson, and the talented folks at University Graphics. Thanks everyone!

At Harvey & Associates, I want to especially thank Shane Gearing for his many contributions to this project, including the "excellent" and informative sample worksheets that appear in the figures along with many invaluable suggestions on how to make learning 1-2-3 fun for the novice user.

(The publisher would like to give special thanks to Patrick J. McGovern, without whom this book would not have been possible.)

Credits

VP & Publisher
David Solomon

Managing Editor
Mary Bednarek

Project Editor
Diane Graves Steele

Production Director
Beth Jenkins

Editor
Patricia A. Seiler

Technical Reviewer
Victor R. Garza

Production Staff
Dana Sadoff
Mary Ann Cordova

Proofreader
Charles A. Hutchinson

Associate Acquisitions Editor
Megg Bonar

Indexers
Dick and Anne Bassler

Book Design
University Graphics, Palo Alto, California

Contents at a Glance

Cartoons at a Glance

By Rich Tennant

Table of Contents

• •

Foreword

Welcome to the world of Lotus 1-2-3!

If you are reading this book, you are probably a new 1-2-3 user. *1-2-3 For Dummies* is an excellent bridge between you, 1-2-3, and the terrific spreadsheets you will soon be creating.

In the pages of this book, you will find that Greg Harvey has combined his talents as a 1-2-3 user, as an author, and particularly as a teacher to present information that skillfully helps you learn the 1-2-3 features and operations you really need to become immediately productive.

Greg shows his understanding of both the software and the new user as he leads you through everything from creating your first spreadsheet to writing your first macro. The lighthearted approach Greg has adopted for this book, the newest entry in IDG Book's highly successful *...For Dummies* series, will accelerate your initiation as a 1-2-3 user, and you'll find yourself enjoying every step along the way.

I am pleased to recommend *1-2-3 For Dummies* to you as an excellent way of rapidly learning how to make the most of your Lotus 1-2-3 software. And may I say that by buying Lotus 1-2-3 and this book you have already proven you are no dummy!

Larry Roshfeld
Senior Product Manager, Spreadsheets
Lotus Development Corporation
Cambridge, Massachusetts
December, 1992

Introduction

●●

*W*elcome to *1-2-3 For Dummies*, the definitive work on using 1-2-3 for those of you who just want to get by without knowing any more than you have to! In this book, you find just enough information to keep your head above water as you accomplish the everyday tasks that normal people (people who don't give a hoot about computers) do with 1-2-3. My intention is to keep things simple and to avoid boring you with a lot of technical details that you neither need nor care a thing about.

1-2-3 For Dummies covers all the fundamental techniques you need to create, edit, format, and print your own worksheets. In addition to learning your way around the worksheet, you get some exposure to the basics of graphing and creating and using the database features offered by 1-2-3.

Keep in mind that this book just touches on the easiest ways to get a few things done with the 1-2-3 features I describe; you'll find no attempt here to cover graphs and databases in anything approaching a definitive way (we'll leave all that to the 1-2-3 wonks). This book concentrates primarily on the worksheet — the part of the program you'll probably be working with almost all the time.

About This Book

As riveting and witty as this book is, I never really thought you would read it from cover to cover! Therefore, although its chapters are loosely organized in a logical manner (progressing as one might when learning 1-2-3 in a classroom situation), the coverage of each topic in a chapter is really meant to stand on its own. Each discussion of a topic attempts to briefly address the question of what a particular feature is good for before launching into how to use it.

In 1-2-3, as with most other sophisticated programs, you can usually find more than just one way to get a particular task done. For the sake of your sanity, I have purposely limited the choices in this book by giving you only what I con- sider to be the most efficient way to do a particular task. Later on, if you're tempted, you can experiment with alternate ways of doing a task — for now, just concentrate on learning how to perform the task as described.

As much as possible, I've made it unnecessary for you to ever have to remember anything that's been covered in another section in the book in order to get something to work in the section you're currently reading. From time to time, however, you will find a cross-reference to another section or chapter in the book. For the most part, these cross-references are meant to help you get more complete information on a subject should you have the time and interest; if you have neither, just ignore the cross-references.

How to Use This Book

This book is like a reference; you can start out by looking up the topic you need information about (either in the table of contents or the index) and then refer directly to the appropriate section. Most topics are explained conversationally (as though you were sitting in the back of my classroom — where you can safely nap).

Sometimes, against my better judgment, the Major General in me takes over, and I list the precise steps that you follow to get a particular task done. These step-by-step sections are meant to be followed like the Seventh Army followed General Patton, unquestioningly and invariably. To put it another way, these steps work just like the numbered footprints on the floor used by Arthur Murray to show the dance steps — the theory is that if you put your feet in the footprints in the order in which they're numbered, well, then you'll be dancing!

What You Can Safely Ignore

When you come across a section that contains the steps you need to take to get something done, you can safely ignore all text accompanying the steps if you find that you have neither the time nor the inclination to wade through more material.

I have, whenever possible, separated the background or footnote type information from the essential facts by exiling the nonessentials to a Technical Stuff section so that you can easily disregard it. Note, too, that the information you find marked with a Tip icon, although designed to help you become more efficient with the program, is also extraneous and can be safely skipped over until you're ready for it.

Foolish Assumptions

I'm going to make only one assumption about you (let's see how close I get): you have access to a PC (at least some of the time) that has installed on it some version of the DOS operating system and Release *x* of 1-2-3 (see "Please Release Me" coming up next). Beyond that, I make only one other assumption about you and that is that you have no previous experience using 1-2-3.

Further, don't worry if you don't have much (okay, any) experience with DOS or you don't really have a clear idea of what 1-2-3 can do for you. If I really feel you need some DOS information that I can't provide within the framework of this little work, I'll let you know that it's time to get out your *DOS For Dummies* book.

Please Release Me

Although you can use this book to learn how to use any version of Release 2 of 1-2-3, this doesn't mean that all the information will pertain to the particular version that you have. (If you are using any version of 1-2-3 Release 3, you can use *1-2-3 For Dummies* to learn the techniques you need as well.)

As of this printing, the four major versions of Release 2 of 1-2-3 are Release 2.0, Release 2.2, Release 2.3, and Release 2.4. As you would expect, with each increase in the release number (most often, but not always, by a tenth of a point), the program contains some new features. Along with new features, you almost invariably find other smaller changes to the way the program operates or appears on-screen in each new release (although in the case of 1-2-3, this is most noticeable when going from Release 2.2 to 2.3; Release 2.0 and 2.2 are almost identical to each other in appearance, as are Release 2.3 and 2.4).

Wherever appropriate in the text, I explicitly point out when an important feature or screen element is not found in all four versions of Release 2. This practice does not, however, guarantee that you won't ever discover undocumented discrepancies in the way a feature is described in the text or appears in a figure (the figures are Release 2.4) and the way it works or looks in your version of 1-2-3. Suffice it to say that if you look for a feature described in the text and you don't find it, or your screen doesn't look exactly the same as the one shown in a particular figure, you probably are not using the same version that I am. But that won't get in your way for learning the program!

How This Book Is Organized

This book is organized in seven parts (so that you get to see seven of these great cartoons!). Each part contains two or more chapters (to keep the editors happy) that more or less go together. Each chapter is further subdivided into loosely related sections that cover the basics of the topic at hand.

You should not, however, get too hung up in following along with the structure of the book because ultimately it doesn't matter at all if you learn how to edit the worksheet before you learn how to format it or learn printing before you learn editing. The important thing is that you are able to find the information and understand it when you need to do any of these things.

Just in case you're interested, here's a brief synopsis of what you'll find in each part:

Part I: The Absolute Basics

As the name implies, this part covers such fundamentals as how to start the program, identify the parts of the screen, enter information in the worksheet, save your document, and so on. If you're starting with absolutely no background in using spreadsheets, you'll certainly want to glance at the information in Chapter 1 before you move on to creating new worksheets in Chapter 2.

Part II: Putting On the Finishing Touches

Part II gives you the skinny on how to make your worksheets look good as well as how to make major editing changes to them without courting disaster. Refer to Chapter 3 when you need information on changing the way your work appears in the worksheet. Refer to Chapter 4 when you need to know about rearranging, deleting, or inserting new information in the worksheet.

Part III: Getting Out and About

Part III is concerned with what you do with the information in a worksheet once you've got it in there. Chapter 5 is full of good ideas on how to keep track of the whereabouts of the information in your worksheet, and Chapter 6 gives you the ins and outs on printing the information.

Part IV: Beyond the Worksheet

Part IV explores some of the aspects of 1-2-3 besides the worksheet. In Chapter 7, you find out just how to graph your worksheet data. In Chapter 8, you find out how useful 1-2-3's database capabilities can be when you have to track and organize a large amount of information. In Chapter 9, you learn how much time and effort you can save yourself by creating and using macros to automate all those repetitive tasks you do day in and day out.

Part V: Wysiwyging through 1-2-3

Part V is for users who are lucky enough to be using Release 2.3 or 2.4 and have enough memory to use the Wysiwyg add-in program and, in the case of 2.4 users, the Icons add-in program. Chapter 10 teaches you how to use Wysiwyg to add fonts, font attributes, borders, and shading to your worksheet. Chapter 10 also covers how to add graphs right in your worksheet and print super-looking reports with the Wysiwyg :**P**rint commands. Chapter 11 teaches you how to use the SmartIcons that have been added in Release 2.4. You also learn how to make your own arrangements on the Custom icon palette, as well as how to assign macros to any of the 12 User Icons.

Part VI: 1-2-3 Function Reference (for Real People)

Part VI gives you valuable information on the use of specific 1-2-3 functions. Chapter 12 covers everyday functions such as @SUM, @AVG, @ROUND, and @NOW. Chapter 13 gets adventurous and covers more sophisticated functions, including the Financial functions @PV and @PMT, the String functions @PROPER, @UPPER, and @LOWER, the special functions @HLOOKUP and @VLOOKUP, and the Logical function @IF.

Part VII: The Part of Tens

Part VII is the Part of Tens. Chapter 14 reviews the ten essential techniques that you'll rely on almost each and every time you use 1-2-3. Chapter 15 lists the 1-2-3 Ten Commandments — the things that you should and shouldn't do when using the program. Chapter 16 contains the ten things that commonly mess up new users. Chapter 17 lists ten important things that will help you be more productive when using 1-2-3.

Conventions Used in This Book

The following information gives you the lowdown on the high points about how things look in this book:

- ✔ When you have to type something exactly, you often find the specific text to type looking like this

```
@SUM(C3..C15,G3..G19,H2..H25)
```

- ✔ Sometimes you are asked to type something that appears right in the text, without its own line. When that happens the word or phrase appears in **bold type.**

- ✔ Text that represents an on-screen message often appears like this

```
Enter address to go to:
```

- ✔ You can also find on-screen information within a sentence or paragraph, such as `C:\>`.

- ✔ The following icons direct you to special kinds of information throughout the book. Just read the explanations to help you decide which ones you want to look for and which ones you want to skip!

This icon flags shortcuts or other valuable hints related to the topic at hand.

This icon flags information you need to keep in mind if you want to meet with a modicum of success.

This icon flags information you need to keep in mind if you want to avert complete disaster!

This icon flags nerdy discussions that you may well want to skip (or save to read when you are alone).

Where to Go from Here

If you've never worked with a computer spreadsheet, I suggest you first go to Chapter 1 and find out what you're dealing with. If you're already familiar with the ins and outs of electronic spreadsheets but don't know anything about creating worksheets with 1-2-3, you might want to jump into Chapter 2 where you'll find out how to get started entering your data and formulas. Then, as specific needs arise (like "How do I copy a formula?" or "How do I print just a particular part of the worksheet?"), you can go to the Table of Contents or the Index to find the appropriate section and then go right to that section for the answers.

Part I
The Absolute Basics

The 5th Wave — By Rich Tennant

The part in which...

You find out that the 1-2-3 worksheet is quite a bit handier than your pocket calculator could ever be, because you learn to create formulas that are automatically recalculated whenever you change the input values the formulas use.

You get a quick look-see at what you're up against, and you learn how to get in and out of 1-2-3 without doing yourself or your computer any irreversible damage. You learn how to get information into a 1-2-3 worksheet — and, more importantly, make it stay there so that you don't have to do your work all over again the next day!

Chapter 1
What's It All About?

As the song says, "the very beginning" is "a very good place to start." So Chapter 1 takes you from the beginning, through the ABCs and 123s, and right to the "how to's" of using the remarkable *spreadsheet!*

After I give you enough info to start 1-2-3, it's only fair that I let you know something about how to behave with your spreadsheets — and how to bail out of the program when you need to. All the while, I'll protect your inalienable right to *not know,* but I'll make sure that you have all the information you need to stay out of trouble.

Who Put the Work in Worksheet?

In the olden days, mankind didn't have computers and sophisticated electronic spreadsheet programs like 1-2-3. Instead, number crunchers used primitive tools: pencils, paper, and hand-held calculators. Our ancestors did financial planning by writing (by hand, mind you) the numbers that they punched up on their calculators onto long green sheets of paper.

These *green sheets* — which, because they were much wider than tall, also became known as *spreadsheets* — had fine gridlines that divided the large sheet into a series of columns and rows. The number cruncher penciled the calculated figures into the spaces created at the intersection of column and row gridlines. The gridlines helped the cruncher line up the numbers in the spreadsheet so that other people could tell whether the numbers referred to widgets, wodgets, or gadgets.

An electronic spreadsheet program like 1-2-3 pays homage to this glorious past by presenting you with a facsimile of the old *green sheet* on your computer screen. In keeping with tradition, the electronic spreadsheet, like its paper spreadsheet counterpart, divides the sheet into a series of columns and rows into which you enter your text and numbers — although the gridlines don't appear in the normal 1-2-3 worksheet (see Figure 1-1).

Note that spreadsheet programs such as 1-2-3 are more apt to refer to their electronic sheets as *worksheets* rather than *spreadsheets*. You should also note that although calling an electronic spreadsheet a *worksheet* is perfectly acceptable (even preferable), you never, never, refer to 1-2-3 as a *worksheet program;* you always call 1-2-3 a *spreadsheet program* (go figure!).

Besides the terminology, the electronic worksheet differs from the traditional paper spreadsheet in one other significant way: the worksheet contains a frame used to label the columns and rows. As you can see in Figure 1-1, columns are labeled by letters of the alphabet, and rows are numbered.

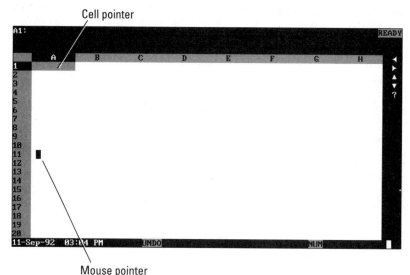

Figure 1-1: Inspired by paper spreadsheets of old, the 1-2-3 *electronic* spreadsheet divides the work area into a series of columns and rows.

The columns and rows are labeled because the 1-2-3 worksheet is humongous. (Figure 1-1 shows only a tiny part of the total worksheet.) Like street signs in a city, the column and row labels help you identify your current location (even when they don't prevent you from becoming lost).

Just how big is this thing?

The 1-2-3 electronic worksheet dwarfs even the largest of paper spreadsheets, consisting as it does of a total of 256 columns and 8,192 rows. If you were to produce the entire worksheet grid on paper, it would be approximately 21 feet wide by 171 feet long!

On a 13-inch monitor screen, you can normally see no more than 8 complete columns and 20 complete rows of the worksheet. Columns are about 1 inch wide, and rows are about ¼ inch high; 8 columns represent a scant 3 percent of the total width of the worksheet, and 20 rows represent about ²⁄₁₀ of one percent of the total length. Now you have some idea of how little of the total worksheet you can see on-screen and just how much area is actually available.

How do I get to 18th and F?

I bring up the facts and figures on the worksheet size not to intimidate you but to make you aware of how important the 1-2-3 worksheet reference system is. This system keeps you informed at all times of your exact position in the worksheet. Because the worksheet is so large, if you do not know where you are placing particular information, you can easily lose track of it.

To help you identify the location of entries and find them again, 1-2-3 not only displays a frame around the worksheet, showing you the column letter and row number, but it also uses these column and row references to keep you constantly informed of your current location.

Figure 1-2 shows you how 1-2-3 gets this vital information to you. In this figure, the current location is the intersection of column F and row 18. The location is indicated in two ways:

✔ In the worksheet, the *cell pointer* highlights this cell.

✔ The column letter and row number appear at the beginning of the first line in the very upper left corner of the screen (the area is identified as the *control panel* in Figure 1-2).

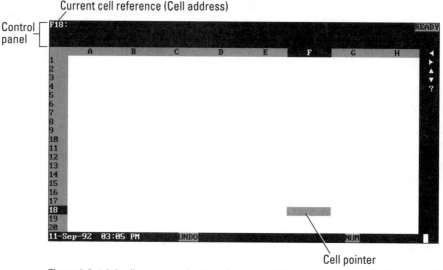

Current cell reference (Cell address)

Control panel

Cell pointer

Figure 1-2: 1-2-3 tells you exactly where in the worksheet world you are by displaying the current column and row reference at the top of the control panel.

In this particular example, because the cell pointer occupies the space at the intersection of column F and row 18, F18 appears at the top of the control panel. F18 identifies your location in the worksheet very similarly to the way that saying to someone, "I'm at the intersection of 18th and F streets," pinpoints your location in town. F18 gives you the current address of the cell pointer relative to a starting point (A and 1st streets, called A1 in 1-2-3).

Pardon me, is this cell occupied?

The space identified by the column letter and row number on the formula bar is called a *cell*. The *cell pointer* highlights the current cell. The worksheet cell works somewhat like a prison cell, at least in the sense that any information that you put into the cell of the worksheet remains *imprisoned* there until you — the warden — either clear the information out or move it to another cell. Unlike cells in a prison, however, a worksheet cell can accommodate only one occupant at a time. If you try to put new information in a cell that is already occupied, 1-2-3 will replace the old occupant with the new one.

Is there life after Z?

Our alphabet, with its mere 26 letters, is certainly not sufficient for labeling the 256 consecutive columns in the 1-2-3 worksheet. To make up the difference, 1-2-3 doubles up the cell letters in the column reference so that column AA immediately follows column Z. Column AA is followed by columns AB, AC, and so on to AZ. After column AZ, you find column BA, then BB, and BC. According to this system for doubling the column letters, the 256th and last column of the worksheet is column IV, and the cell reference of the very last cell in the worksheet is IV8192.

So, what can I do with this thing?

At this point, here's is all you really know about 1-2-3:

- 1-2-3 uses an electronic worksheet modeled after a paper spreadsheet.
- The worksheet is divided into columns and rows. It contains a frame that labels the columns with letters and the rows with numbers.
- You enter information in the areas formed by the intersections of columns and rows, which are known as cells.

With just this much information, you could easily get the mistaken idea that a spreadsheet program such as 1-2-3 is little more than a word processor with gridlock that forces you to enter information in tiny, individual cells instead of offering you the spaciousness of full pages. Who would want to bother with such a disaster?

Read on. The big difference between the cell of a worksheet and the pages of a word processor is that *each cell offers computing power along with text editing and formatting capabilities.* Ahhhh, the light begins to dawn.

This computing power takes the form of formulas that you create. Yes, you. Even if math wasn't your best subject, you can learn to create formulas that do all the dirty work. And if you are a math whiz, you'll probably stay up all night thinking up ways to fill up those cells.

- Quite unlike a paper spreadsheet that contains only values computed somewhere else, an electronic worksheet can store both the formulas and the computed values returned by these formulas. Even better, the formulas can use values stored in other cells of the worksheet, and, as you see later in the book, 1-2-3 automatically updates the computed answer returned by such a formula anytime you change these values in the worksheet.

✔ 1-2-3's computational capabilities — combined with its editing and formatting capabilities — make it perfect for generating any kind of document that utilizes text and numeric entries and requires calculations.

✔ Because you can make formulas dynamic — so that their calculations are automatically updated when you change referenced values stored in other cells of the worksheet — 1-2-3 makes it easy to keep the calculated values in a worksheet document both current and correct.

Get That Spreadsheet Up and Running

You can start 1-2-3 directly from DOS or you can start it from the Lotus Access Menu.

✔ To start 1-2-3 from the DOS prompt (that weird-looking C:\> thing), type **123** and press Enter.

✔ To start 1-2-3 from the Lotus Access Menu, you first have to start the Lotus Access system. Type **LOTUS** at the DOS prompt and press Enter. The Lotus Access Menu screen in Figure 1-3 appears, with 1-2-3 highlighted. Simply press Enter to start 1-2-3.

```
 Create worksheets, graphs, and databases
 1-2-3        PrintGraph      Translate        Install      Exit


                           Lotus
                     1-2-3 Access Menu
                       Release 2.4

            Copyright 1990, 1991, 1992 Lotus Development Corporation
                         All Rights Reserved.


     To select a program to start, do one of the following:

        * Use ←, →, HOME, or END to move the menu pointer
          to the program you want and then press ENTER.

        * Type the first character of the program's name.

     Press F1 (HELP) for more information.
                                                           NUM
```

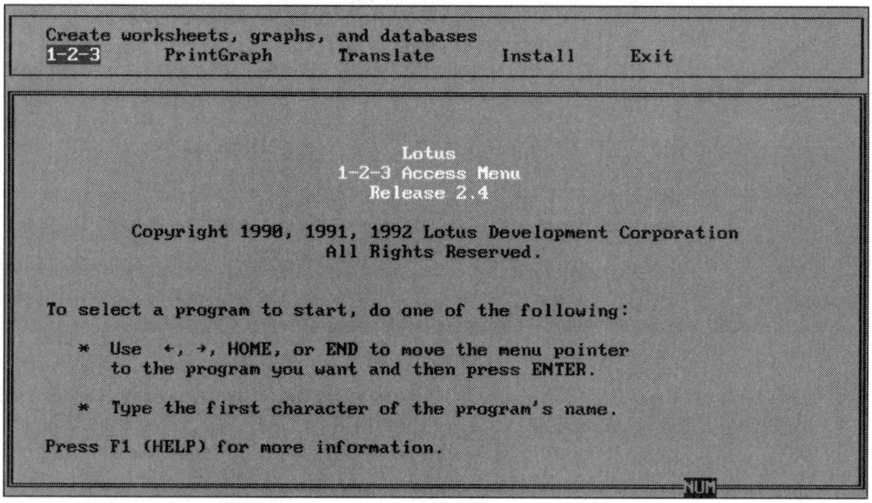

Figure 1-3: The Lotus Access Menu.

Just remember that the full name of the program is Lotus 1-2-3. You type the first part of the name, **LOTUS,** when you want the Lotus Access Menu and type the second part of the name, **123,** (sans hyphens) to start the worksheet.

As you can see, the Lotus Access Menu gives you access to a number of other programs besides 1-2-3.

✔ PrintGraph prints the graphs you create in 1-2-3.

✔ Translate translates files to and from 1-2-3.

✔ Install updates changes to your computer system, such as going from a dot-matrix printer to a laser printer.

What Goes on Here?

Figure 1-4 identifies the different parts of the 1-2-3 screen that appear when you start 1-2-3 (either from DOS or from the Lotus Access Menu). As you can see, the opening 1-2-3 window is full of all kinds of useful, though potentially confusing, stuff.

Help! My computer says I have a bad command or file name!

If you type the 123 or LOTUS startup command and DOS displays the message Bad command or file name, one of three things is going on:

1. You mistyped the startup command.

2. You typed the startup command flawlessly but the technicians forgot to install 1-2-3 on your computer.

3. You typed the startup command flawlessly, and 1-2-3 is properly installed, but it is in its own directory such as C:\123R24. Because you are not in this directory, DOS can't match the startup command you typed with the 123.EXE and LOTUS.EXE command files that actually load the program into memory.

In this case, you need to type the CD (Change Directory) DOS command (as in **CD\123R24**) to make the 1-2-3 program directory current; then enter the startup command again.

✔ To avoid this problem in the future, pull out your copy of *DOS for Dummies* and find out how to add the name of the 1-2-3 program directory to the PATH statement of your computer's AUTOEXEC.BAT file. If that sounds like gobbledygook, then bribe some nerd in the office who knows DOS to add it for you!

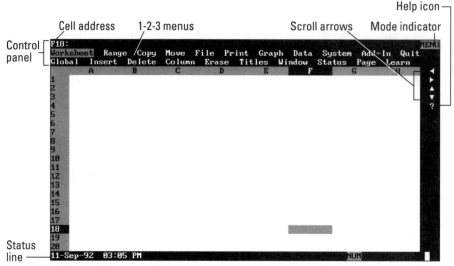

Figure 1-4: The parts of the 1-2-3 screen.

Getting control from the panel

The first three lines of the 1-2-3 screen are known collectively as the *control panel*. The first line of the control panel gives you vital information about the current cell (the one with the cell pointer) and the condition of the program.

On the left side of the first line you see the address of the current cell, followed by whatever you've put into the cell. (When the cell is blank, as they all are when you open a new worksheet, you don't see anything after the cell address.)

Having 1-2-3 á la mode

The *mode indicator* on the right side of the first line of the control panel gives you information about the current condition of the program. The mode indicator normally shows READY, meaning that 1-2-3 is ready to accept the entry of new information in the current cell or to process the next command. As you choose various commands, the mode indicator changes. For example, when you activate the command menus, the mode indicator changes from READY to MENU.

> ✔ The only mode that enables you to move the cell pointer and select a new cell or choose a program command is READY mode.

> ✔ 1-2-3 uses several other mode indicators, but most of them are either self-explanatory or of little interest to non-nerds.

Slashing through the menus

The second line of the control panel is where the command menus appear. You use these menus to choose 1-2-3 commands so that you can get things done in the program. To display the command menus, you press the / (slash) key. Some people refer to them as the slash-command menus (original, huh?). For complete information on how to choose commands from menus, jump ahead to the section, "Have You Seen What's on the Menu?"

When trying to display the command menus, be sure that you're pressing the forward slash key — the same key that the ? (question mark) is on — instead of the \ (backslash) key — the one with the | (vertical bar) on it.

Scrolling around and helping yourself

If your computer has a mouse (the pointing device that lies next to the keyboard — not the kind your cat is interested in), your 1-2-3 screen displays five icons down the right-hand side of the screen. (These icons are identified in Figure 1-4.)

✔ The scroll icons are the four triangles pointing in different directions (left, right, up, and down). You click on these icons to scroll new parts of your worksheet into view. (To learn how to scroll, see "Scroll!," coming up soon in this chapter.)

✔ The Help icon is the question mark. You click on this icon to display the Help index so that you can choose a particular topic from 1-2-3's on-line help. (See "Help Is At Hand" later in this chapter.)

Knowing the state of the program

The line at the very bottom of the 1-2-3 screen is called the status line because it displays information that keeps you informed of the current state of 1-2-3.

✔ The left part of the status bar normally displays the current date and time, but you can change it to a display of the filename. (You learn to change the display in Chapter 2.)

✔ To the right of the clock/calendar display, you see various *status indicators*. These indicators tell you when you've placed 1-2-3 in a particular state that somehow affects how you work with the program. (Not to be confused with the state you're in; that also affects how you work with the program, but 1-2-3 doesn't keep track of it. Hey, if you need a break, take one.)

For example, when you first start 1-2-3, the NUM indicator normally appears in this part of the status bar, indicating that you can use the numbers on the numeric keypad to enter values in the worksheet. Should you press the

Num Lock key, the NUM indicator disappears. This signal tells you that the cursor-movement functions (also assigned to this keypad) are now in effect. Pressing the 6 key, for example, moves the cell pointer one cell to the right, instead of entering this value in the cell.

Make That Mouse Less of a Drag

1-2-3 Release 2.3 and later releases enable you to use a mouse to move around the worksheet, select the cells you want to work with, or even choose 1-2-3 commands. You can tell whether your version of 1-2-3 is set up to work with a mouse because, in addition to the normal cell pointer, you see a mouse pointer — the rectangular block shown in cell A11 in Figure 1-1.

✔ If you're using Release 2.3 of 1-2-3, the mouse works only when the Wysiwyg (pronounced *wizzy-wig* — honest, I'm not making this up) add-in program is loaded into the computer's memory. If you don't see the mouse pointer, you need to jump ahead to Chapter 10 to find out how to load this program.

✔ Don't confuse the *mouse pointer* with the *cell pointer* (shown in cell A1 in Figure 1-1). To move the mouse pointer around the worksheet, you need to move the mouse on your desk. You can, however, also move the cell pointer with the mouse. You simply position the pointer in a new cell and click the left mouse button. (You learn more about how to move the cell pointer with the mouse and with the keyboard later in this chapter.)

✔ Like it or not, the mouse is one of the more challenging computer tools. These little rats demand a level of hand-and-eye coordination that make touch-typing on the keyboard seem like a walk in the park. After all, your brain has to learn how to correlate the movement of the mouse pointer across a slightly curved vertical plane (your monitor screen) with the smaller movements that you make with the mouse on a flat horizontal plane (your desk). Then again, it could also be that most of us are just klutzes.

✔ Whatever the reason, you may find mastering mouse techniques some-what of a challenge. However, I'm quite sure that with just a modicum of mouse experience under your belt, you too will be double-clicking with the best of them.

Although, all of 1-2-3's worksheet capabilities are accessible with the keyboard, in a few cases, using a mouse is a more efficient way to choose a command or perform a particular procedure.

1-2-3 uses three basic mouse techniques to choose and manipulate various objects in the program and document windows:

✔ Click on an object.

   Position the pointer on it and then press and immediately release the left or the right mouse button.

✔ Double-click on an object.

   Position the pointer on it and then press and immediately release the left mouse button rapidly twice in a row.

✔ Drag and drop an object.

   Position the pointer on it and then press and hold down the left mouse button as you move the mouse in the direction you want to drag the object. When you have positioned the object in the desired position on the screen, you then release the left mouse button to drop and place it.

Taming the mouse

To make using the mouse easier, keep the following tips in mind:

✔ When clicking on an object, make sure that the mouse pointer (the block) is touching the object you want to select before you click. To avoid moving the pointer slightly before you click, grasp the sides of the mouse between your thumb and your ring and little fingers; then click the left mouse button with your index finger.

✔ If you run out of room to move the mouse on your desktop, just pick up the mouse and reposition it on the desk. (This action does not move the pointer.)

✔ The mouse emphasizes a different set of muscles from the keyboard, so you may experience some initial discomfort in your upper back and shoulder. Keep that Ben-Gay handy!

Switch-clicking (or looking out for lefties)

Sinister or not, we left handers have to stick together. As a fellow southpaw, I feel that I have to let you know that you can save a lot of wear and tear on your left shoulder by swapping the left and right mouse buttons.

After you move the mouse to the left side of the keyboard, every time you click the left mouse button, you twist your left hand so that your index finger can reach the button. If you switch the left and right buttons, you can keep your hand perfectly aligned over the mouse, and your index finger can still reach and click the left button (which is *physically* the right button).

To switch the left and right buttons, follow these simple steps:

1. Turn on your computer and then use the CD DOS command to change to the directory that contains your 1-2-3 program files.

   Type **CD\123R24,** for example, if your copy of 1-2-3 is installed in the directory C:\123R24.

2. Load the Lotus Access Menu by typing **LOTUS** at the DOS prompt (the C:\> thing) and pressing Enter.

3. Press I to choose the Install command on the Lotus Access system.

   The opening screen for the Lotus Install Program appears.

4. Press Enter to display the main menu, press the ↓ key to highlight the Change Selected Equipment option, and then press Enter.

5. Press the ↓ key until you highlight the Switch Mouse Buttons option and then press Enter.

6. Press the ↓ key to highlight the Right option and then press Enter.

7. Press the End key or the ↓ key until you highlight the End Install option and then press Enter.

8. Press the ↓ key to highlight the Yes option and then press Enter to save your change and return to the Lotus Access Menu.

9. Press the Enter key to start 1-2-3.

   Otherwise, press E to choose the Exit command and return to the DOS operating system.

After you swap the left and right buttons, every time you see "click the left mouse button" or even more commonly just "click the mouse button," click the *physical* right button of your mouse. And, on those rare occasions (and there are some in 1-2-3) when you see "click the right mouse button," click the *physical* left button. Sounds crazy, but I know that you can handle it. You've been making left-to-right conversions all your life.

How Do I Get from Here to There?

1-2-3 provides several methods for getting around its big worksheet. For mouse users, one the easiest ways to get around is to use the scroll icons (displayed to the right of the worksheet) to bring new parts of a worksheet into view. Don't worry if you don't have a rodent, however. 1-2-3 provides a wide range of keystrokes that enable you not only to move a new part of the worksheet into view but also to make a new cell active by placing the cell pointer in it.

Scroll!

If you have a pet mouse and your version of 1-2-3 supports it, you can use the scroll icons to move the cell pointer and scroll new parts of the worksheet into view. When you click on the scroll icons, 1-2-3 moves the cell pointer one cell in the direction of the scroll arrow. So, for example, to move the cell pointer from cell A1 to cell C3 in the worksheet, you click on the icon pointing right two times and then click on the icon pointing down two times.

✔ While clicking away, you will find that as soon as the cell pointer reaches the edge of the worksheet display, the next click on the same icon not only moves the cell pointer but begins to scroll part of the new column or row into view as well. The scrolling of the columns or rows of the worksheet occurs in the opposite direction of the scroll icon that you're clicking on.

✔ When you continue to click on the right scroll icon after reaching the right edge of the worksheet, for example, the columns begin scrolling off the left edge in order to display new columns on the right. Likewise, if you click on the downward pointing scroll icon until you reach the last row on the screen and then continue to click on this icon, the rows at the top of the worksheet begin to scroll off the screen as new rows of information begin to appear at the bottom.

✔ When you need to cover large distances in the worksheet, you can scoot across it like a mouse running away from the family cat by clicking on the appropriate scroll icon and keeping the mouse button depressed. When the portion of the worksheet that you want to see comes into view, release the mouse button.

Stroke!

If you're the type who wouldn't be caught dead using a mouse, you can forget all about scroll icons. Fortunately for you (and all the people out there with early versions of Release 2 that don't even support these critters), 1-2-3 offers a wide variety of keystrokes for moving the cell pointer to a new cell. (In truth, many of these keystrokes are even more efficient than cranking on the old scroll icons anyway.)

When you use these keystrokes, 1-2-3 automatically scrolls a new part of the worksheet into view if scrolling is required in moving the cell pointer. Table 1-1 summarizes the keystrokes and tells where they move the cell pointer.

Getting around the block

The keystrokes that combine the End key with an arrow key are among the most helpful for moving quickly from one edge to the other in large blocks of cell entries or in moving from block to block in a section of the worksheet that contains many blocks of cells.

Table 1-1	Keystrokes for Moving the Cell Pointer
Keystroke	*Where the Cell Pointer Moves*
→	To the cell one column right
←	To the cell one column left
↑	To the cell up one row
↓	To the cell down one row
Home	To the first cell (A1) of the worksheet
End, Home	To the last cell in the active area (diagonal opposite of home) in the worksheet
PgUp	To the cell one screenful up in the same column
PgDn	To the cell one screenful down in the same column
Tab or Ctrl-→	To the cell one screenful to the right in the same row
Shift-Tab or Ctrl-←	To the cell one screenful to the left in the same row
End, →	To the first occupied cell to the right in the same row that is either preceded or followed by a blank cell
End, ←	To the first occupied cell to the left in the same row that is either followed or preceded by a blank cell
End, ↑	To the first occupied cell above in the same column that is either followed or preceded by a blank cell
End, ↓	To the first occupied cell below in the same column that is either preceded or followed by a blank cell

For example, if the cell pointer is positioned on a blank cell somewhere to the left of a table of cell entries that you want to view, pressing End, → moves the cell pointer to the first cell entry at the leftmost edge of the table (in the same row, of course). When you then press End, → a second time, the cell pointer moves to the last cell entry at the rightmost edge (assuming that there are no blank cells in that row of the table).

If you then switch direction and press End, ↓, 1-2-3 moves right to the last cell entry at the bottom edge of the table (again assuming that there are no blank cells below in that column of the table). If, when the cell pointer is at the bottom of the table, you press End, ↓ again, 1-2-3 moves the pointer to the first entry at the top of the next table located below (assuming that there are no other cell entries above this table in the same column).

If you press End and an arrow key combination and there are no more occupied cells in the direction of the arrow key, 1-2-3 advances the cell pointer to the cell at the very edge of the worksheet in that direction. For example, if the cell pointer is located in cell C15 and there are no more occupied cells in row 15, when you press End, →, 1-2-3 moves the cell pointer to cell IV at the rightmost edge of the worksheet. Likewise, if you are in cell C15 and there are no more entries below in column C and you press End, ↓, 1-2-3 moves the pointer to cell C8192 at the very bottom edge of the worksheet.

When you use End and an arrow key combination, you must press and then release the End key *before* you press the arrow key (indicated by the comma in keystrokes such as *End,* →). Pressing and releasing the End key causes the END indicator to appear on the status bar. This indicator is a signal that 1-2-3 is ready for you to press one of the four arrow keys.

Where will you GoTo?

1-2-3's GoTo function key provides an easy method for moving directly to a distant cell in the worksheet.

1. Press F5 (a.k.a. the GoTo key).

   The following prompt appears in the control panel:

   ```
   Enter address to go to:
   ```

   The prompt is followed by the address of the current cell.

2. Type the address of the cell you want to go to.

   You can type the column letter(s) in upper- or lowercase. 1-2-3 replaces the current address with the new cell reference.

3. Press Enter.

   1-2-3 moves the cell pointer to the new cell.

Freeze!

You can use the Scroll Lock key to *freeze* the position of the cell pointer in the worksheet so that you can scroll new areas of the worksheet into view with keystrokes, such as PgUp and PgDn or Tab and Shift-Tab, without changing the cell pointer's original position.

When you press the Scroll Lock key, 1-2-3 displays the SCROLL mode indicator on the status bar as a sign that scroll lock is engaged. Then, when you scroll the worksheet with the keyboard, 1-2-3 does not select a new cell as it brings a new section of the worksheet into view.

To *unfreeze* the cell pointer, just press the Scroll Lock key again so that SCROLL disappears from the status bar.

Have You Seen What's on the Menu?

The 1-2-3 menus that appear on the second line of the control panel provide the primary means for choosing program commands. You can use either the mouse or the keyboard to make your choices.

✔ To display the menus with the mouse, move the mouse pointer over the second line of the control panel. Voilà! The menus appear as if by magic. (And much faster than at most restaurants.)

✔ To display the command menus from the keyboard, press the / (forward slash) key — the one with the question mark above it. Voilà! More magic.

✔ When your have finished making choices from the menus, simply move the mouse pointer from the control panel to somewhere on the worksheet itself. To get rid of the menus that were displayed by pressing the / key, you must press the Esc key.

When the 1-2-3 menus are displayed, you choose a command either by positioning the mouse pointer somewhere on its name and clicking the left mouse button or by typing its first letter. For example, if you need to choose a command on the **File** menu, you press F, if you need to choose a command on the **Print** menu, you press P, and so on.

Menu trivia you can safely ignore

1-2-3 uses the / key to activate its menus because its predecessor, VisiCalc (the granddaddy of electronic spreadsheets), used the / key. And why did VisiCalc use this key instead of a sensible function key such as F10? Because it was developed to run on the original Apple computer. The Apple was so primitive that its keyboard didn't have any function keys. And the / key was chosen because there's no usage (at least in English) that has / as the initial character.

Here's another piece of menu trivia you'll never use: You can display the 1-2-3 menus by pressing the < (less than) key instead of the / key. Of course, to use this method you have to press two keys — Shift, plus the key with the comma on it — instead of one /. Who has time to bother with that nonsense?

If you're not sure which 1-2-3 menu contains the command you need, press → to highlight each menu name. The third line of the control panel then shows you either a list of the commands on the next level that become available when you choose that menu or a brief description of the command's usage. (You can also press the ← key to highlight a previous command.) When you identify the menu you need, you choose it by pressing the Enter key or typing its initial letter.

As soon as you choose a menu that shows a list of further commands, this list of commands replaces the original menus on the second line of the control panel. For example, Figure 1-5 shows you the control panel after you choose the **Worksheet** command on the first level of the slash command menus (shown in Figure 1-4).

Choose **Worksheet** and the list of commands **G**lobal through **L**earn replaces the original list, **W**orksheet through **Q**uit, on the second line of the control panel. You can also see the list of commands, **F**ormat through **Z**ero, that becomes available when you choose the **G**lobal command on the second line.

After a new menu level appears on the second line of the control panel, you can then choose one of its commands either by clicking on it (if you're into the mouse) or by typing its initial letter. As before, you can get a list of the commands attached to a particular command option or a description of a command's function by using the → or ← key to highlight the command and then reading the list or prompt that appears on the third line of the control panel.

Figure 1-5: The 1-2-3 menus after choosing the Worksheet command on the main menu.

✔ Some tasks in 1-2-3 require you to choose several commands on subsequent menu levels. For example, to widen a column in the worksheet, you must display the 1-2-3 menus and choose the **W**orksheet command from the main menu (the first level). Next you choose the **C**olumn command ·rom the second menu level. Then you choose the **S**et-Width command from the third level. Finally (whew!), you set the new column width in response to a prompt.

All of this sounds a lot more complicated than it really is. Thanks to the power of 1-2-3, you can make the change in a matter of seconds — once you get the hang of it.

✔ Other tasks require only one or two command selections from the menus. Suppose that you want to copy a cell or a group of cells. You display the 1-2-3 menus and choose the **C**opy command from the main menu. Then you respond to a couple of prompts asking you define what to copy and where.

After you've copied them, you change your mind — or the boss tells you to change it. To erase the contents of a cell or a group of cells, you display the 1-2-3 menus and choose the **R**ange command from the main menu and the **E**rase command on the next level. Then you press Enter to erase the contents of the current cell or you highlight the block to be erased and then press Enter. Poof! The cells are blank once more.

Let me outta here!

One day when you're just traipsing your merry way through the menu woods, picking commands by typing their initial letters, whoa, all of a sudden you find yourself in a completely alien menu. What are you doing there? How do you get out of there?

The answer to the first question is that if you're not watching the control panel as you type the first letters of commands, you can easily choose the wrong commands by making typos — a common problem for touch typists.

The answer to the second question is: No problem, just press the Esc key. It backs you out of the menu system one level at a time. Sooner or later you'll probably come to a menu you recognize. Or, if you are at the main menu level and want to quit the menus entirely, you can press Esc to deactivate the menus and return 1-2-3 to READY mode. Then you can take a deep breath and start over. (Bet you'll pay closer attention this time.) But what if the menu you're in is so alien that you know you're deep in the menu woods and you want to get out of there quickly?

You can bail out of the menus by pressing Ctrl-Break. That key combination is the ultimate Esc key in 1-2-3. No matter where you are in the menu woods, it immediately takes you out of the menu system and returns the program to

READY mode. *Note:* On older keyboards, the Break key is located on the Scroll Lock key, and on newer keyboards it's usually located on the Pause key rather than the Esc key.

Save me from the dreaded /FS typo!

You need to be aware of one really scary menu command typo. You usually make this typo when you intend to type the command sequence **/FS** to choose the **F**ile **S**ave command to save your worksheet on disk. Instead, you transpose the menu letters and type **/SF.** This transposition causes 1-2-3 to choose the **S**ystem command on the main menu as soon as you type **/S.** Unfortunately, the **S**ystem command jumps out of 1-2-3 and returns to the DOS operating system. There you see only the obscure message

```
(Type EXIT and press ENTER to return to 1-2-3)
```

above the equally obscure DOS prompt

```
C:\>
```

At this point, you must *not* panic and try to restart 1-2-3 by typing the **123** startup command (however much you're tempted to do so). Doing this would start a second copy of the 1-2-3 program (should your computer have a lot of memory), and this new copy of the program would not contain your unsaved worksheet.

What you really want to do is just return to the copy of the program that's currently running. So keep your wits about you and simply type **EXIT** at the DOS prompt. Then press the Enter key. Exit command immediately returns to 1-2-3 and the unsaved worksheet. Breathe a sigh of relief, choose the real /File Save command, and save your work.

The /System command is really quite useful. It enables you to do all kinds of DOSy things, such as formatting new disks or even starting other programs without having to quit 1-2-3 first (if your computer has enough memory). You should, however, *never, ever* use this command without first saving all your work in 1-2-3.

Once, a few years back, when I was writing a book on using 1-2-3, I developed a great example worksheet that I was eager to write about. So I used the 1-2-3 /System command to return to DOS and start my word processor — without first saving my example worksheet. I then spent the rest of the afternoon writing all about my wonderful 1-2-3 example worksheet. When I was finished, I saved my document, exited the word processor, and returned to DOS (which no longer displayed the message Type EXIT and press ENTER to return to 1-2-3, as this message had long since scrolled off the screen). I decided to call it a day and turn off the computer; you got it — the very second after I flipped that off switch, I realized in horror that 1-2-3 had still been running with my *unsaved* sample worksheet (which I had to reconstruct from scratch). From that day on, I have never, ever intentionally used the /System command without first saving all my work in 1-2-3.

You mean I have to memorize these things?

Even for you folks out there who hunt and peck at the keyboard, typing the first letters of the commands to choose them on each menu level is probably the most efficient way to choose 1-2-3 command sequences. The hard part, of course, is remembering the exact command sequence so that you know which letters to type.

You're most apt to get stuck at the beginning, right after you've displayed the main menus (with the / key or the mouse pointer), and you have to choose the proper menu. When you're new to 1-2-3, the assignment of commands to menus can seem very arbitrary, making them hard to remember.

For example, many beginners find it strange that commands for setting a new column width are found on the /Worksheet menu rather than on the /Range menu. (This location actually makes sense after you realize that when you change a column width, you are changing the width of the column down the entire length of the worksheet.) Others find it hard to associate the Erase command, used to delete the contents of a cell or group of cells, with the /Range menu.

To help my new students become familiar with the syntax of the 1-2-3 menu system, I sometimes tell them to think of 1-2-3 as being from the "old country," where the languages frequently put the modifiers after the noun. The French say *Moulin Rouge* (Mill Red), for example, whereas we would say *Red Mill*; and the Germans say *haus braun* (house brown), whereas we would say *brown house*. In a similar manner, 1-2-3 command sequences put the modifiers after the major commands they describe. /Range Erase erases a range of cells, and /Worksheet Column Set-Width sets the width of a column.

Of course, 1-2-3 command sequences are set up this way because the menus are arranged in a hierarchy from the most general to the most specific, but we all know that foreign languages use this construction to make it hard for English speakers to learn them!

Whatever works. When you learn new commands, just keep in mind that you need to find a way to associate the command with its menu. Then you'll find it easier to reproduce and remember the entire command sequence.

Is Meaningful Dialog Possible?

Versions of Release 2 of 1-2-3 that are later than Release 2.2 have taken to displaying dialog boxes at a certain point in the command sequences. Figure 1-6 shows you the Global Settings dialog box that appears as soon as you choose the /Worksheet Global commands in Release 2.3 or 2.4. (If this dialog box doesn't appear when you choose /Worksheet Global, then you know that you're using Release 2.0 or 2.2. The precise version is listed on the startup screen that appears briefly before the worksheet appears when you first start the program.)

As you can see in Figure 1-6, the Global Settings dialog box shows you the current settings for the various commands currently available on the command line. (Note that these settings are arranged in a slightly different order from the commands; the Protection setting is first in the Global Settings dialog even though the **P**rotection command is fifth on the command line.)

Dialog boxes in 1-2-3 are designed not only to give you all the current settings at a glance but also to enable you to change any of the current settings right in the dialog box. In earlier versions of 1-2-3, the only way to change these settings is by choosing individual commands on the command line. But before you can change a setting in a displayed dialog box, you need to press F2 (the Edit function key) to activate the dialog box. Figure 1-7 shows you what happens to the Global Settings dialog box when you press F2.

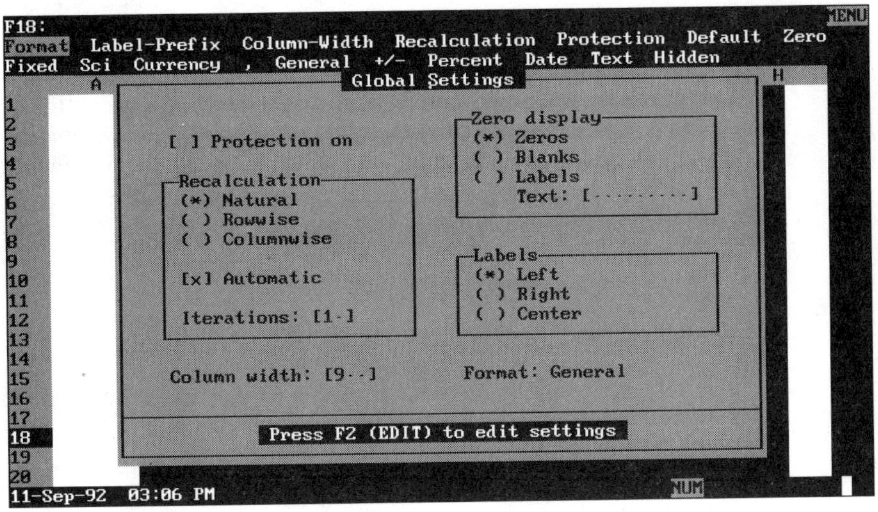

Figure 1-6: The Global Settings dialog box.

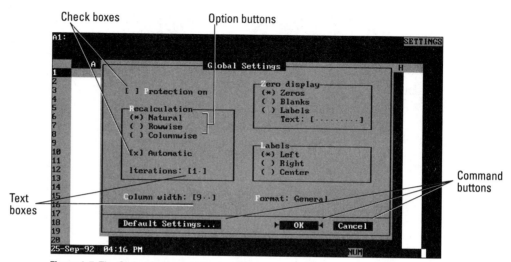

Figure 1-7: The Global Settings dialog box after you press F2.

When you activate a dialog box with the F2 (Edit) key, the following changes occur:

- 1-2-3 blanks out the command line in the control panel.
- It replaces the message

```
Press F2 (EDIT) to edit settings
```

at the bottom of the dialog box with various buttons that you can use either to put changes into effect or to restore the original settings.

- Some letters in the dialog box are displayed in another intensity or color. You type these letters to choose items when you want to change their settings. (Note that most often, but not always, these letters are the first letters of the item name.)

Changing settings

To change a setting in a dialog box, you can use either the mouse or the keyboard.

- To use the mouse, position the mouse pointer anywhere on the item you want to change and click the left mouse button.
- To use the keyboard, press F2 — a step you don't have to take when using the mouse — and then type the letter that is shown in a different intensity or color.

If you're not much for typing command letters, you can also choose a particular option in a dialog box with the keyboard by pressing the Tab or Shift-Tab keys.

✔ Pressing Tab selects the next setting in a dialog box (moving left to right and then down the options).

✔ Pressing Shift-Tab selects the previous setting.

1-2-3 indicates which setting is selected by highlighting it (or if the option is already highlighted, as in the case of some of the buttons, the program encloses it in left- and right-pointing arrowheads).

Consider your option button

Some dialog boxes group related settings together as a single item. For example, in the Global Settings dialog box shown in Figure 1-7, a number of settings are grouped together for the item called **R**ecalculation. (All the settings are enclosed in a box.)

Notice that the first settings (Natural, **R**owwise, and Columnwise) are all preceded by a set of closed parentheses, and the set in front of Natural contains an asterisk (meaning that it's selected). Settings grouped together and preceded by a pair of parentheses are known as *option buttons.* Option buttons are used in dialog boxes when you are confronted by mutually exclusive choices (in other words, you can set **R**ecalculation to Natural *or* to **R**owwise *or* to Columnwise, but not to Natural *and* **R**owwise or to **R**owwise *and* Columnwise).

To choose a new option button, either click on it with the mouse or activate the item by typing its menu letter (**R** in the case of **R**ecalculation) and then type the menu letter of the particular setting (**N** for Natural, **R** for **R**owwise, or **C** for Columnwise). As soon as you choose a new option button, 1-2-3 puts the asterisk in its parentheses at the same time that it removes the asterisk from the former selection.

Turn on a check box

Below the **R**ecalculation options buttons, you find the **A**utomatic setting. This setting uses a *check box.* A check box setting can be either on or off. When the setting is turned on, the box in front of the item contains an *X.* When the setting is turned off, the box is empty. To change the setting for a check box item such as **A**utomatic, click on the item or type its menu letter. If the check box is selected when you do this, 1-2-3 turns it off (by removing the *X*). If, however, the check box is not selected when you do this, the program turns it on (by adding an *X*).

A check box forms what computer people never tire of referring to as a *toggle* or *toggle switch* because each time you choose it, it assumes the opposite state (on when off or off when on).

Fill in a text box

Beneath the **A**utomatic check box, you find the **I**terations setting (*Iteration* is just a fancy, three-dollar word from the Latin word for *repetition* — it refers to how many times the formulas in your worksheet should be recalculated). This setting uses a *text box*. A text box contains either the current setting (1 in the case of the Iterations text box) or a place where you can enter a setting enclosed in square brackets following its description. (The text box indicates the maximum number of characters you can enter by displaying a dot for each character.)

To change a text box setting, you click on the item or type its menu letter. 1-2-3 then positions the *cursor* (the flashing underscore) under the first character (or the dot marking its position), and you can type the new setting. When you're done typing the new setting, you press Enter to take yourself out of the text box.

Pop-up a box

Sometimes choosing a particular setting causes 1-2-3 to display what's called a *pop-up dialog box*. This box contains more choices. For example, in the Global Settings dialog box, choosing the **F**ormat setting leads to the Format pop-up dialog box shown in Figure 1-8. Here you see a two-column list of option buttons from which you can choose the new global format.

Order a command button

At the bottom of each dialog box (regular as well as pop-up), you find the box's *command buttons,* which you can use to put a particular action into effect. The most common command buttons are the OK and Cancel buttons.

- ✔ To put the new settings you've chosen in a dialog box into effect, you click on the OK button (or press Enter).

- ✔ To deactivate the dialog box without recording your changes, you click on the Cancel button (or press Esc).

Some dialog boxes contain other command buttons besides the more common OK and Cancel buttons. For example, the Global Settings dialog box contains a **D**efault Settings button that you can use to change various program settings.

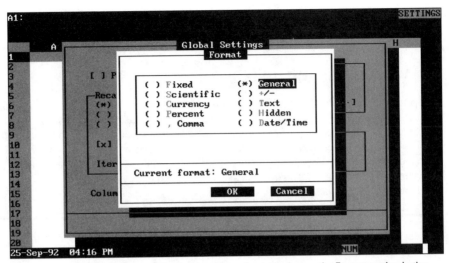

Figure 1-8: The Format pop-up dialog box appears when you choose the Format setting in the Global Settings dialog box.

When you choose this command button, 1-2-3 displays a completely new dialog box (called appropriately enough, the Default Settings dialog box) where you can change as many or as few of the settings as you like.

You can always tell when choosing a command button in a dialog box opens another dialog box because the name of the command button is followed by three periods . . . (known in highbrow circles as an ellipsis).

Getting back to more practical matters, note that when you finish changing your settings in the Default Settings dialog box and choose the OK button, 1-2-3 returns to the Global Settings dialog box rather than to READY mode in the worksheet. You will find this to be true anytime you use a command button to open another dialog box.

Totally inane word derivation coming up

For those among you who don't know, *ellipsis* is derived from the ancient Greek verb *elleipein,* which simply means *to leave out* (which is exactly what I should have done to this note).

TIP

If you've got 'em, use 'em

If you're lucky enough to have dialog boxes in your version of 1-2-3, by all means use them. Changing any of the settings listed in a dialog box by choosing the appropriate commands on the command line is possible — and your only option when using an earlier version of Release 2. But changing them in a dialog box has it all over using the menu commands. The dialog box allows you to change as many settings in the box as you want with one shot; when you change settings with the command menus, you have to change each setting individually by reentering all or part of its command sequence.

Go down a list

In addition to option buttons, check boxes, text boxes, pop-up dialog boxes, and command buttons, the only other element you'll ever run into in a 1-2-3 dialog box is the *list box*. A list box, as the name implies, is simply a box that contains an alphabetical listing of all your choices.

- ✔ To choose a new setting in a list box, click on the option or press the ↑ or ↓ key to highlight your selection and then press Enter.

- ✔ If the list box contains more options than can possibly be displayed at one time in the list box, you can click on the ↑ and ↓ scroll arrows on the right side of the box to bring new or previously seen options into view (scrolling happens automatically when you press the ↑ and ↓ keys).

Help Is at Hand

You can get on-line help anytime you need it while you are using 1-2-3. To display the Main Help Index (shown in Figure 1-9), you press the F1 (Help) key or click on the Help icon (the question mark beneath the scroll icons on the right side of the worksheet). After you open the Main Help Index, you can display help screens that provide great information about particular topics. Simply choose the topic you are interested in by using the ↑ and ↓ keys to highlight a topic and then press Enter or click on the topic.

- ✔ The only problem with the Main Help Index system is that it is truly helpful only when you are familiar with the 1-2-3 jargon. If you don't know what 1-2-3 calls a particular feature, you will have trouble locating it in the help topics (just like trying to look up a word in a dictionary when you have no idea how to spell it).

✔ Fortunately, the 1-2-3 Help system can also give you context-sensitive help on commands. Suppose that you display the 1-2-3 main menus and then choose the **Worksheet** menu. In looking over the commands on the **Worksheet** menu, you become curious about the purpose of the **Window** command. To display the on-line help information about the **Window** command, you press → until this command is highlighted. (In this case, you use the arrow keys to highlight the command rather than typing its menu letter, which would activate the command rather than just select it.) Then you press the F1 (Help) key or click on the Help icon. The 1-2-3 Help system then displays help information on just the /**Worksheet Window** command.

✔ Many of the help topics contain more information than can fit in the Help dialog box. When this is the case, you can scroll through the text by pressing ↑ and ↓ keys or by clicking on the ↑ and ↓ scroll arrows. If you're into using the keyboard, you can take bigger jumps in the help information by pressing the PgUp and PgDn keys. Also, you can move directly to the end of a help topic by pressing End or to the top by pressing Home.

✔ When you finish using on-line help, you simply press Esc to return to the program. If you got on-line help while choosing a 1-2-3 command, 1-2-3 returns to the command line where you can either continue or back out and return to READY mode. Otherwise, 1-2-3 goes back to your worksheet.

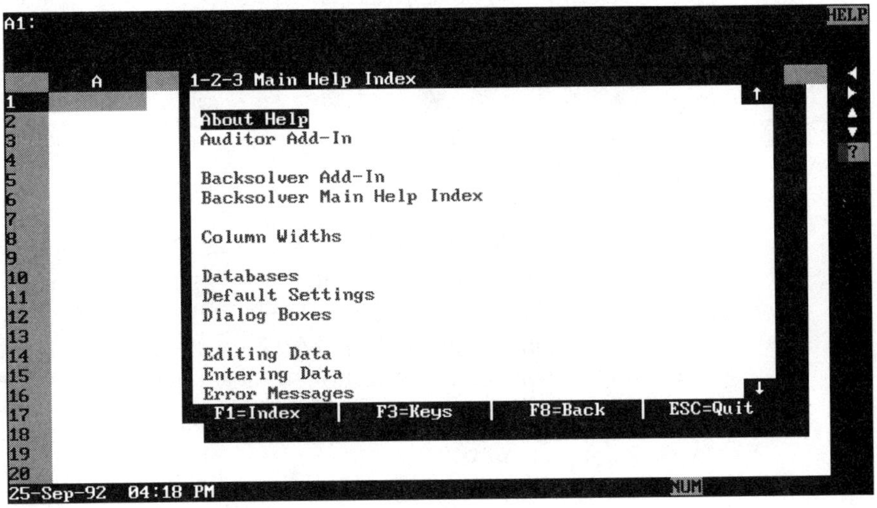

Figure 1-9: The 1-2-3 Main Help Index.

When Quitting Time Rolls Around

When you're ready to call it a day and quit 1-2-3, shut down the program by choosing the /Quit command. When you choose the /Quit command, the main menu on the second line of the control panel is replaced with a No and Yes option, and the following prompt appears on the third line of the control panel:

```
Do not end 1-2-3 session; return to READY mode?
```

✔ If you chose the /Quit command in error, simply press Enter to return to the program.

✔ However, if you really want to get out — in fact, you're more than ready to get out — you have to choose the Yes option. (Isn't it cute the way 1-2-3 assumes no one would ever voluntarily leave the program, and it makes the No option the default instead of the Yes option?)

As soon as you type **Y** or click on **Yes** to finally get out of the program, you are dropped back at the DOS prompt where you can choose your next DOS command (lots of luck) or shut your computer off.

If you choose the **Yes** option to quit 1-2-3 without saving the latest changes on your worksheet (for shame!), the program does not immediately drop you at the DOS prompt. Instead, it scolds you soundly by beeping at you and then displaying a new set of No and Yes menu options. This time the following scary prompt appears on the third line of the control panel:

```
WORKSHEET CHANGES NOT SAVED! End 1-2-3 anyway?
```

This is your last chance to avoid being a dodo and losing all your unsaved work (which means the entire worksheet if you never bothered to save it in the first place).

✔ To return to 1-2-3, where you can then straightway save your work with the /File Save command (see Chapter 2 for details on using this command), choose the No option or press Enter.

✔ If you are really, really, really sure (beyond the slightest shadow of a doubt) that you don't need to save the changes you made since the last time you saved your work, go ahead and choose the Yes option to return to DOS. (Just don't say I didn't warn you.)

Chapter 2
Worksheets Easy as 1-2-3

. . . .

In This Chapter

▶ Starting a new worksheet

▶ Entering different types of information in a worksheet

▶ Creating simple formulas

▶ Correcting mistakes in entering information

▶ Using built-in functions in formulas

▶ Saving a worksheet

. . . .

*N*ow that you know how to get into 1-2-3 and display that big blank worksheet on the screen, the time has come to learn what to do with it. This chapter focuses on the ins and outs of getting information into the worksheet.

It begins with tips on the most efficient way to arrange information in the worksheet and then moves on to the essential techniques for entering text, numbers, dates, and formulas.

After you learn how to fill a worksheet with raw data and formulas, you learn the most important lesson of all: how to save all this information on disk so that you never, ever have to enter all that stuff again.

Getting Organized

When you start 1-2-3, the program opens a blank worksheet in a new document window. To begin a new worksheet, you simply start entering information.

Here are a few simple guidelines to keep in mind when you're filling up the worksheet:

  ✔ Whenever possible, organize the information into tables of data that use adjacent (neighboring) columns and rows. Start a table in the upper left corner of the worksheet and work your way down the sheet, rather than across the sheet, whenever possible. When it's practical, separate each table by no more than a single column or row.

✔ When setting up tables, don't skip columns and rows just to "space out" the information. In Chapter 3, you learn how to add as much white space as you want between adjacent columns and rows by widening columns and changing the alignment.

✔ Reserve a single column at the left edge of the table for the table's row headings. (Make them feel special.)

✔ Reserve a single row at the top of the table for the table's column headings. (Make them feel special too.)

✔ If the table requires a title, put it in the row above the column headings and in the same column as the row headings. You can center the title across the columns of the entire table if you follow the directions in Chapter 3.

Chapter 1 makes such a big deal about how large the worksheet is that you are probably wondering why these guidelines emphasize keeping the information as close together as possible. After all, given the vast amount of wide-open space in a 1-2-3 worksheet, you probably think that saving space is low on the list of 1-2-3 priorities.

The thing is, saving space in a worksheet equals saving memory. As the table grows and expands into new areas of the worksheet, 1-2-3 allocates a certain amount of computer memory for the cell entries. If you skip columns and rows unnecessarily, you waste computer memory that could otherwise be used to store more information in the worksheet.

The amount of computer memory available to 1-2-3 — not the total number of cells in the blank worksheet — determines the ultimate size of the worksheet. When you run out of memory, you effectively run out of space, no matter how many columns and rows are left to fill. To maximize the amount of information you can fit into a worksheet, always follow the example of our pioneer forebears and use the covered wagon approach to worksheet design.

To check out how much computer memory is available to 1-2-3 at any given time, choose the /Worksheet Status command. The program provides information in a dialog box or a screen that shows the percentage of computer memory (in bytes) still available to the program. After viewing this information, press Enter to return to the worksheet. Note that the MEM indicator automatically begins flashing at the bottom of the screen whenever the amount of memory available to the program falls to 4 percent or below.

Entering at Your Own Risk

To enter information in your new worksheet, simply select the cell where you want the information to appear and begin typing. As soon as you type the first character of the entry, 1-2-3 activates the second line of the control panel. The character that you typed appears, followed by the *cursor* (the flashing under-score).

As you continue to type the entry, 1-2-3 displays your progress only on the second line of the control panel, as shown in Figure 2-1. If you make a mistake while typing the entry, just press the Backspace key (the ← above the Enter key — not the ← on the cursor pad or the one on the numeric keypad next door to the right).

After you finish typing the entry, you still have to get it from the control panel into the current cell. You can put it in its place three different ways:

✔ Press the Enter key, which enters the information in the cell without mov-ing the cell pointer from that cell.

✔ Press one of the cursor-movement keys (↑, ↓, ←, or →). This method en-ters the information in the cell and moves the cell pointer to the next cell in the direction of the arrow (up, down, left, or right).

✔ Position the mouse pointer somewhere on the entry and click the left mouse button. This method enters the information in the cell without moving the cell pointer from the cell or the mouse pointer from the control panel.

As soon as you enter information in a cell, 1-2-3 blanks out the second line of the control panel. Zap! The information appears in the cell, but it doesn't show up on the control panel again until you select the cell by moving the cell pointer into it.

If you discover that you're about to put information in the wrong cell, you can clear the second line of the control panel without completing the entry in the cell by pressing the Esc key. If you're into mice, clicking the *right* mouse button does the same thing (and you don't even need to have the mouse pointer any-where near the entry for this to work).

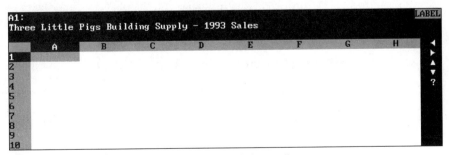

Figure 2-1: Entering a worksheet title in a blank worksheet cell.

Typecasting Your Data

1-2-3 checks each entry you make to see whether you've entered a formula that should be calculated. When checking the entry, the program classifies it either as a *label* (any type of text entry) or as a *value* (straight numeric entries, as well as formulas that the program calculates).

1-2-3 needs to make this determination because it aligns labels in their cells differently from the way it aligns values. Also, most formulas work properly only when you feed them values. You can get the wrong answer if you feed them labels where a value ought to be. (They're finicky, like Morris.)

If 1-2-3 finds that your entry falls into the value category *and* is indeed a *bona fide* formula (you learn how 1-2-3 tells a *bona* formula [a good one] from a *male* formula [a bad one] in the next section), the program calculates it and displays the computed result in the worksheet cell. The formula itself, however, continues to be displayed on the formula bar.

In contrast to formulas, text and numbers are considered to be *constants* because they change only when you edit or replace them. Formulas, on the other hand, update their computed values as soon as you modify any of the values they use.

Placing a value on it

1-2-3 is a master of snap judgments when it comes to categorizing a new entry as either a value or a label. 1-2-3 looks only at the very first character that you type. If it sees any of the following characters, as far as the program is concerned, you're well on the way towards entering a value in the cell:

0 1 2 3 4 5 6 7 8 9 + − . (@ # $

As you can see from this list, you would associate most of these characters — the digits 0 through 9, the decimal point, the plus sign, and the minus sign — with the entry of a value in a cell. The others — (, @, #, and $ — are not nearly so self-evident.

You don't need to waste time memorizing the characters on this list because 1-2-3 always lets you know when you hit pay dirt. It immediately changes the mode indicator from READY to VALUE. (If you don't believe me, try it out for yourself. Just type one of these characters and check the mode indicator. And remember to press the Esc key to clear the control panel without entering the character.)

Labeling the text

1-2-3 considers any entry that begins with a character other than 0, 1, 2, 3, 4, 5, 6, 7, 8, 9, +, –, ., (, @, #, and $ as a label (making labels the catchall category of 1-2-3 entries). Most label entries consist of a combination of letters and punctuation or letters and numbers, and you use them for the titles and headings in the worksheet.

1-2-3 makes it easy for you to tell that it considers your entry a label.

1. You can tell right away when you're on the road to entering a label in a cell because the mode indicator changes from READY to LABEL as soon as you type a character that doesn't fall into the value category.

2. If you don't happen to catch this action in the control panel, just look at the entry's alignment in the cell. 1-2-3 automatically aligns labels at the left edge of the cell.

3. Also, 1-2-3 automatically adds an apostrophe as the first character of any label entry. For example, on the control panel, you type

```
Sleeping Beauty Cosmetics
```

In the cell, 1-2-3 enters

```
'Sleeping Beauty Cosmetics
```

Of course, the initial apostrophe is not used as a text character, so it doesn't show in the cell. Instead, it is a formatting character that determines how the label is aligned in its cell. After you enter the label in the cell, the apostrophe appears in the control panel when the cell is highlighted.

As you may have guessed, the apostrophe is the *label-prefix character* that left-aligns labels in their cells. (You learn the other label prefix characters in the next chapter.)

If the label has more characters than fit in the current width of the cell, the display of the entry spills over into the neighboring cell on the right, provided that the next cell is blank (as shown in Figure 2-2). Should you later enter information in the cell next door, 1-2-3 cuts off that messy spillover (as shown in Figure 2-3).

Not too worry, however, for 1-2-3 doesn't actually lop off the characters of the cell entry; it simply shaves the display to make room for the new neighbor next door. You can easily make the first column wider so that all the characters are visible. (Skip ahead to Chapter 3 for instructions on how to fatten up that column.)

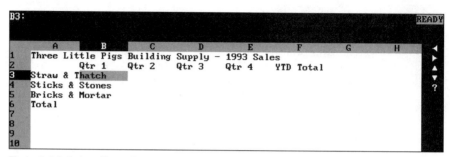

Figure 2-2: Labels spill over into neighboring blank cells when they are too long to fit in their own cells.

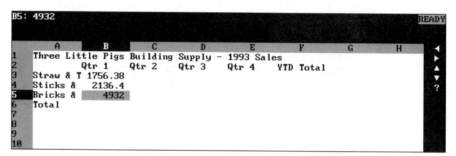

Figure 2-3: Making an entry in the cell next door cuts off the spillover of a long label.

Accepting different values

Values in 1-2-3 can be

- ✔ numbers that represent quantities, such as 10 departments or –100 dollars
- ✔ numbers that represent dates, such as January 11, 1993
- ✔ numbers that represent times, such as 11:59 a.m.
- ✔ formulas, such as 15+25 or +A3–A4, that return some new calculated value

You can tell when 1-2-3 has accepted a cell entry as a value because a numeric entry is automatically aligned at the right edge of the cell. If the value is wider than the cell can display, 1-2-3 automatically converts the value in the cell to *scientific notation* (for example, 6E+08 indicates that the 6 is followed by eight zeros, for a grand total of 600,000,000). To change a value that has been converted to scientific notation back to a normal number, simply widen the column that contains its cell.

WARNING!

Beware the hateful space!

The space, though undetectable to the eye, is considered as much a label character as is a letter such as *A* or *Z*. So if you introduce a space into what would otherwise qualify as a value, 1-2-3 does not accept your value in the cell.

A rather rude beep and a change of the mode from VALUE to EDIT when you try to complete the cell

entry tells you that 1-2-3 finds your entry unacceptable. To get the value into the cell, you have to delete the bothersome space from the entry and then press Enter or click on the entry with the mouse.

Number, please

To enter a numeric value in a cell, select the cell and then type the number as you normally would — sort of. 1-2-3 requires certain very specific (and, at first, startling) exceptions:

✔ Always enter negative values with a – (minus sign or hyphen), as in **–175.** Don't try to enclose the number in a pair of parentheses, as in **(175)**, as accountants do. 1-2-3 treats such a value as a positive number enclosed in parentheses. To make 1-2-3 enclose negative numbers in parentheses (and display them in red on a color monitor), assign the *Comma* or *Currency number format* to the entry. (What are they? See Chapter 3 for details.)

✔ When entering a numeric value in a cell, don't include the dollar signs ($) and commas (,) that may appear in the printed or handwritten numbers you are working from. The comma is considered a label character. If you add it to a numeric entry, 1-2-3 does not accept the entry. If you enter a dollar sign before a financial figure, 1-2-3 enters the value but ignores the dollar sign. In 1-2-3, you add commas and dollar signs to the numbers entered in the worksheet by assigning a Comma or Currency number format to them (again, see Chapter 3 for details).

✔ When the numeric value uses decimal places, use the period as the decimal point. When entering decimal values, the program automatically adds a zero before the decimal point (putting 0.34 in a cell when you enter **.34**), and drops trailing zeros entered after the decimal point (putting 12.5 in a cell when you enter **12.50**). In 1-2-3, you display trailing zeros in values by assigning the Fixed, Comma, or Currency number format to them and choosing the number of decimal places to be used (Chapter 3 again).

✔ When entering a numeric value that represents a percentage, you have a choice: either divide the number by 100 and enter the decimal equivalent, (**.12** for 12 percent, for example), or enter the number followed by the percent sign (**12%**). Either way, 1-2-3 stores the decimal value in the cell (0.12 in this example). In 1-2-3, you display values with a percent sign in the cell (such as 12%) by assigning the Percent number format to them (Chapter 3 again — but you knew that).

Of the weirdnesses you have to be mindful of when entering values in a 1-2-3 worksheet, remembering to leave all the commas and dollar signs out of numeric entries is among the hardest. When entering a column or row of figures into a worksheet from a written report, you have to concentrate on the digits and learn to ignore all the (now) irrelevant dollar signs and commas.

Also try to remember not to waste time entering any trailing zeros after the decimal point. For example, you enter the amount $1,205.20 in its cell as **1205.2**, instead of typing **1205.20**. (1-2-3 drops the final zero and puts 1205.2 in the cell regardless of what you do.)

The cursor/numeric keypad conundrum

Worksheets often require many numeric entries. To make this type of data entry as easy and efficient as possible, you probably want to enter numbers with the numeric keypad, which is arranged like a 10-key pad on an adding machine.

The only problem is that the keyboards on older computers don't have a numeric keypad that is separate from the cursor keypad. Instead, their functions are combined so that the same keys that move the cell pointer when Num Lock is off enter the 10 digits (0 through 9) and the decimal point when Num Lock is on. (Remember that you turn Num Lock on and off by pressing the Num Lock key and that 1-2-3 indicates when Num Lock is on by displaying the NUM indicator on the status line.)

This double duty as both cursor and numeric keypad is especially bad news in 1-2-3, where you first want to use the keypad as a numeric keypad to enter the value in the control panel, and immediately thereafter you want to use it as a cursor keypad to enter the value in the cell (while at the same time moving the cell pointer to the next cell that requires data entry). Whew! How many hands does that take?

Believe you me, pressing the Num Lock key to turn on Num Lock and entering your value with the keypad, then pressing the Num Lock key a second time to turn off Num Lock, and then pressing one of the arrow keys on the keypad to enter your value and move the cell pointer is a totally unacceptable method. You'd be much better off keeping Num Lock off, entering values from the top row of the typewriter keys, and using the keypad solely to move the cell pointer.

The work around for this problem is provided compliments of the Shift key. If you're at your computer, take a quick look at the cursor/numeric keypad. Notice how 7 appears above Home on the first white key in the upper left corner, 4 appears above ←, 1 appears above End, and so on. This arrangement is no different from the one used by the key for the / (slash) and the ? (question mark). To type a question mark, you hold down Shift as you press the /? key (otherwise, you get a slash). So, too, if you hold down Shift as you press the Home key on the cursor/numeric keypad, you get the number 7 instead of moving the cell pointer to cell A1.

The only catch is that you must keep Num Lock turned off (otherwise, everything works backwards so that you get numbers until you press the Shift key, and then you move the cell pointer).

I must warn you that using the Shift key to switch in and out of numeric-key mode, while it has it all over the Num Lock key, takes some getting used to. This method has its own kind of rhythm — something like *Shift-while-punching-numbers, release Shift, press arrow* — and then you repeat the entire sequence — *Shift-while-punching-numbers, release Shift, press arrow*. (It has a good beat, but I can't dance to it.)

Star date 34296

If you thought entering regular numbers in 1-2-3 was a strange experience, wait till you get a load of what you have to go through to enter dates as values in a worksheet. Of course, you may wonder why anyone would even bother to enter a date as some sort of value rather than just as a plain old label.

No dancing on the laptop

If you use 1-2-3 on a laptop computer, you have to learn a variation of this Shift/numeric keypad dance to do anything even close to 10-key numeric entry in your 1-2-3 worksheets. Laptop keyboards are so squeezed for space that the keys for the numeric keypad are embedded somewhere in the midst of the regular typewriter keys (with the numbers appearing on the lower edge of the keys rather than on the face).

In this arrangement, a special function key (sometimes simply marked *Fn*) acts like the Shift key does on a full-size keyboard. It temporarily switches the typewriter keys into numeric mode so that you can type numbers. Of course, on a laptop, when you release the Fn key after you enter a value in the control panel, you still have to find and press the appropriate arrow key (none of which do double duty) to enter the value and move the cell pointer. (Sorry, laptoppers, this method doesn't even have a good beat.)

Entering dates as values makes it possible to use them in calculations performed by other formulas. For example, if you enter two dates as values, you can then set up a formula that subtracts the more recent date from the older date and returns the number of days between them. Should you, however, enter these two dates as labels in the worksheet, rather than as values, 1-2-3 will be unable to calculate such a difference by formula.

Now that you understand the rationale for entering dates as values, you're ready to learn how to do it. But, before I spring this one on you, let me first present you with the problems you encounter if you try to enter dates as any normal person would do in a 1-2-3 worksheet.

Ordinarily, you enter dates (especially when you've got a lot of them) in one of two familiar formats. You either separate the month, day, and year with dashes, as in 11-23-93, or you separate them with slashes, as in 11/23/93.

✔ Consider what a cold-blooded calculator like 1-2-3 does with an entry like 11-23-93. Instead of interpreting it as the date November 23, 1993, as anyone with half a brain would do, the program treats it like a math problem. It subtracts 23 from 11 and then subtracts 93 from that result, leaving you with -105 in the cell. Thanks, 1-2-3, that's just what I wanted. *Not!*

✔ And what if you enter this date in the form of 11/23/93? Does 1-2-3 do any better? Of course not! This time, the program thinks you've set up a division problem, so it dutifully divides 11 by 23, and then it divides that result by 93, leaving you with 0.005143 in the cell. (Obviously, 1-2-3 is not even *close* to getting it.)

Okay, so what's a poor non-nerd to do? Short of giving up and entering dates as labels in the form **November 23, 1993**, or a somewhat shorter version, such as **Nov. 23, 1993** (which can't be calculated in formulas), how do you enter dates as values in the worksheet? Voilà! The magic answer is *special Date functions.* You'll discover that 1-2-3 has all kinds of special, built-in functions that perform specific calculations when you feed in the right information. Date functions are just a part of what the special functions have to offer.

To enter a particular date in the worksheet, you use the function *@DATE*. (All 1-2-3 functions start with the @ symbol, which is why they are called *@functions* — pronounced *at functions* — and why the program switches into VALUE mode.)

When using the @DATE function, you need to give the program three pieces of pertinent information — the year, the month, and day (yes, in that strange and partially inverted order).

You enter these three pieces of information separated by commas within a set of closed parentheses (all @functions require such parentheses). For example, to enter the date November 23, 1993, with the @DATE function, you type the following in the cell where you want the date to appear:

```
@DATE(93,11,23)
```

When you press an arrow key or the Enter key to enter this @DATE function in the cell, the value 34296 appears in the cell. So what is this *34296* number anyway — the star date?

Well, no. 1-2-3 has nothing to do with *Star Trek,* so this is not the star date. It's the *serial date,* representing the number of days between November 23, 1993, and the preceding turn of the century.

Serial numbers entered with Date functions, like @DATE, indicate the number of days that have elapsed from January 1, 1900, (otherwise known as *serial number 1*). It's precisely because dates entered with date functions are stored as serial numbers that 1-2-3 is able to perform mathematical calculations between dates in formulas.

Star date, serial date, whatever. . . After entering a date in your worksheet with a Date function, you still have to convert the serial number to a form that a human being (as opposed to a 24th century android) can understand. To convert a serial number, you simply assign one of 1-2-3's five Date number formats to the cell that contains it. (For the particulars on how you accomplish this formatting, see Chapter 3.)

To enter dates in the 21st century, you use three digits to enter the year information, instead of the normal two digits that you use for years in the 20th century. For example, you enter the last day of this century as **@DATE(99,12,31)** and the first day of the next century as **@DATE(100,1,1).**

Changing identities: labels into values and values into labels

You already understand that 1-2-3 determines whether you are entering a label or a value by evaluating the very first character that you type. Most of the time, the program correctly anticipates what kind of entry you are making. In a couple of situations, however, 1-2-3 consistently makes the wrong determination, and you have to override the program manually in order to get the results you want:

- ✔ when you enter text in a cell that begins with a number or other character that 1-2-3 sees as a value
- ✔ when you create a formula that begins with a value stored in a cell reference

In the first situation, perhaps you want to enter a street address, such as **125 Maple Avenue**, or a telephone number, such as **(555) 777-3333.** As soon as you type the **1** of 125 or the **(** of (555), the program goes into VALUE mode. And as soon as you press Enter or an arrow key to enter these *values* into their cells, 1-2-3 beeps at you, goes into EDIT mode, and absolutely refuses to complete your entries because they contain *spaces*, which are allowed only in labels.

To prevent 1-2-3 from going into VALUE mode and embarrassing you in public when you make such entries, you need to trip the program into LABEL mode before you begin typing the entry.

This trick is simple. Just type the apostrophe (') that the program uses to left-align a label in its cell before you begin typing the erstwhile value. After you type the apostrophe label prefix to put the program into LABEL mode, 1-2-3 accepts any combination of numeric and text characters that you then type, and it obediently enters them as a label in the current cell of your worksheet (no more EDIT mode and no more embarrassing noises in front of everyone else in the office).

The second situation where 1-2-3 consistently guesses wrong is when you are creating a formula that begins with a value stored in a cell reference (see the next section for details on how to enter formulas). For example, you want to add the value stored in cell A2 to the value stored in cell B2 and have the sum appear in cell C3. In cell C3 you enter the following formula:

```
A2+B2
```

Seems logical enough, but 1-2-3 doesn't work that way. When you type the A of the cell address A2, the program goes into LABEL mode. Then when you complete the formula entry in cell C3, the following label shows up in the cell where the new sum ought to appear:

```
-A2+B2
```

WARNING!

All it wants to do is calculate!

Even entries without spaces (for example, Social Security numbers such as 666-66-6000 and telephone numbers without their areas codes, such as 555-4000) need to be entered as labels by prefacing them with an apostrophe. Otherwise, 1-2-3 treats them as numbers to be subtracted from one another, and — you got it — this calculating-happy program hands you a bogus computed value where your entry ought to be.

To combat this particular problem, you need to use the opposite technique of finding a character like the apostrophe that trips the program into LABEL mode. Here you must find a character that trips the program into VALUE mode before you enter the first cell reference of the formula. To do this, use the + (plus sign), and enter

```
+A2+B2
```

The reason for using the plus sign, rather than some other value-type character, is that the plus sign has a completely neutral effect on the number stored in the cell. Regardless of whether the number stored in cell A2 is positive or negative, prefacing its cell reference with a plus sign has no affect on its value.

The same is not true if you use a character such as the hyphen (-) to get into VALUE mode. The hyphen is used as the minus sign and, while entering **–A2+B2** would have the desired effect of entering the formula as a value rather than as a label, it would also have the undesired effect of changing the sign of the value in cell A2. The sign would change to positive if the value were negative and to negative if the value were positive. (Remember two negatives make a positive, just like two wrongs make a right. Gotcha!)

Having a formula for success

As entries go in a 1-2-3 worksheet, formulas are the real work horses. If you set formulas up properly, not only will they compute the correct answers when first entered into a cell, but they will thereafter keep themselves up to date, recalculating their results whenever you change any of the values they use.

To enter a formula, you must make sure that 1-2-3 is in VALUE mode. If a formula begins with a number such as 9, –10, or .025, or with one of the built-in functions, such as @SUM or @DATE, the program goes into VALUE mode as soon as you type the first character. If, however, a formula begins with a reference to a cell in the worksheet that contains a value (as is very often the case), you need to type the + (plus sign) to put 1-2-3 into VALUE mode before you indicate the cell address.

Formulas that you build in a worksheet can consist of a built-in function, such as @SUM or @DATE (see "Becoming Fully Functional" later in this chapter for more information on using functions in formulas). They can also consist of a series of values or a series of cell references (that contain values), separated by one or more of the following mathematical operators:

✔ + (plus sign) for addition

✔ – (minus sign or hyphen) for subtraction

- ✔ * (asterisk) for multiplication
- ✔ / (slash) for division
- ✔ ^ (caret) for raising a number to a power

For example, to create a formula in cell C5 that multiplies a value entered in cell A5 by another value next door in cell B5, enter the following formula in cell C5:

```
+A5*B5
```

To enter this formula after selecting cell C5, you can type the entire formula as shown above in the formula bar, or you can follow these steps:

1. Press + (to put 1-2-3 in VALUE mode).
2. Select cell A5 in the worksheet with the mouse or keyboard (which places the cell reference +A5 in the control panel).
3. Press * (the asterisk is used for multiplication rather than x, which you used in school).
4. Select cell B5 in the worksheet (to place the cell reference B5 in the formula).
5. Click on the formula or press Enter to put the formula into cell C5.

The method of actually selecting the cells that you use in a formula, rather than typing in their cell references, is known as *pointing*. Even though pointing may seem to involve more steps than typing cell references, it is quicker.

More important, using the pointing method reduces the risk of putting in the wrong cell reference. When you type a cell reference, you can easily type the wrong column letter or row number and not discover your mistake by just looking at the calculated result returned in the cell. By selecting the cell you want to use, either by clicking on it or moving the cell pointer to it, you reduce the risk of inserting the wrong cell reference in your formula.

When you complete the formula +A5*B5 in cell C5 of your worksheet, 1-2-3 displays the calculated result, which depends on the values currently entered in cells A5 and B5. Here are some examples:

- ✔ If cell A5 contains the value 20 and cell B5 contains the value 100, the program displays the result 2000 in cell C5 of the worksheet.
- ✔ If you change the value in cell A5 to 10, the calculated value in cell C5 immediately changes to 1000.
- ✔ If you clear cell B5 of its entry without replacing it with a new one, the calculated value in cell C5 changes to 0. (Empty cells carry a zero value, so the formula +A5*B5 is equivalent to 20*0 when you clear cell B5.)

The major strength of the electronic spreadsheet is the capability of formulas to change their calculated results automatically to match changes in the cells referenced in the formulas.

Following the pecking order

Many formulas that you create perform more than one mathematical operation. 1-2-3 performs each operation from left to right, according to a pecking order which says that multiplication and division pull more weight than addition and subtraction, and, therefore, they are to be performed first. Consider the following formula:

```
+A2+B2*C2
```

If cell A2 contains the number 5, B2 contains the number 10, and C2 contains the number 2, in essence, 1-2-3 is evaluating the following formula:

```
5+10*2
```

In this formula, 1-2-3 multiplies 10 times 2 to make 20, and then it adds this result to 5 to produce 25.

If you want 1-2-3 to perform the addition between the values in cells A2 and B2 before it multiplies the result by the value in cell C2, you need to enclose the addition operation in parentheses as follows:

```
(A2+B2)*C2
```

The parentheses around the addition tell 1-2-3 that you want this operation performed before the multiplication. (Note that because the left parenthesis triggers VALUE mode, you don't have to put a plus sign before the cell reference to A2.) If cell A2 contains the value 5, B2 contains the value 10, and C2 contains 2, 1-2-3 adds 5 to 10 to make 15 and then multiplies this result by 2 to produce 30.

In fancier formulas, you may need to add more than one set of parentheses, one within another (like the sets of wooden Russian dolls that nest within each other) to indicate the order in which you want calculations to take place. When you nest parentheses, 1-2-3 first performs the calculation contained in the inmost pair of parentheses; then it uses that result in further calculations as it works its way outward. For example, consider the following formula:

```
(A4+(B4-C4))*D4
```

1-2-3 subtracts the value in cell C4 from the value in cell B4, adds the difference to the value in cell A4, and, finally, multiplies that sum by the value in D4. Note that without the additions of the two sets of nested parentheses, 1-2-3 would first multiply the value in cell C4 by that in D4, then it would add the value in A4 to the value in B4, and finally, it would subtract that sum from the result of the multiplication.

When nesting parentheses in a formula, you need to pair them properly so that you have a right parenthesis for every left parenthesis in the formula. 1-2-3 does not tolerate unbalanced parentheses.

If you are impolite enough to omit one of the parentheses, 1-2-3 beeps at you and goes into EDIT mode when you try to enter the formula in the cell. After flipping into EDIT mode, 1-2-3 positions the cursor as close as possible to the place in the formula that is missing the parenthesis.

You can then humbly position the cursor, insert the missing parenthesis in the exact position, and press Enter to correct the unbalanced condition. Another crisis survived.

Keeping your cool when a formula freaks

Under certain circumstances, even the best formulas can freak out in your worksheet. You can tell right away that your formula has gone haywire because when you enter the formula, instead of the nice calculated value that you expected, 1-2-3 places ERR in the cell (no beeps, just a nice, quiet ERR). This weirdness is known, in the parlance of spreadsheets, as an *error value*, and it lets you know that some element, either in the formula or referred to in the formula, prevents 1-2-3 from returning the anticipated calculated value.

- ✔ When an error value shows up in a cell, you have to discover what caused the error and edit the worksheet to replace it with the desired calculation.

- ✔ The worst part about error values is that they can contaminate other formulas in the worksheet. If a formula returns an error value to a cell, and a formula in another cell uses its calculated value, that formula returns the error value as well.

Correcting Those Nasty Little Typos

When entering information in a cell, you can easily make a mistake while typing the entry. If you catch the mistake before you complete the entry, you can delete it simply by pressing the Backspace key (the key immediately above the Enter key) until you have removed all the incorrect characters from the control panel. Then you can retype the rest of the entry in the control panel before you insert it into the current cell.

If you don't discover your mistake until after you've completed the cell entry, you can either replace the entry in its entirety or just edit the incorrect parts. To replace a cell entry, you simply select the cell and start typing your replacement.

Cell entry, you can be replaced!

Note that until you complete the entry 1-2-3 doesn't actually replace the current information in the cell (which is shown after the cell address on the first line of the control panel) with the new information that you enter on the second line. You complete the entry by pressing the Enter key, clicking on the entry on the second line, or pressing one of the arrow keys.

So if you discover that you're in the wrong cell (how embarrassing), you have an opportunity to not replace the current entry. Just quietly clear the control panel of what you've typed by pressing the Esc key or clicking the *right* mouse button and ease on over to the cell where you're supposed to be.

It's time for a change!

If the entry is long and the error is relatively easy to fix, you probably want to edit the contents of the cell instead of replacing it. To edit it, follow these steps:

1. Select the cell.

2. Put the program in EDIT mode by pressing F2.

   Putting 1-2-3 in EDIT mode returns the entry to the second line of the control panel, where you make corrections, and positions the cursor after the last character on this line.

   1-2-3 does not allow you to edit the contents of a cell within the worksheet itself. (You may find this hard to get used to, especially if your background is word processing.)

3. Use the arrow keys to move to the place in the entry that needs editing.

   Table 2-1 lists the keystrokes that you can use to reposition the cursor in the cell entry and delete unwanted characters. If you need to insert new characters at the cursor's position, simply start typing. If you want to delete existing characters at the cursor's position as you type the new ones, press the Insert key to switch from the normal insert mode to overtype mode. 1-2-3 lets you know that you have switched to overtype mode by displaying the OVR mode indicator on the status line. To return to normal insert mode, press the Insert key a second time.

4. When you have completed the corrections in the cell entry, enter the edited information by pressing the Enter key, clicking on the entry in the control panel, or pressing ↑ or ↓. (You can't use → or ← to complete your entry because the program is still in EDIT mode and these keys are reserved for moving the cursor through the entry.)

1-2-3 updates the contents of the cell (both in the cell in the worksheet and on the first line of the control panel). As soon as you complete an edit, 1-2-3 switches from EDIT to READY mode.

Table 2-1	Keystrokes for Editing Cell Entries
Keystroke	**What the Keystroke Does**
Del	Deletes the character at the cursor
Backspace	Deletes the character to the immediate left of the cursor
→	Positions the cursor one character to the right
←	Positions the cursor one character to the left
↑ or ↓	Enters the edited entry in the cell and moves the cell pointer one cell up or down
Home	Moves the cursor to the first character of the cell entry
End	Moves the cursor to the position after the last character in the cell entry
Tab or Ctrl-→	Moves the cursor five characters to the right in the cell entry
Shift-Tab or Ctrl-←	Moves the cursor five characters to the left in the cell entry
Ins	Switches between insert and overtype mode (indicated by the OVR indicator on the status line)

Becoming Fully Functional

Earlier in this chapter, you learned how to create formulas that perform a series of simple mathematical operations, such as addition, subtraction, multiplication, and division. For more complex calculations, instead of creating the formula from scratch out of an intricate combination of these operations, you can find a 1-2-3 function that gets the job done.

A *function* is a predefined formula that performs a particular type of computation. All you have to do to use a function is supply the values that the function uses when performing its calculations. (Such values are known as the *arguments* of the function.) As with simple formulas, you can enter the arguments for most functions either as a numerical value, such as **22** or **–4.56**, or, as is more common, as a cell reference, such as **B10**, or a cell range, such as **C3..F3**.

Unlike a formula that you build yourself, each function in 1-2-3 starts with the @ (at) symbol. Following the @ symbol, you enter the name of the function (in upper- or lowercase — it doesn't matter, just as long as you don't misspell the name). Following the name of the function, you enter whatever arguments are required to performed the calculations. All function arguments are enclosed in a pair of parentheses.

If you type the function on the second line of the control panel, remember not to insert spaces between @, the function name, and the arguments enclosed in parentheses. Some functions use more than one value when performing their designated calculations. In this case, you separate each function with a comma (not with a space).

After you type the @ symbol, the function name, and the left parenthesis that marks the beginning of the arguments for the function, you can then point to any cell or cell range that you want to use as the first function argument, instead of typing in the cell references. When the function uses more than one argument, you can point to the cells or cell ranges you want to use for the second argument immediately after you press , (comma) to complete the first argument.

After you finish entering the last argument, don't forget to type a right parenthesis to mark the end of the argument. Then press Enter or click on the formula to insert the function in the cell and have 1-2-3 calculate the answer.

Pointing It Out

Although you can enter a function by typing its entire contents, you are much better off typing as little as you can and pointing out as much information as you can. To get an idea of how to do this, follow along with the steps for creating formulas using the @SUM function to total the sales in 1993 for the Three Little Pigs Building Supply company.

Figure 2-4 shows the company's worksheet after entering the sales figures for all four quarters for all three categories of sales — Straw & Thatch, Sticks & Stones, and Bricks & Mortar. (Note that you can see only part of these names in column A because the Qtr 1 sales figures in column B cut them off. The next chapter teaches you how to fix this problem.) This figure also shows you the beginnings of the @SUM function that will total the first quarter sales in cell B6.

To begin building this formula, first position the cell pointer in cell B6 and then type

```
@SUM(
```

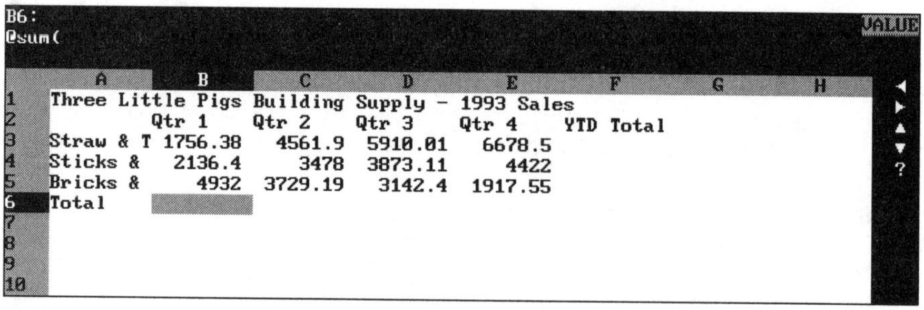

Figure 2-4: Starting the @SUM function.

After entering this much of the first part of the @SUM function, including the left parenthesis that marks the beginning of the arguments, you are ready to start pointing.

To use the @SUM function, you need to indicate which cells are to be totaled as its argument. In this particular example, you want to indicate cells B3 (the Straw & Thatch first quarter total), B4 (the Sticks & Stones first quarter total), and B5 (the Bricks & Mortar first quarter total) as the argument of the @SUM function. A block of neighboring cells like this is called a *cell range*.

To indicate this cell range by pointing, simply move the cell pointer up to cell B3 or click on the cell. 1-2-3 adds this cell reference to the @SUM function so that on the second line of the control panel you see

```
@sum(B3
```

To add the other two cells (B4 and B5), you first need to *anchor* the range on cell B3. Anchoring the range on this first cell enables you to extend the range to include the other two cells.

To anchor a range on the current cell, you press the period (.) key. (Think of the period as a wad of sticky chewing gum that you place right on the cell.) 1-2-3 then indicates that the range is anchored on the current cell by replacing the single cell reference with a doubled cell address separated by periods. Figure 2-5 shows the @SUM function just after you select cell B3 and type the period. Note how 1-2-3 indicates that the range is securely anchored (stuck with gum) on cell B3 by changing the reference in the @SUM function to

```
B3..B3
```

```
B3: 1756.38                                                          POINT
@sum(B3..B3
       A        B        C        D        E        F        G        H
1  Three Little Pigs Building Supply - 1993 Sales
2              Qtr 1    Qtr 2    Qtr 3    Qtr 4    YTD Total
3  Straw & T 1756.38   4561.9   5910.01   6678.5
4  Sticks &   2136.4     3478  3873.11     4422
5  Bricks &     4932  3729.19   3142.4  1917.55
6  Total
7
8
9
10
```

Figure 2-5: Anchoring the range on the first cell to be summed.

After you anchor the cell range, you can move the cell pointer to extend it so that the range includes the other cells in the block. In this example, you press ↓ twice to include cells B4 and B5. Each time you press ↓, 1-2-3 updates the second cell reference in the cell range. When you position the cell pointer in cell B4, the argument of the @SUM function becomes

```
B3..B4
```

Then when you press ↓ again to select cell B5, the range in the function changes again. As shown in Figure 2-6, this time it becomes

```
B3..B5
```

Because the cell range is anchored on cell B3, only the second cell reference changes.

✔ If you discover that you've anchored a range on the wrong cell, you need to press the Esc key to unanchor the range before you try to move the cell pointer to the correct first cell. 1-2-3 does not provide a way to change the reference of the first cell in a range address when the range is anchored. In anchored ranges, only the second cell reference changes as you move the cell pointer.

✔ Note that if you type the @SUM argument, rather than pointing it out, you can enter the range address by typing either **B3..B5** or **B3.B5.** Although 1-2-3 accepts entries with only one period between the first and last cell addresses in the range, it automatically adds a second period. To visually reinforce the idea that the range includes all the (unlisted) cell references between the first and last cell addresses, I use two periods in all range addresses in this book. (Just keep in mind that regardless of how a range address is shown, you can get away with typing only one period.)

✔ To indicate a cell range with a mouse, just drag through the block of cells. You don't need to type a period after you click on the first cell. Simply click and hold the mouse button as you move the mouse pointer through the cells in the range.

After pointing out the range, you finish off the @SUM function by typing the right parenthesis. As soon as you type this character to close off the argument list, 1-2-3 returns the cell pointer to the original cell (B3) where the @SUM argument will be entered (as shown in Figure 2-7).

At this point, you have an opportunity to check out both the location of the @SUM function and its argument.

✔ If you realize that you are about to enter the formula in the wrong cell (especially one that already contains an entry that you don't want to replace), you can bail out and clear the formula from the control panel by pressing Esc.

✔ Likewise, if you review the cell range listed as the argument and notice that you've included the wrong cells in the range, you can fix the cell range by backspacing over the right parenthesis and the range address to delete them. Then you can select the first cell, anchor it with the period, move the cell through the other cells in the block to indicate the correct range, and retype the right parenthesis.

When the @SUM function checks out, you can enter it in the highlighted cell by pressing Enter or clicking on the function in the control panel. Figure 2-8 shows the Three Little Pigs Building Supply sales worksheet after you enter the @SUM function that totals the first quarter sales in cell B6. Notice that the computed total of 8824.78 appears in this cell and the formula @SUM(B3..B5) appears after the cell address on the first line of the control panel.

```
B5: 4932                                                          POINT
@sum(B3..B5

        A         B         C        D        E         F       G       H      ◄
1   Three Little Pigs Building Supply - 1993 Sales                                ►
2             Qtr 1     Qtr 2     Qtr 3    Qtr 4    YTD Total                      ▲
3   Straw & T  1756.38   4561.9   5910.01   6678.5                               ▼
4   Sticks &   2136.4    3478     3873.11   4422                                  ?
5   Bricks &   4932      3729.19  3142.4    1917.55
6   Total
7
8
9
10
```

Figure 2-6: Extending the range to be summed.

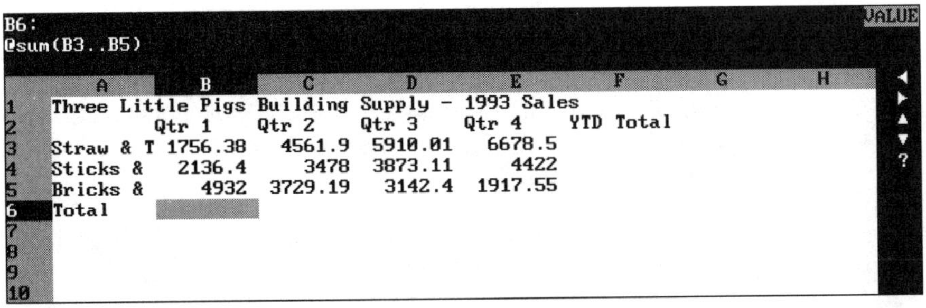

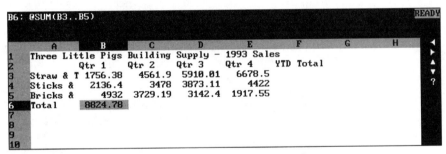

Figure 2-7: Typing) closes the argument list.

Figure 2-8: Worksheet after the @SUM function has been entered.

After building the formula with the @SUM function in cell B6 to total the first quarter sales, you can then copy this formula across the row to have 1-2-3 calculate the totals for the other three quarters (as well as the grand total in the Total column). To copy this formula across the row, you use the /Copy command.

TIP

Using the SUM SmartIcon

If you're using Release 2.4 of 1-2-3 (as of this writing, the latest and greatest version), you don't have to go through these laborious steps. You can click on the SUM SmartIcon and have it create @SUM formulas and select the cells to be summed. See Chapter 11 for details on how to display and use SmartIcons, including the SUM SmartIcon.

Figure 2-9 shows the two prompts that you have to deal with when you use this command. On the left side of the control panel, you see the first prompt, which asks what you want to copy. This prompt appears as soon as you choose the /Copy command. Because the cell pointer was in cell B6 when this command was chosen, the program automatically supplies the current address, B6..B6, as the range to be copied.

Note that 1-2-3 automatically anchors the range on the current cell, as evidenced by the doubling of the cell address and the two periods. If you need to select a different cell, you first have to press the Esc key to unanchor the range.

To accept the current cell as the one you want to copy, press the Enter key. When you press Enter, 1-2-3 displays the second prompt, which is on the right side of the control panel. This prompt asks where you want the selected cell range copied to. The program also supplies the current cell address as the response to this new prompt, except that this time the cell address is not anchored. The unanchored cell address gives you the option of moving the cell pointer without extending the cell range.

For this particular example, it is not necessary to move the cell pointer at all because all the cells where you want to copy the formula are in a single block to the right. (You do no harm if you include the cell with the original formula in the copy to range. The program simply copies the same formula onto itself.) You type a period to anchor the range on the current cell and then press → until you reach cell F6 to highlight the cells and put the cell range B6..F6 on the control panel in response to the To where? prompt.

After indicating the range to copy to, you are ready to copy the formula in cell B6 to the cell range B6..F6 by pressing Enter. Figure 2-10 shows the worksheet after you copy the @SUM formula in cell B6 to the other columns in the table. Note that the answer supplied by the @SUM function copied to cell F6 (where

```
F6:                                                                    POINT
Copy what? B6..B6                              To where? B6..F6

        A         B         C         D         E         F      G      H     ◀
 1  Three Little Pigs Building Supply - 1993 Sales                             ▶
 2            Qtr 1     Qtr 2     Qtr 3     Qtr 4    YTD Total                 ▲
 3  Straw & T 1756.38   4561.9   5910.01   6678.5                             ▼
 4  Sticks &   2136.4     3478   3873.11     4422                             ?
 5  Bricks &     4932  3729.19    3142.4  1917.55
 6  Total     8924.78
 7
 8
 9
10
```

Figure 2-9: Copying the @SUM function across the row.

```
B6: @SUM(B3..B5)                                                           READY

      A         B        C        D        E        F      G       H      ◀
1   Three Little Pigs Building Supply - 1993 Sales                         ▶
2            Qtr 1     Qtr 2    Qtr 3    Qtr 4    YTD Total                ▲
3   Straw & T 1756.38  4561.9  5910.01   6678.5                            ▼
4   Sticks &   2136.4    3478  3873.11     4422                            ?
5   Bricks &     4932 3729.19   3142.4  1917.55
6   Total     8824.78 11769.09 12925.52 13018.05            0
7
8
9
10
```

Figure 2-10: Worksheet with copied formulas.

the grand total of '93 sales is to appear) is 0. This is because the cell range F3..F5, which is used as the argument of the @SUM function, contains only empty cells, and all empty cells (or cells that contain labels for that matter) carry a value of zero.

To complete this sales worksheet, all you have to do is build an @SUM formula that calculates the sales totals for all four quarters for the Straw and Thatch category in cell F3 and then copy this formula to cells F4 and F5. The steps for building this formula are as follows:

1. Put the cell pointer in cell F3 where you want the total to appear.

2. Type **@SUM(** and then move the cell pointer to cell B3, the first cell to be summed.

3. Press . (period) to anchor the range on cell B3 (making the @SUM argument B3..B3).

4. Press → to extend the range to cell E3 (making the @SUM argument B3..E3).

5. Press) to finish off the @SUM function. The cell pointer returns to cell F3. Then press Enter to enter the formula in cell F3.

After building this @SUM formula in cell F3, you are ready to copy it with the /Copy command, as follows:

1. With the cell pointer in cell F3, type **/C** to choose the /Copy command.

2. Press Enter to accept the cell range F3 as the one to copy (listed as the cell range F3..F3 after the Copy what? prompt).

3. Press . (period) to anchor the range to copy to (changing range F3 to F3..F3 after the To where? prompt).

4. Press ↓ twice to include cells F4 and F5 in the range to copy to (changing the range to F3..F5 after the To where? prompt).

5. Press Enter to copy the @SUM formula in cell F3 to cells F4 and F5 (see Figure 2-11).

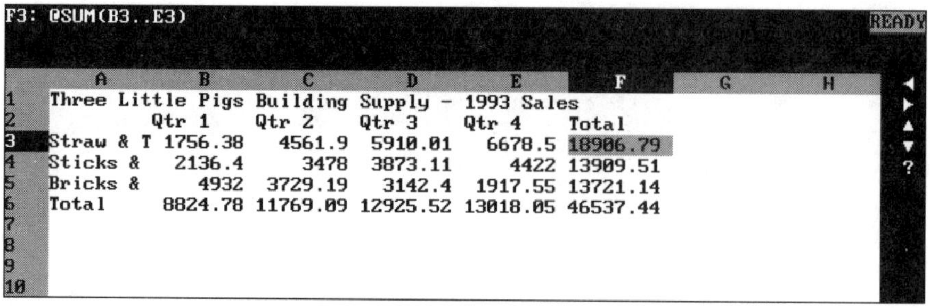

```
F3: @SUM(B3..E3)                                                          READY

        A          B        C        D        E        F       G      H
1  Three Little Pigs Building Supply - 1993 Sales
2              Qtr 1    Qtr 2    Qtr 3    Qtr 4    Total
3  Straw & T 1756.38   4561.9  5910.01   6678.5 18906.79
4  Sticks &   2136.4     3478  3873.11     4422 13909.51
5  Bricks &     4932  3729.19   3142.4  1917.55 13721.14
6  Total     8824.78 11769.09 12925.52 13018.05 46537.44
7
8
9
10
```

Figure 2-11: Worksheet after the @SUM function has been copied down the column.

Saving for the Future

All the work that you do in a worksheet is at risk until you save the file on disk. If your computer crashes or loses power before you have a chance to save the document, you're out of luck. You have to re-create each and every keystroke — a painful task, made all the worse because it's so unnecessary.

To avoid this unpleasantness altogether, adopt this rule of thumb: Save your worksheet anytime that you enter more information than you can possibly bear to lose.

Kindly steer me in the right directory

To save a worksheet, choose the /File Save command. The first time you choose this command, 1-2-3 displays the following prompt on the second line of the control panel (see Figure 2-12):

```
Enter name of file to save:
```

Following this prompt, you see the name of the current directory (G:\123R24 in Figure 2-12), followed by the pattern

```
*.wk1
```

This very strange-looking thing is just DOS talk for *list all the files that use the file extension WK1* (the * is the DOS wildcard character that stands for any filename). The WK1 filename extension indicates that the file is a worksheet created by some version of Release 2 of 1-2-3. (Don't ask me why, but all versions of Release 2 worksheet files use the WK1 extension, when WK2 makes a lot more sense.) The program automatically adds this extension to whatever filename you assign to the worksheet.

On the third line of the control panel, an alphabetical listing of all the worksheet files in the current directory appears (well, at least those files that use the WK1 extension), along with any *subdirectories* (directories below the level of the current directory listed on the second line). If this is too deep for you, grab *DOS For Dummies* and start poring through it.

✔ To save the file in the current directory, simply type the filename (I know it doesn't look as if there's anywhere to type the name, but, trust me, as soon as you start typing, the first character wipes out the *.wk1 thing on the second line of the control panel, and the name appears at the end of the current directory path.)

✔ If you don't want to save your worksheet in the current directory (and it's not a good idea to save your work in the directory with the 1-2-3 program files), you need to choose a new directory before you name the worksheet. If the directory where you want to stash the worksheet file is a sub-directory of the current directory, you can choose it by pressing → until the subdirectory is highlighted and then press Enter. In Figure 2-12, the PIGS directory has just been selected. (Where else would you store this worksheet?) The PIGS directory is a subdirectory of 123R24. When you press Enter, the program adds the subdirectory to the path on the second line of the control panel. It appears as

```
G:\123R24\PIGS\*.wk1
```

You then replace the *.wk1 part of this statement by typing a filename for your worksheet.

And what if the directory where you want to save your file is not a subdirectory of the current directory? What if it's on the same level — or even on a level above?

```
List  ◄  ►  ▲  ▼  ?  ..   A:  B:  C:  D:  E:  F:  G:  H:              FILES
Enter name of file to save: G:\123R24\*.wk1
COLORTST.WK1     SAMPMACS.WK1     PIGS\        TUTOR\        WYSIWYG\
     A        B        C        D        E        F        G        H
1  Three Little Pigs Building Supply - 1993 Sales
2          Qtr 1    Qtr 2    Qtr 3    Qtr 4   YTD Total
3  Straw & T 1756.38   4561.9  5910.01   6678.5 18906.79
4  Sticks &  2136.4     3478  3873.11     4422 13909.51
5  Bricks &    4932  3729.19   3142.4  1917.55 13721.14
6  Total     8824.78 11769.09 12925.52 13018.05 46537.44
7
8
9
10
```

Figure 2-12: Selecting the directory where you want the file saved.

In that case, your best bet is the current directory. If you are using Release 2.3 or 2.4 and have a mouse, you can use the various icons shown on the first line of the control panel.

- ✔ To choose a new drive, click on its icon (D:, E:, and so on).

- ✔ To back up a directory level, click on the two-period icon (..) which represents the parent directory on the DOS family tree — the one on the level above the current directory.

- ✔ To get a full-screen listing of all files and subdirectories, click on LIST (or press F3, the Name key). Then you can use the arrow keys or click on the various scroll icons to move to the subdirectory you want to use and press Enter to choose it.

If you aren't using Release 2.3 or 2.4 and you don't have a mouse, you can choose a different directory by pressing the Esc key twice in a row (the first time to remove `*.wk1` from the pathname and the second time to remove the directory path itself). Then type the filename along with its complete path.

Suppose that you want to save a worksheet with the name *DANNYQ* in the subdirectory called BROWN in the MURPHY directory on drive D of your computer. At the `Enter name of file to save:` prompt, type

```
d:\murphy\brown\dannyq
```

Then press Enter. Just be very, very careful when separating the different parts of the pathname and the path from the filename. Be sure that you press the \ (back slash), rather than the / (forward slash) that you use either for calling up the 1-2-3 command menus or for dividing in a formula.

Please help me name the baby

Believe you me, for most people (Murphy Brown excepted), coming up with a proper name for a baby is a lot easier than coming up with one for a worksheet file. Stingy old DOS doesn't let you use more than eight characters for the main filename, and it doesn't allow any spaces. As a result, you're forced to waste all kinds of time coming up with terrible, clever abbreviations to use in your filenames, and you end up creating names so cryptic that even the CIA can't decode them.

So, once you've thought up your eight-letter (or less) obscurity, you just type it in response to the `Enter name of file to save:` prompt, as shown in Figure 2-13. When typing the letters in the filename, you don't need to capitalize

```
                                                                    EDIT
Enter name of file to save: G:\123R24\PIGS\93sales
       A          B         C        D        E        F      G      H
1  Three Little Pigs Building Supply - 1993 Sales
2              Qtr 1     Qtr 2    Qtr 3    Qtr 4    YTD Total
3  Straw & T 1756.38    4561.9  5910.01   6678.5  18906.79
4  Sticks &   2136.4      3478  3873.11     4422  13909.51
5  Bricks &     4932   3729.19   3142.4  1917.55  13721.14
6  Total     8824.78  11769.09 12925.52 13018.05 46537.44
7
8
9
10
```

Figure 2-13: Naming the worksheet you're saving.

them. The program capitalizes them automatically when you save the file. So, for example, to name a worksheet file *DRXLICST.WK1* (for Drexel income statement worksheet, of course), you just type

```
drxlicst
```

Then you press Enter. You don't need to add the filename extension WK1 because 1-2-3 automatically adds it to the main filename.

Save it again, Sam

Saving a worksheet is not a one-time deal. You need to save your changes at regular intervals to guard against permanent, irretrievable loss of data due to a power outage or your computer's suddenly giving up the ghost. After saving a worksheet the first time, however, you no longer have to fool with the filename (unless you want to save a copy of it with a new name). To save changes in a

Correlating filename extensions with versions of 1-2-3

1-2-3 automatically appends the file extension WK1, to the main filename of worksheet files created with any version of Release 2. Worksheet files created with a version of Release 1 get the extension WKS. Worksheet files created with a version of Release 3 (or 1-2-3 for Windows) get the extension WK3. As you can see, it wasn't until Release 3 of 1-2-3 that Lotus learned to count properly!

worksheet, you choose the /File Save command, just as you did the first time. This time, however, the program shows you the current name of the file (including the path and file extension) after the `Enter name of file to save:` prompt.

If the filename and its current location are cool, just press Enter. A new menu with three commands appears on the second line of the control panel:

```
Cancel    Replace    Backup
```

So many choices . . . how to decide?

✔ To bail out of this operation *without* saving your changes, choose the Cancel command.

✔ To save the previous version of the worksheet as a backup file with the BAK extension, before saving the current version with the WK1 extension (so that you end up with both a DRXLICST.BAK file and a DRXLICST.WK1 file), choose the **B**ackup command.

✔ To save changes without creating a backup file, choose the **R**eplace command.

The whole procedure of having to choose the /File Save command, press Enter to accept the filename, and then choose the **R**eplace command just to save a couple of lousy changes in your worksheet is pretty bogus. To make things easier, flip to Chapter 9 and learn to create a Save macro. Then all you have to do is press Alt-S.

Watching Time March On

You may have noticed that 1-2-3 keeps you constantly informed on how slowly the workday is passing by displaying the date and time at the left edge of the status line. Assuming that you have a wristwatch or you always know the time without having to look at a clock (it's too early to go home and too late to get anything meaningful accomplished), you can get rid of the clock/calendar display and replace it with the name of the worksheet.

The filename display enables you to quickly identify a worksheet that you've retrieved for editing (see Chapter 4 for details). Also, when you're working on a new worksheet, the absence of the filename on the status line reminds you that you haven't yet bothered to save your work and that all of it could be lost if you lose power. (In other words, it reminds you to get it in gear and fire up the old /File Save command.)

To replace the clock/calendar display on the status line with the filename, follow these steps:

1. Choose the /**W**orksheet **G**lobal **D**efault **O**ther **C**lock command (just type /**WGDOC**).

2. Choose the **F**ilename command on the **C**lock menu.

3. Choose the **U**pdate command on the **D**efault menu (to save the change so that you don't have to go through this each time you use 1-2-3).

4. Choose the **Q**uit command on the **D**efault menu to return to the worksheet. The name of the worksheet file you're working on should appear at the beginning of the status line — if not, choose /**F**ile **S**ave and then. . .

Part II
Putting On the Finishing Touches

The 5th Wave   By Rich Tennant

"We see it as a form of copy protection".

The part in which...

You have to admit, especially given the ugly way 1-2-3 displays values, that a newly created worksheet is nothing to write home about. Here's where you find out how to perform some face-lifting by formatting and editing your worksheet.

You learn how to format values, change the alignment of labels, and widen or hide altogether various columns in the worksheet. You learn how to deal effectively with that unending series of changes that the worksheet seems to demand. As part of this process, you learn how to undo your faux pas and how to duplicate information and move it around to new places in the worksheet. And besides all that, you learn to add rows or columns just where you need them and to delete those you don't want to look at anymore — without obliterating the entire worksheet in the bargain!

Chapter 3
Prettying Up the Information

. . . .

In This Chapter

▶ Selecting ranges of cells

▶ Applying built-in number formats to a cell range

▶ Changing the widths of columns in the worksheet

▶ Hiding columns in the worksheet

▶ Changing the alignment of the labels in a cell range

. . . .

*N*ow that you know how to get information into a worksheet and how to make it stay there, you're ready to learn how to make it look pretty. In spreadsheet programs like 1-2-3, you normally don't play with formatting the information until you have done the drudge work of entering all the data in the worksheet.

Because putting information in a cell and formatting a cell are two distinct procedures, when you change the data in a cell that is formatted, the new data assumes the cell's formatting. Also, you can format blank cells in a worksheet, and 1-2-3 automatically applies the formatting to data that you later enter in the cells. (It's sort of like moving into an apartment that has already been decorated.)

After you decide what formatting you want to apply to a portion of the worksheet, you have a choice about how to apply the formatting.

> ✔ Keyboard users first choose the formatting command that they want to use and then select the cell range to apply it to.

> ✔ Mouse users usually do just the opposite. First they select the cell range that they want to format, and then they choose the formatting command that they want to apply.

Regardless of which you do first, you need to know how to pick out the range of cells that you want to format in order to be able to dress up your cells.

Home, Home on the Range

A *cell range* is whatever collection of neighboring cells that you pick out for formatting or editing in some way. Given the extremely rectangular nature of the worksheet and its components, you should not be surprised to find that all the cell ranges in the worksheet have the same kind of Mondrian-like feel. Basically, all of them are just cell blocks made up of different numbers and arrangements of cells.

✔ The smallest possible cell range in the worksheet consists of just one cell. (The so-called current cell, that is, the one with the cell pointer, is really just a single cell selection.)

✔ The largest possible cell range in the worksheet is all the cells in the worksheet (the whole enchilada, so to speak).

✔ Most of the cell ranges that you need to format are probably somewhere in between, consisting of cells in several adjacent columns and rows.

1-2-3 shows a cell range in the worksheet by highlighting the block of cells. Figure 3-1 shows how the cell range B3..E5 (consisting of four columns across and three rows down) appears when you select the range for formatting.

Cell ranges à la keyboard

Whenever you select a 1-2-3 command that requires you to designate a cell range, the program anchors the range on the current cell. Remember that you can tell when the range is anchored on the current cell because the current cell address (B3 for example) is repeated and two periods are added (B3..B3, for example).

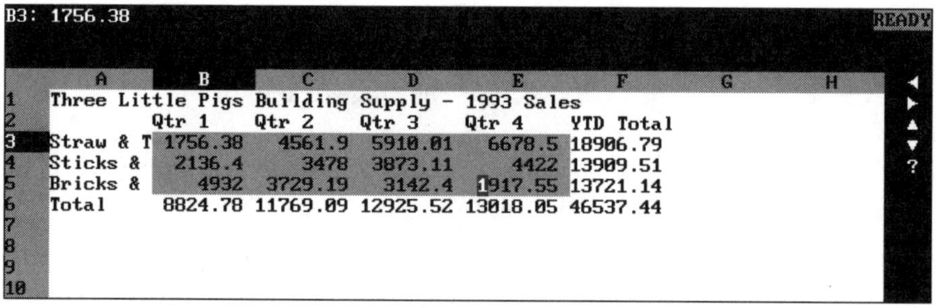

Figure 3-1: Selecting the cell range B3..E5.

When a range is anchored on a cell, you can extend the range in one direction and then in another by pressing one of the keystrokes that move the cell pointer (for a complete list refer to Table 1-1 in Chapter 1). For example, to extend a range two columns to the right and then three rows down, you press → twice and then ↓ three times (or you could first press ↓ three times and then → twice).

If you need to select all the entries in a table of information, remember that you can use the End key plus the arrow keys to quickly extend a cell range to the borders of the table. But first you have to remember to position the cell pointer in one of the cells in the corner of the table *before* you choose the formatting or editing command that anchors the cell range.

Sometimes you realize that you don't have the cell pointer in the correct position *after* you've selected the formatting or editing command and 1-2-3 has anchored the range on the current cell. What to do?

Simply *unanchor* the range by pressing Esc. Then correctly position the cell pointer and once again anchor the range by typing a period. Finally, extend the range with the keys that move the cell pointer. At last.

In Release 2.3 or 2.4 of 1-2-3, you can use the F4 (Abs) key to select a cell range before you choose the 1-2-3 editing or formatting command that you want to apply. Simply position the cell pointer in the first cell of the range (the one in the upper left corner) and then press the F4 (Abs) key. 1-2-3 anchors the range on the current cell, and you can use the arrow keys to extend the range in response to the Range: prompt. After you highlight the entire range, press Enter to set the range (the Range: prompt disappears, but the range remains highlighted). Then choose the 1-2-3 editing or formatting command you want to apply.

When you select a range first, the cell range remains selected after you execute the formatting command. You can then choose another command and apply it to the same range without having to hassle with selecting the cell range again.

Cell ranges à la mouse

The mouse is a very natural tool for selecting cell ranges in 1-2-3. To select a cell range with the mouse, you simply position the mouse pointer on the first cell of the range and then drag the little critter in the direction that you want to extend the range. For example, to extend the cell range to columns to the right, you drag right, highlighting neighboring cells as you go. To extend the range to rows below, you drag downward. To extend the range down and to the right at the same time, you drag diagonally towards the cell in the lower right corner of the block you're highlighting.

- ✔ If you notice that you've included the wrong cells before you release the mouse button, you can deselect the cells and resize the selection by moving the mouse pointer in the opposite direction.

- ✔ If you've totally messed up and you need to start all over again, you can click the *right* mouse button to unanchor the range. (This method leaves only the current cell selected, and you can then move the pointer to the correct cell.) A more direct method is to use the normal left mouse button to click on the cell that you should have selected in the first place and then drag through the cells to highlight the correct range.

When you've highlighted all the cells you want in the cell range, you can release the mouse button.

- ✔ If you've selected the range to be formatted or edited *before* choosing the formatting or editing command (a possibility that is not open to you when you select ranges with the keyboard), the range remains selected, and you can then choose the appropriate menu command. Note that after you apply formatting or editing, the cell range remains selected so that you can apply another format or editing change to it without having to first reselect the range. (This is the real advantage of selecting the range before the command, rather than vice versa.)

- ✔ If you've selected the range with the mouse *after* choosing the appropriate formatting or editing menu command (as you must when selecting ranges with the keyboard), 1-2-3 applies that format or editing change to the highlighted range. It then unanchors the range, leaving only the current cell selected. If you want to apply another format to the same range, you have to choose that command and then reselect the range.

Give Me a Format

As you can see in the example worksheet in Figure 3-1, 1-2-3 displays the numbers you enter and calculate in a worksheet in a variety of ways. The program retains only the significant digits in any value, trashing anything, such as trailing zeros, whose demise doesn't actually reduce the accuracy of the value.

Regardless of the reason, the result is that very often values in the same column of a table don't line up with each other because they aren't aligned on a common decimal point. The table looks as if it has been hit by a whirlwind, but, more important, this haphazard arrangement makes it easier to misinterpret the numbers.

In the Three Little Pigs Building Supply worksheet, the first quarter sales figures in cells B3, B4, and B5 provide a perfect example of this problem. Although the little pigs sold almost three times more bricks and mortar than straw and

Generalities about the General format

1-2-3 formats all calculated values and values that don't follow the pattern of some predefined number format with a general purpose format called, appropriately enough, the General format. The problem with the General format is that it has the nasty habit of dropping all leading and trailing zeros from entries. This makes it very hard to line up numbers in a column on their decimal points. Ergo, enter the number formats!

thatch in the first quarter of 1993, at first glance you can easily get the mistaken impression that straw and thatch was their barn burner (pardon the pun).

To remedy such problems with values, you need to apply one of the 1-2-3 number formats to their cells. The number formats are selected from the /**R**ange Format command menu. (See Table 3-1 for a run-down on the formats.)

Table 3-1	1-2-3 Number Formats	
/Range Format Command	**Control Panel Abbreviation (assuming default number of decimal places)**	**What the Format's Good for**
Fixed	(F2)	Fixes the number of decimal places displayed in values. When setting this format, you decide how many decimal places to display (between 0 and 15, with 2 the default).
Sci (for Scientific)	(S2)	Displays values in scientific notation, using exponents. When setting this format, you decide how many decimal places to display (between 0 and 15, with 2 the default).
Currency	(C2)	Displays values as dollars and cents. This format adds a dollar sign, puts commas between thousands and multiples thereof, and places negative numbers in parentheses. When setting this format, you decide how many decimal places to display (between 0 and 15, with 2, naturally, the default).

(continued)

Table 3-1	1-2-3 Number Formats *(continued)*	
/Range Format Command	**Control Panel Abbreviation (assuming default number of decimal places)**	**What the Format's Good for**
, (for Comma)	(,2)	This format adds commas between thousands and multiples thereof and places negative numbers in parentheses. When setting this format, you decide the number of decimal places to use (between 0 and 15, with 2 the default).
General	(G)	Displays the significant digits of values as entered or calculated, with up to 10 decimal places. If the widths of the cells are too narrow to display all digits, this format converts them to scientific notation.
+/–	(+)	Displays values with symbols. Positive values are represented with plus signs (+), negative values with hyphens (–), and zeros with periods (.).
Percent	(P2)	Displays your values as percentages by multiplying them by 100 and adding a % sign. As with the Currency and Comma formats, you decide the number of decimal places to display (between 0 and 15, with 2 the default).
Date	(D1) through (D5) for the Date formats; (D6) through (D9) for the Time formats	Displays values as one of the five date formats or four time formats. This format converts data serial numbers or time fractions to dates and times that humans can read.
Text	(T)	Displays the contents of each cell in the cell range as it appears in the control panel.
Hidden	(H)	Hides the display of all entries in the range. Note that this format affects both labels and values in the cell range. The contents of cells in a hidden range continue to be displayed after the cell address in the control panel.
Reset		Returns values to the program default (which is **General** unless you change it to something else with the **/W**orksheet **G**lobal **F**ormat command).

To select the cell range to be formatted with the keyboard, follow these steps:

1. Position the cell pointer in the first cell of the range.

2. Choose the appropriate number format from the /**R**ange Format menu.

3. Use the cursor keys to extend the range to be formatted.

If you are using the mouse, reverse this process:

1. Select the cell range to be formatted by dragging through the block of cells.

2. Choose the number format you want to apply to the range on the /**R**ange Format menu.

After applying a format to a cell range, 1-2-3 indicates what format was used by displaying an abbreviation in front of the value in the control panel. For example, if you apply the Currency format with two decimal places to the value 12.75 entered in cell B3, you see the following at the top of the control panel when the cell pointer is in cell B3:

```
B3: (C2) 12.75
```

In the worksheet itself, however, the value appears in the cell as

```
$12.75
```

Money, money, money...

Given the financial nature of most worksheets, you probably will use the Currency format more than any other. This format is really easy to apply because the Currency format adds a dollar sign, commas between thousands of dollars, hundreds of thousands of dollars (trillions of dollars, of course, if you're in government work), and adds two decimal places to any values in a selected range. If any values in the cell selection are negative, the Currency format displays them in parentheses — the way accountants like them — and displays them in red on a color monitor — the way governments are used to seeing them.

Figure 3-2 shows the Three Little Pigs Building Supply 1993 sales worksheet after cell range F3..F6 has been selected with the mouse and the /**R**ange Format Currency command has been chosen. To format this cell range with the Currency format with two decimal places, you simply press Enter twice the first time to accept 2 as the number of decimal places and the second time to apply the format to the selected cell range.

```
F3: @SUM(B3..E3)                                                    MENU
Fixed  Sci  Currency  ,  General  +/-  Percent  Date  Text  Hidden  Reset
Currency format ($x,xxx.xx)
          A          B          C          D          E          F          G          H
1    Three Little Pigs Building Supply - 1993 Sales
2              Qtr 1      Qtr 2      Qtr 3      Qtr 4    YTD Total
3    Straw & T 1756.38    4561.9    5910.01     6678.5  18906.79
4    Sticks &   2136.4      3478    3873.11       4422  13909.51
5    Bricks &     4932   3729.19     3142.4    1917.55  13721.14
6    Total     8824.78  11769.09  12925.52   13018.05  46537.44
7
8
9
10
```

Figure 3-2: First quarter sales totals before the Currency format is applied.

International Financiers take note!

If you work in the world of high finance and your worksheets deal in foreign currencies such as Pounds, Yen, Pesetas, and so on, you can change the currency symbol that 1-2-3 displays when you apply the Currency format. Also, if necessary, you can select a new thousands separator and decimal point indicator (for countries where the comma serves as the decimal point and the period serves as the thousands separator).

To change the currency symbol, choose the **/W**orksheet **G**lobal **D**efault **O**ther International

Currency command, delete the $ sign, enter the new symbol (press Alt-F1 and then type **L=** for the Pound symbol, **Y=** for the Yen symbol, or **PT** for the Pesetas symbol, and then choose the **P**refix or **S**uffix command.

To change the thousands separator and decimal point indicator, choose the **/W**orksheet **G**lobal **D**efault **O**ther International **P**unctuation command and then choose the appropriate setting.

Where'd those numbers go?

Figure 3-3 shows the Three Little Pigs Building Supply 1993 sales worksheet after the Currency format with two decimal places has been applied to cell range F3..F6. As you can see, something must have gone wrong because the formatted cell range now displays ********* instead of the yearly sales totals. In fact, this string of asterisk symbols where a dollar amount should appear merely indicates that the Currency format (with its dollar sign, commas to separate thousands, and two decimal places) added so many characters to the values in this range that 1-2-3 can no longer display them all, given the current width of the cells.

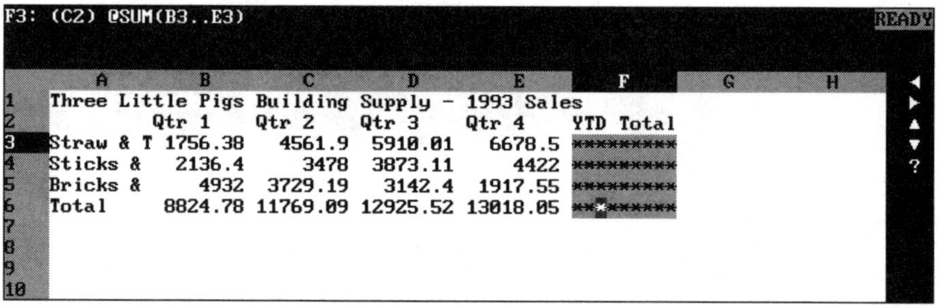

Figure 3-3: Worksheet after the Currency format has been applied to the totals column.

To get rid of the asterisk symbols and bring back the totals in cell range F3..F6, you need to widen column F. (If you can't wait to find out how to widen it, jump ahead to "If the Column Fits..." later in this chapter.)

Let's all remain comma

The Comma format (appearing as **,** between the Currency and General formats on the **/R**ange Format menu) offers a good alternative to the Currency format. Like Currency, it inserts commas in larger numbers to separate thousands, hundred thousands, millions, and, you get the idea. This format also naturally displays two decimal places (although you can choose between 0 and 15 decimal places), and it displays negative values in parentheses and in red on a color monitor. What it doesn't display is dollar signs. It's perfect for formatting tables where you are obviously dealing with dollars and cents and for larger values that have nothing to do with money.

The Comma format also works well for the bulk of the values in the Three Little Pigs Building Supply 1993 sales worksheet. Figure 3-4 shows the cell range B3..E5 after the Comma format with two decimal places has been applied. Note that the helter-skelter look is gone. The Comma format gives each number two decimal places and aligns the numbers on the decimal point.

Playing the percentages

Many worksheets use percentages in the form of interest rates, growth rates, inflation rates, and so on. To insert such a value in a cell, you can either enter the value with the percent sign (for example, **15%**) or enter the decimal

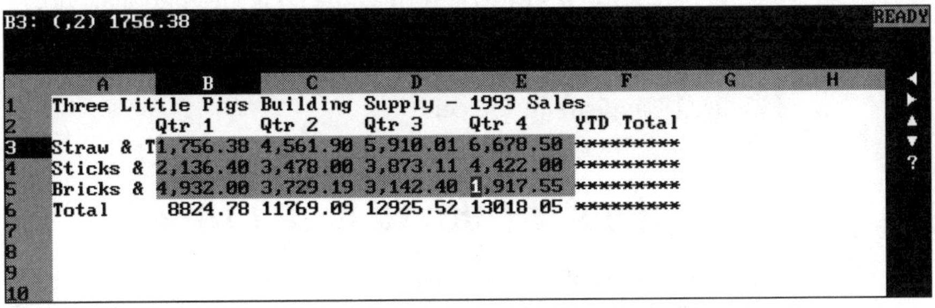

Figure 3-4: Quarterly sales figures displayed in the Comma format.

equivalent (for example, **.15**). Either way, 1-2-3 displays the value In the decimal form until you assign a Percent number format to its cell. Follow these steps to display 15 percent as 15% in the worksheet:

1. Select the value's cell.

2. Choose the **/R**ange **F**ormat **P**ercent command.

3. Enter **0** as the number of decimal places.

4. Press Enter to apply the format to the cell.

Can you make it a date?

As Chapter 2 explains, you enter dates as values by using special Date functions, which return serial numbers that only a computer could love. To transform a date serial number to something intelligible to humans, select its cell, choose the **/R**ange **F**ormat **D**ate command, and select a date format from the following menu commands:

```
1 (DD-MMM-YY) 2 (DD-MMM) 3 (MMM-YY) 4 (Long Intn'l) 5 (Short Intn'l)Time
```

To get an idea of what all this DD, MM business means, here's how a sample date, 34380 (that's February 15, 1994, for you humans out there), appears in the different date formats:

- In Date Format 1 (also known as the Lotus standard long format), 15-Feb-94 appears in the cell.

- In Date Format 2 (also known as the Lotus standard short format), 15-Feb appears in the cell.

- In Date Format 3, Feb-94 (should be, but is not, known as the Lotus non-standard even shorter format) appears in the cell.

- In Date Format 4 (also known as the Long International date format), 02/15/94 appears in the cell.

- In Date Format 5 (also known as the Short International date format), 02/15 appears in the cell.

What does it take to be on time?

Like dates, times of the day are entered as values with a special Time function, called (what else?) @TIME. To use the @TIME function, you enter the number of the hour, minutes, and (if you're really into details) seconds. For example, to enter 8:30 a.m. in a cell of the worksheet, you enter

```
@TIME(8,30,0)
```

Just for our European friends

Whereas we, in the Colonies, tend to like seeing the month ahead of the day in our dates, as in 05/03/93, and whereas most of you, in the Mother Countries, prefer to see it the other way around, as in 03/05/93, be it resolved, therefore, that you can, if you wish, modify the Long and Short International date formats so that any dates that you format with either the D4 or D5 Date format put the day ahead of the month.

To this end, therefore, first choose the **/W**orksheet **G**lobal **D**efault **O**ther **I**nternational **D**ate command and then choose the **B** (DD/MM/YY) or **C** (DD.MM.YY) command. (Note, however, that you need to choose carefully. Option C separates the dates with periods, and Option B separates them with slashes.)

Considering what 1-2-3 does to dates, you won't be surprised to learn that the program converts your entry into a decimal number that represents what percentage the time is of a 24-hour period. This number is called a *time fraction*. If you enter 8:30 a.m., the following time fraction appears in the cell:

```
0.3541666
```

Note that to enter 8:30 p.m. in the worksheet, instead of 8:30 a.m., you have to add 12 hours to the hour argument in the @TIME function. You enter

```
@TIME(20,30,0)
```

The function places the following value in the cell:

```
0.8541666
```

Of course, time fractions are no more legible than date serial numbers (although, like date serial numbers, they enable you to perform calculations), so you need to format them. To format a time fraction, you choose the **/R**ange Format **D**ate **T**ime command (remember that the **T**ime command is the last command to appear on the **D**ate menu). The following Time format commands appear:

```
1 (HH:MM:SS AM/PM) 2 (HH:MM AM/PM) 3 (Long Intn'l) 4 (Short Intn'l)
```

The first two formats express the times before noon with the AM designation and those after noon with the PM designation. The only difference between them is that Time format 1 displays seconds, but Time format 2 does not display them.

Both Time format 3 (the Long International) and Time format 4 (the Short International) express the time on a 24-hour clock (you know, 1:00 p.m. is 1300). The only difference between them is that the Long International Time format includes the number of seconds, but the Short International Time format does not display them.

What you see is not always what you get

Make no mistake about it, all these fancy number formats do is spiff up the presentation of the values in your worksheet. Like a good illusionist, a particular number format may sometimes appear to have magically transformed some of your entries, but, in reality, they are the same old numbers you started with. Suppose that a formula returns the following value in a cell:

```
25.6456
```

If you apply the Currency format, the following value appears in the cell, just as if 1-2-3 had rounded the value up to two decimal places:

```
$25.65
```

In fact, the program has rounded up only the display of the calculated value. The cell still contains the same old value of 25.456. If you use this cell in another worksheet formula, keep in mind that 1-2-3 uses the behind-the-scenes value in its calculation, not the spiffed-up value you see in the cell.

But what if you need the values to match their formatted appearance in the worksheet? Well, to make them the same, you use the @ROUND function to round off the values and then replace the original values with the rounded values (see Chapter 12 for details).

If the Column Fits...

Adjusting the column widths is one of those never-ending worksheet chores that's on a par with housekeeping chores like doing dishes or cleaning. Yuck. No sooner do you finish putting all your columns in order than you make a change to the worksheet (such as formatting a table of figures) that requires new column-width adjustments.

Fortunately, 1-2-3's **/W**orksheet **C**olumn **S**et-Width command makes short work of changing the width of any column in the worksheet. Take the display problem in column F of the Three Little Pigs Building Supply sales worksheet in Figures 3-3 and 3-4. Adding the Currency format adds so many characters that 1-2-3 can no longer display them all in its standard nine-character column.

To display the dollar amounts in column F, put the cell pointer somewhere in the column, type **/WCS** (for **/W**orksheet **C**olumn **S**et-Width), press the → key *x* times until all the formatted totals are visible on the screen, and then press Enter. Voilà! Numbers appear in column F, as shown in Figure 3-5. What could be easier! (It's almost as magical as cleaning house in those TV commercials.)

To reiterate, here are the four easy steps you follow to make your windows shine. . . . er, widen or narrow a column in the worksheet:

1. Position the cell pointer in any cell in the column you want to widen or narrow.

2. Choose the **/W**orksheet **C**olumn **S**et-Width command (just type **/WCS**).

3. Enter the number of characters (between 1 and 240) you want in the column, in response to the control panel prompt

   ```
   Enter column width (1..240):
   ```

   If you don't know exactly how many characters you want, press → or ←.

   Each time you press one of these keys, 1-2-3 not only changes the column-width number listed on the control panel but also modifies the display of the selected column accordingly.

4. Press Enter to set the new width of the column.

   When you change the width of a column, 1-2-3 indicates the current width after the cell address on the first line of the control panel. The characters are enclosed in brackets. For example, it displays [W11] when you widen the column to 11 characters.

```
F3: (C2) [W11] @SUM(B3..E3)                                    POINT
Enter column width (1..240): 11
     A         B         C         D         E         F         G
1    Three Little Pigs Building Supply - 1993 Sales
2              Qtr 1     Qtr 2     Qtr 3     Qtr 4     YTD Total
3    Straw & T1,756.38 4,561.90 5,910.01 6,678.50 $18,906.79
4    Sticks & 2,136.40 3,478.00 3,873.11 4,422.00 $13,909.51
5    Bricks & 4,932.00 3,729.19 3,142.40 1,917.55 $13,721.14
6    Total      8824.78 11769.09 12925.52 13018.05 $46,537.44
7
8
9
10
```

Figure 3-5: Worksheet after widening column F to display the formatted totals.

Dealing with a bunch of columns

Sometimes you have a situation where a bunch of neighboring columns all need widening (or narrowing). Provided that you like uniformity, you can set all of them to the same width in one quick operation. (Unless you're using Release 2.0 — sorry kids, this feature wasn't added until Release 2.2.)

Figure 3-6 illustrates a time when this feature comes in handy. Here you see the Three Little Pigs Building Supply sales worksheet after the Currency format with two decimal places has been applied to the quarterly totals in the cell range B6..E6. Adding the Currency formatting kinda broke the bank. This worksheet has stars in some cells where moola oughta be!

The following steps provide an example of how to widen a range of columns at the same time, instead of widening each one individually (sorry, 2.0 users):

1. Put the cell pointer in one of the cells in the first column to be widened, such as cell B6.

2. Choose the /**W**orksheet **C**olumn **C**olumn-Range **S**et-Width command.

   1-2-3 displays the prompt

   ```
   Enter range for column width change:
   ```

   The prompt is followed by the address of the current cell anchored as a range. If you've already used a mouse to select a cell range, this prompt does not appear, and you can skip to the information on the prompt in item 4.

3. Press the → key to extend the range of columns to include all four columns to be widened (the range B6..E6 in this example).

```
B6: (C2) @SUM(B3..B5)                                              READY

        A        B        C        D        E        F        G      ◄
1  Three Little Pigs Building Supply - 1993 Sales                       ►
2           Qtr 1    Qtr 2    Qtr 3    Qtr 4    YTD Total               ▲
3  Straw & T1,756.38 4,561.90 5,910.01 6,678.50 $18,906.79             ▼
4  Sticks & 2,136.40 3,478.00 3,873.11 4,422.00 $13,909.51             ?
5  Bricks & 4,932.00 3,729.19 3,142.40 1,917.55 $13,721.14
6  Total    ***************************************$46,537.44
7
8
9
10
```

Figure 3-6: Worksheet after the Currency format has been applied to the totals in row 6.

4. Press Enter.

1-2-3 then displays the prompt

```
Select a width for range of columns (1..240):
```

5. Type the number of characters you want to be able to include in each cell or press → or ← until the columns are the width you want them to be.

6. Press Enter.

1-2-3 sets all the columns to the selected width.

Figure 3-7 shows the sample worksheet after the width for range of columns B through E has been set to 11 characters. All the formatted quarterly totals appear in row 6.

Column Hide 'n Seek

The skinniest you can make a column with the /Worksheet Column Set-Width command is one character wide (pretty skinny, but still clearly visible). If you want to make the column display disappear completely, you have to use the /Worksheet Column Hide command instead.

Now why in the world would you spend all kinds of time entering and formatting information and then go and hide it? Actually, you mostly play hide and seek with worksheet information when you are setting up printed reports. For example, you may have a worksheet that contains a column listing employee salaries. Although you need the information in the column to calculate departmental budget figures, you probably prefer to leave it off most printed reports. Instead of wasting time moving the column of salary figures outside the area to be printed, you can simply hide it until after you've printed the report.

```
B6: (C2) [W11] @SUM(B3..B5)                                        POINT
Select a width for range of columns (1..240): 11
         A          B         C         D         E         F
1  Three Little Pigs Building Supply - 1993 Sales
2             Qtr 1     Qtr 2     Qtr 3     Qtr 4     YTD Total
3  Straw & T  1,756.38  4,561.90  5,910.01  6,678.50 $18,906.79
4  Sticks &   2,136.40  3,478.00  3,873.11  4,422.00 $13,909.51
5  Bricks &   4,932.00  3,729.19  3,142.40  1,917.55 $13,721.14
6  Total      $8,824.78 $11,769.09 $12,925.52 $13,018.05 $46,537.44
7
8
9
10
```

Figure 3-7: Worksheet after columns with totals have been widened.

Hiding columns is a lot like changing their width. You can use the /Worksheet Column Hide command to hide just the column with the cell pointer or to hide a range of columns.

For an idea of how this command works, follow along with the steps for hiding columns B through E in the Three Little Pigs Building Supply sales worksheet so that the column of the yearly totals appears right next to the row headings in column A:

1. Place the cell pointer in one of the cells in column B, the first column that you want to hide (cell B6, for example).

2. Choose the /Worksheet Column Hide command.

   The program displays the prompt

   ```
   Specify column to hide:
   ```

   The current cell address appears after the prompt. If you wanted to hide only the column with the cell pointer, you would press Enter at this point.

3. Anchor the cell pointer by typing a period so that you can hide a range of columns, starting with the one containing the cell pointer.

   The program changes the cell address to a cell range. In this example, it changes B6 to B6..B6.

4. Extend the range to include all the columns to be hidden by pressing → or ←.

   In this example, you press → three times to highlight the range B6..E6.

5. Press Enter.

   The program hides the columns in the highlighted range from view.

Figure 3-8 shows the results. After you hide columns B through E, it looks like the year-to-date totals were entered next to their associated headings. The only

```
F6: (C2) [W11] @SUM(F3..F5)                                    READY

         A            F       G      H      I      J      K      ◄
1  Three Little Pigs Building Supply - 1993 Sales               ►
2                    YTD Total                                  ▲
3  Straw & Thatch  $18,906.79                                   ▼
4  Sticks & Stones $13,909.51                                   ?
5  Bricks & Mortar $13,721.14
6  Total           $46,537.44
7
8
9
10
```

Figure 3-8: Worksheet after columns B, C, D, and E have been hidden.

way you can tell that some columns are missing from this worksheet is from the frame. Notice that column F follows column A. The information stored in columns B, C, D, and E is safe and sound; it's just not visible at the moment. If you print the worksheet in this condition, it appears on paper as if the entries had never existed.

Bring 'em back!

Redisplaying a hidden column or range of columns is simply the reverse of hiding them. When you choose the /**W**orksheet **C**olumn **D**isplay command, 1-2-3 *temporarily* redisplays all hidden columns in the worksheet display. The columns that are hidden are indicated on the screen by an asterisk following their column letters (for example, B*) and the prompt

```
Specify hidden columns to redisplay:
```

The address of the current cell follows the prompt.

- ✔ To redisplay a single column, place the cell pointer in one of its cells and press Enter.

- ✔ To redisplay more than one column, highlight a range and press Enter.

Figure 3-9 shows the Three Little Pigs Building Supply sample worksheet after you choose the /**W**orksheet **C**olumn **D**isplay command and indicate which columns to redisplay. Note how 1-2-3 shows which columns are hidden by placing an asterisk after the column letter. To display hidden columns B through E, simply press ← to move the cell pointer to cell E6, type a period to anchor the cell range, press ← three times to extend the cell range (it appears as E6..B6 in the control panel), and press Enter to bring back the columns permanently to the worksheet display.

```
B6: (C2) [W11] @SUM(B3..B5)                                                POINT
Specify hidden columns to redisplay: E6..B6

         A          B*        C*        D*        E*        F              ◄
1  Three Little Pigs Building Supply - 1993 Sales                          ►
2                   Qtr 1     Qtr 2     Qtr 3     Qtr 4     YTD Total       ▲
3  Straw & Thatch   1,756.38  4,561.90  5,910.01  6,678.50 $18,906.79      ▼
4  Sticks & Stones  2,136.40  3,478.00  3,873.11  4,422.00 $13,909.51      ?
5  Bricks & Mortar  4,932.00  3,729.19  3,142.40  1,917.55 $13,721.14
6  Total            $8,824.78 $11,769.09 $12,925.52 $13,018.05 $46,537.44
7
8
9
10
```

Figure 3-9: Displaying the hidden columns in the worksheet.

As soon as you press Enter, the asterisk disappears from the frame of each selected column, and its entries in the visible area of the worksheet remain on the screen. Note that the cell pointer jumps back to whatever cell it was in when you first selected the command.

Put 'em in Their Places

In Chapter 2 you learned that the initial alignment of a cell entry depends on what type of entry it is. The program left-aligns all labels and right-aligns all values. Although 1-2-3 gives you no choice over the way *values* are aligned, you can change the alignment of any *labels* from left-aligned to centered or right-aligned.

Being smarter than a computer program, you can fool 1-2-3 into accepting a value as a label simply by starting its entry with an apostrophe or with another label prefix.

  ✔ If you start an entry with an apostrophe, the program *left-aligns* the entry in its cell.

  ✔ If you know at the time you're entering a label that you want to *center* it in its cell, start it with the circumflex (^), which acts as the label prefix for centering a label. (Hold down the Shift key as you press 6 on the top row of the typewriter keys.)

  ✔ If you prefer to *right-align* the label in its cell, start the entry with the double quotation mark ("), the label prefix for right-aligning a label. (Hold down the Shift key as you press the same key that gives you the apostrophe.)

Most of the time you don't know whether you want to change the alignment of various column and row headings in your worksheet until after you have adjusted the column widths. No problem. You can use the /**R**ange **L**abel command to easily modify the alignment of labels after the fact. As soon as you choose this command, 1-2-3 displays the following menu commands on the second line of the control panel:

```
Left    Right  Center
```

  ✔ Choose **Left** to restore the label(s) in a cell or cell range to their original left alignment.

  ✔ Choose **Right** to change their alignment to right alignment.

  ✔ Choose **Center** to center them.

Figure 3-10 shows the column headings in the cell range B2..F2 after you use the /**R**ange **L**abel Center command to center the labels in their columns. You should note two things about this figure.

```
B2: [W11] ^Qtr 1                                                    READY

         A            B            C            D            E          F
1  Three Little Pigs Building Supply - 1993 Sales
2                     Qtr 1        Qtr 2        Qtr 3        Qtr 4    YTD Total
3  Straw & Thatch     1,756.38     4,561.90     5,910.01     6,678.50 $18,906.79
4  Sticks & Stones    2,136.40     3,478.00     3,873.11     4,422.00 $13,909.51
5  Bricks & Mortar    4,932.00     3,729.19     3,142.40     1,917.55 $13,721.14
6  Total             $8,824.78   $11,769.09   $12,925.52   $13,018.05 $46,537.44
7
8
9
10
```

Figure 3-10: Worksheet after the labels in the cell range B2..F2 have been centered.

1. Not only are the column headings nicely centered over the values in their columns, but they will remain centered — even if you start fooling with the widths of the columns.

2. Using the /**R**ange **L**abel **C**enter command has simply changed the original left-align label prefix (') to the center label prefix (^). (This prefix is in the first line of the control panel, where the contents of cell B2 are listed after the cell address.) In fact, you can change the alignment of any label simply by editing the label to change its label prefix character.

Centering a Title over Several Columns

Sometimes you want to center a label over several columns in the worksheet, instead of just within its own cell. For example, in the 1993 sales table, it would be nice to center the worksheet title, Three Little Pigs Building Supply - 1993 Sales, over the entire table of data (columns A through F). As it stands now, this title is entered as a label in cell A1, and it spills over into the blank cells to the right in columns B through D.

To center this title over all the columns in the table, you need to edit the long label in cell A1 and pad it with spaces. (You can't tell how many spaces to add. You just have to do it by trial and error.)

To edit this label so that it's centered, this is what you have to do:

1. Put the cell pointer in cell A1.

2. Press F2 (Edit).

3. Move the cursor under the T in Three. (Be sure that it's not under the apostrophe label prefix.)

4. Press the spacebar to insert blank spaces before the first character.

5. Press Enter.

6. Look at the worksheet. If the label isn't centered, go back to step 1 and try again.

Figure 3-11 shows the worksheet after 10 spaces have been inserted between the apostrophe label prefix and the first character. As you can see, the title now appears perfectly centered over the table.

Note that this "perfect" centering exists only as long as the table remains at its present width. If you change the column widths or add columns to the table, the title no longer appears perfectly centered over the entries. In that event, you have to go back and tinker with the number of spaces padding the label.

```
A1: [W16] '          Three Little Pigs Building Supply - 1993 Sales          READY

            A             B           C           D           E           F      ◄
1                Three Little Pigs Building Supply - 1993 Sales                   ►
2                    Qtr 1       Qtr 2       Qtr 3       Qtr 4     YTD Total       ▲
3     Straw & Thatch   1,756.38    4,561.90    5,910.01    6,678.50 $18,906.79     ▼
4     Sticks & Stones  2,136.40    3,478.00    3,873.11    4,422.00 $13,909.51     ?
5     Bricks & Mortar  4,932.00    3,729.19    3,142.40    1,917.55 $13,721.14
6     Total           $8,824.78 $11,769.09 $12,925.52 $13,018.05 $46,537.44
7
8
9
10
```

Figure 3-11: Worksheet after the title has been centered over its table.

Centering a title with Wysiwyg

If you are using Release 2.3 or 2.4 of 1-2-3 and your computer has sufficient memory to load the Wysiwyg add-in (see Chapter 10), you can use a much superior method for centering a label over a range of columns.

1. Position the cell pointer in the cell with the label.

2. Choose the :Text Align Center command.

3. Extend the range to the right to include all the columns over which the label is to be centered.

4. Press Enter.

Voilà! The label is centered over all the columns in the range. Better still, this label remains perfectly centered over these columns no matter what adjustments you later make to their widths.

If you're using Release 2.4 of 1-2-3, you can simplify this process even further by using the "Center Across Columns" SmartIcon. Simply select the cell range (starting with the cell containing the label) within which the title is to be centered and then click the SmartIcon at the very bottom of the second icon palette.

Chapter 4
Going through Changes

● ●

In This Chapter

▶ Opening the worksheet that needs editing

▶ Using Undo to recover from a boo-boo

▶ Moving and copying entries in a worksheet

▶ The ins and outs of copying formulas

▶ Erasing entries from a cell range

▶ Deleting rows and columns

▶ Inserting new rows and columns

● ●

*P*icture this: you've just finished creating, formatting, and printing a major project with 1-2-3, a worksheet with your department's budget for the next fiscal year. Because you finally understand a little bit about how this thing works, you've gotten the job done in crack time. You're actually ahead of schedule; it's Wednesday, and the budget isn't due until Friday.

You've turned the printed worksheet over to your boss so that she can check the numbers. But not to worry. You have plenty of time to make those inevitable last-minute corrections. For a change, you're feeling on top of the situation. Maybe, just maybe, learning to use 1-2-3 isn't going to be as painful as trying to learn that last program.

Then comes the reality check. Your boss comes over, and she's plainly agitated. "We forgot to include the estimates for the temps and our overtime hours. They've got to go right here. While you're adding them, can you move these rows of figures up and those columns over?"

As she continues to "suggest" improvements to go along with the major additions that she wants you to make, your heart begins to sink. These modifications are in a different league from "let's change these column headings from bold to italics and add shading to that row of totals." Clearly, you're looking at a lot more work on this baby than you had contemplated. Even worse, however, you're looking at making structural changes that threaten to unravel the very fabric of your beautiful worksheet!

The point of this fable is that editing a worksheet can occur on two different levels. You can make changes that affect the contents of the cells, such as copying a row of column headings or moving a table to a new area in the worksheet, or you can make changes that affect the structure of the worksheet itself, such as inserting new columns or rows or deleting unnecessary columns or rows.

In this chapter, you learn how to make both types of changes to a worksheet safely. The mechanics of copying and moving data or inserting and deleting rows from a worksheet are simple to master. The impact that these changes have on the worksheet takes a little more effort to understand. Not to worry. You can always fall back on the Undo feature for those (rare?) times when you make a little, tiny change that throws your entire worksheet into complete and utter chaos.

Help, My Document's Gone and I Can't Get It Back!

Before you can do any damage (um, I mean, make any changes) to your worksheet file, you have to retrieve it in 1-2-3. To retrieve a worksheet, you choose the /File **R**etrieve command, select the file you want to edit (either by moving the highlight bar to the filename with the cursor keys or by clicking on it with the mouse), and press Enter.

Figure 4-1 shows the control panel after you choose the /File **R**etrieve command when the \PIGS directory is current. This sample directory has only four worksheet files. In real situations, you might well have hundreds and hundreds of worksheet files in a single directory (well, at least more than can be displayed on the last line of the control panel). 1-2-3 always lists the filenames in alphabetical order.

- ✔ To bring files later in the list into view on the control panel, press → to move to the next file in the list or Ctrl—→ to move five files at a time. When you press these keys after you have reached the last file displayed on the right, 1-2-3 begins scrolling the filenames to the left.

- ✔ To jump directly to the last file in the list, press the End key.

- ✔ To return to the first file, press the Home key.

At the most, the control panel can display a group of five files at any one time. If you get tired of scrolling through the list, you can switch to a full-screen display of the files in the current directory simply by pressing the F3 (Name) key. If you press this key again, the program returns to the normal worksheet screen.

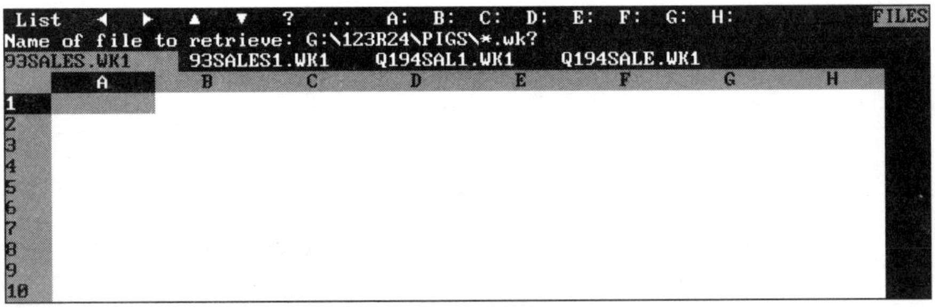

Figure 4-1: The control panel lists files you can retrieve in the current directory.

Figure 4-2 shows you how this full-screen file listing looks when the \TUTOR directory is current. (1-2-3 stashes all the practice files in the \TUTOR directory.)

✔ To retrieve one of the files shown on this screen, you select the filename by moving the highlight bar with the cursor keys and pressing Enter or by clicking on the filename with the mouse (which doesn't require you to press Enter).

✔ If you have more files than can fit on a single screen (heaven forbid!), you can scroll up the next screenful by pressing the ↓ key when you're on the last file in the last column, or you can press the PgDn key to advance to the next screen and the PgUp key to return to the previous screen.

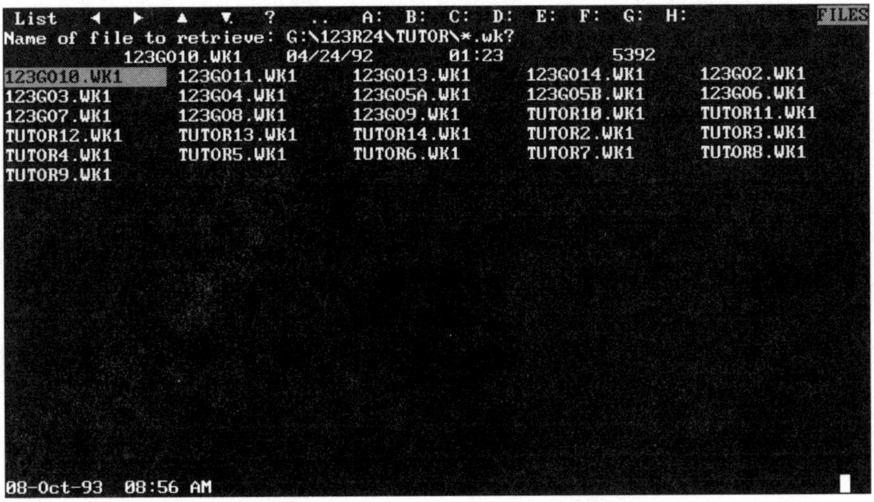

Figure 4-2: A full-screen file listing.

Release 2.0 of 1-2-3 can deal with only one worksheet at a time (which for most of us is plenty). If you retrieve a worksheet file with the /File Retrieve command when you already have one on-screen, the new worksheet replaces the one you were just looking at. This is fine (it's better than having them mishmashed together) as long as you've saved all the changes to the first worksheet prior to retrieving the new one. But if you haven't saved the changes, you can get into serious trouble.

✔ In Release 2.3 and 2.4, 1-2-3 is actually kind enough to warn you that you're about to do something really stupid. Without even giving you time to select a file in the list, it beeps at you and displays the following prompt beneath **No** and **Yes** options on the control panel *as soon as you choose* the /File Retrieve command:

```
WORKSHEET CHANGES NOT SAVED! Retrieve file anyway?
```

✔ Unfortunately, earlier versions of Release 2.0 are not so charitable, and they give you no warning of the impending loss of data. Instead, they just blithely go ahead and retrieve the file you select, while at the same time discarding the changes that you've forgotten to save. If you're using a vintage version of Release 2, you ought to cultivate the habit of always saving the worksheet currently on the screen with /File Save before you retrieve a new worksheet with /File Retrieve.

Clear the decks

Sometimes you may need to start a brand new worksheet after you finish working on the worksheet currently displayed on-screen. To clear the screen of the current worksheet and bring up a blank worksheet grid where you can enter your new work, you use the /Worksheet Erase command.

Now, please don't confuse the /Worksheet Erase command with the /File Erase command (as everybody else does, due to the confusing job Lotus did in naming the /Worksheet Erase command; why didn't they just call it the /Worksheet Clear command.

✔ Clearing a worksheet from the screen with /Worksheet Erase only removes the worksheet from the computer's memory without affecting the disk file version in any way.

✔ Deleting a worksheet with the /File Erase command only removes the file from your disk without affecting the worksheet on-screen (if the file happens to be retrieved at the time) in any way.

When you choose the /Worksheet Erase command to clear the worksheet on the screen, 1-2-3 displays the prompt beneath **No** and **Yes** options on the control panel:

```
Erase the entire worksheet from memory
```

The **Yes** option is automatically highlighted, meaning that you can clear the decks by pressing either Y or Enter. (Except in Release 2.4. where **No** is highlighted.)

If you've forgotten to save all the changes you've made to the worksheet currently on the screen, 1-2-3 lets everyone in the office know you've probably done something wrong by beeping at you and displaying the following message beneath **No** and **Yes** options on the control panel:

```
WORKSHEET CHANGES NOT SAVED! Erase worksheet anyway?
```

This time, however, the **No** option is highlighted so that you can crawl out from under your desk and bail out of the /Worksheet Erase command by pressing N or Enter. You can then save the worksheet with /File **S**ave before you try to clear the screen again with /Worksheet Erase — without a beep.

Of course, if all is well and you have saved all your editing changes, 1-2-3 clears the worksheet display without further ado the moment you choose the **Yes** option in response to the Erase the entire worksheet from memory prompt.

One last chance when you goof up and erase a worksheet that hasn't been saved

If you blow away a worksheet with unsaved changes by selecting the Yes option in response to the WORKSHEET CHANGES NOT SAVED! Erase worksheet anyway? warning, you can still save your bacon if you press the Alt-F4 (Undo) key before you do anything else.

I'm assuming, of course, that the Undo feature was enabled before you started editing the worksheet. (See "What's the Big To-Do about Undo?" later in this chapter for more information on the ins and outs of using Undo.)

The file that got away

When you want to retrieve a worksheet, the only problem you're likely to have is finding it. Misplacing files is an all-too-common experience, and most of the blame can be laid at the doorstep of DOS, that inscrutable old operating system. DOS's directory hierarchy, with its backslashes (\) and double periods (..), is so hard to understand (unless, of course, you've read *DOS For Dummies*) that most users just give up and try to ignore the whole thing (hoping it will go away).

Unfortunately, programs such as 1-2-3 must play by the DOS rules or they don't get to play at all. So, what can you do to stop losing your worksheet files? Well, the easiest thing to do is simply to pay attention to where you're saving the worksheet, because — guess what? — the place where you save the file is the *same* place where you retrieve it.

Directory assistance

Keep in mind that when you start 1-2-3, the program selects one of the directories on the hard disk (the disk you can't see) and makes it the *default directory*. The default directory is usually the one with the 1-2-3 program files, so it has a name like C:\123, D:\123R24, or something like that), unless you (very unlikely) or someone who knows DOS (more likely) has changed it. (See the information on changing the default directory if you really want to know more.)

For those of you who really want to know how to change the default directory

To change the default directory, choose the **/W**orksheet **G**lobal **D**efault **D**irectory command, type in the complete path name (drive letter, colon, and then the string of directories separated by backslashes — all that jazz), and press Enter. To save this directory change for future work sessions, choose the **U**pdate command and then the **Q**uit command.

The name of the default directory doesn't matter. Just keep in mind that the default directory is the place where all the worksheets are saved unless you change directories either before or during the saving process. (For information on how to choose a new directory when saving a file, see Chapter 2.)

Because the directory with all the 1-2-3 program files is already full of junk, you don't want to save worksheets there. Usually, you want to choose a subdirectory made for a particular type of worksheet, such as C:\123\DEFICITS for all budget worksheets, or a directory on a higher level made just for you, such as C:\GREGORY.

You use the /File **D**irectory command to change the directory when you want to save worksheets in a different place *or* when you want to retrieve worksheets that have been saved in a different place. When you choose the /File **D**irectory command, the program lists the name of the current directory (which is the default directory unless you've used this command before in your current work session). You can replace this pathname by typing in the pathname of the directory you want and then pressing Enter. (In later versions of Release 2, you can edit the pathname by pressing → or ← to move the cursor to the place where you want to delete or insert characters.)

✔ After you change the current directory with the /File **D**irectory command, the program automatically suggests the new directory as the place to save all new worksheet files (so that all you have to do is enter their filenames) until you either change the directory again with /File **D**irectory or you quit 1-2-3. (Remember, the default directory becomes the current directory the next time you start 1-2-3.)

✔ After you change the directory, whenever you choose the /File **R**etrieve command, the program displays files that are in the new directory.

A file with a view

Even when you're really good at remembering which directory contains which file, you can still forget which file contains the information you need to edit. Blame it on DOS again. Keeping those files straight would be much easier if you didn't have to use all sorts of cryptic abbreviations in order to name your files with only eight characters.

When you print a rough draft of a worksheet, you can save yourself a lot of hassle if you enter the filename (including its directory path if there's any chance you'll forget it) as part of the footer for the printout. (See Chapter 6 for details on how to create footers.) Then when your boss marks it up with all the changes you have to make, you'll know exactly which file you need to retrieve (as well as precisely where it is!).

If it's inappropriate to include the filename as part of the footer, pencil it in. If it's verboten to pencil it in, put the info on one of those sticky Post-it notes and slap it on the first page of the printout.

When you're retrieving a file, sometimes you feel like a game show contestant. Is the file behind door number 1, door number 2, or door number 3? (Of course, when you guess right, you don't collect big bucks.)

Wouldn't it be nice if you could peek into a file and preview its contents before you select it, instead of having to guess which file is the one you want? Well, guess what, if you're lucky enough to be using Release 2.4, you can peek at worksheet files before you open them, thanks to a new add-in program called the Viewer.

Before you can use the Viewer add-in, however, you have to load the thing into memory and attach it to a function key. (You can use F7, F8, F9, or F10 as long as you haven't already used one of them for something else.) Follows these steps to load the Viewer:

1. Choose the /Add-In **A**ttach command.

2. Press → until you highlight the file named VIEWER.ADN on the control panel.

3. Press Enter.

4. Type the number of the key you want to use to select the Viewer (**7** for F7, **8** for F8, **9** for F9, or **10** for F10), or press → until you highlight it.

5. Press Enter.

6. Choose the **Q**uit command to return to READY mode.

After you load the Viewer, you can use it whenever you need to retrieve a worksheet by following these steps:

1. If necessary, choose the /**F**ile **D**irectory command, enter the name of the directory containing the worksheet files you want to work with, and then press Enter.

2. Instead of choosing the normal /**F**ile **R**etrieve command, press Alt plus the function key you assigned to the Viewer (for example, Alt-F7, if you assigned the add-in to F7).

3. Choose the **R**etrieve command (which appears along with **L**ink and **B**rowse).

   A screen similar to the one shown in Figure 4-3 appears.

4. Press ↓ or ↑ to select different subdirectories or worksheet files in the current directory in the left part of the Viewer screen.

5. To view the worksheet files in a particular subdirectory, press → after highlighting the directory name.

   The Viewer then lists all the worksheet files in that directory in the left part of the screen.

6. Use ↓ and ↑ to select files.

   As you select each file, the Viewer displays the first part of the worksheet on the right.

7. If you can't tell from the first part of the worksheet whether it's the file you want to use, press → once to select the first cell in the representation of the worksheet. You can then use any of the normal keystrokes for moving the cell pointer or the Scroll arrow icons to move the cell pointer and scroll the worksheet.

8. When you've identified the worksheet you want to retrieve in the Viewer, press Enter to retrieve it into 1-2-3.

```
Lotus Magellan Viewer      Specify file to retrieve and press ENTER    VIEW
◄ ► Directory: G:\123R24\PIGS\*.W??
  93SALES.WK1      A1: [W16] '          Three Little Pigs Building Supply READY
  93SALES1.WK1
  Q194SAL1.WK1              A              B        C        D          ◄
  Q194SALE.WK1    1            Three Little Pigs Building Supply - 1993 S ►
                  2                     Qtr 1    Qtr 2    Qtr 3          ▲
                  3    Straw & Thatch   1,756.38  4,561.90  5,910.01     ▼
                  4    Sticks & Stones  2,136.40  3,478.00  3,873.11     ?
                  5    Bricks & Mortar  4,932.00  3,729.19  3,142.40
                  6    Total           $8,824.78 $11,769.09 $12,925.52
                  7
                  8
                  9
                  10
                  11
                  12
                  13
                  14
                  15
                  16
  File 2 of 4        93SALES1.WK1      10-05-93    9:05a        2,155 Bytes
  F1     F2    F3    F4    F5        [F6]        F7    F8    F9    F10
  Help  Reset            Date Sort  Name Sort
```

Figure 4-3: The Viewer enables you to preview the contents of a worksheet before you retrieve it.

What's the Big To-Do about Undo?

Before you start fooling with your work of art, you need to know how to get to the Undo feature — just in case you somehow manage to do something that messes it up. Strangely enough, the Undo feature is not automatically turned on when you first install the program. You have to do it yourself (figures, somehow, doesn't it?).

To turn the Undo feature on and off, follow these steps:

1. Choose the /Worksheet Global Default Other Undo command.

2. Choose the Enable command to turn Undo on. Choose the Disable command to turn it off.

3. To save a change for future sessions of 1-2-3, choose the Update command and then choose Quit.

   When you return to READY mode, you should see the UNDO mode indicator on the status line if you turned on the feature. If you turned off the feature, this indicator should be nowhere to be found.

Do it with Undo

To undo the last action in the worksheet when the Undo feature is turned on (indicated by the UNDO mode indicator), press the Alt-F4 (Undo) key. For example, if you delete the contents of a cell range with the /Range Erase command by mistake, you press Alt-F4, and presto, like magic, 1-2-3 restores the deleted entries to their cells. Likewise, if you move a cell range to a new part of the worksheet and then suddenly decide that you liked it better where it was, 1-2-3 restores it to the original position when you press Alt-F4.

In fact, the Undo feature undoes whatever changes you've made to the worksheet since the last time the program was in READY mode. Not only that, should you then decide that you prefer your mistake (after all, it is yours) to the original, untouched version you just restored, you can get it back by pressing the Alt-F4 (Undo) key again.

So, for example, if you move a range to a new area of the worksheet and then press Alt-F4 to move it back to its original position, 1-2-3 returns it to the new area if you press Alt-F4 a second time. (In fact, you can waste the rest of the workday toggling back and forth between the *worksheet before move* and the *worksheet after move.* Just don't tell your boss it was my idea.)

The only problem with the Undo feature is that it hogs so darn much computer memory, which you may need to enter more data or to load a particular add-in program. That's why it's not on when you install the program.

✔ It requires so much memory because, in order to restore a worksheet to its previous pristine state, 1-2-3 has to make a backup copy of the worksheet as it was before you messed it up and keep the pristine copy in memory along with the messed-up copy. According to my arithmetic, you use twice as much memory when you work with the Undo feature turned on as you do when you work with it turned off.

✔ When you're working on some large worksheets, you may have to turn off Undo in order to finish your work. If the MEM indicator starts flashing, try turning off Undo to see whether you have enough memory to finish your changes. Just remember that editing a large worksheet with Undo turned off is kind of like doing a high-wire act without a safety net — one stupid mistake and . . . well, just be careful out there. If you have to turn it off to get one editing job done, for goodness' sake, don't forget to turn it back on before you start the next one.

This is not a paid advertisement

Versions of Release 2 prior to Release 2.2 do not have an Undo feature. I repeat, they DO NOT have Undo. Therefore, anything that you do wrong in the worksheet can and will be held against you.

If you're the type who makes big editing boo-boos that would take a lot of time to fix manually, I think

you just might want to seriously consider forking over the bucks to Lotus Development Corporation to upgrade to their latest version of Release 2. Tell your boss it's worth it!

When Undo just won't do

Just when you thought it was safe to begin gutting the company's most important worksheet, I really feel I have to inform you that Undo doesn't work in all
situations. Sorry.

✔ You can undo your latest erroneous cell deletion, bad move, or unwise
copy, but you can't undo your latest inaccurate file erasure or imprudent
save (for example, when you meant to change the filename at the time you
saved your latest changes, or at least make a backup copy of the previous
version of the worksheet, but you neglected to do either one).

✔ Undo doesn't work at all when you're using external utility programs, such
as PrintGraph, Translate, or Install (all available from the Lotus Access
Menu). Whenever you use these programs, you're completely on your
own, kid.

Move It or Lose It

Moving a range of cell entries to a new part of the worksheet is a housekeeping
chore that everybody has to tackle sooner or later. Luckily, moving a range of
cells in 1-2-3 is not a big deal. You just select the range you want to move and
then indicate the place where you want to move it.

You do, however, need to keep one little detail in mind when you're moving
stuff around the worksheet: if any of the cells in the range that you are moving
to contain data, 1-2-3 replaces their entries with the data in the cells that are
being moved.

So the long and short of it is simply this:

✔ If you don't want to lose any data when you're relocating a range, make
sure that you don't move one cell that contains data on top of another cell
that contains data.

✔ If you do replace some entries by mistake, remember to press that Alt-F4
(Undo) key right away to restore the worksheet to the way it was before
the move.

You use the /**M**ove command (one of the few that doesn't require more than
one menu level) to move a range of cells. When you choose this command, 1-2-3
anchors the range on the current cell address and displays the following
prompt on the left side of the control panel:

```
Move what?
```

To save time (because you know that the first thing that you have to do is indicate the range to move), position the cell pointer in the first cell of the range to be relocated before you choose /**M**ove. That way you can just go about highlighting the rest of the range to be moved. If you use the mouse, you can really save time by selecting the cell range to move before choosing the /**M**ove command. The cell range appears after the `Move what?` prompt, and you are moved right along to the `To where?` prompt.

After you highlight the cell range to be moved, you press Enter, and 1-2-3 displays the following prompt on the right side of the control panel:

```
To where?
```

You then designate where you want the cell range moved. Although the address of the current cell is displayed after the `To where?` prompt, notice that it is unanchored so that you can move the cell pointer in the worksheet without extending the cell range.

To indicate where to move a range in response to the `To where?` prompt, all you need to do is select the cell that's in the upper left corner of the destination cell range. (Don't waste time trying to highlight a range that's the same size and shape as the one you're moving into the new area.)

When you select the first cell, 1-2-3 can figure out where to put the rest of the range. It just uses however many columns to the right and rows down from this cell that it needs to fit the range you're moving. All you have to do is check to see whether these cells contain data that you don't want replaced. After you select the first cell of the destination range, you press Enter, and 1-2-3 moves the cells.

To see how easily you can move a range of cells, follow along with the steps for moving the lower part of a sales table down to make room for a new row of figures. Figure 4-4 shows the worksheet that tracks the first quarter sales in 1994 for the Three Little Pigs Building Supply. In this table, you need to make room to track the sales of a brand new building material — Twigs & Branches — that was introduced in February 1994. You need to move the last two rows of the sales table (cell range A5..E6) down to open a blank row for the Twigs & Branches sales.

Because you are inserting the new row between Sticks & Stones and Bricks & Mortar, instead of at the end of the table between Bricks & Mortar and the Totals, 1-2-3 automatically expands the cell range in the @SUM formulas in the Totals row to include the new sales. If you place the Twigs & Branches sales at the end of the table, you have to edit the argument list in the @SUM formula in the first cell and then copy this revised formula to the other total cells in the table. Why go to all that trouble when you can easily avoid it?

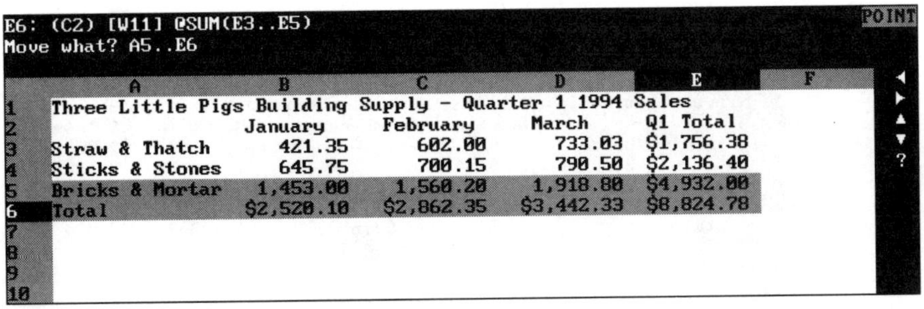

```
E6: (C2) [W11] @SUM(E3..E5)                                    POINT
Move what? A5..E6
       A          B          C          D          E       F
1  Three Little Pigs Building Supply - Quarter 1 1994 Sales
2                  January    February    March     Q1 Total
3  Straw & Thatch    421.35    602.00     733.03   $1,756.38
4  Sticks & Stones   645.75    700.15     790.50   $2,136.40
5  Bricks & Mortar 1,453.00  1,560.20   1,918.80   $4,932.00
6  Total           $2,520.10 $2,862.35  $3,442.33  $8,824.78
7
8
9
10
```

Figure 4-4: Selecting the cell range to move.

To move the last two rows of the sales table down one row, follow these steps:

1. Place the cell pointer in cell A5.

2. Choose the /**M**ove command.

3. Highlight the cell range A5..E6 (as shown in Figure 4-4).

4. Press Enter.

5. Position the cell pointer down one row in cell A6.

6. Press Enter again.

As you see in Figure 4-5, 1-2-3 moves the last two rows of this table down, making room for the new category. Figure 4-6 shows you this sales table after the new label and sales figures for the first quarter have been entered. Note two things in Figure 4-6:

1. The totals in the cells in row 7 are automatically updated.

2. The values entered in the cell range B5..D5 are not automatically formatted (they pick up that unattractive General format used by all the blank cells), so you still have to use the /**R**ange **F**ormat command to get them to match the other cells in the table.

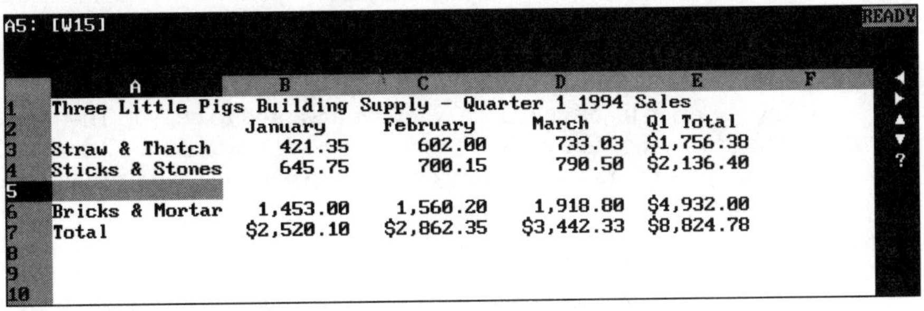

```
A5: [W15]                                                     READY
       A          B          C          D          E       F
1  Three Little Pigs Building Supply - Quarter 1 1994 Sales
2                  January    February    March     Q1 Total
3  Straw & Thatch    421.35    602.00     733.03   $1,756.38
4  Sticks & Stones   645.75    700.15     790.50   $2,136.40
5
6  Bricks & Mortar 1,453.00  1,560.20   1,918.80   $4,932.00
7  Total           $2,520.10 $2,862.35  $3,442.33  $8,824.78
8
9
10
```

Figure 4-5: The sales table after the cell range has been moved.

```
D5: [W12] 2001                                                           READY

              A            B            C            D          E          F    ◄
1    Three Little Pigs Building Supply - Quarter 1 1994 Sales                   ►
2                    January     February      March     Q1 Total              ▲
3    Straw & Thatch      421.35      602.00      733.03  $1,756.38             ▼
4    Sticks & Stones     645.75      700.15      790.50  $2,136.40             ?
5    Twigs & Branches         0     1776.04        2001
6    Bricks & Mortar   1,453.00    1,560.20    1,918.80  $4,932.00
7    Total            $2,520.10   $4,638.39   $5,443.33  $8,824.78
8
9
10
```

Figure 4-6: The sales table after the sales for the new category have been added.

Copy Cats

Copying a range of cell entries to a new part of the worksheet is a lot like moving a range:

1. Put the cell pointer in the first cell of the range to be copied.

2. Choose the /Copy command.

3. Extend the range to be copied (if necessary).

4. Press Enter.

5. Move the cell pointer to the first cell of the range where the copies are to appear.

6. Press Enter again.

You can use the /Copy command to copy all sorts of things in a worksheet, including titles and headings as well as formulas.

If the copy procedure sounds simple, well, it is. Unfortunately, just because it's simple doesn't mean that screwing it up is hard. For example, you try to copy a single entry to several cells in a neighboring cell range, and instead of ending up with a bunch of copies in the cell range, the worksheet looks the same. Here's what you did wrong: Instead of just selecting the single cell you wanted to copy in response to the Copy what? prompt, you selected both this cell and the neighboring blank cell range where you wanted to copy it. Then you selected the same range in response to the To where? prompt. 1-2-3 copied the one cell entry plus the range of empty cells on top of themselves, resulting in an unchanged worksheet.

When you're creating a worksheet table, you can use the /Copy command to copy a formula that you've just created to a bunch of neighboring cells that need to perform the same type of calculation (such as totaling columns of figures). You saw this use of the /Copy command in the creation of the Three

Little Pigs Building Supply 1993 sales worksheet in Chapter 2. There the formula using the @SUM function to total sales for each quarter in the last row of the table was copied to neighboring cells to the right. Also, the formula with the @SUM function that totals sales for each sales category in the last column of the table was copied down the rows.

You can also use the /Copy command to copy one of the existing @SUM formulas that total the sales for each category to the new Twigs & Branches category added to the first quarter 1994 sales table shown in Figure 4-6. You use the /Copy command, instead of building a new @SUM formula in cell E5 of this revised table, because 1-2-3 copies not only the formula but also the Currency number format. If you build a new formula from scratch, not only can you make a mistake in selecting the cell range to be summed, but you also have to waste time formatting the cell with the /Range Format Currency command.

Format the cell or cell range before you copy it whenever you want the copies to use the same formatting. This suggestion works for aligning labels as well as for applying number formats to values (numbers as well as formulas).

It's all relative

Figure 4-7 shows the worksheet after the formula in cell E4 has been copied to cell E5. To copy the formula to that one cell, you position the cell pointer in cell E4, choose /Copy, press Enter to accept the single cell range E4..E4 as the range to copy, press ↓ once to select cell E5 as the cell to copy to, press Enter, and, boom, the copy's made. As you can see, 1-2-3 copies not only the @SUM formula in cell E4, but the Currency formatting as well.

Note how 1-2-3 handles the copying of this formula behind the scenes. The original formula in cell E4 is as follows:

```
@SUM(B4..D4)
```

```
E5: (C2) [W11] @SUM(B5..D5)                                          READY

          A            B           C          D          E         F
1   Three Little Pigs Building Supply - Quarter 1 1994 Sales
2                     January     February    March      Q1 Total
3   Straw & Thatch     421.35      602.00      733.03    $1,756.38
4   Sticks & Stones    645.75      700.15      790.50    $2,136.40
5   Twigs & Branches     0.00    1,776.04    2,001.00    $3,777.04
6   Bricks & Mortar   1,453.00    1,560.20    1,918.80   $4,932.00
7   Total            $2,520.10   $4,638.39   $5,443.33  $12,601.82
8
9
10
```

Figure 4-7: The sales table after the @SUM formula has been copied to cell E5.

When the formula is copied down one row to cell E5, 1-2-3 changes it slightly so that it becomes

```
@SUM(B5..D5)
```

1-2-3 adjusts the row reference, changing it from 4 to 5, because you are copying down the column.

When you copy a formula to a cell range that extends across columns instead of down the rows, 1-2-3 adjusts the column letters in the copies, rather than the row numbers, to suit the position of each copy. For example, cell B7 in the first quarter 1994 sales tables contains the following formula:

```
@SUM(B3..B6)
```

When you copy this formula to the next column to the right (cell C7), 1-2-3 changes the copy of the formula to the following:

```
@SUM(C3..C6)
```

It adjusts the column reference to keep current with the new column C position. Because 1-2-3 adjusts the cell references in copies made of a formula relative to the direction of the copying, they are known as *relative cell references*.

Make it absolute

All new formulas that you create contain relative cell references unless you say otherwise. Because most copies of formulas require adjustments of their cell references, you rarely have to give this arrangement a second thought. Then out of the blue, you come upon an exception that calls for limiting when and how cell references are adjusted in copies.

One of the most common exceptions is when you want to compare a range of different values to a single value. You do this most often when you are computing what percentage each part is of a total. For example, in the first quarter 1994 sales worksheet, you encounter this situation in creating and copying a formula that calculates what percentage each monthly total (in the cell range B7..D7) is of the first quarter total in cell E7.

Suppose that you want to enter these formulas in row 9 of the first quarter 1994 sales worksheet, starting in cell B9. The formula for calculating the percentage for the January total in cell B9 is very straightforward:

```
+B7/E7
```

The formula divides the January total in cell B7 by the first quarter total in E7. (What could be easier?) Look, however, at the formula that would result if you copied this formula from cell B9 to cell C9:

```
+C7/F7
```

The adjustment of the first cell reference from B7 to C7 is just what the doctor ordered. However, the adjustment of the second cell reference from E7 to F7 is a disaster. It doesn't calculate what percentage the February sales are of the first quarter sales, and, besides that, you end up with one of those horrible ERR error things in cell C9.

To stop 1-2-3 from adjusting a cell reference in a formula in any copies you make, you convert the cell reference from relative to *absolute.* You change the cell reference by pressing the F4 (Abs for Absolute) key at the same time you select the cell reference in the formula (with the mouse or the keyboard).

1-2-3 indicates that the cell reference is absolute by displaying dollar signs in front of the column letter and row number. For an example, look at Figure 4-8. Cell B9 in this figure contains the correct formula to copy to the cell range C9..D9:

```
+B7/$E$7
```

Figure 4-9 shows the worksheet after this formula is copied to cell range C9..D9 with the /Copy command. Notice in the control panel that cell C9 contains the first copy of the formula:

```
+C7/$E$7
```

Because E7 was changed to $E$7 in the original formula, all the copies divide by this same cell reference.

```
B9: (P2) [W12] +B7/$E$7                                              READY

        A              B           C           D          E      F    ◄
1   Three Little Pigs Building Supply - Quarter 1 1994 Sales            ►
2                     January     February    March      Q1 Total      ▲
3   Straw & Thatch     421.35      602.00      733.03   $1,756.38      ▼
4   Sticks & Stones    645.75      700.15      790.50   $2,136.40      ?
5   Twigs & Branches     0.00    1,776.04    2,001.00   $3,777.04
6   Bricks & Mortar   1,453.00    1,560.20    1,918.80  $4,932.00
7   Total            $2,520.10   $4,638.39   $5,443.33 $12,601.82
8
9   Month/Qtr %          20.00%
10
11
```

Figure 4-8: Cell B9 contains a formula for computing the percentage of the quarterly total for each monthly total.

```
C9: (P2) [W12] +C7/$E$7                                          READY
```

	A	B	C	D	E	F
1	Three Little Pigs Building Supply – Quarter 1 1994 Sales				
2		January	February	March	Q1 Total
3	Straw & Thatch	421.35	602.00	733.03	$1,756.38
4	Sticks & Stones	645.75	700.15	790.50	$2,136.40
5	Twigs & Branches	0.00	1,776.04	2,001.00	$3,777.04
6	Bricks & Mortar	1,453.00	1,560.20	1,918.80	$4,932.00
7	Total	$2,520.10	$4,638.39	$5,443.33	$12,601.82
8					
9	Month/Qtr %	20.00%	36.81%	43.19%	
10					
11					

Figure 4-9: The worksheet after the formula in cell B9 has been copied to the range C9..D9.

If you goof up and copy a formula where one or more of the cell references should have been absolute, but you left them all relative, edit the formula as follows:

1. Select the cell with the formula.

2. Press F2.

3. Position the cursor somewhere on the reference that you want to convert to absolute.

4. Press the F4 (Abs) key.

5. Edit the formula.

6. Press Enter.

7. Copy the formula to the messed-up cell range with the /Copy command.

Out, Out, Darn Stuff

You can snuff out something from a worksheet in one of two ways:

- ✔ *Erasing a range* deletes or empties the cell's contents without removing the cells from the worksheet, which would alter the layout of the neighboring cells.

- ✔ *Deleting a column or row* gets rid of the whole kit and caboodle — the cell structure along with all its contents and formatting. When you delete a range of columns or rows (as described in the following section), 1-2-3 shuffles the position of entries in the remaining cells in the neighborhood to plug up any gaps made by its demise.

Note: 1-2-3 does not support the deletion of partial columns and rows; it supports only their erasure.

Eraser games

Follow these steps to erase a cell range with the /**R**ange **E**rase command:

1. Position the cell pointer in the first cell to be erased.

2. Choose /**R**ange **E**rase.

3. Extend the range if necessary.

4. Press Enter.

If you made a mistake and erased some cells that you shouldn't have erased, remember to press the Alt-F4 (Undo) key right away before you do anything more to the worksheet.

✔ If you're using Release 2.3 or 2.4 and you want to erase only the current cell, just press the Delete key. You don't have to go to all the trouble of choosing the /**R**ange **E**rase command and then pressing Enter to erase one cell, as you do with earlier versions. Note, however, that you still have to use /**R**ange **E**rase to erase an entire range of cells. If you select a range with the mouse and then press Delete, 1-2-3 erases only the first cell in the highlighted range.

✔ Keep in mind that the /**R**ange **E**rase command removes only the entries from the selected cells; it does not remove their formatting. So, if you erase a number from a cell that has been formatted with the Currency format and two decimal places, the cell continues to use this formatting, as indicated by the display of (C2) after the cell address in the control panel. If you later enter a new number or formula in this cell, 1-2-3 formats the value as currency.

✔ If you want to change a number format in an erased cell or cell range to General format, like the other blank cells in the worksheet, choose the /**R**ange **F**ormat **R**eset command and then select the cell range.

✔ To change the number format used by the erased cell or cell range to a different number format, you simply choose the alternate number format on the /**R**ange **F**ormat menu and then apply it to the appropriate cell range.

Note: When cell contents that contain a label are erased, the cell reverts to the default left-alignment used by blank cells. The reason for this is simple: In 1-2-3 you assign a new alignment to a label by adding a label-prefix character at the time you enter the label in its cell. When you erase the contents of the cell, 1-2-3 gets rid of the label prefix along with all the other characters in the label.

Don't fall prey to the evil spacebar!

I'm well aware that versions of 1-2-3 prior to Release 2.3 and 2.4 force you to choose the **/R**ange **E**rase command and then press Enter when all you want to do is erase a single cell. That's four keystrokes — **/RE** and Enter — where you should be able to get away with one. What a pain.

I'm also aware that to get around this serious annoyance, many people just press the spacebar and then press Enter. I'm here to tell you, don't do it.

It's not at all the same as clearing a cell with **/R**ange **E**rase; for although the cell appears to be empty, it contains a space that you can't see. "So, it's got a space," you may be thinking, "big deal."

Unfortunately, it can be a big deal if you use the @COUNT function (see Chapter 12) on a range "erased" with the spacebar, or if you use this method to "erase" a criteria range when you're using the database feature (see Chapter 8). In both cases, the invisible spaces throw off the results.

Because spacing out the cell instead of actually erasing it can get you into trouble at times like these, don't take the risk. Instead, turn to Chapter 9 and find out how to create a macro that enables you to erase a single cell simply by pressing Alt-E. Using the macro is just as easy, if not easier, than pressing the spacebar and Enter.

Worksheet demolition derby

Deleting a column or row is easy:

1. Position the cell pointer in the column or row to be deleted.

2. Choose the **/W**orksheet **D**elete command.

3. Choose either the **C**olumn or **R**ow option.

   Zap! The row or column is gone in a flash.

When you want to erase a range of cells and fill in the gaps that they leave in the worksheet, deleting a range of columns or rows is more efficient than erasing a range of cells and then moving the remaining cell ranges. When you delete a row from a worksheet, 1-2-3 automatically moves up all the remaining rows of data to fill in the gap. Likewise, if you delete a column, 1-2-3 automatically adjusts the columns of remaining data to the left.

Deleting entire columns and rows from a worksheet is a much riskier business than erasing cells, unless you're absolutely certain that the columns and rows in question contain nothing of value. Remember, when you delete an entire row from the worksheet, you delete _all information from column A through IV_ in that row (and you can see only a few columns in the row). Likewise, when you delete an entire column from the worksheet, you delete _all information from row 1 through 8192._

To be sure that you're not about to take out the middle of some unseen table of data in the outback of your worksheet; check what's out there in the great beyond before you proceed.

 ✔ When deleting a row, position the cell pointer in the last occupied cell (that you know about) in that row and then press the End key, followed by →. If the cell pointer jumps all the way to column IV in that row, you know that all is clear.

 ✔ To check whether the column you're about to demolish is clear, position the cell pointer in the last occupied row, and then press End, ↓. This time, if the cell pointer jumps all the way down to row 8192, you know you've got a green light to blow that column out of the water.

You can use the /**W**orksheet **D**elete command to delete a range of columns or rows, rather than just the column or row that contains the cell pointer. For example, to delete a range of columns, follow these steps:

 1. Put the cell pointer somewhere in the first column. (Any row will do because they're all going to be history.)

 2. Choose /**W**orksheet **D**elete **C**olumn.

 3. Press → to highlight all the columns to be taken out.

 4. Press Enter.

Building a Better Mousetrap

For those inevitable times when you need to squeeze new entries into an already populated region of the worksheet, you can use the /**W**orksheet **I**nsert command to insert new columns or rows in the worksheet instead of having to go through all the trouble of moving individual cell ranges. The /**W**orksheet **I**nsert command is like the /**W**orksheet **D**elete command on two counts: it enables you to insert only entire columns and rows, and it automatically adjusts the location of remaining entries in the neighboring columns and rows.

Keep in mind that, just as when you delete whole columns and rows, inserting entire columns and rows affects the entire worksheet, not just the part you see. If you don't know what's in the unseen areas of the worksheet, you can't be sure how your insertion will impact (perhaps, sabotage) entries that are out there in the boonies. So be sure to scout out those distant areas of the worksheet.

Make it bigger and better

If the way is clear, inserting a new column or row when you need to make room for additions to your worksheet can really make your work a lot easier. To illustrate, let's look again at the revised first quarter 1994 sales table for the Three Little Pigs Building Supply.

Boss Hog has decided that he wants a row of equal signs to underscore the totals in the blank row (currently row 8) and separate them from the percentages in the row below. No problem. You can add the row of equal signs to the blank row that already separates the totals from the percentages.

Boss Hog also wants a row of dashes to separate the totals at the bottom of each column (currently in row 7) from the sales figures in the rows above. A little more trouble. Before you can insert the dashes, you need to insert a new row. At least you already know that this table is the only one on the worksheet, so you don't have to worry about whether the hinterlands are clear.

To insert a new row for the dashes, follow these steps:

1. Position the cell pointer in cell B7.

   Any cell in row 7 will do, but you use this one because you're thinking ahead. It's the first column where you'll put dashes in the new row.

2. Choose the /**W**orksheet **I**nsert **R**ow command.

3. Press Enter to insert a single row when you see the following prompt:

   ```
   Enter row insert range: B7..B7
   ```

Figure 4-10 shows the worksheet after a new row has been inserted.

```
B7: [W12]                                                              READY
            A             B            C            D           E      F    ◄
1  Three Little Pigs Building Supply - Quarter 1 1994 Sales                 ►
2                     January      February      March      Q1 Total        ▲
3  Straw & Thatch       421.35       602.00       733.03   $1,756.38        ▼
4  Sticks & Stones      645.75       700.15       790.50   $2,136.40        ?
5  Twigs & Branches       0.00     1,776.04     2,001.00   $3,777.04
6  Bricks & Mortar    1,453.00     1,560.20     1,918.80   $4,932.00
7
8  Total             $2,520.10    $4,638.39    $5,443.33  $12,601.82
9
10 Month/Qtr %          20.00%       36.81%       43.19%
11
12
```

Figure 4-10: The worksheet after a new row has been inserted.

Repeat after me

Now that you have room for the dashes, you can enter them across the row by first inserting them in the new empty cell, B7, and then using the /Copy command to copy them to the cell range C7..E7. To insert a repeated string of characters such as the dash (hyphen) in a cell, you start the entry with \ (the backslash). The backslash acts as the *repeating label prefix* when you start a text entry with it.

- ✔ After pressing \, you only need to enter the character you want repeated *one* time — so to fill a cell with dashes, you enter \- (backslash, hyphen) in the cell.

- ✔ If you want 1-2-3 to repeat more than one character across the cell, you enter all the characters once after the backslash. For example, if you want to repeat dash-star-dash-star, you enter \-* in the cell and 1-2-3 enters -*-*-*-* as many times as fit in the current cell width.

- ✔ Note a most important point about using the \ to repeat characters in a cell: 1-2-3 automatically adjusts the number of repeated characters to fill the entire cell, no matter how wide or narrow you make its column.

To enter the row of dashes in the table, take these steps:

1. With the cell pointer still in cell B7, type \-.

2. Press Enter.

   1-2-3 fills the cell with a string of dashes, as shown in Figure 4-11.

3. Choose the /Copy command.

4. Press Enter to accept the cell range B7..B7 as the range to copy.

5. Press . (the period) to anchor the range.

6. Press → to highlight the range B7..E7.

7. Press Enter to make the copies.

Follow the same steps to enter a row of equal signs, filling cell B9 with equal signs and using B9..B9 as the range to copy. Use the range B9..E9 as the range to copy to.

Figure 4-12 shows the worksheet with the totals separated and underscored.

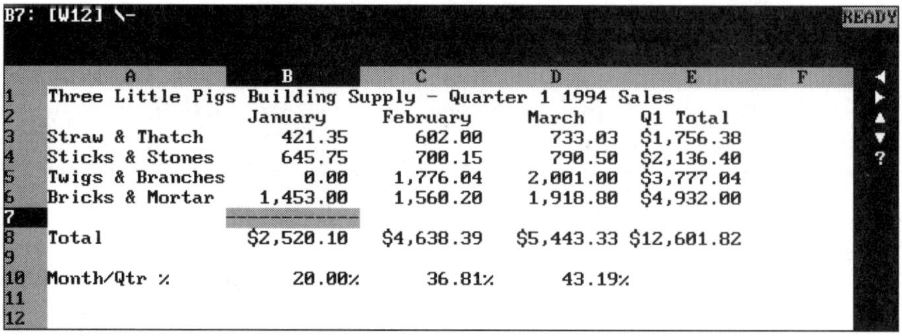

```
B7: [W12] \-                                                              READY

        A              B            C          D          E        F    ◀
1  Three Little Pigs Building Supply - Quarter 1 1994 Sales             ▶
2                   January     February      March     Q1 Total        ▲
3  Straw & Thatch     421.35      602.00      733.03  $1,756.38         ▼
4  Sticks & Stones    645.75      700.15      790.50  $2,136.40         ?
5  Twigs & Branches     0.00    1,776.04    2,001.00  $3,777.04
6  Bricks & Mortar   1,453.00    1,560.20    1,918.80  $4,932.00
7            ─────────────
8  Total            $2,520.10   $4,638.39   $5,443.33 $12,601.82
9
10 Month/Qtr %         20.00%      36.81%      43.19%
11
12
```

Figure 4-11: The worksheet with a string of dashes in cell B7.

If you're using Release 2.3 or 2.4 and you have enough memory to run the Wysiwyg add-in program, you don't have to resort to this chintzy method of inserting new rows and then repeating hyphens or equal signs in the cell range. Instead, you can use the Wysiwyg :Format Lines command (see Chapter 10) to draw different kinds of lines around various borders of a cell range to emphasize and underscore its entries.

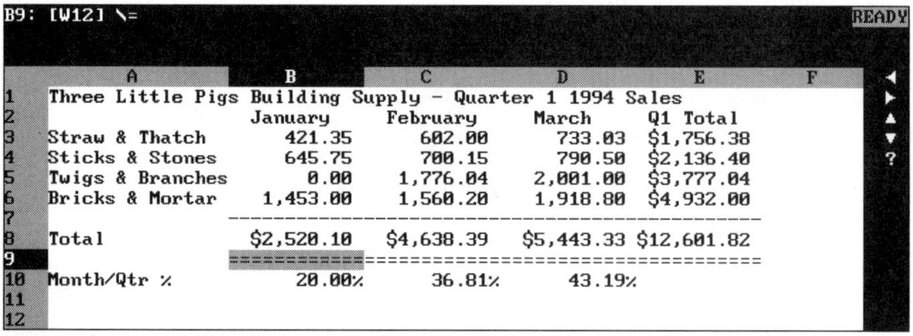

```
B9: [W12] \=                                                              READY

        A              B            C          D          E        F    ◀
1  Three Little Pigs Building Supply - Quarter 1 1994 Sales             ▶
2                   January     February      March     Q1 Total        ▲
3  Straw & Thatch     421.35      602.00      733.03  $1,756.38         ▼
4  Sticks & Stones    645.75      700.15      790.50  $2,136.40         ?
5  Twigs & Branches     0.00    1,776.04    2,001.00  $3,777.04
6  Bricks & Mortar   1,453.00    1,560.20    1,918.80  $4,932.00
7  ───────────────────────────────────────────────────────────
8  Total            $2,520.10   $4,638.39   $5,443.33 $12,601.82
9  ═══════════════════════════════════════════════════════════
10 Month/Qtr %         20.00%      36.81%      43.19%
11
12
```

Figure 4-12: The completed worksheet with rows of dashes and equal signs.

Part III
Getting Out and About

The 5th Wave   By Rich Tennant

"I'm afraid I don't understand all the reports of our upgrade having a delayed release date. Unless... wait a minute — How many people here DIDN'T KNOW I was speaking in dog-months?"

The part in which...

You find out how to climb a few important "ladders" for keeping on top of the information in your worksheet. Then you learn to get down and get your worksheet down in print.

After you learn how to split the worksheet display into two windows so that you can view distant parts of the same worksheet on the screen, how to assign English-like names to worksheet cells that you can then use with the GoTo feature to zip straight to the cells, how to use the Search feature to locate and, if necessary, replace specific information in your formulas or labels, how to manually control when the worksheet is recalculated, and how to protect the worksheet from any unwanted or unauthorized changes (whew!), you will know how to keep track of — that is, not lose — important information.

You'll be such a pro at printing that you will effortlessly add page numbers and other useful stuff to headers and footers, print (only) certain rows and columns with worksheet headings on each page, insert your own page breaks, and print a copy of your worksheet showing the formulas in each cell along with the worksheet row and column frame. Awesome!

Chapter 5
Finders Keepers
(Losers Weepers)

●　●

In This Chapter

▶ Splitting the screen to view different parts of the same worksheet

▶ Freezing information on-screen with worksheet titles

▶ Using range names to move to new locations in the worksheet

▶ Locating information with the Search feature

▶ Replacing existing entries with new ones

▶ Controlling when a worksheet is recalculated

▶ Protecting a worksheet from further changes

●　●

*B*y this point, you are aware of how humongous the 1-2-3 worksheet is. Because a computer monitor can show only a tiny bit of the total worksheet at any one time, keeping on top of the information it contains is a challenge that's right up there with keeping track of kids at an amusement park.

The 1-2-3 worksheet uses a very coherent cell coordinate system that enables you to get anywhere in the worksheet. But you have to admit that this A1, B2 stuff, although highly logical, is rather artificial and alien to human thought processes. (I mean, saying, "Go to cell BA70," just doesn't have anywhere near the same impact as saying "Go to the corner of Haight and Ashbury.") Consider for a moment how hard it is to come up with a meaningful association between a table of data for the fourth quarter 1994 sales for the Three Little Pigs Building Supply and a cell range like Z56..BB621. How can you possibly remember where to find the table?

This chapter describes techniques that can keep you from losing information in the worksheet and other techniques that can keep you from losing your mind when you do misplace a table or two. Don't panic, 1-2-3 can help you find information that you lose — sometimes. You learn how to split the screen into separate windows (to view different parts of the same worksheet) and how to keep particular rows and columns on the screen at all times. You learn how to add descriptive, regular English-type names (like Haight and Ashbury) to cell ranges and how to use the Search and Replace features to locate and, if necessary, replace entries anywhere in the worksheet. Finally, you learn how to control when 1-2-3 recalculates the worksheet and how to limit where changes can be made.

Windows on the Worksheet

In 1-2-3, you can bring together two separate sections of the same worksheet and compare their data on the same screen. To manage this kind of trick, you split the screen into separate windows and then scroll the worksheet in each window so that you can see the parts that you want to compare. You can split the screen at a particular row (creating *horizontal* windows) or at a particular column (creating *vertical* windows).

Splitting the screen into windows is a very easy process. Figure 5-1 shows an income statement used to project probable income and expenses during the upcoming year (1994) for the Three Little Pigs Building Supply. This worksheet is so long that you can't see both the gross and net profits in the same screen. To remedy this situation so that Boss Hog can see what he thinks he'll make (revenues), what he thinks Uncle Sam will take (taxes), and what, if anything, will be left over (net profits), the first little pig has split the screen into two horizontal windows at row 10. Now, how do you do that?

1. Place the cell pointer somewhere in row 10. (It doesn't really matter which cell the pointer is in.)

2. Choose the /**W**orksheet **W**indow **H**orizontal command.

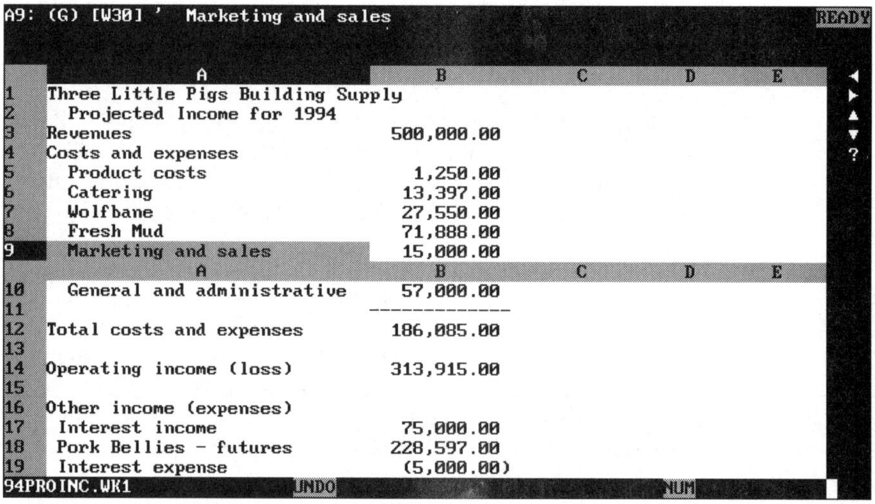

```
A9: (G) [W30] '  Marketing and sales                                    READY

              A                    B           C          D          E    ◄
1   Three Little Pigs Building Supply                                      ▶
2      Projected Income for 1994                                          ▲
3   Revenues                   500,000.00                                 ▼
4   Costs and expenses                                                    ?
5     Product costs              1,250.00
6     Catering                  13,397.00
7     Wolfbane                  27,550.00
8     Fresh Mud                 71,888.00
9   Marketing and sales         15,000.00
              A                    B           C          D          E
10    General and administrative 57,000.00
11                              ------------
12  Total costs and expenses    186,085.00
13
14  Operating income (loss)     313,915.00
15
16  Other income (expenses)
17    Interest income            75,000.00
18    Pork Bellies - futures    228,597.00
19    Interest expense          (5,000.00)
94PROINC.WK1            UNDO                              NUM
```

Figure 5-1: The screen split into two horizontal windows at row 10.

Note that the worksheet in Figure 5-1 contains two rows of identical column letters — one above row 1 and another above row 10 (where the split occurred).

✔ To move the cell pointer back and forth between worksheet windows, press the F6 (Window) key, which activates each window in turn.

✔ To scroll different parts of the worksheet into view in the active window, position the cell pointer against the edge of the window frame or the edge of the worksheet itself and then press one of the keys for moving the cell pointer. (Don't forget the Scroll arrow icons if you use the mouse.) Alternatively, you can freeze the cell pointer in its current position and start scrolling from there if you press the Scroll Lock key to turn on scroll lock. (SCROLL appears on the status line.)

You thought you had to be a rocket scientist to understand this stuff, but just remember the following universal truths:

✔ You can always tell what kind of window split you have in a worksheet by looking at which part of the frame is *duplicated* (as opposed to *split*). If the column letters are duplicated, you've got horizontal windows; if the row numbers are duplicated, they're vertical windows.

✔ The type of windows determines which type of scrolling is *synchronized* on the screen. Horizontal scrolling is synchronized in horizontal windows; vertical scrolling is synchronized in vertical windows.

✔ The type of scrolling that works *independently,* as opposed to being synchronized, is the opposite of the window's type. Vertical scrolling works independently in horizontal windows; horizontal scrolling works independently in vertical windows.

Figure 5-2 shows the projected income statement after you position the cell pointer at the top of the lower window with the F6 (Window) key, engage scroll lock with the Scroll Lock key, and then press ↓ until the last rows of the worksheet are visible, literally showing the "bottom line."

With both the top and bottom parts of this worksheet in view, you can do little what-if scenarios to see what effect different projected revenues have on the net income. Figure 5-3 shows the worksheet after you make the upper window active (with the F6 key), turn off scroll lock (with the Scroll Lock key), and then position the cell pointer in cell B3 and replace the original value of $500,000 with $650,000. Note what effect this new figure for projected revenues in B3 has on the net earnings in B30, to say nothing of the taxes in B29. Boss Hog must be having a cow!

```
A22: [W30] ' Video Royalties                                        READY

             A                       B            C       D     E    ◄
1 Three Little Pigs Building Supply                                  ►
2   Projected Income for 1994                                       ▲
3 Revenues                        500,000.00                        ▼
4 Costs and expenses                                                ?
5   Product costs                   1,250.00
6   Catering                       13,397.00
7   Wolfbane                       27,550.00
8   Fresh Mud                      71,888.00
9   Marketing and sales           15,000.00
             A                       B            C       D     E
22  Video Royalties                92,375.00
23  Coloring Books                  4,972.00
24  Other                           1,000.00
25                                 --------------
26 Total other income (expenses)  436,376.00
27
28 Income (loss) before taxes     750,291.00
29 Provision for taxes            187,572.75
30 Net earnings (loss)            562,718.25
31                                ==============
94PROINC.WK1              UNDO                        NUM      SCROLL
```

Figure 5-2: The split screen with the "bottom line" of the income statement — the last row of the worksheet — displayed in the lower window.

When doing what-if scenarios like this, remember that you can use the Alt-F4 (Undo) key to flip back and forth between the before and after versions of the worksheet so that you can compare the original values with those returned by the new scenario.

You use horizontal windows when you want to compare two areas that are above and below one another in the worksheet, but what about comparing

```
B3: (,2) [W13] 650000                                              READY

             A                       B            C       D     E    ◄
1 Three Little Pigs Building Supply                                  ►
2   Projected Income for 1994                                       ▲
3 Revenues                        650,000.00                        ▼
4 Costs and expenses                                                ?
5   Product costs                   1,250.00
6   Catering                       13,397.00
7   Wolfbane                       27,550.00
8   Fresh Mud                      71,888.00
9   Marketing and sales           15,000.00
             A                       B            C       D     E
22  Video Royalties                92,375.00
23  Coloring Books                  4,972.00
24  Other                           1,000.00
25                                 --------------
26 Total other income (expenses)  436,376.00
27
28 Income (loss) before taxes     900,291.00
29 Provision for taxes            225,072.75
30 Net earnings (loss)            675,218.25
31                                ==============
94PROINC.WK1              UNDO                        NUM
```

Figure 5-3: The split screen shows the effect on the "bottom line" after the projected revenues figure is changed.

sections that are side by side? Then you want to split the screen into two vertical windows do the following:

1. Position the cell pointer somewhere in the column where you want the window split to occur.

2. Choose the /Worksheet Window Vertical command.

In splitting the screen vertically, 1-2-3 duplicates the part of the frame with the row numbers and places the cell pointer at the edge of the window on the left. To jump the cell pointer back and forth between the window on the left and the window on the right, you press the F6 (Window) key. Keep in mind that when the screen is split into vertical windows, vertical scrolling through the rows is synchronized in each window, but horizontal scrolling left and right through the columns happens only in the active window. Got it?

So far, so good. But what do you do if you want to compare two sections of a worksheet that are not only side by side, but also above and below one another? Suppose that you have a table of data in the cell range A1..F9, and you want to compare some of its figures with figures in a table located in the cell range K22..P29 of the same worksheet. How are you going to manage that?

If you split the screen horizontally and then scroll up the rows in the lower window so that you can see rows 22 through 29 while rows 1 through 10 are displayed in the window above, you still won't see both tables. Only columns A through F will be visible in *both* windows, and the second table will still be off to the right in columns K through P.

If you scroll the columns to the left to bring columns K through P into view so that you can see the second table in the lower window, the first table in columns A through F will no longer be in view (arrghh!).

Okay, so horizontal windows won't work. How about a vertical split? Suppose that you split the screen vertically at column D and then scroll columns K through M into view in the window on the right while you keep columns A through C visible in the window on the left. Still no good, because by the time you scroll the rows up to see the second table, starting in row 22, the entries in the first table in rows 1 through 9 are long gone. Now what?

You've probably already guessed that 1-2-3 has a solution. The answer to this mystery is the /Worksheet Window Unsync (for unsynchronize) command. When you choose this command, 1-2-3 enables you to scroll horizontal or vertical windows independently in both directions.

If you are using horizontal windows in the example worksheet, use the following steps to bring the two tables into view:

1. Make the lower window active.

2. Scroll up until row 22 is at the top of the window.

3. Choose the /Worksheet **W**indow **U**nsync command.

4. In just the lower window, scroll the columns left until columns K through P appear.

   Column K in the lower window should appear beneath column A in the upper window, column L below column B, and so on.

For vertical windows, use the following steps:

1. Make the window on the right active.

2. Scroll columns K through P into view.

3. Choose the /Worksheet **W**indow **U**nsync command.

4. Scroll up the rows in just the right window.

   Row 22 should be at the top of the window, with row 22 next to row 1, row 23 next to row 2, and so on.

When you finish comparing different areas of the worksheet, wipe those windows off the screen by choosing /Worksheet **W**indow **C**lear.

Freeze Those Titles in Their Tracks

Worksheet windows are great for viewing different parts of the same worksheet that normally can't be seen together. You use worksheet *titles,* however, when you need to freeze the headings in the top rows and/or first columns so that they stay in view at all times, no matter how you scroll through the worksheet. This feature is especially helpful when you're working with a table which is so large that its information extends beyond the rows and columns that can be shown on the screen.

Figure 5-4 shows just such a table. Here you see the worksheet that holds the client list for the Three Little Pigs Building Supply. This table contains many more columns and rows than you can view on-screen at one time. If you scroll up rows to view new clients in the list, the column headings scroll off the screen, and you can't tell what the information in each column refers to. Likewise, if you scroll columns to the left to see the information in the other columns to the right, the columns with the client names scroll off the screen and you can't tell what information is whose.

To avoid this kind of problem, you freeze the first few rows with the column headings and the first few columns with the row identifiers by designating them as the titles of the worksheet. When setting titles with /Worksheet Titles, you choose one of three commands:

- ✔ The Horizontal command designates the rows above the one with the cell pointer as the worksheet titles.

- ✔ The Vertical command designates the columns to the left of the one with the cell pointer as the worksheet titles.

- ✔ The Both command designates both the rows above the one with the cell pointer and the columns to the left as the worksheet titles.

In the client list shown in Figure 5-4, you want to designate rows 1 and 2, as well as columns A and B, as the worksheet titles. You freeze these columns and rows by following these steps:

1. Position the cell pointer in cell C3.

   C3 is the cell that is below rows 1 and 2 and to the right of columns A and B.

2. Choose the /Worksheet Titles Both command.

   The program freezes the titles, and you can no longer move the cell pointer into any of the cells in these rows and columns (either with the normal keys on the keyboard or with the mouse). These cells remain off limits until you clear the titles from the worksheet.

```
C3: (G) [W11] 'Michael                                                    READY

        A          B          C              D                E          ◀
1   Three Little Pigs Building Supply -- Client List                     ▶
2      ID No    Last Name  First Name        Street          City        ▲
3     101-001   Bryant     Michael     326 Chef's Lane       Paris       ▼
4     102-002   Gearing    Shane       1 Gunfighter's End    LaLa Land   ?
5     102-003   Wolfe      Big Bad     3 West End Boulevard  London
6     103-004   Cupid      Eros        97 Mount Olympus Road Greece
7     104-005   Gookin     Polly       4 Feathertop Hill     Hawthorne
8     102-006   Cinderella Poore       8 Lucky Maiden Way    Oxford
9     103-007   Baum       L. Frank    447 Toto Too Road     Oz
10    105-008   Harvey     Chauncey    60 Lucky Starr Place  Shetland
11    106-009   Sunnybrook Rebecca     21 Last Week          Portland
12    106-010   White      Snow        552 Magic Mirror Circle Dwarf Place
13    104-011   Dragon     Kai         2 Pleistocene Era     Ann's World
14    102-012   Gondor     Aragorn     2956 Gandalf          Midearth
15    102-013   Baggins    Bingo       99 Hobbithole         Shire
16    101-014   Andersen   Hans        341 The Shadow        Scholar
17    101-015   Humperdinck Engelbert  654 Hansel & Gretel Trail Gingerbread
18    103-016   Oakenshield Rex        Mines of Goblins      Everest
19    103-017   Jacken     Jill        Up the Hill           Pail of Water
20    104-018   Ridinghoode Crimson    232 Cottage Path      Wulfen
CLIENTS.WK1                     UNDO                          NUM
```

Figure 5-4: Creating worksheet titles at C3 in the client list.

```
C25: (G) [W11] 'Johnny                                                READY
```

	A	B	C	D	E
1	Three Little Pigs Building Supply -- Client List				
2	ID No	Last Name	First Name	Street	City
25	103-023	Appleseed	Johnny	6789 Fruitree Trail	Along The Way
26	103-024	Oakley	Anney	Six Shooter Path	Target
27	102-025	Washington	George	8 Founders Diamond	Hamilton
28	104-026	Brown	Charles	59 Flat Plains	Saltewater
29	105-027	Laurel	Stan	2 Oliver Hardy	Celluloyde
30	101-028	Cassidy	Butch	Sundance Kidde	Hole In Wall
31	101-029	Oow	Lu	888 Sandy Beach	Honolulu
32	101-030	Liberty	Statuesque	31 Gotham Centre	Big Apple
33	104-031	Eaters	Big	444 Big Pigs Court	Dogtown
34	101-920	Andersen	Christian	340 The Shadow	Scholar

```
CLIENTS.WK1                    UNDO                          NUM
```

Figure 5-5: The frozen row titles remain in view at the top of the worksheet when the client list is scrolled up.

Figure 5-5 shows you what happens when you scroll the worksheet up after setting up vertical and horizontal worksheet titles at cell C3. In this figure, rows 25 through 34 are displayed under rows 1 and 2. Note that because the first two rows are designated as vertical titles, they remain displayed. Normally they would have been the first to disappear as you scrolled the worksheet up.

Figure 5-6 shows what happens if you then scroll the worksheet to the left. In this figure, columns G through J appear after columns A and B. Because the first

```
J25: (G) [W10] ^Yes                                                  READY
```

	A	B	G	H	I	J
1	Three Little Pigs Buil					
2	ID No	Last Name	Anniversary	In Years	Grs Rcpts	Cash Only
25	103-023	Appleseed	02/24/88	4.6	$4	Yes
26	103-024	Oakley	04/03/88	4.5	$17	No
27	102-025	Washington	05/20/88	4.4	$19,700	No
28	104-026	Brown	07/09/88	4.3	$956	No
29	105-027	Laurel	09/13/88	4.1	$5	No
30	101-028	Cassidy	11/11/88	3.9	$12	No
31	101-029	Oow	12/26/88	3.8	$2,116	No
32	101-030	Liberty	01/03/89	3.8	$459	No
33	104-031	Eaters	09/02/92	0.1	$66,666	Yes
34	101-920	Andersen	12/29/86	5.8	$12,000	Yes

```
CLIENTS.WK1                    UNDO                          NUM
```

Figure 5-6: The frozen column titles remain displayed when the client list is scrolled left.

two columns are designated as horizontal worksheet titles, they remain on the screen, helping you identify who belongs to what information.

To get rid of the frozen worksheet titles, you choose the /Worksheet Titles Clear command. They are outta here, and you can move the cell pointer into any of the columns and/or rows that were previously out of bounds.

The Name Game

Where did you put that table? Is it in AA48..AG95, or is it in BB48..BB95, or is it in CC48..CC95? And how long will it take to find it again?

Instead of trying to remember random cell coordinates, you can assign descriptive names to cells and cell ranges to help yourself keep track of important information. Then you just have to remember the name, instead of meaningless combinations of letters and numbers. And best of all, after you've named a cell or cell range, you can select it by using its name with the F5 (GoTo) key.

Unless you have Release 2.3 or 2.4, when assigning range names to a cell or cell range, you need to follow a few guidelines:

✔ Range names must begin with a letter of the alphabet, rather than with a number. For example, you use HOGWASH93, instead of 93HOGWASH.

✔ Range names cannot contain spaces. Instead of a space, use the underscore (Shift-hyphen) to tie the parts of the name together. For example, you enter HOG_HEAVEN, instead of HOG HEAVEN.

✔ Range names cannot correspond to cell coordinates in the worksheet. For example, you can't name a cell A1 because this is a valid cell coordinate. Instead, use something like A1_PIGMENT.

Follow these steps to name a cell or cell range:

1. Position the cell pointer in the cell or in the upper left cell of the cell range that you want to name.

2. Choose the /Range Name Create command.

   A listing of the names already defined in the worksheet appears on the third line of the control panel to help you avoid entering a range name that you've already used.

3. Type the name for the cell or cell range in response to the Enter name: prompt.

4. Press Enter.

   The Enter range: prompt with the current cell address anchored as a range appears on the right side of the control panel.

Creating a list of range names

Naming a range is all well and good — and a big improvement over trying to remember those letters and numbers. But you still have to remember the range name, and a name that seems obvious when you create a worksheet may be hard to recall a few weeks later when the boss tells you that he wants the quarterly figures on Sticks and Stones right away.

1-2-3 has a command that you can use to create a list of all the range names and their cells ranges. Not only that, but you conveniently store the list right in the worksheet.

To create the list of range names and their ranges, position the cell pointer in the first cell of the area where you want the table to appear, choose the /**R**ange **N**ame **T**able command, and press Enter. Be sure to choose an area of the worksheet that has enough blank cells to accommodate the list of range names and addresses. The range name table uses two columns and as many rows as there are range names.

5. Indicate the range to be named. If you're naming just the current cell, press Enter to accept the current single cell range. If you're naming a range with more than one cell, highlight the range and press Enter.

To move the cell pointer to a named cell or to the first cell of a named range in a worksheet, follow these steps:

1. Press the F5 (GoTo) key.

2. Type the range name in response to the Enter address to go to: prompt or press the F3 (Name) key to display a list of all range names and highlight the range name.

3. Press Enter.

Note: If you're using Release 2.0, you have to type the range name in response to the Enter address to go to: prompt. Unfortunately, the Name key trick does not work.

Hunters of the Lost Cells

When all else fails and you just can't seem to find the information you need, 1-2-3 comes to the rescue with the /**R**ange **S**earch command. You can use this command to locate specific information in the worksheet — provided that you are using Release 2.2 or higher.

The Search feature enables you to search for any characters in labels, in formulas, or in both of them. Unfortunately, you cannot search for particular values — either those that you entered manually or those returned by a formula. You just have to wander around the worksheet and hunt for those values on your own.

As soon as you choose the **/R**ange **S**earch command, the following prompt appears on the second line of the control panel:

```
Enter range to search:
```

1-2-3 doesn't anchor the range on the current cell address that's listed after the prompt as it does with the other **/R**ange commands that you've learned so far (**/R**ange **F**ormat, **L**abel, **E**rase, **N**ame, and so on).

To indicate which cells are to be searched, you move the cell pointer to the first cell, anchor the range with the period (remember that old ball of sticky chewing gum?), and then extend and highlight the range with any of the keys that move the cell pointer. After you highlight the range, press Enter.

To make it easy to search for information in a really big table, assign a range name to the table, choose **/R**ange **S**earch and then enter the range name in response to the `Enter range to search:` prompt.

After you indicate the range to search, 1-2-3 asks you to enter just what it is that you're looking for with the prompt

```
Enter string to search for:
```

String is techie talk for a series of characters, so *search string* just means the characters you want to find. When you type the characters to look for, you don't need to worry about capitalization because the search operation is not case sensitive. For example, if you enter *PIG* as the search string, 1-2-3 considers *Pig, PIG,* or *pig* to be a match.

Also be aware that 1-2-3 considers any occurrence of the search string within another word to be a match, so if you use *PIG* as the search string, the program considers *piggy* or *Piglet* a match.

If you don't know the exact spelling of the word or name or the precise formula you're searching for, you can use the question mark (?) to stand for a single unknown character or the asterisk (*) to stand for any number of missing characters. Suppose that you enter the following as the search string:

```
7*4
```

1-2-3 stops at cells containing formulas that include *74, 704,* and *7,5234* and even at cells with a label such as *782 4th Street.*

Keep in mind that 1-2-3 uses the asterisk as the times sign for multiplication. When you want to search for an asterisk in a formula, you cannot precede it with another character. For example, to search the formulas in the worksheet for one that multiplies by the number 2, you enter

```
*2
```

Suppose that you enter the following search string, with characters before the asterisk:

```
W?1*w
```

1-2-3 treats the asterisk as if it represents missing characters, rather than as the sign for multiplication. When you perform the search, it stops at cells that contain the labels wolf, Wolverine, wildcat, William, and so on.

After you type in the search string, you press Enter, and the following commands appear on the second line of the control panel:

```
Formulas    Labels    Both
```

To search only the formulas in the search range, choose the Formulas command. To search only the labels in this range, choose **Labels.** If you want 1-2-3 to search for the search string in both the labels and the formulas, choose **Both.**

After you indicate where to conduct the search, 1-2-3 displays the following commands on the second line of the control panel:

```
Find    Replace
```

To simply locate the search string without making any changes to the entry, choose the **Find** command. To locate the string and replace it with some new text, choose the **Replace** command. (See the following section for details.)

As soon as you choose the **Find** command, 1-2-3 starts the search. When the program locates a cell in the search cell range that contains the characters you're searching for, it selects that cell, highlights the search string in the contents of the cell displayed on the first line of the control panel, and displays the following commands on the second line of the control panel:

```
Next    Quit
```

Choose **Next** to have the program search for the next occurrence of the search string. Choose **Quit** to terminate the search and return to READY mode.

When 1-2-3 is unable to find the search string in the formulas and/or labels in the search range, it beeps at you and displays one of these error messages:

```
No more matching strings
```

```
String not found
```

At that point, you press Esc to return to READY mode. If you want to continue to search for the missing information, you can begin the search operation again and perhaps widen the search by using the question mark (?) or asterisk (*) wildcard characters.

Now that you know every last little detail, here are the bare-bones instructions for searching for a string of characters in labels and formulas:

1. Choose the **/R**ange **S**earch command.

2. Select the range to be searched.

3. Press Enter.

4. At the `Enter string to search for:` prompt, enter the search string.

5. Press Enter.

6. Choose **F**ormulas, **L**abels, or **B**oth.

7. Choose **F**ind.

8. If 1-2-3 finds the string, choose **N**ext to continue the search or **Q**uit to end the search. If the string is not found, press Esc to return to READY mode.

Send in the Substitutes

If you search for a particular entry so that you can find and change it, you can automate this process by choosing the **R**eplace command instead of the **F**ind command.

After you choose **R**eplace, 1-2-3 displays the following prompt on the control panel:

```
Enter replacement string:
```

When you enter the replacement text in response to this prompt, enter it exactly as you want it to appear in the cells that you replace. In other words, if you are replacing all occurrences of the label *Pig* in the search range with *Piggy*, you enter

```
Piggy
```

You need to use the uppercase *P* in the replacement string, even though you can enter pig as the search string.

After you enter the replacement string and press Enter, 1-2-3 looks for the search string. If it locates the string, it displays these commands on the second line of the control panel:

```
Replace   All   Next   Quit
```

✔ If you want to replace the search string highlighted in the entry shown on the first line of the control panel with the replacement string, choose the **R**eplace command.

✔ If you want to pass on changing this particular entry and search for the next occurrence, choose the **N**ext command.

✔ If you want to replace this entry and all subsequent occurrences of the search string, choose the **A**ll command.

✔ When you finish replacing all the entries that you want to change and you're ready to quit, choose (what else?) the **Q**uit command.

Just like the regular search operation, when 1-2-3 is unable to find the search string in the search range, it makes one of those beeping noises and displays the No more matching strings message. At that point, you can press Esc to terminate the search-and-replace attempt and return to READY mode.

Be very careful about choosing the **A**ll command to perform a global search-and-replace in the search range. You can really mess up a worksheet in a hurry if you replace parts of formulas or characters in the titles and headings that you hadn't intended to change. As a precaution, ***never undertake a global search-and-replace operation on an unsaved worksheet.*** If you do make a mess, press the Alt-F4 (Undo) key to restore the worksheet to its pre-search-and-replace condition. If you don't discover the problem in time to use Undo, close the messed-up worksheet without saving the changes (/**W**orksheet **E**rase **Y**es) and then open (/**F**ile **R**etrieve) the unreplaced version that you saved — thanks to reading this warning!

Now that you've been duly warned, here are the steps to follow when you want to send 1-2-3 on a search-and-replace mission:

1. Choose the /**R**ange **S**earch command.

2. Select the range to be searched.

3. Press Enter.

4. At the Enter string to search for: prompt, enter the search string.

5. Press Enter.

6. Choose **F**ormulas, **L**abels, or **B**oth.

7. Choose **R**eplace.

8. At the `Enter replacement string:` prompt, type the replacement text.

9. Press Enter.

10. When 1-2-3 finds the search string, choose **R**eplace, **A**ll, **N**ext, or **Q**uit. If the search does not find the string, press Esc to return to READY mode.

To Calc or Not to Calc...

Although extremely important, being able to locate information in a worksheet is only part of what you need to know to keep on top of worksheet information. You must know how to control recalculation — particularly in really large worksheets.

Often, when 1-2-3 recalculates the formulas that aren't up to date throughout the worksheet each time you enter or change information, your work can slow down to a crawl.

By switching to manual recalculation, you can control when the formulas in the worksheet are calculated. You can hold off the recalculation until you are ready to save or print the worksheet so that you can work without interminable delays.

To switch the recalculation of the worksheet to manual, you choose the /**W**orksheet **G**lobal **R**ecalculation **M**anual command. Then 1-2-3 displays the CALC indicator on the status bar any time you make a new entry or change an existing entry. This is your signal that some of the calculated values in the worksheet may no longer be correct.

To make sure that everything's up to date before you save the worksheet or print it, press the F9 (Calc) key. 1-2-3 recalculates the formulas that aren't up to date in the worksheet, and the CALC indicator disappears.

If you find that remembering to use the F9 (Calc) key is too much of a hassle and you think you've about finished making changes to the worksheet, you can turn the recalculation back to automatic by choosing the /**W**orksheet **G**lobal **R**ecalculation **A**utomatic command.

Protective Custody

When you've more or less finalized a worksheet by checking out its formulas and proofing its text, you often want to guard against any unplanned changes by *protecting* it. Simply choose the /**W**orksheet **G**lobal **P**rotection command and then choose the **E**nable option.

After you protect the worksheet, 1-2-3 refuses to process any changes that you try to make to any of the entries. You can't make new entries, copy and move information to new places, or erase or edit existing entries. Furthermore, when you press Enter after you select the appropriate editing commands, 1-2-3 beeps at you and displays this error message:

```
Protected cell
```

Then you have to press Esc to get out of ERROR mode and return to READY mode — without getting to process your changes.

Normally, your intention in protecting a worksheet is not to prevent all changes but, instead, to prevent changes in certain areas of the worksheet. For example, in a sales worksheet, you may want to protect all the cells with column headings and @SUM formulas but allow changes in all of the cells where you enter the sales figures. That way, you can't inadvertently wipe out a title or formula in the worksheet simply by entering a value in the wrong column or row (a common occurrence).

To leave certain cells unprotected so that you can change them even after you turn on global protection in the worksheet, you choose the /**R**ange **U**nprotect command and apply it to the cell or cell range which you want to be able to edit. All cells that are unprotected with the /**R**ange **U**nprotect command display U after the cell address on the first line of the control panel. (Protected cells sport a PR in this area when global protection is turned on.)

To remove global protection from a worksheet so that you can once again make changes to any of its cells, you choose the /**W**orksheet **G**lobal **P**rotection command and then choose the **D**isable option.

If protecting the worksheet doesn't provide sufficient security for the sensitive nature of your work (in other words, it's CONFIDENTIAL), you can also password-protect the file so that only those privileged souls who know the password can even open the worksheet. To assign a password to a file, follow these steps:

1. Choose the /**F**ile **S**ave command.

2. Enter the filename.

3. Press the spacebar.

4. Press P.

    Yes, P for password.

5. Press Enter.

    1-2-3 prompts you to enter a password.

6. Type the password.

    1-2-3 masks each character that you enter with a little square dot.

7. Press Enter.

    1-2-3 prompts you to reenter the password to verify it.

8. Type the password again.

(Yeah, there are a lot of steps. You don't want to do this a lot unless your worksheets are really, really confidential or you are really, really paranoid.)

From then on, you cannot open the worksheet unless you can reproduce the password exactly as you assigned it. Be very careful about password-protecting files. If you forget the password, you can never open the worksheet again (let alone unprotect it and alter its contents).

Chapter 6
Putting It Down on Paper

. . . .

In This Chapter

▶ Printing a cell range

▶ Changing the margins and other print settings

▶ Adding headers and footers

▶ Printing titles on each page of the report

▶ Inserting page breaks

▶ Printing the formulas in the worksheet

. . . .

*O*kay, so now you know how to get information into a 1-2-3 worksheet. But how do you get it onto paper so you can share it with other people? (After all, you can't very well have them all gather 'round your monitor — especially if they don't work in your office.) In this chapter, you learn the basics of printing 1-2-3 worksheets. You find out how to make sure that the program prints all the information you want to include in your report and learn how to add headers, footers, and borders that make your report clearer.

The only catch in printing a worksheet is that you have to get used to the way that the program pages the printout and learn how to control it. As you are well aware, many worksheets are not only longer than one printed page, but also wider. Spreadsheet programs such as 1-2-3 often have to break up pages both vertically and horizontally when they print a worksheet document. In contrast, a word processor only has to page documents vertically because it doesn't let you create a document that's wider than the page size.

When paging a worksheet, 1-2-3 first pages the document vertically down the rows in the first columns of the print area, just as a word processor does. After it finishes paging the first columns, the program then moves to the right and pages down the rows of the second set of columns in the print area. The program continues paging down, and then over, until it finishes paging everything you've included in the print area (which can be all or just sections of the worksheet).

When 1-2-3 pages a document, you need to keep in mind that the program does not break up the information in a row or column. If all the information in a row doesn't fit at the bottom of the page, the program moves the entire row to the following page. So, too, if all the information in a column doesn't fit at the right edge of the page, the program moves the entire column to a new page. (Remember that because 1-2-3 pages down and then over, chances are that the *new* page is not going to be the *next* page in the report.)

This chapter describes a couple of ways to deal with paging problems. When you get them under control, printing a worksheet is as easy as 1-2-3!

Printing 101

If you don't mind using 1-2-3's standard print settings, printing a worksheet is a snap:

1. Turn on the printer and make sure that it has plenty of paper and that the cable between the computer and the printer are secure.

   (Otherwise, when you call for help, the office computer whiz is going to post your name on the bulletin board as the winner of the Computer Blooper of the Week Award.)

2. Retrieve the worksheet file that you want to print.

   (No, you can't print a file until you retrieve it from the disk.)

3. Choose the **/P**rint **P**rinter **R**ange command.

4. If a print range has already been defined for the worksheet, press Esc to unanchor the range before you go on to the next step.

5. Select the cell range. (Position the cell pointer at the very beginning of the range you want to print, type a period to anchor the range, and highlight all the cells that you want to include in the range.)

   If the print range contains long labels that spill over into blank cells, be sure to include the blank cells in the print range. (Otherwise, 1-2-3 will print only the characters that are displayed in the cells you do include.)

6. Press Enter.

7. Make sure that the paper is properly positioned in the printer.

   The print head needs to be at the top of the new page if you're using a dot-matrix printer, and the paper tray needs to be firmly in place if you're using a laser printer.

8. Choose the **A**lign **G**o **P**age command.

9. If you're using a dot-matrix printer, choose the **P**age command a second time to advance the paper another complete page.

Advancing the paper another page makes it easy to tear off the last sheet without ripping the last page of the report in half. (Leave that for the boss to do when she sees the low sales figures.)

10. If the printout looks okay, choose the **Q**uit command to leave the /**P**rint **P**rinter menu and return to READY mode.

Printout, go where I send thee

Initially, having to choose the **P**rinter command right after you've chosen the /**P**rint command might strike you as kinda' redundant — but you have to do this in 1-2-3. Actually, you have to choose **P**rinter because the printer is not the only possible destination for your worksheet information.

You can send the worksheet to a text file, with the **F**ile command; a special encoded file that contains all the formatting codes the printer needs to print the data, with the **E**ncoded command; or in some later versions, a file with all the formatting codes that prints in the background while you continue to work in 1-2-3, with the **B**ackground command.

To print or not to print

When you choose the /**P**rint **P**rinter command, 1-2-3 displays the following menu:

```
    Range  Line  Page  Options  Clear  Align  Go  Quit
```

The /**P**rint **P**rinter menu, unlike other menus that you're familiar with (such as the /**R**ange Format menu or the /**R**ange Label menu), is a "sticky" menu; it remains displayed, or sticks around, until you choose the **Q**uit command. A sticky menu enables you to choose several different commands from the same menu without having to activate the 1-2-3 menu system with the / (backslash) key and then choose the higher level menu commands (/**P**rint **P**rinter in this case) each time.

As the printing directions indicate, you need to define what cells you want printed with the **R**ange command before you print. You can select the print range by pointing or by indicating the range name (see Chapter 5). If you find yourself printing the same cell range over and over again in a worksheet, don't mess around. Assign a clever name to the range and use it!

1-2-3 is a creature of habit. It remembers the last print range that you defined and highlights this range as soon as you choose the **R**ange command. If you don't want the program to highlight the same old range, choose the **C**lear and **R**ange commands to clear the old range from memory before you choose the **R**ange command. 1-2-3 then displays just the current cell address (unanchored) after the `Enter print range:` prompt on the control panel.

After indicating the print range, you choose the **A**lign and **G**o commands. The **A**lign command tells 1-2-3 to start counting lines at the current position of the print head (which should be at the top of the page when you are printing with a dot-matrix printer). That way, the program knows to start a new page after it has printed 66 consecutive lines.

When you choose the **G**o command, the program finally sends the print job to the printer and goes into WAIT mode (during which time you might as well send out for a pizza, because you can't do anything with your computer). As soon as the program finishes sending the print job, the mode changes to MENU. (It doesn't go back to READY mode because that sticky /**P**rint **P**rinter menu remains displayed on the screen.)

If you want to stop the printing altogether, press Ctrl-Break (Break may be located on the same key as Pause on your keyboard) and then press Esc or Enter. (1-2-3 then clears the error message and returns from ERROR mode to READY mode.) Note that after you press Ctrl-Break the printer may continue to print for a while until it empties its memory of all the information that 1-2-3 sent before you pulled the plug on the printing.

Someday, my prints will come

1-2-3 stops printing the report as soon as the last row in the print range has been printed. Because the printing just kinda, stops dead in its tracks, the print head remains wherever it finishes on the last page of the printout without advancing to the top of the next page. (In contrast, a word processor, such as WordPerfect, always completes the print job by automatically advancing the printer to the top of next blank page.) What's even worse, if you're using a laser printer, the last page remains stuck in the printer.

To advance the print head (or eject the last page from a laser printer), you choose the **P**age command on the /**P**rint **P**rinter menu. If you're using a dot-matrix printer, the **P**age command issues a form-feed to the printer, and the printer then advances the paper another full page. You waste a sheet of paper, but you can detach the last sheet of the printout more easily. If you don't want to advance the paper that far, you can use the **L**ine command to advance it line by line.

Whatever you do, don't ever manually advance the paper in the printer to the top of the next page and then forget to choose the **A**lign command before you choose the **G**o command. If you do, you'll totally screw up 1-2-3's line count so that it no longer breaks the pages at the right places. Then you'll have to deal with the dreaded "creep down" problem. The printing will start too far down on the first page and continue to creep down on each succeeding page of the printout. Imagine the havoc that creep down can wreak when you're printing out a really big worksheet.

Including lots of cell ranges in a printout

1-2-3's inability to advance the last page automatically to the next top of form (forcing you to rely on the **P**age command) is normally a real nuisance. It does, however, come in quite handy when you need to include more than one cell range in a printed report.

To print multiple ranges from a worksheet in a single printout, follow these steps:

1. Print the first cell range just as you normally would, but don't choose the **P**age command to advance the last page.

2. When 1-2-3 finishes printing the first range, use the **R**ange command to define the second range to be printed.

    (Remember, you can use the **C**lear **R**ange command to clear the first range before you try to define the second one.)

3. To print the second range, choose the **G**o command, but this time do not choose the **A**lign command.

    If you want to separate the two print ranges with a few blank lines, use the **L**ine command to advance the page a line at a time before you choose **G**o.

4. Continue to follow steps 2 and 3 to print all the other cell ranges to be included in the report. When 1-2-3 finishes printing the last cell range in the report, choose the **P**age command to advance the last page to the next top of form.

Putting 1-2-3 on Report

1-2-3's normal print settings are fine when all you need is a quickie rough draft of the information in a worksheet. However, you often need to change the print settings when you are preparing more formal presentations. In the next several sections, you learn how to change individual print settings, such as the margins and page length, and how to turn on compressed printing. You also learn how to add a header, a footer, and borders to help identify the information and pages in a multipage report.

If you can use the Wysiwyg add-in program, you probably want to use it, in-stead of 1-2-3, to format and print worksheet reports. Wysiwyg enables you to preview on-screen not only the formatting that you apply to worksheet data but also the pages of your report. (See Chapter 10 for previews of coming attrac-tions.)

Massaging the margins

Many times you can squeeze the last column or few rows that you need onto a page just by adjusting the margins. By default, 1-2-3 sets the top margin 2 lines down from the top of the paper and the bottom margin 2 lines up from the bot-tom of the paper. It sets the left margin 4 spaces from the left edge of the paper and the right margin 76 spaces from the left edge of the paper. To get more columns on a page, you can try reducing the left margin setting and/or increas-ing the right margin setting. To fit more rows on a page, you can try reducing the top and bottom margin settings.

The default left and right margin settings used by 1-2-3 presuppose that you are printing on 8½ x 11-inch paper with the standard pica type (which gives you 10 characters per inch). You have approximately ½ inch of white space on both the left and right sides of each page. If you switch to a different size paper or a different size type, you need to adjust at least the right margin setting.

For example, if you use 14 x 11-inch paper (the so-called computer paper) with pica type, you increase the right margin setting from 76 to 132. You increase the right margin setting using the same numbers if you use 8 ½ x 11-inch paper, but you switch from pica to compressed type, which is a change from 10 characters per inch to about 17 characters per inch. (See "What a setup!" later in this chap-ter.) If you use 14 x 11-inch paper and switch from pica to compressed type, you can increase the right margin setting to accommodate the maximum of 240 characters!

To change the margin settings, you choose the **O**ptions and **M**argins commands on the /**P**rint **P**rinter menu. 1-2-3 then displays the following menu on the second line of the control panel:

```
Left  Right  Top  Bottom  None
```

After you choose the appropriate margin command, 1-2-3 displays the current setting, which you can edit or replace with a new setting.

✔ You set new left and right margins by entering a value between 0 and 240 (representing the number of spaces from the left edge of the paper) and pressing Enter.

✔ You set new top and bottom margins by entering a value between 0 and 32 (representing the number of lines up or down from the top or bottom edge of the paper) and pressing Enter.

✔ You choose the **None** command to set the top, bottom, and left margin settings to the minimum of 0 and the right margin setting to the maximum of 240 characters. Use this command to max out the amount of data per page *only* when you are using 14-inch wide paper and have changed to compressed type.

Pushing the page length

The default page length is 66 lines, which is the number of lines available when you are printing on a standard, letter-size, 11-inch long page using single spacing (which gives you 6 lines per vertical inch). If you are printing on paper with a different length (such as legal size, rather than letter size) or with different vertical spacing (such as 8 lines per inch, instead of the normal 6 lines per inch), you need to adjust the page length setting accordingly.

Also, when you are using a laser printer, such as one of the HP LaserJet printers, you need to reduce the page length from 66 to 60 lines even when you are printing on an 11-inch page with single spacing. (These printers have a nonprintable area at the top and bottom of each page that reduces the total number of lines available.)

To determine the page length setting, simply multiply the number of lines in each vertical inch by the total number of inches in the length of the page. For example, you enter **84** as the page length setting when you are printing on legal-size paper using the standard single spacing. (Six lines per inch times 14 inches equals 84.) Likewise, you enter **88** as the page length setting when you are printing with letter-size paper using the compressed vertical spacing of 8 lines per inch. (Eight lines per inch times 11 inches equals 88.)

To change the page length setting, follow these steps:

1. Choose the **Options** and **Pg**-Length commands on the **/Print P**rinter menu.

2. Edit or replace the number of lines per page (between 1 and 100).

3. Press Enter.

What a setup!

Printers vary greatly in the number of type sizes and attributes (stuff like bold, italics, and underlining) that they can produce. Most dot-matrix printers give you a choice between only three type sizes: normal (10 characters per inch), compressed (17 characters per inch), and expanded (6 characters per inch). Most laser printers, on the other hand, give you a much wider choice of type sizes, depending upon which fonts you own and which ones are built into the printer itself.

Unfortunately, 1-2-3 really discourages you from utilizing whatever capabilities your printer does have by making it as hard as possible to use them in a report. The program could be set up so that you choose a menu command when you want to change such things as the type size or line spacing or when you want to add a particular attribute. Instead, it makes you stoop to the level of looking up and entering the program codes that your printer uses for these things and then entering the codes in what's known as a *setup string.*

In order to create a setup string, you not only have to have access to your printer's manual (no small feat in many cases), but you also have to understand how to enter its gobbledygook codes properly as a setup string. Many printer manuals give you the Esc codes (pronounced *escape codes*, as in, "Isn't there any way to *escape* all this setup nonsense?") used by your printer to perform such things as switching to compressed or expanded type or turning on and off attributes such as bold or italics. For example, if you're using an Epson dot-matrix printer, the printer manual may list the following code for changing the line spacing to 8 lines per vertical inch (sometimes called *compressed spacing*):

```
Esc 0
```

A setup string can consist of several different codes that control different printer functions, such as switching to compressed printing and to 8 lines per inch. The total length of the string cannot, however, exceed 39 characters. You separate different printer codes in the same setup string by entering a \ (backslash).

Now, to enter this escape code as a 1-2-3 setup string, you have to know enough to replace the *Esc* in Esc 0 with its code number equivalent (which happens to be 027, as in zero, two, seven). In place of Esc 0, you enter **0270.** Furthermore, when you enter this code as the setup string after you choose the **O**ptions and **S**etup commands on the /**P**rint **P**rinter menu, you need to preface it with a backslash (just like the one you use between DOS file directories):

```
\0270
```

As if you don't have more than enough to worry about, you may find that instead of listing the printer code as Esc 0, your printer manual lists it as Esc 48 or Esc 048 (48 is the numerical code equivalent of 0). If that's the case, you need to separate the code equivalent for 0 from the code equivalent for Esc with a \ (backslash), and you need to enter the code equivalent for 0 in its three-digit form with a leading 0:

```
\027\048
```

Also keep in mind that when you enter escape codes that use *code letters*, rather than numbers, you need to enter the letters exactly as they appear in the manual. For example, the Escape code for switching to 8 lines per inch with the HP LaserJet is &l8D (as in the ampersand, the lowercase letter *l*, the numeral eight, and the uppercase letter *D*). When you enter this code as a setup string, you must enter

```
\027&l8D
```

You have to enter it just as it's shown above. If you mess up and uppercase the *l* or lowercase the *D*, this setup string does not work.

To summarize, you enter a setup string by choosing the /**P**rint **P**rinter **O**ptions **S**etup, typing the setup string, and pressing Enter.

1-2-3 remembers whatever setup string you enter, and when you save the worksheet, it saves the setup string as part of the file. Follow these steps if you want to remove a setup string before you print from the same worksheet again:

1. Choose the /**P**rint **P**rinter **O**ptions **S**etup command.

2. Press Esc to clear the control panel.

3. Press Enter to confirm the deletion of the setup string.

You can also clear out the setup string by choosing the /**P**rint **P**rinter **C**lear **F**ormat command. Keep in mind, however, that when you use this command, you not only delete the setup string but also restore the margin and page length settings to their default values — which you may not want to do.

There has to be a better way!

If at all possible, print with the Wysiwyg add-in, rather than with 1-2-3, whenever you need to use a different type size or add various attributes to parts of the report. Wysiwyg enables you to make all these changes with its menu commands, instead of forcing you to deal with those nasty setup strings. (See Chapter 10 to learn how to escape from Esc.)

After you print a report with a setup string, the printer often retains the print setting(s) which that string put into effect. For example, you print a report with a setup string that turns on compressed type. Then the person in the cubicle next to yours prints a report from a worksheet that uses normal type. From the look on your colleague's face, you can tell right away that the second report came out in compressed print too. To save some paper and keep everything friendly in the office, do your good deed for the day. If your printer has a long memory, turn the printer off and then turn it on again to make it forget it ever heard of the setup string.

Put your header on my shoulder

Headers and footers are simply standard text that appears in the same place on every page of the report. The header is printed at the top of each page on the first line below the top margin (the third line down from the top of the page when you are using the default top margin setting of 2 lines). The footer is printed at the bottom of each page on the first line above the bottom margin (the third line up from the bottom of the page when you are using the default bottom margin setting of 2 lines).

1-2-3 always separates the text of any header and footer from the body of the report with two blank lines.

- ✔ It puts the two blank lines beneath the line of the header.
- ✔ It puts the two blank lines above the text of the footer, after the last line of the body of the report.

Note that 1-2-3 reserves these three lines (one for the header or footer and two lines to separate it from the rest of the text) at the top and bottom of the page whether or not you define a header and footer for your report. (These lines are in addition to the number of lines that are used for the top and bottom margins — 2 by default).

You can use a header and a footer in a report to identify the document used to produce the report, the page numbers, and the date of the printout.

You add a header or footer by following these steps:

1. Choose **/Print Printer Options Header** or **/Print Printer Options Footer**.

   On the second line of the control panel, the prompt Enter header: or Enter footer: appears.

2. Type the text that you want to appear as the header or footer.

3. Press Enter.

When you enter the text for your header or footer, you can use any of the codes shown in Table 6-1.

Table 6-1	Codes for Headers and Footers
Code	*What It Does*
@	Produces the current date, formatted as in 01-Nov-94
#	Produces the current page number, as in Page #
\ (backslash) followed by a cell address or range name	Uses the contents of the cell as the text of the header or footer; for example, **\B2** to use the label in cell B2 as the header or footer
I (vertical bar, same as Shift-\)	Aligns various parts of the header or footer text; the text following the first I is centered, and the text following the second I is right justified

Figures 6-1 and 6-2 illustrate how you can use these codes in headers and footers. Figure 6-1 shows the Print Settings dialog box after you define a header and a footer for a two-page report. Notice that the label entered in cell A1 supplies the text for the report header (as indicated by the \A1 in the Header text box).

As you can see in the Footer text box, the footer is divided into three parts:

- The first part of the footer displays the current date (designated by the @ symbol) after the stock text, Report Date. It is aligned with the left margin because it is entered before the first vertical bar.

- The second part of the footer displays the word Confidential and is centered because it follows the first vertical bar.

- The third part displays the page number (designated by the # symbol) after the word Page and is aligned with the right margin of the report because it follows the second vertical bar.

Figure 6-2 shows the printed results on the first page of the report. As you can see, the long label, Three Little Pigs Building Supply—Client List, which is entered in cell A1, is printed as the header for this report as well as in the first row. In the footer, you can see that @ has been replaced with the current date and # has been replaced with the actual page number.

When you use the vertical bar to align parts of a header or footer, keep in mind that the header or footer doesn't have to include all three parts. For example, if you just want to center the page number in the footer, you enter I**Page #** as the footer text (with no space between I and **Page #**). Likewise, if you just want the current date to appear in the header and you want it to be right justified, you

```
A1: (G) [W10] 'Three Little Pigs Building Supply -- Client List      MENU
Header  Footer  Margins  Borders  Setup  Pg-Length  Other  Quit
Create a footer
┌───────────────────────────── Print Settings ─────────────────────────────┐
│1                                                                          │
│2    Range: [A1..J34········]          ┌Destination──────────────────────┐ │
│3                                      │ (*) Printer      ( ) Encoded file│ │
│4    ┌Margins────────────────┐         │ ( ) Text file    ( ) Background  │ │
│5    │ Left:  [4··]  Top:  [2·]│                                          │ │
│6    │ Right: [76·]  Bottom: [2·]│        File name: [···················]  │ │
│7    └────────────────────────┘                                           │ │
│8    ┌Borders─────────────────┐                                           │ │
│9    │ Columns: [··············]│      Page length: [60·]                   │ │
│1    │ Rows:    [··············]│                                          │ │
│1    └────────────────────────┘      Setup string: [············]          │ │
│1                                                                          │ │
│1    Header: [\A1·····························]    [ ] Unformatted pages    │ │
│1    Footer: [Report Date: @│Confidential│Page #]  [ ] List entries        │ │
│1   ─────────────────────────────────────────────────────────────────────│ │
│1    Interface: Parallel 1              Name: HP LaserJet series           │ │
│1   ─────────────────────────────────────────────────────────────────────│ │
│1              Press F2 (EDIT) to edit settings                            │ │
│1   ─────────────────────────────────────────────────────────────────────│ │
│20   104-018  Ridinghoode Crimson      232 Cottage Path      Wulfen        │
│CLIENTS.WK1                                              NUM               │
└───────────────────────────────────────────────────────────────────────────┘
```

Figure 6-1: The Print Settings dialog box with a header and a footer entered.

enter | |@ as the header text. (Don't put spaces between the vertical bars or the bars and the @ symbol.) Also note that when you use a cell address to supply the text for a header or footer, you can't preface the cell or range address with vertical bars to align the text; it must remain alone, making it left aligned.

Border patrol

Just as you can freeze rows and columns of information as worksheet titles so that you can always identify the data that you're looking at on your monitor, you can have 1-2-3 print particular rows and columns on each page of the report. 1-2-3 refers to such rows and columns in a printed report as *borders*.

Don't confuse borders with the header in the report. Even though both are printed on each page, the header information is printed just below the top margin of the report, but the borders always appear in the body of the report.

✔ When you use rows as borders, they appear at the top of the report.

✔ When you use columns as borders, they appear on the left side of the report.

```
Three Little Pigs Building Supply -- Client List


Three Little Pigs Building Supply -- Client List
ID No    Last Name   First Name        Street           City
101-001  Bryant      Michael     326 Chef's Lane        Paris
102-002  Gearing     Shane       1 Gunfighter's End     LaLa Land
102-003  Wolfe       Big Bad     3 West End Boulevard   London
103-004  Cupid       Eros        97 Mount Olympus Road  Greece
104-005  Gookin      Polly       4 Feathertop Hill      Hawthorne
102-006  Cinderella  Poore       8 Lucky Maiden Way     Oxford
103-007  Baum        L. Frank    447 Toto Too Road      Oz
105-008  Harvey      Chauncey    60 Lucky Starr Place   Shetland
106-009  Sunnybrook  Rebecca     21 Last Week           Portland
106-010  White       Snow        552 Magic Mirror Circle Dwarf Place
104-011  Dragon      Kai         2 Pleistocene Era      Ann's World
102-012  Gondor      Aragorn     2956 Gandalf           Midearth
102-013  Baggins     Bingo       99 Hobbithole          Shire
101-014  Andersen    Hans        341 The Shadow         Scholar
101-015  Humperdinck Engelbert   654 Hansel & Gretel Trail Gingerbread
103-016  Oakenshield Rex         Mines of Goblins       Everest
103-017  Jacken      Jill        Up the Hill            Pail of Water
104-018  Ridinghoode Crimson     232 Cottage Path       Wulfen
104-019  Fudde       Elmer       8 Warner Way           Hollywood
102-020  Franklin    Ben         1789 Constitution      Jefferson
106-021  Horse       Seabisquit  First Place Finish     Raceway
106-022  Foliage     Red         49 Maple Syrup         Waffle
103-023  Appleseed   Johnny      6789 Fruitree Trail    Along The Way
103-024  Oakley      Anney       Six Shooter Path       Target
102-025  Washington  George      8 Founders Diamond     Hamilton
104-026  Brown       Charles     59 Flat Plains         Saltewater
105-027  Laurel      Stan        2 Oliver Hardy         Celluloyde
101-028  Cassidy     Butch       Sundance Kidde         Hole In Wall
101-029  Oow         Lu          888 Sandy Beach        Honolulu
101-030  Liberty     Statuesque  31 Gotham Centre       Big Apple
104-031  Eaters      Big         444 Big Pigs Court     Dogtown
101-920  Andersen    Christian   340 The Shadow         Scholar




Report Date: 14-Oct-93      Confidential              Page 1
```

Figure 6-2: The first page of the printout, showing the printed header and footer.

To define a row or range of rows as the border rows for a report, follow these steps:

1. Choose the **O**ptions **B**orders **R**ows command from the /**P**rint **P**rinter menu.

2. Position the cell pointer in one of the cells in the first row containing the column headings that you want to be printed at the top of each page of the report. If you also want to use information from rows below the first one, type a period to anchor the range and then press ↓ to highlight the rows.

3. Press Enter.

To define a column or range of border columns, follow similar steps:

1. Choose the **O**ptions **B**orders **C**olumns command from the /**P**rint **P**rinter menu.

2. Position the cell pointer in one of the cells in the first column that contains the row headings that you want printed on the left side of each page in the report. If you also want to use information in other columns on the right, type a period to anchor the range and then press → to highlight the columns.

3. Press Enter.

When you define columns and rows as borders for a report, watch out for one catch: You must *not* include these columns and rows as part of the print range. If you do, 1-2-3 prints the information in the border rows and columns twice on the first page — one time because these cells are defined as the borders for the report and another time because they are included in the print range.

If you have already selected the print range and it includes cells that are in the same rows and columns as those you defined as borders for the report, you can avoid printing the same rows or columns twice. Before you print the report, choose the **R**ange command on the /**P**rint **P**rinter menu and reduce the extent of the print range so that it doesn't include any of the border columns or rows.

Figures 6-3 through 6-5 illustrate the usefulness of borders in reports. Figure 6-3 shows the Print Settings dialog box after you define column A (which contains the row headings that identify the sales listed in each row) as the border column. It is listed in the Columns text box as the range A3..A3. Row 2 (row 2

```
A1: [W18] ^Three Little Pigs Building Supplies - 1992 Sales          MENU
Header  Footer  Margins  Borders  Setup  Pg-Length  Other  Quit
Print border columns and/or rows
┌────────────────────────────── Print Settings ──────────────────────────┐
│1                                                                        │
│2    Range: [B3..R19········]        ┌─Destination─────────────────────┐ │
│3                                    │ (*) Printer      ( ) Encoded file│ │
│4    ┌─Margins─────────────────┐     │ ( ) Text file    ( ) Background  │ │
│5    │ Left:  [4··]  Top:  [2·]│                                        │ │
│6    │ Right: [76·]  Bottom: [2·]│   │ File name: [················]  │ │
│7    └─────────────────────────┘     └──────────────────────────────────┘ │
│8    ┌─Borders─────────────────┐                                         │
│9    │ Columns: [A3..A3········]│     Page length: [60·]                 │
│1    │ Rows:    [A2..A2········]│                                         │
│1    └─────────────────────────┘     Setup string: [············]       │
│1                                                                        │
│1    Header: [¦¦1992 Sales Report··············]    [ ] Unformatted pages│
│1    Footer: [Date: @¦Confidential¦Page #·······]   [ ] List entries     │
│1                                                                        │
│1    Interface: Parallel 1              Name: HP LaserJet series         │
│1                                                                        │
│1    ┌──────────── Press F2 (EDIT) to edit settings ─────────────┐       │
│20   └─────────────────────────────────────────────────────────┘        │
│92SALES.WK1                                                     NUM      │
└─────────────────────────────────────────────────────────────────────────┘
```

Figure 6-3: The Print Settings dialog box after the border column and border rows have been defined.

contains the column headings that identify when the sales in each column were made) has been defined as the border row. It is listed in the Rows text box as the range A2..A2. Please note too, that the print range (B3..R19) shown in the Range text box does not contain any cells that are in column A or in row 2.

Figures 6-4 and 6-5 show the first and second pages of a report with a border column. Notice that defining the row headings in column A as the border column has caused 1-2-3 to repeat these headings on the left side of both Pages 1 and 2. If you hadn't defined column A as the border column, its row headings

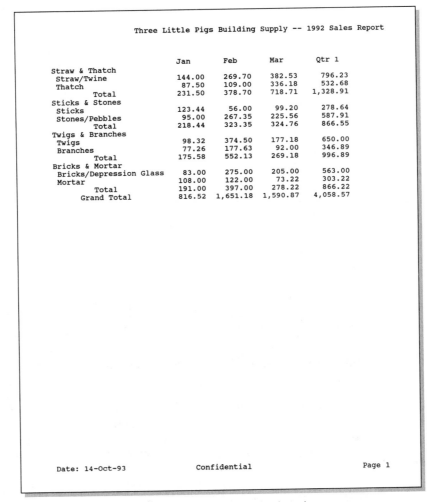

```
              Three Little Pigs Building Supply -- 1992 Sales Report


                          Jan        Feb        Mar       Qtr 1
         Straw & Thatch
          Straw/Twine     144.00     269.70     382.53     796.23
          Thatch           87.50     109.00     336.18     532.68
              Total       231.50     378.70     718.71   1,328.91
         Sticks & Stones
          Sticks          123.44      56.00      99.20     278.64
          Stones/Pebbles   95.00     267.35     225.56     587.91
              Total       218.44     323.35     324.76     866.55
         Twigs & Branches
          Twigs            98.32     374.50     177.18     650.00
          Branches         77.26     177.63      92.00     346.89
              Total       175.58     552.13     269.18     996.89
         Bricks & Mortar
          Bricks/Depression Glass  83.00  275.00  205.00   563.00
          Mortar          108.00     122.00      73.22     303.22
              Total       191.00     397.00     278.22     866.22
          Grand Total     816.52   1,651.18   1,590.87   4,058.57
```

```
     Date: 14-Oct-93            Confidential              Page 1
```

Figure 6-4: The first page of a four-page report with a border column.

```
              Three Little Pigs Building Supply -- 1992 Sales Report


                            Apr        May        Jun        Qtr 2
        Straw & Thatch
         Straw/Twine      153.00     109.54     279.42       541.96
         Thatch           116.25     247.98     321.00       685.23
              Total       269.25     357.52     600.42     1,227.19
        Sticks & Stones
         Sticks            56.85      93.00      75.50       225.35
         Stones/Pebbles   116.06     212.37     301.00       629.43
              Total       172.91     305.37     376.50       854.78
        Twigs & Branches
         Twigs             38.50      56.00      63.95       158.45
         Branches          99.36     132.19     283.50       515.05
              Total       137.86     188.19     347.45       673.50
        Bricks & Mortar
         Bricks/Depression Glass  108.00     198.00      93.00       399.00
         Mortar            82.25      73.66      33.59       189.50
              Total       190.25     271.66     126.59       588.50
          Grand Total     770.27   1,122.74   1,450.96     3,343.97
```

```
        Date: 14-Oct-93            Confidential              Page 2
```

Figure 6-5: The second page of a four-page report with a border column.

would not have been repeated on Page 2, and you would have no way of identifying the categories of the second quarter sales figures printed on this page.

You're probably wondering what happened to the border rows that were defined for the report. Well, because the rows in the print range all fit on a single page, 1-2-3 does not use the border rows in this particular report. If you later add more rows of data to the worksheet so that all the rows no longer fit on one page, 1-2-3 will automatically print the column headings in row 2 at the top of all the pages containing information from the rows that are forced onto their own pages.

To clear print borders from a report when you no longer need them, you choose the /**P**rint **P**rinter **C**lear **B**orders command.

Gimme a (page) break

Sometimes, after you print a report, you notice that 1-2-3 has put in a bad page break that caused rows of information that should always be together to appear on different pages. So how do you fix that? Easy. Just insert a manual page break to force 1-2-3 to print the information from a particular row farther down on the same page.

To insert a manual page break, you need to be in READY mode so that you can move the cell pointer. If you still have the sticky old **/Print Printer** menu displayed, you need to unglue it by choosing the **Quit** command.

1. Move the cell pointer to the intersection of the row where you want the manual page break to appear and the first column that has been included in the print range.

   For example, if the print range is defined as the cell range B3..T50 and you want to insert a manual page break starting at row 23, you place the cell pointer in cell B23.

2. Choose the **/Worksheet Page** command.

3. Press Enter.

   1-2-3 then inserts a blank row in the worksheet at the cell pointer's position and enters : : (a double colon), which is the manual page break symbol, in the current cell. Any rows of data in the print range that are below this symbol will be printed on a new page when you next print the report with the **/Print Printer Align Go Page** command.

Be sure that you don't put the manual page symbol in a cell in a column that has been defined as part of the borders for the report. If you do, 1-2-3 will print the report with that silly looking manual page break symbol (::) on the first page, and each page of the report that includes that row will feature a blank line at that row.

After you print the report, you can easily remove a manual page break from the worksheet:

1. Position the cell pointer somewhere in the row that contains the double colon (: :).

2. Choose the **/Worksheet Delete Row** command.

3. Press Enter.

   1-2-3 immediately removes the blank row, manual page break symbol and all.

Formula Printing

Another basic printing technique that may come in handy every once in a while is printing the formulas, rather than the more normal calculated results. For example, you can use a printout of the formulas to check them over and make sure that you haven't done anything stupid — such as replacing a formula with a number or using the wrong cell references in a formula — *before* you distribute the worksheet company wide. (Which can be really embarrassing.)

To print the contents of each cell in the print range, you choose the **O**ptions **O**ther Cell-Formulas command from the /**P**rint **P**rinter menu before you print a report (or simply put an *X* in the List entries check box in the Print Settings dialog box).

Figure 6-6 shows the kinds of results that you get when you choose the Cell-Formulas option. This figure shows the first page of the report introduced in Figures 6-4 and 6-5 when you print the contents of the cells. As you can see, in this format 1-2-3 simply displays a long laundry list that includes the cell address followed by the contents of the cell.

Although having this list is somewhat helpful, you can't easily correlate this inventory of cell goodies with the results shown in the printed report in Figures 6-4 and 6-5. That report doesn't display the column letters and row numbers, so you can't identify the cell references. (See the next section for tips on printing the column letters and row numbers as part of a report.)

After you print a report that shows the formulas in the print range, be sure to remember to switch back to the normal display of cell results before you print the report again. Just choose the /**P**rint **P**rinter **O**ptions **O**ther **A**s-Displayed command (or remove the *X* from the List entries check box in the Print Settings dialog box).

You can choose the Unformatted command on the /**P**rint **P**rinter **O**ptions **O**ther menu to print a rough draft of a report with as many lines of data on each page as possible. To maximize the number of lines per page, 1-2-3 ignores the top and bottom margin settings and suppresses any header or footer used in the report. When you are ready to print a final draft of the report, be sure to return to the /**P**rint **P**rinter **O**ptions **O**ther menu and choose the Formatted option before you send the report to the printer with the **A**lign **G**o commands on the /**P**rint **P**rinter menu.

```
                                                1992 Sales Report

        B4: (,2) [W10] 144
        C4: (,2) [W10] 269.7
        D4: (,2) [W10] 382.53
        E4: (,2) [W11] 796.23
        F4: (,2) [W11] 153
        G4: (,2) [W11] 109.54
        H4: (,2) [W11] 279.42
        I4: (,2) [W13] 541.96
        J4: (,2) [W10] 211.5
        K4: (,2) [W10] 187.25
        L4: (,2) [W10] 415.93
        M4: (,2) [W11] 814.68
        N4: (,2) [W10] 153
        O4: (,2) [W10] 109.54
        P4: (,2) [W10] 279.42
        Q4: (,2) [W11] 1389.67
        R4: (,2) [W11] @SUM(E4,I4,M4,Q4)
        B5: (,2) [W10] 87.5
        C5: (,2) [W10] 109
        D5: (,2) [W10] 336.18
        E5: (,2) [W11] 532.68
        F5: (,2) [W11] 116.25
        G5: (,2) [W11] 247.98
        H5: (,2) [W11] 321
        I5: (,2) [W13] @SUM(F5..H5)
        J5: (,2) [W10] 97
        K5: (,2) [W10] 111.25
        L5: (,2) [W10] 289.17
        M5: (,2) [W11] 497.42
        N5: (,2) [W10] 116.25
        O5: (,2) [W10] 247.98
        P5: (,2) [W10] 321
        Q5: (,2) [W11] 833.24
        R5: (,2) [W11] @SUM(E5,I5,M5,Q5)
        B6: (,2) [W10] @SUM(B4..B5)
        C6: (,2) [W10] @SUM(C4..C5)
        D6: (,2) [W10] @SUM(D4..D5)
        E6: (,2) [W11] @SUM(E4..E5)
        F6: (,2) [W11] @SUM(F4..F5)
        G6: (,2) [W11] @SUM(G4..G5)
        H6: (,2) [W11] @SUM(H4..H5)
        I6: (,2) [W13] @SUM(I4..I5)
        J6: (,2) [W10] @SUM(J4..J5)
        K6: (,2) [W10] @SUM(K4..K5)
        L6: (,2) [W10] @SUM(L4..L5)
        M6: (,2) [W11] @SUM(M4..M5)
        N6: (,2) [W10] @SUM(N4..N5)
        O6: (,2) [W10] @SUM(O4..O5)
        P6: (,2) [W10] @SUM(P4..P5)
        Q6: (,2) [W11] @SUM(Q4..Q5)


     Date: 14-Oct-93          Confidential            Page 1
```

Figure 6-6: The first page of a report that lists the contents of the cells in the print range.

But I Was Framed!

As mentioned in the preceding section, sometimes you want to print the column letters and row numbers on a report so that you can easily identify the worksheet location of printed data. Such a draft is especially helpful when you've printed the formulas in the worksheet (as described previously) and want to check the contents of a cell listed in this special report against the result shown in a normal report.

Unfortunately, the folks at Lotus didn't add a command for printing the frame. Unless you can use the Wysiwyg add-in, you have to go into the worksheet itself and add a row of column letters at the top of the print range and a column of row numbers at the left of the print range. After that, you have to define the new row and column as part of the borders. (If you can use the Wysiwyg add-in, get outta' here as fast as you can, and go immediately to the tip at the end of this section.)

Here's how you add letters and numbers to a report:

1. Position the cell pointer in the first cell of the print range. If you've already defined border columns and rows in the worksheet, place the cell pointer in the cell at the intersection of the first border column and row instead of in the first cell in the print range.

2. Choose the /Worksheet Insert Row command and press Enter.

3. Choose the /Worksheet Insert Column command and press Enter.

4. Move the cell pointer to the next cell on the right.

5. Turn on Caps Lock.

6. Type the letter of *the column on the left.* (In other words, if the pointer is in column B, you press A.) Press → to move to the next cell, and type the letter of the column that comes next.

   Continue in this manner until you have entered column letters (using the letters displayed on the frame for the *preceding* column) for all the columns in the print range.

7. Press Enter, instead of →, when you enter the last column letter.

8. Turn off Caps Lock.

9. Choose /Range Label Center and press End-←.

10. Press Enter.

11. Press End-← and then press ← again and ↓ to put the cell pointer in the first cell that needs a row number.

12. Choose the /Data Fill command.

13. Type a period to anchor the range and press ↓ until you highlight all the rows in the column that require row numbers; then press Enter.

14. Type the number of the first row (one less than the real row number listed on the frame) in response to the Start: prompt; then press Enter three times to fill this range with sequential numbers.

15. Use the /Worksheet Column Set-Width command to narrow the column that contains the row numbers.

16. If necessary, use the **Columns** and **Rows** commands on the **/Print Printer Options Borders** menu to define the column with the row numbers and the row with the column letters as borders for the report.

17. Make sure that the print range does not include the border columns and rows that contain the row numbers and column letters.

18. Use the **Align Go** commands on the **/Print Printer** menu to print the report with the made-up frame.

19. Use the **/File Save** command and then enter a new name for the version of the worksheet with the made-up frame. That way, you can use the original when you want to print a report without the worksheet frame. And when you do want to print a report of the worksheet with the frame, you'll never ever have to go through these 19 steps again.

20. Put your feet up and take a nap. Or take the rest of the day off. Or take a hike.

Wysiwyg users take note: You don't have to go through all this nonsense to print the column letters and row numbers on a report. You lucky people can simply choose the Wysiwyg **:Display Options Frame** command before you print the report with the Wysiwyg **:Print Go** command. (See Chapter 10 for details on using Wysiwyg to format and print your worksheets.)

Figures 6-7 and 6-8 show you the first part of a worksheet and the first page of the accompanying report after you add a row of column letters and column of row numbers to the worksheet and define them as part of the border rows and columns for the report.

```
A3: [W5] 2                                                          READY

        A          B              C         D         E         F      ◄
   1                                                                   ►
   2                 A             B         C         D         E      ▲
   3        2                     Jan       Feb       Mar       Qtr 1   ▼
   4        3 Straw & Thatch                                            ?
   5        4    Straw/Twine     144.00    269.70    382.53    796.23
   6        5    Thatch           87.50    109.00    336.18    532.68
   7        6         Total      231.50    378.70    718.71  1,328.91
   8        7 Sticks & Stones
   9        8    Sticks          123.44     56.00     99.20    278.64
  10        9    Stones/Pebbles   95.00    267.35    225.56    587.91
  11       10         Total      218.44    323.35    324.76    866.55
  12       11 Twigs & Branches
  13       12    Twigs            98.32    374.50    177.18    650.00
  14       13    Branches         77.26    177.63     92.00    346.89
  15       14         Total      175.58    552.13    269.18    996.89
  16       15 Bricks & Mortar
  17       16    Bricks/Depression Glass  83.00  275.00   205.00  563.00
  18       17    Mortar          108.00    122.00     73.22    303.22
  19       18         Total      191.00    397.00    278.22    866.22
  20       19    Grand Total     816.52  1,651.18  1,590.87  4,058.57
92SALESF.WK1              UNDO                           NUM
```

Figure 6-7: The first part of the worksheet after you add the column letters and row numbers.

```
                                                        1992 Sales Report


                        A                  B          C          D          E
                  2                       Jan        Feb        Mar        Qtr 1
                  3  Straw & Thatch
                  4    Straw/Twine      144.00     269.70     382.53       796.23
                  5    Thatch            87.50     109.00     336.18       532.68
                  6         Total       231.50     378.70     718.71     1,328.91
                  7  Sticks & Stones
                  8    Sticks          123.44      56.00      99.20       278.64
                  9    Stones/Pebbles   95.00     267.35     225.56       587.91
                 10         Total       218.44     323.35     324.76       866.55
                 11  Twigs & Branches
                 12    Twigs            98.32     374.50     177.18       650.00
                 13    Branches         77.26     177.63      92.00       346.89
                 14         Total      175.58     552.13     269.18       996.89
                 15  Bricks & Mortar
                 16    Bricks/Depression Glass   83.00   275.00   205.00     563.00
                 17    Mortar          108.00     122.00      73.22       303.22
                 18         Total      191.00     397.00     278.22       866.22
                 19      Grand Total   816.52   1,651.18   1,590.87     4,058.57
```

```
         Date: 15-Oct-93              Confidential                   Page 1
```

Figure 6-8: The first page of a report with column letters and row numbers.

Part IV
Beyond the Worksheet

The 5th Wave By Rich Tennant

"Kevin here heads our software development team. Right now he's working on a spreadsheet program that's sort of a combination 1-2-3 Lotus and Donkey Kong."

The part in which...

You learn that yes, Virginia, there's life beyond the 1-2-3 worksheet, and this part proves it! You tap into your artistic talents and learn how easy it is to create super looking graphs that literally give your worksheet data (and you?) a whole new image.

You learn how you can use 1-2-3 to maintain and organize the great quantities of facts and figures that you need to track. You learn how to sort the information in any preferred order as well as how to search for and retrieve just the data you're interested in at the time — instant gratification!

Finally, you learn how to create and use simple macros that streamline and automate repetitive tasks — which is a smooth way to say that you can remove a lot of the drudgery from your work!

Chapter 7
"Every Picture Tell a Story, Don't It?" — Rod Stewart

*I*n keeping with the old Chinese proverb, "A picture is worth a thousand words," this chapter tells you how to use graphs to represent the data in a worksheet. Graphs can add zest and spice to otherwise ho-hum reports, heighten interest in the data, and illustrate trends and anomalies that might not be apparent from looking at the numbers alone. Because 1-2-3 makes it so easy to graph the information in a worksheet, you can experiment with different types of graphs until you find the one that best represents the data.

Just a general word about graphs before you start learning how to make them with 1-2-3. Remember when your high school algebra teacher valiantly tried to teach you how to graph equations by plotting different values on an x-axis and a y-axis on graph paper? You were probably too busy with more important things to pay too much attention to your old algebra teacher. Besides, you probably told yourself, "I'll never need this junk when I'm out on my own and get a job!"

Well, see, you just never know. It turns out that even though 1-2-3 automates almost the entire process of graphing worksheet data, you may need to be able to tell your x-axis from your y-axis, just in case 1-2-3 doesn't draw the graph the way you had in mind. To refresh your memory, the *x-axis* is the horizontal axis, and the *y-axis* is the vertical one.

In most graphs that use these two axes (pronounced *axees,* as in taxies, not axes, as in taxes), 1-2-3 plots the categories along the x-axis and their relative values along the y-axis. The x-axis is sometimes referred to as the *time axis* because the graph often depicts values along this axis at different time periods, such as months, quarters, years, and so on.

Pretty as a Picture

Well, enough of that boring background information on graphs. Now to get on with the fun part. To create a graph in 1-2-3, all you need is a worksheet with a table of data — something like the Three Little Pigs Building Supply first quarter 1994 sales table shown in Figure 7-1.

When you graph the data in a worksheet table, you first need to decide how you want the values to be compared. For example, in the table shown in Figure 7-1, either you can have the graph group the sales figures and compare them to each other by month (January, February, and March), or you can have it group and compare them by the type of sales (Straw & Thatch, Sticks & Stones, and Bricks & Mortar).

Whichever way you decide to go, I think you'll agree that, for this table, the graph you create will compare three data ranges. You can compare the data rowwise, using the ranges B3..D3, B4..D4, and B5..D5, or columnwise, using the ranges B3..B5, C3..C5, and D3..D5. Each data range is given a letter of the alphabet between A and F, so you can compare up to six different ranges in one graph.

```
A1: [W15] 'Three Little Pigs Building Supply - Quarter 1 1994 Sales        READY
         A              B            C            D            E         F
1  Three Little Pigs Building Supply - Quarter 1 1994 Sales
2                   January     February      March     Q1 Total
3  Straw & Thatch    421.35      602.00       733.03    $1,756.38
4  Sticks & Stones   645.75      700.15       790.50    $2,136.40
5  Bricks & Mortar  1,453.00    1,560.20     1,918.80   $4,932.00
6                  --------------------------------------------------
7  Total           $2,520.10   $2,862.35    $3,442.33   $8,824.78
8
9                                      ▉
10
11
12
13
14
15
16
17
18
19
20
Q1SALES.WK1                  UNDO                            NUM
```

Figure 7-1: A worksheet table with the data to be graphed.

After you decide how to compare the data, you simply define each data range of the graph, add some titles, and away you go. When you define data ranges for the graph and do that other graph-type stuff, you use (what else?) the **/Graph** menu. The **/Graph** menu, like the **/Print** menu, is a sticky menu that enables you to define each part of the graph without returning to READY mode all of the time. When you are ready to return to READY mode from this menu, you simply choose its **Quit** command or press Esc.

To see how easy creating a graph really is, follow along with the steps for defining the three data ranges to graph the Three Little Pigs first quarter sales by month:

1. Choose **/Graph A** to define the first data range for the graph.

2. Position the cell pointer in cell B3 and type a period to anchor the range. Press → to highlight the range B3..D3 and press Enter.

3. Press **B** to define the second data range. Position the cell pointer in cell B4 and type a period to anchor the range. Press → to highlight the range B4..D4 and press Enter.

4. Type **C** to define the last data range. Position the cell pointer in cell B5 and type a period to anchor the range. Press → to highlight the range B5..D5 and press Enter.

5. Choose the **View** command or press the F10 (Graph) key to look at the graph so far. (It looks similar to the graph shown in Figure 7-2.) Press a key (any key, such as Enter, F, or the spacebar) to return to the **/Graph** menu and the normal worksheet screen.

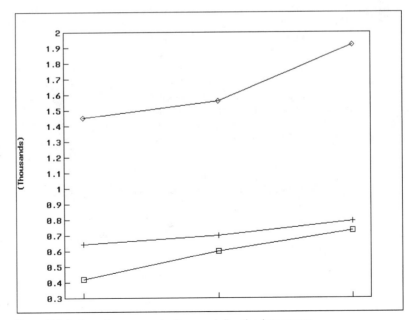

Figure 7-2: A view of a new graph after you define the data ranges.

When you create a new graph, such as the one shown in Figure 7-2, 1-2-3 automatically draws it as a *line graph,* with each data range represented by a different line. (You learn how to choose another graph type in the next section.) The values in each data range are plotted against the y-axis (the vertical one running up the left side of the graph), which is automatically generated and labeled.

Except for the y-axis, however, 1-2-3 does not add any labels or titles to a new graph. You have to add them yourself. Most notably absent from this graph are the labels along the x-axis that identify just what it is that each of the *data points* (the diamonds, plus signs, and boxes) represents. You remedy the lack of x-axis labels by defining the **X** data range as follows:

1. Choose the **X** command on the **/G**raph menu and then position the cell pointer in cell B2. Type a period to anchor the range. Press → to highlight the range that has the column headings `January`, `February`, and `March` (B2..D2), and press Enter.

2. Choose the **V**iew command or press the F10 (Graph) key to view the graph.

3. Press any key to return to the **/G**raph menu and the normal worksheet screen.

The names of the months `January`, `February`, `March` appear as x-axis labels centered beneath each *tick mark* (those little vertical and horizontal lines along the x-axis and y-axis that indicate where the values or categories occur).

You can save time by defining all the data ranges, as well as the x-axis labels for the graph, in one operation. Choose the **G**roup command on the **/G**raph menu and then select the range of cells in the worksheet that contains the x-axis labels as well as the values to be graphed. As soon as you press Enter to record this group range, you can choose the **C**olumnwise or **R**owwise option. Choose **C**olumnwise if the x-axis labels are in the first column and the values are in the columns to the right; choose **R**owwise if the x-axis labels run across the first row with the values in the rows below. For example, to graph the Three Little Pig first quarter '94 sales with the **/G**raph **G**roup command, you select the cell range B2..D5 as the group range and then choose **R**owwise as the direction.

This graph is really not my type

Although 1-2-3 draws every new graph as a line graph, you can easily change the graph type. Choose the **T**ype command on the **/G**raph menu and then choose the new type of graph. You can choose between the following graph types:

✔ Line graphs, which are the default, use each line to represent a data range and each point on a line to represent a particular value in that range.

✔ Bar graphs use different sized bars to compare individual values or sets of values. You define the **A** data range to produce a single-range bar graph where each bar represents a different value. You define the **A** through **F** data ranges when you want to compare many sets of values in different ranges and have each bar in each group represent a different value.

✔ XY graphs, also known as scatter graphs, correlate two different types of numeric data. This is the only graph type that displays values along the x-axis as well as along the y-axis. You use the **X** data range for the x-axis values and the **A** through **F** data ranges for the set of values to plot.

✔ Stack-Bar graphs compare individual and total values by stacking different types of bars on top of each other. Each value in a stacked bar is represented by a different pattern or color. You define the **A** through **F** data ranges to indicate the set of values that you want to compare. Each section of the stacked bar then represents a different value.

✔ Pie charts identify the relationship of each value in a single data range to the values in the entire data range. Define the **A** data range to indicate the set of values to compare, where each slice of the pie represents its percentage of the whole pie.

✔ HLCO (High Low Close Open) graphs are available only in Release 2.3 and 2.4. You use HLCO graphs to track the fluctuations of stock prices over time. You define the **A, B, C,** and **D** data ranges, with the ranges containing the high, low, closing, and opening values, respectively.

✔ Mixed graphs, which are available only in Release 2.3 and 2.4, combine the use of lines and bars in the same graph. You define the **A** through **C** data ranges with the values you want represented by bars and the **D** through **F** data ranges with the values you want represented by lines.

Changing from one graph type to another is easy, so have fun experimenting with different graph types. After you use the /Graph Type command to change types, you can take a look at the new graph by choosing the View command or pressing the F10 (Graph) key. Figure 7-3 shows the sample graph after you change it from a line graph to a bar graph. Figure 7-4 shows the same graph, this time as a stack-bar graph.

Viewing the feature presentation

If you're fortunate enough to be using Release 2.3 or 2.4 of 1-2-3, you can use the Features command on the /Graph Type menu to make some nifty enhancements to the basic graph types. When you choose the /Graph Type Features command, the following sticky menu appears on the control panel:

```
Vertical Horizontal Stacked Frame 3D-Effect Quit
```

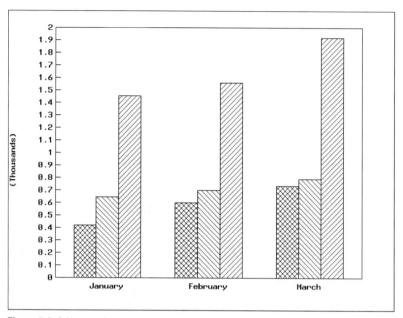

Figure 7-3: A bar graph.

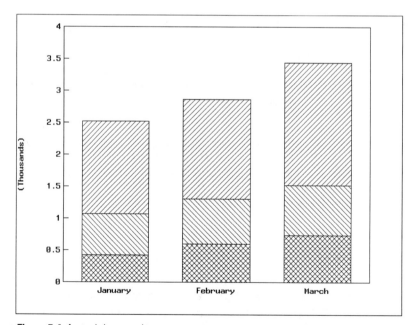

Figure 7-4: A stack-bar graph.

✔ You use the Horizontal and Vertical commands to switch the orientation of a graph. Figure 7-5 shows the stack-bar graph introduced in Figure 7-4 after you choose the Horizontal command to turn it on its side.

✔ You use the **Stacked** command to stack or unstack data ranges. For example, you can use it to change a basic bar graph into a stack-bar graph or a stack-bar graph into a simple bar graph.

✔ You use the **Frame** command to change the way the basic box, or frame, around the graphed data appears. You can remove all or part of the frame.

✔ You use the **3D-Effect** command to make the bars in a simple bar or stack-bar graph appear three-dimensional or to switch back to the normal flat, two-dimensional representations. (A nice feature of this 3-D effect is that you don't have to wear those funny glasses with the cardboard frames to see it.) Figure 7-6 shows how the horizontal bar graph in Figure 7-5 looks after you turn on the 3-D effect. Not only the bars, but also the top of the graph frame, appear to have some depth because they've been drawn slightly in perspective.

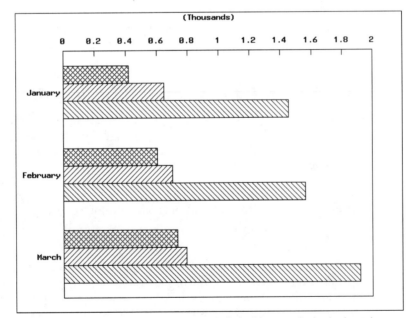

Figure 7-5: A stack-bar graph that has been switched from vertical to horizontal orientation.

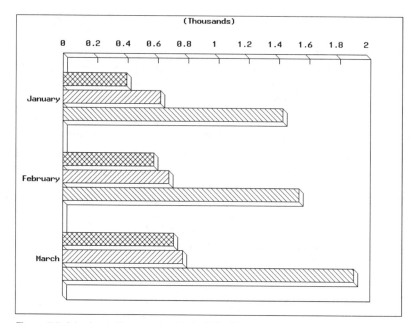

Figure 7-6: A horizontal bar graph with the 3-D effect.

Coming up with some really graphic titles

You can assign up to four lines of text as various kinds of titles for the graph. You can have a main title that appears centered at the top of the graph in two lines, a y-axis title that runs up the y-axis of the graph, and an x-axis title that runs along the x-axis at the bottom of the graph.

To add any or all of these titles to a graph, choose the /Graph Options Titles command to display the following menu on the control panel:

```
First  Second  X-Axis  Y-Axis
```

Choose the command for the type of title that you want to add and then either type the text of the title after the prompt on the control panel or enter the address of the cell that contains the label you want to use, preceded by a backslash. Suppose that you want to use the label entered in cell A1 as the **First** title in the graph. In response to the `Enter first line of graph title` prompt, you simply enter

```
\A1
```

Note that if you use a cell address as a graph title, 1-2-3 automatically updates the text of the title whenever you edit the label in that cell in the worksheet. If, however, you choose to type the text of a title yourself, you have to edit it yourself if you want to change it. Return to the /Graph Options Titles menu, choose the particular title command, and then edit the text.

Figure 7-7 shows the bar graph (in the normal vertical orientation) after you add first, second, x-axis and y-axis titles. Note that 1-2-3 centers the first and second lines of the main title at the top the graph, the x-axis title (First Quarter) at the bottom of the graph, and the y-axis title (Sales) on the left side of the graph (running up the side).

Creating a legend in your own time

What's really missing from the sample graph at this point is a *legend* that identifies the symbols, patterns, or colors assigned to the various data ranges that are represented. This information is essential whenever a graph includes more than a single data range. Otherwise, someone looking at it doesn't have the foggiest idea what the elements in the graph mean.

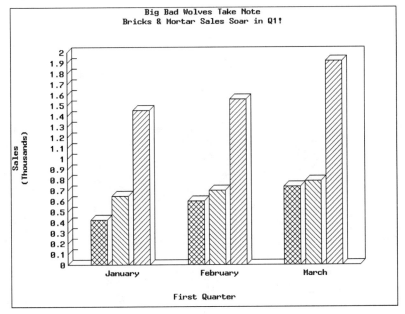

Figure 7-7: A bar graph with titles.

To add a legend to a graph, you choose the **O**ptions **L**egend command from the /**G**raph menu, which brings up the following menu:

A B C D E F Range

Choose the letter of the data range to which you want to assign a legend and then type the text that identifies that data range. You can, instead, type the address of a worksheet cell that already contains such an identifier (preceded, of course, by a backslash). For example, to add a legend in the sample graph for the **A** data range (B3..D3, which contains the monthly sales figures for Straw & Thatch), you can enter the cell reference **\A3** because this cell in the worksheet already contains the row heading, Straw & Thatch.

If the worksheet already contains a range of headings that you can designate as the legend for all of the data ranges, you can save time by choosing the **R**ange command on the /**G**raph **O**ptions **L**egend menu and selecting the range that has the appropriate labels (instead of choosing the **A, B, C, D, E,** and **F** commands individually to define a legend for each data range).

For example, in the worksheet table used to create the sample graph, you can use the **R**ange command to define the legend for all three data ranges (**A, B,** and **C**) because the cell range A3..A5 contains three appropriate row headings. Figure 7-8 shows the bar graph after you designate this cell range as the legend for the data ranges.

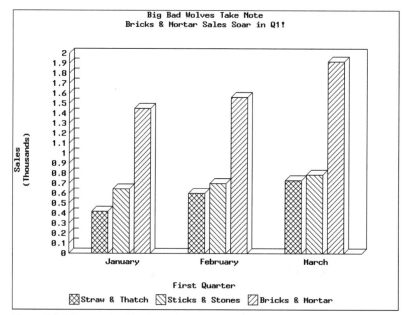

Figure 7-8: A bar graph with a legend.

Grid lines, if you wouldn't mind

When you created graphs back in high school, you probably did it in pencil, using graph paper with grid lines that divided the page into a bunch of columns and rows. You used the grid lines on the graph paper to create an x-scale and a y-scale for the graph's x-axis and y-axis.

When you create a 1-2-3 graph, the program does not automatically add vertical and horizontal grid lines to the background, although it does draw tick marks along the x- and y-axes to indicate where these lines would go. In some graphs, adding vertical and/or horizontal grid lines really helps clarify when values in a particular data range exceed or fall below certain points on the y-scale. To add grid lines to a graph, you choose the **O**ptions **G**rid commands on the /Graph menu and then choose from the following menu options:

```
Horizontal      Vertical        Both       Clear
```

- ✔ Choose the **H**orizontal command to draw grid lines across the graph from the horizontal tick marks on the vertical y-scale.

- ✔ Choose the **V**ertical command to draw the grid lines from the vertical tick marks along the x-axis.

- ✔ Choose the **B**oth command to draw both horizontal and vertical grid lines.

- ✔ Choose the **C**lear command to tell 1-2-3 to make those grid lines go away.

Figure 7-9 shows the sample graph after you add horizontal grid lines. Note how much the grid lines help to indicate when a particular bar goes above or falls below a particular mark on the y-axis, especially when you use the 3-D effect.

Formatting the y-axis

You may have noticed that when 1-2-3 generates the y-axis for a graph, it divides the values displayed on the scale by one thousand and puts the (Thousands) note along the axis. Other than that, it doesn't seem to do any formatting. Actually, it does use the General number format, which often has an unformatted look to it.

If you are so inclined, or if your boss suggests it, you can format the numbers on the y-scale with the same number formats that you apply to values in a range of cells in a worksheet. As a matter of fact, when you are working with an XY graph that displays values along both the x- and y-axes, you can also format the x-scale. Fun, fun, fun.

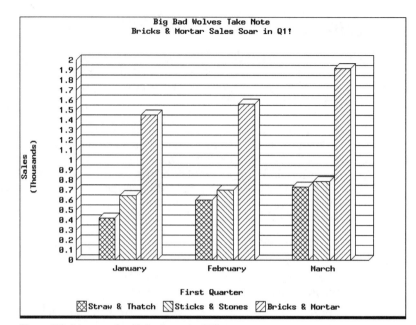

Figure 7-9: A bar graph with horizontal grid lines.

To format the values on the y-scale, follow these steps:

1. Choose the **O**ptions **S**cale **Y**-Scale **F**ormat command on the **/G**raph menu.

2. Choose a number format option and designate the number of decimal places, just as you do when you are applying one of these formats with the **/R**ange Format command.

Although you may be tempted to use the Currency format to indicate when values on the y-scale represent dollars and cents, the addition of dollar signs to each value on the scale may be a bit much. Instead, consider formatting the y-scale with the Comma format and suppressing the display of the (Thousands) indicator. (Choose the **I**ndicator and **N**o commands from the **/G**raph **O**ptions **S**cale **Y**-Scale menu.) You can add a note as part of the y-axis title to indicate that values are in thousands of dollars. Figure 7-10 shows the sample graph after you format the y-scale, suppress the (Thousands) indicator, and edit the y-axis title.

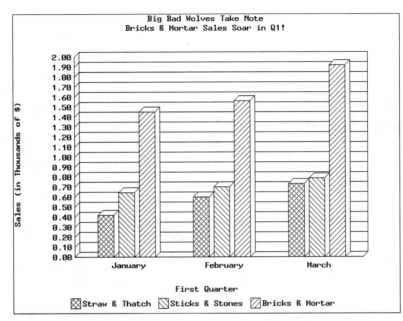

Figure 7-10: A bar graph after the y-axis scale has been formatted.

Label that data!

Some graphs benefit from having the actual value printed next to the symbol or bar in the graph that represents it. In many cases, however, adding the values to the graph is overkill and can be quite distracting — especially when you're plotting data ranges with lots of values. To display the values being graphed next to their symbols, you define the cell in the worksheet that contains the value as the *data label* for that particular data range.

1. Choose the **O**ptions **D**ata-Labels command from the **/G**raph menu.

2. Choose the data range to which the labels are to be applied (**A, B, C, D, E,** or **F**).

   1-2-3 prompts you to enter the data label range.

3. Select the cell range in the worksheet that contains the values you want to display.

4. Press Enter to record the range.

   1-2-3 displays these options on the control panel:

   ```
   Center  Left  Above  Right  Below
   ```

5. Choose the option that best represents the desired position for the data label in relation to the symbol or bar that represents the data. (By default, 1-2-3 uses the **C**enter option to place the data label right on its data point in the graph.)

If you assigned all the data ranges for the graph in a single operation with the /Graph Group command, chances are good that you can assign the data labels for all the data points in the graph in another single operation by using the /Graph Options Data-Labels Group command. After you choose this command, select the cell range in the worksheet that contains all the values represented in the graph. (Just be sure that you don't include the cells with the headings that became the x-axis labels.) After you press Enter to record the range, 1-2-3 prompts you to choose between a **C**olumnwise option and a **R**owwise option. Simply choose the same option that you chose when you originally defined the data ranges for the graph with the /Graph Group command.

Figure 7-11 shows how the sample bar graph looks after you define data labels for the graph, remove the horizontal grid lines, and turn the graph on its side with the /Graph Type Features Horizontal command. Only this orientation gives you enough room to display all of the data labels without having the bars in their way. (When you switch orientation, 1-2-3 does not correspondingly switch the orientation in the legend; we'll have to wait for a new release for the fix.)

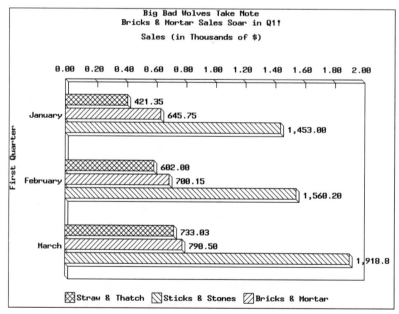

Figure 7-11: A horizontal bar graph with data labels.

Color my graphic world

1-2-3 automatically draws the graphs that you create in black and white. If you have a color monitor, you can liven them up by choosing the /Graph Options Color command. When you switch to color, 1-2-3 represents the different data ranges with various colors. In the case of bar and stack-bar graphs, the program uses colored bars and bands, rather than cross-hatch patterns, to differentiate the data ranges and the individual values represented. While this is all well and good on a fancy color screen, it's no use at all when you print the graph with a black-and-white printer and all the colors become black (ugh).

So if you turn on color to view a graph on the screen and you don't have a color printer or plotter, you'd better remember to switch the graph back to black and white with the /Graph Options B&W command before you save it for printing. (See "Putting Out the Graph" later in this chapter.)

Pie charts baked to perfection

The pie chart is different from other graphs in three ways:

- ✔ It doesn't use an x-axis or a y-axis.
- ✔ The values that it displays are restricted to a single data range (**A**).
- ✔ It's highly explosive (grin).

Figure 7-12 shows a pie chart that compares the sales made in each category to the first quarter total. Here's the recipe for this delectable pie chart:

1. Choose **Pie** as the graph type.

2. Designate the cell range E3..E5 (the totals for each category) as the **A** data range.

3. Define the cell range A3..A5 as the **X** data range to label the pieces of the pie.

4. Enter the worksheet title in cell A1 as the **First** title (by entering **A1**).

As you can see, when 1-2-3 creates a pie chart, it merely draws the outline of a circle with dividing lines that create the pie wedges. This pie is rather plain-looking and unappealing — not like Mom's. Fortunately, you can add a little pizzazz by using cross-hatch patterns. You can also explode particular wedges of the pie. (No, you don't have to look out for flying blueberries. When 1-2-3 *explodes* a pie chart wedge, it draws the wedge slightly apart from the rest of the pie in order to emphasize it.)

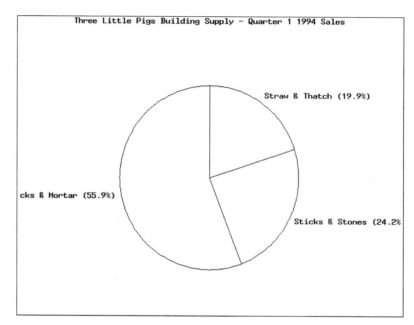

Figure 7-12: A typical pie chart.

✔ To add cross-hatch patterns, you enter code numbers in a range of the worksheet and then choose the /**Graph B** command to assign this range as the **B** data range for the pie chart. 1-2-3 offers you seven different cross-hatch patterns (with code numbers 1 through 7). Figure 7-13 shows how the various cross-hatch patterns appear in a pie chart.

✔ To explode a wedge of a pie chart, you simply enter **100** as the code number in the **B** data range. If you want to both explode a wedge and assign a cross-hatch pattern to it, you add the cross-hatch pattern code to 100. For example, if you want to explode the first section of the pie chart and assign pattern 3, you enter **103** as the first value in the range assigned as the **B** data range.

Figure 7-14 shows the pie chart first shown in Figure 7-12 after you jazz it up with cross-hatch patterns and explode the last wedge. To bake this pie, enter the code **2** in cell F3, the code **5** in cell F4, and the code **107** in cell F5 of the Three Little Pigs first quarter 1994 sales worksheet (in the column right next to the totals). Then assign the range F3..F5 as the **B** data range for the pie chart.

You can mask the pattern codes that you enter in the worksheet and assign as the **B** data range for the graph by using the /**R**ange Format **Hi**dden command to hide the range.

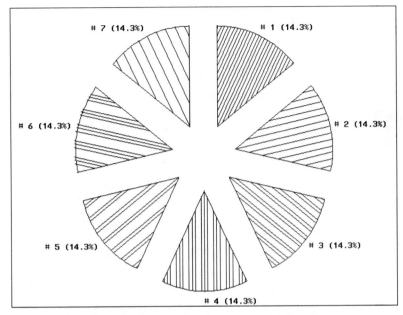

Figure 7-13: A pie chart showing cross-hatch patterns and their codes.

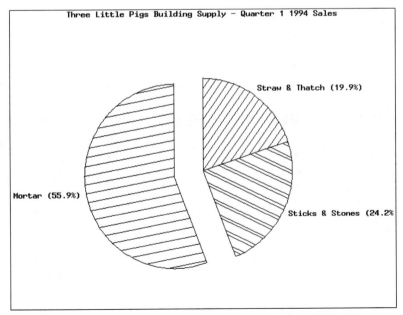

Figure 7-14: A pie chart after patterns have been assigned and a wedge has been exploded.

Name That Graph

When you save the worksheet with the /**F**ile **S**ave command, 1-2-3 automatically saves the graph as part of the worksheet file. Then the next time you retrieve the worksheet, you can view the graph simply by pressing the F10 (Graph) key. You don't even have to choose the /**G**raph **V**iew command.

You can make more than one graph for each worksheet. In fact, you can make as many graphs as your little heart desires — or your boss orders — and save all of them as part of the worksheet. However, before you begin to create a second graph, you need to remember to name the first graph. If you don't name the first graph, you'll lose it. It will literally turn into the second graph as you assign the new graph type, data ranges, titles, and other graph options.

To name a graph and save it, do the following:

1. Choose the /**G**raph **N**ame **C**reate command.

2. Type the name in response to the `Enter graph name:` prompt.

    You can enter a name of up to 15 characters. Just as when you name ranges, if your 1-2-3 version requires it, you need to use underscores instead of spaces, and begin a name with a letter rather than a number.

3. Press Enter to record the name.

    1-2-3 returns to the /**G**raph menu.

4. To save the named graph as part of the worksheet, choose the **Q**uit command and save the file with /**F**ile **S**ave.

Resetting the graph settings

When you create a second graph in a worksheet (after you've named the first one), clearing away some or, in a few extreme cases, all of the settings used by the first graph is often helpful. To clear settings, choose the **R**eset command on the /**G**raph menu. 1-2-3 then presents you with this menu:

`Graph X A B C D E F Ranges Options Quit`

✔ Choose the **G**raph command to clear all of the graph settings so that you can start building the new graph from scratch.

✔ Choose the **X** or **A** through **F** commands to clear specific data ranges.

✔ Choose the **R**anges command to clear all of the data ranges in a single operation (leaving all titles, grid lines, and so on intact).

✔ Choose the **O**ptions command to clear all settings on the /**G**raph **O**ptions menu (including the legends, titles, grid lines, scale formatting, and so on).

Putting Out the Graph

To print the graphs that you create in a 1-2-3 worksheet, you need to save each graph in a separate graphics file and then exit 1-2-3 and use the PrintGraph utility to print the graphics files.

To save a graph, follow these steps:

1. Choose the **/G**raph **N**ame **U**se command, highlight the name of the graph that you want to save for printing, and then press Enter.

   1-2-3 makes the graph that you selected the current one and displays it on the screen.

2. Press a key to return to the **/G**raph menu and then choose the **S**ave command.

3. Enter a filename for the graphics file in response to the `Enter graph file name:` prompt, following the same rules (if you have to) you use when you save a worksheet file (8 characters max, no spaces, that kind of thing); then press Enter.

1-2-3 saves the current graph as a graphics file in the current directory. The file has the name you just entered, followed by the PIC file extension (which marks it as a special graphics file).

 If you used the **/G**raph **O**ptions **C**olor command to display graphs in color on a color monitor, but you will print your graphs on a black-and-white printer, be sure to switch back to black and white with the **/G**raph **O**ptions **B&W** command *before* you use **/G**raph **S**ave to save the graph files.

Repeat this three-step procedure for each graph in the worksheet. When you have finished saving all the graphs that you want to print in their own graphics files, you are ready to quit 1-2-3 with the **/Q**uit command so that you can start the PrintGraph program. Be sure to save any changes to the worksheet, especially if you named the graphs just prior to saving them in graphics files and did not save their names as part of the worksheet.

If you started 1-2-3 directly from DOS, instead of from the Lotus Access Menu, you need to type the following startup command at the DOS prompt to start the Lotus Access Menu:

```
LOTUS
```

You can then choose the PrintGraph command. Alternatively, you can start the PrintGraph program directly from DOS by typing

```
PGRAPH
```

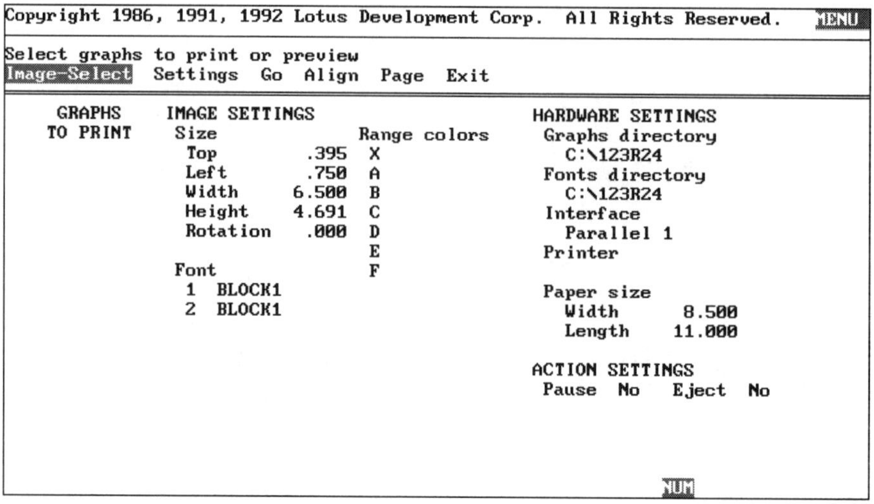

```
Copyright 1986, 1991, 1992 Lotus Development Corp.  All Rights Reserved.  MENU

Select graphs to print or preview
Image-Select  Settings  Go  Align  Page  Exit

     GRAPHS      IMAGE SETTINGS                    HARDWARE SETTINGS
     TO PRINT    Size              Range colors     Graphs directory
                   Top       .395  X                  C:\123R24
                   Left      .750  A                Fonts directory
                   Width    6.500  B                  C:\123R24
                   Height   4.691  C                Interface
                   Rotation  .000  D                  Parallel 1
                                   E                Printer
                 Font              F
                 1  BLOCK1                          Paper size
                 2  BLOCK1                            Width      8.500
                                                      Length    11.000

                                                  ACTION SETTINGS
                                                    Pause  No    Eject  No



                                                                    NUM
```

Figure 7-15: The PrintGraph main menu.

Any way you do it, provided that you installed the PrintGraph utility with the 1-2-3 program, the PrintGraph startup screen appears, followed by the Print-Graph main menu shown in Figure 7-15.

The PrintGraph menus work just like the 1-2-3 menus, except that you never have to type a character (like /) to display the menus. They remain displayed at all times. Before you can print the graphs, you need to make sure that the Hardware and Image settings shown below the PrintGraph main menu are correct and then select the graph files to be printed.

Lining up the hardware

When you check over the HARDWARE SETTINGS, be sure that the directory listed as the Graphs directory is current. (It needs to be the directory that contains the PIC graph files.) Also, check that the directory listed below the Fonts directory is the same one that contains the PrintGraph and 1-2-3 program files. (Most of the time, this will be the case.) The first time you use PrintGraph, you need to select a printer. After that, its name appears below the Printer heading. If you are printing graphs on a paper size other than letter size (8½ x 11 inches), you need to change the Paper size settings as well.

To change the HARDWARE SETTINGS, you need to choose the **S**ettings and **H**ardware commands to display the **H**ardware menu:

Graphs-Directory   Fonts-Directory   Interface   Printer   Size-Paper   Quit

Then choose the menu command for the setting that you want to change.

✔ When you change the Graphs or Fonts directory, you need to type the drive and directory path.

✔ When you select a new printer, choose the printer name from the list, press the spacebar to select it (indicated by a # symbol in front of the name) and press Enter to record the change.

✔ If the graphics printer is not the printer that you use for printing worksheets, you may need to change the Interface setting as well. (To find out exactly what kind of interface the graphics printer uses, check with your resident nerd or whip out your copy of *PCs For Dummies*.)

✔ When you select a new paper size with the Size-Paper command, you need to specify the width and the length of the page.

After you change all the HARDWARE SETTINGS that you want to change, choose the Quit command on the Hardware menu to return to the Settings menu. When you arrive there, choose the Save option to save the HARDWARE SETTINGS so that you don't have to go through the chore of selecting the printer and its interface each time you use PrintGraph.

Changing your image

Normally, PrintGraph sizes graphs so that two can fit on a page. The program also prints graphs in black and white, using its built-in Block1 font for all the titles. To change any of these settings, choose the Image command on the Settings menu. PrintGraph displays these options:

```
Size   Font   Range-Colors   Quit
```

✔ If you want to change the size of a graph, choose the Size command on this menu and then choose from these commands:

```
Full   Half   Manual   Quit
```

✔ To increase the size of each graph so that PrintGraph prints one per page (turned sideways in landscape mode), choose the Full command.

✔ To determine the size of the graph and its position on the page, choose the Manual command and indicate the top and left margin of the graph, as well as its width and height, with the Top, Left, Width, and Height commands, respectively.

✔ You can rotate the graph so that it prints sideways (landscape) by choosing the Rotation command and entering **90** as the number of degrees to rotate the graph.

PrintGraph uses two different fonts when it prints a graph: Font 1 is used to print the title on the first line; Font 2 is used to print all the other titles and text (such as the labels used as the **X** data range or for data labels).

When you first start PrintGraph, the program assigns the Block1 font to both Font 1 and Font 2. Instead of using Block1, you can choose from ten other built-in fonts for Font 1 and/or Font 2. Many of these fonts are paired, as in Block1 and Block2 or Italic1 and Italic2, and the second version is a slightly bolder rendition of the same font. Figure 7-16 shows a sample printed graph that uses the Bold font as Font 1 and the Lotus font as Font 2.

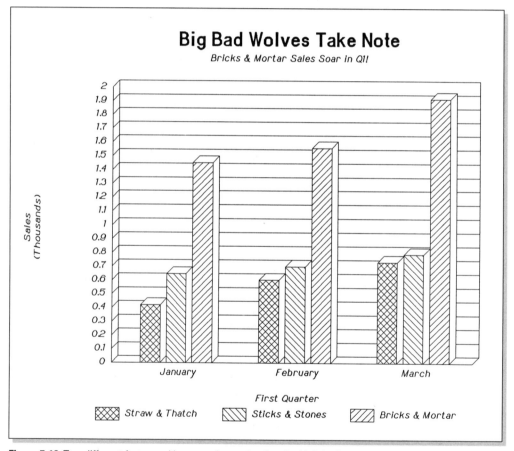

Figure 7-16: Two different fonts used in a sample graph printed with PrintGraph.

Here's what to do when you want to jazz up a graph by changing the fonts:

1. Choose the **F**ont command and then choose **1** or **2** to identify which font you want to change.

2. Select the name of the font that you want to use by highlighting it and then pressing the spacebar (to put the # symbol in front of it).

3. Press Enter.

If you're using a color printer or plotter, you can use the **R**ange-Colors command on the **I**mage menu to assign particular colors to specific data ranges.

1. Choose **R**ange-Colors.

2. Choose the letter of the range (**X** or **A** through **F**).

3. Choose the color that you want to assign to each of the data ranges from among those listed on the menu for the printer. (If you have a black-and-white printer selected in the **H**ardware settings, **B**lack is the only color option displayed. Do not pass GO. Do not collect $200.)

4. Choose **Q**uit to return to the **I**mage menu.

Choosing and printing the graphs

After you choose the Hardware and Image settings, you are ready to select the graphs to print. Use the **Q**uit command from whatever menu you're on until the PrintGraph main menu appears and then choose its **I**mage-Select command.

As soon as you choose this command, PrintGraph displays a screen listing all of the graph files (the ones with the PIC extension) saved in the directory listed as the Graphs directory in the HARDWARE SETTINGS.

If this directory is particularly lacking in PIC files (in other words, there aren't any), PrintGraph beeps at you and displays a warning that it can't find any graph files. If the graph files are on a floppy disk and you specified a floppy disk drive, such as drive A or drive B, as the Graphs directory, you may have put the wrong disk in the drive. While the error message is displayed for everyone to see, announce loudly that the pizza has arrived and quickly switch disks while everyone is looking the other way. Then press Enter to have PrintGraph look for PIC files on the new disk. Another embarrassing moment averted by quick thinking! (No pizza? But I thought I saw someone in a red shirt.)

If the graph files are on a directory of the hard disk and you simply entered the wrong directory as the Graphs directory, press Esc, go back and correct the directory with the **S**ettings **H**ardware **G**raphs-Directory command, choose the

Quit command twice, and then choose the Image-Select command again. You can see that this process takes quite a bit longer than replacing a floppy disk and pressing Enter. To get out of this one, you may actually have to order a pizza.

When you finally get the graph files properly displayed on the Select graphs to print screen, you need to wipe the tomato sauce off your fingers and choose each one in the order in which you want them printed.

1. To select a graph file, highlight it and then press the spacebar to put a # symbol in front of its name.

   If you select a graph by mistake, deselect it by highlighting it and pressing the spacebar again. (The # symbol disappears.)

2. When you finally get all the graphs straight, press Enter to return to the PrintGraph main menu. Miraculously, the files you selected are listed under Graphs to Print.

To print the graphs displayed under the PrintGraph main menu, make sure that the graphics printer is turned on, that it has paper, and that the print head is properly positioned at the top of the first page. Then choose the Align and Go commands. PrintGraph will go into WAIT mode as it prints each graph file you've selected. (This can, by the way, take a really long time, so you might not want to start the printing until you're ready to go on break or to lunch. Too bad you just had that pizza.)

- ✔ If, while your printer is chugging away, you discover that something terrible has gone wrong and you need to stop the printing, press Ctrl-Break. (Don't forget that Break is located on the same key as Pause on many newer keyboards.) Then press Esc or Enter to clear the error message and return the program from ERROR mode to MENU mode.

- ✔ When you finish printing the graphs and you're ready to return to 1-2-3, choose the Exit and Yes commands.

- ✔ If you started PrintGraph from the Lotus Access Menu, you can then start 1-2-3 by pressing 1 or Enter. If you started the PrintGraph program from DOS, you need to type **123** and press Enter.

Chapter 8
Just Give Me the Facts, Ma'am

*T*he main purpose of the worksheet tables you've worked with so far has been to perform important calculations, such as totaling monthly or quarterly sales figures, and to present this information in an intelligible form. In this chapter, you learn about *databases,* which are another kind of 1-2-3 worksheet table. You use a database not so much to calculate new values as to store lots of information in a consistent manner. For example, you can create a database that contains the names and addresses of all your clients, or you can create a database that contains the lowdown on your employees, products, or sales.

From your experience with creating other types of worksheet tables, you already know everything you need to know about setting up and creating a database. You begin by entering a row of column headings (technically known as *field names*) that identify the different kinds of items you need to keep track of (such as First Name, Last Name, Street, City, State, and so on). After you enter the row of field names, you then enter the information for the database in the appropriate columns of the rows immediately below the field names.

As you proceed, notice that each column of the database contains information for a particular item, such as a company name or a telephone extension. The columns are known as the *fields* of the database. Notice, also, that each row of the database contains complete information about a particular person or thing that you are keeping track of — perhaps a corporation, such as Stinko Broadcasting Corp., or a particular employee, such as Billy D. Kid. The entities or individuals described in the rows are also known as the *records* of the database.

Maintaining vast quantities of data in a tabular format, however, is only one small part of 1-2-3's database story. The program also has very powerful features that you can use to organize the data and locate just the information you need. For example, you entered the clients alphabetically by company name, but now you want to see them both listed alphabetically by company name and grouped by their states and cities. No problem. You simply sort the records of the database by State, City, and then Company fields.

What if you want a list of the clients in Boston and New York who have purchased at least $10,000 worth of merchandise from you? No big deal. You simply enter **Boston** and **New York** under the City field name and **>=10000** under the field name Total Sales in a special region of the worksheet known as a *criteria range*. Then you perform a data *extract operation,* and presto! 1-2-3 searches the fields in the database and extracts only those records that meet the criteria (in this case, where the city is Boston or New York and the total sales is $10,000 or more) in a special place in the worksheet called the *output range*.

On What Do You Base Your Data?

Setting up a database in a 1-2-3 worksheet is really no different from setting up any other table of data, except that instead of identifying the data with both a row of column headings and a column of row headings, you identify the data with only a row of column headings. The column headings are known in the database as *field names* — a rose by another name.

Duplicate field names in the same database confuse 1-2-3 when you ask it to search for information, so be sure that each name is unique. You can't use a value for a field name; you have to use a label.

When you come up with the field names, you also have to decide how you want to represent the information that you track in the database. For example, will the database store the full name of each person in a single field, or will it have separate fields for the first name, middle initial, and last name? Likewise, will it store the entire address in a single field, or will it contain separate street, city, state, and ZIP code fields?

When you make these decisions, you need to think about the various ways you might use the information. For example, if you intend to use names from a database in form letters created with a word processor, you probably want to store the first and last names in separate fields so that you can isolate the first name from the last name in different parts of the same letter but combine the first and last names when you need to. You may use *Dear Ms. Smith* in the heading, *Congratulations, Mary!* in the body of the letter, and *Ms. Mary Smith, 111 Elm Street...* in the inside address or on the envelope.

In addition to considering the various ways you might use the information, you also have to figure out how you may want to arrange the information. For example, in a client database, you may want to work with the records in alphabetical order by client name most of the time. However, just prior to using the information to generate form letters with a word processor, you may want to change the order of the database and have the records in ZIP code order (so that the letters are already in the order preferred by the post office as they come off the printer).

Later in this chapter you learn how to change the order of the records in a database by sorting the information by a particular field or by more than one field. To sort a client database by ZIP code, you need a database with a separate ZIP code field. If you maintain a single address field that contains all the information for the street, city, state, and ZIP code, you can't sort the database in ZIP code order because the ZIP code is only a piece of information in the address field.

So, too, if you maintain the client's full name in a single field with the first name first and the last name last, you can't put the records in alphabetical order by last name, as is the usual practice. Instead, when you sort on the name field, the records appear primarily in first name alphabetical order because the first name precedes the last name in each cell. Your best bet, when in doubt, is to create separate fields in the database for first and last names; you will have more flexibility in the long run.

Figure 8-1 shows a worksheet with the first few field names for a new Three Little Pigs Building Supply client database. After you enter the field names in each column, you can then format these labels with the /**R**ange **L**abel **C**enter or the /**R**ange **L**abel **R**ight command to center them (as shown in Figure 8-1) or right justify them over the data in each database field.

Putting Humpty-Dumpty together again

In 1-2-3, you can join labels stored in separate cells (such as a first name stored in a First Name field and a last name stored in a Last Name field) by creating a formula that uses the & (ampersand) as the *concatenation*, or joining, operator. Suppose that you have John Paul entered in cell A2 and Jones entered next door in cell B2, and you want to put them together in cell H2. To combine them, you enter the formula +A2&" "&B2 in cell H2. Note that this formula joins the label John Paul in cell A2 to a blank space (the space identified by the " " that's sandwiched between the two ampersands) and then joins both of them to the label Jones in cell B2. The result in cell H2 is John Paul Jones, rather than John PaulJones, which is what you get if you enter +A2&B2 as the formula.

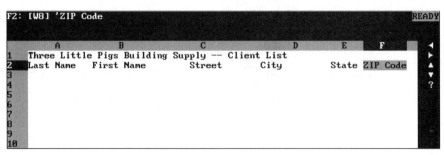

Figure 8-1: Field names for a new database.

Remember that you can use the **/W**orksheet **T**itles **H**orizontal command to freeze the row with the field names on the screen so that the field names remain displayed at all times as you scroll through records in the database.

Put another record in...

After you enter the row of field names for the new database, you are ready to begin entering its records. Entering the information for each field of a new record in a database is no different from making any other cell entry. Just make sure that you don't skip any rows in the database. Put the first record right under the row of field names and put each subsequent record in the next blank row.

When you enter information for some of the fields in the database, you have to remember to preface the information with a label prefix (such as the apostrophe) just to get the information to go into the cell. For example, if you're entering the street address for a client in the Street field and you forget to start the address with a label prefix (entering **123 Maple Street**, rather than **'123 Maple Street**), 1-2-3 beeps at you and goes into EDIT mode the minute you try to complete the entry by pressing an arrow key or Enter. Remember that when you type a number as the first character, 1-2-3 immediately goes into VALUE mode, which simply doesn't accept a mix of numbers and text characters. The only way you can mix numbers and text is by making the entry a label.

In addition to field entries that just won't go in unless you add a label prefix, you also have to deal with entries which do go in without a label prefix but are not displayed correctly. This problem occurs in two cases:

- ✔ When you enter ZIP codes
- ✔ When you enter numbers that contain hyphens (such as Social Security numbers or telephone numbers)

Because ZIP codes consist entirely of numbers, you won't have a problem entering them as values in a database. However, if you enter a ZIP code such as **03049**, which starts with a zero, 1-2-3 displays it as 3049 in the cell. None of the 1-2-3 number formats restores the leading zero, so the only way to put this ZIP code in the database correctly is to enter it as a label with one of the label prefixes. (The zero, which is so important to the post office, is of absolutely no consequence to a mathematician.) You can use **'03049** to left-align the ZIP code, **^03409** to center-align it, or **"03049** to right-align it.

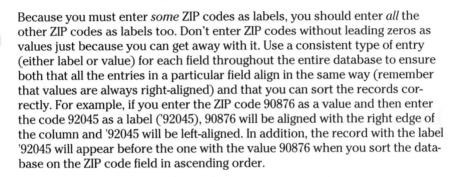

Because you must enter *some* ZIP codes as labels, you should enter *all* the other ZIP codes as labels too. Don't enter ZIP codes without leading zeros as values just because you can get away with it. Use a consistent type of entry (either label or value) for each field throughout the entire database to ensure both that all the entries in a particular field align in the same way (remember that values are always right-aligned) and that you can sort the records correctly. For example, if you enter the ZIP code 90876 as a value and then enter the code 92045 as a label ('92045), 90876 will be aligned with the right edge of the column and '92045 will be left-aligned. In addition, the record with the label '92045 will appear before the one with the value 90876 when you sort the database on the ZIP code field in ascending order.

Another problem occurs when you are entering numbers separated by hyphens (dashes), such as Social Security numbers (666-01-6790) and telephone numbers (555-4567). If you don't add label prefixes to such entries, 1-2-3 treats them as subtraction problems, and you wind up with nasty negative numbers where a nice string of numbers should appear.

Also keep in mind that when you enter dates for a date field, you need to use the @DATE function (see Chapters 2 and 3 for a quick review) and then format the resulting serial number (you remember the star dates, don't you?) with the **/R**ange Format **D**ate command. For example, to enter the date 02/01/81 in a date field, you enter the following formula in the cell:

```
@DATE(81/2/1)
```

Then you format the resulting serial number, 29618, with the **/R**ange Format **D**ate **4** (Long Intn'l) command.

When you are entering the same information in a particular field, you can speed things up by using the **/C**opy command to copy the last entry you made to the other records that use the same information. Before you copy an entry down to new records in a field, always be sure that you've formatted it. (Remember that 1-2-3 copies the formatting as well as the contents of the cell, relieving you of having to format after the fact.)

You can also use the /Copy command to copy dates in a date field, even when the dates in subsequent records are not the same. After you copy the formatted date down for your new records, you can replace it with the correct date by editing just the arguments of the copied @DATE functions.

1. Put the cell pointer in the cell with the date that needs to be edited.

2. Press the F2 (Edit) key.

3. Use the arrow keys to position the cursor under the arguments in the @DATE function that need to be changed.

4. Press Delete to remove them.

5. Type in the correct values.

6. Press Enter to have the correct (formatted) date appear in the cell.

Keep in mind that you can use the F2 (Edit) key to correct an entry in any field of the database that contains some kind of error, not just an entry in a date field.

In some cases, a database has fields whose entries are calculated by formula, rather than entered by hand — for example, the In Years field in Three Little Pigs client database. Figure 8-2 shows the original formula in cell H3 for calculating the number of years someone has been a Three Little Pigs client. This formula is

```
(@NOW-G3)/365
```

The @NOW function is a 1-2-3 date function that returns the current date (see Chapter 13 for more information on using @NOW). This date is then subtracted from the date when the client first did business with Three Little Pigs Building Supply, which is entered in the Anniversary field (G3 in this first formula). The result of this subtraction (in days) is then divided by 365 to return the approximate number of years.

Whenever you have a calculated field in a 1-2-3 database, you always use the /Copy command to copy its formula down the calculated field for the new records in the database. Figure 8-3 shows the Three Little Pigs client database

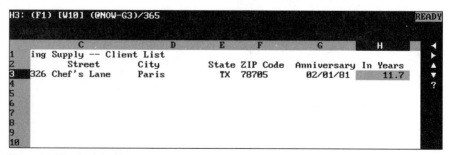

Figure 8-2: The formula for calculating the entry for the In Years field follows the cell address on the control panel.

```
H34: (F1) [W10] (@NOW-G34)/365                                    READY

        A        E     F         G          H        I          J
 1   Three Little
 2   Last Name   State ZIP Code  Anniversary In Years Grs Rcpts Cash Only
19   Jacken      OK    45678      03/01/87    5.7          $55   No
20   Ridinghoode PA    15201      05/27/87    5.4      $18,900   No
21   Fudde       FL    33461      08/13/87    5.2           $2   Yes
22   Franklin    WV    20178      10/21/87    5.0      $34,400   Yes
23   Horse       KY    23986      11/02/87    5.0         $195   No
24   Foliage     VT    05452      12/18/87    4.9       $4,200   Yes
25   Appleseed   SD    66017      02/24/88    4.7           $4   Yes
26   Oakley      ND    66540      04/03/88    4.6          $17   No
27   Washington  DC    01776      05/20/88    4.4      $19,700   No
28   Brown       UT    84001      07/09/88    4.3         $956   No
29   Laurel      NM    82128      09/13/88    4.1           $5   No
30   Cassidy     CO    80477      11/11/88    3.9          $12   No
31   Oow         HI    99909      12/26/88    3.8       $2,116   No
32   Liberty     NY    10011      01/03/89    3.8         $459   No
33   Eaters      AZ    85257      09/02/92    0.1      $66,666   Yes
34   Andersen    MN    58764      12/29/86    5.8      $12,000   Yes
35
36
CLIENTS.WK1                   UNDO                        NUM
```

Figure 8-3: The database after the last record has been entered and the formula for the In Years field has been copied.

after the last of the first batch of records in row 34 of the worksheet is entered. Here, as in all the preceding records, the value in the In Years field was entered by a formula that was copied from the field in the record above.

Establishing a new database order

Every database that you put together in 1-2-3 has some kind of preferred order for maintaining and viewing the records. Depending on the database, you may want to see the records in alphabetical order by last name or, perhaps, by company name. In an employee database, the preferred order may be numerical order by the employee's Social Security number or by a special employee number that the company has assigned.

When you initially enter the records for a new database, you may enter them in the preferred order. However, despite your best efforts, before long you'll have to enter new records that will undoubtedly mess up the preferred order. After all, you'll tack the new records onto the bottom of the database by entering the information in the first blank row below the last record. (Remember that you can zip to the last record in the database by pressing End, ↓ when the cell pointer is in one of the fields that doesn't have any blanks.)

If, for example, you enter all of the original records in alphabetical order by the client's last name (from Andersen, as in Christian, to Wolfe, as in Big Bad) and then Peter Pumpkin signs on as a client, you add his record at the bottom of the barrel. It winds up in the row below the one with the Big Bad Wolfe's record, even though it really belongs somewhere between Christian Andersen and that old Wolfe.

And this problem isn't the only one you'll have with the order you used when you originally entered the records. For even if you don't change many of the records in the database, the preferred order is merely the order you use most of the time.

What about those times when you need to see the records in another, special order? Suppose that you usually like to work with the database in alphabetical order by the client's last name. When you need to use the records to generate mailing labels for a mass mailing, you want them in ZIP code order. Then, when you want to generate a list for your salespeople that shows which clients are in whose territory, you want them in alphabetical order by state, and maybe even by city.

1-2-3 to the rescue! The **/D**ata **S**ort command offers you flexibility in the record order so that you can use the database to fill many different needs. To have 1-2-3 correctly sort the records in a database, you need to specify which fields are the key to the new order (rightfully known as the *sorting keys*). You also need to specify what type of order you want the information in. You get only two choices:

- ✔ Ascending order, where text entries are placed in alphabetical order (A to Z) and values are placed in numerical order (smallest to largest)

- ✔ Descending order, which is the exact reverse of alphabetical order (Z to A) and numerical order (largest to smallest)

When you sort the records in a database, you can specify up to two fields (keys) on which to sort. (You also can choose between ascending and descending order for each key you use.) However, you need to use more than one key only when the field you really want to sort (technically known as the *primary key*) contains duplicates and you want a say in how the records with duplicate entries are arranged. If you don't specify another key, 1-2-3 just puts the duplicate records in the order in which you entered them.

The best and most common example of when you need more than one key is when you sort a large database alphabetically in last name order. Suppose that you have several people with the last name Andersen, Hood, or Wolfe (which is certainly the case at the Three Little Pigs Building Supply). When you specify the Last Name field as the sorting key (using the default ascending order), all the duplicate Andersens, Hoods, and Wolfes are simply placed in the order in which their records were originally entered.

To sort these duplicates, however, you can specify a second key. For example, you might well specify the First Name field (again using the default ascending order) as the *secondary* or *tie breaker key* so that Red Riding Hood's record comes after Grandma Hood's record and Big Bad Wolfe's record precedes Harry Wolfe's.

Choosing a new collating sequence

1-2-3 sorts data in ascending and descending order according to the *collating sequence* in use. By default, 1-2-3 uses the Numbers first collating sequence, which puts labels beginning with numbers before those beginning with letters (which precede labels starting with other characters).

If you wish, you can change to the Numbers last or the ASCII (pronounced *ass-key*) collating sequence. Both of them put labels beginning with letters before those beginning with numbers. In all three collating sequences, blanks precede the labels, and values always come after the labels. In the case of the Numbers first and Numbers last collating sequences, 1-2-3 ignores capitalization and puts labels with lowercase and uppercase letters together. In the ASCII sequence, however, uppercase letters precede lowercase letters.

To change the collating sequence, you choose the Install command on the Lotus Access Menu, and then you press Enter to display the Main Menu screen. Use the ↑ and ↓ on succeeding screens to choose the Change Selected Equipment command, the Modify The Current Driver Set command, and then the Collating Sequence command.

Select the new collating sequence (ASCII, Numbers first, or Numbers last) on the Collating Sequence Selection screen by highlighting it and pressing Enter (the current sequence is marked with an arrowhead). Press Enter or Esc twice to return to the Change Selected Equipment screen and then choose the End Install command. Press Enter at the Saving Your Changes screen and then press Enter again when prompted with the name of the driver set.

To sort the records of the database, you follow these steps:

1. Choose the **/Data Sort Data-Range** command, position the cell pointer in the first field of the first record of the database, and type a period to anchor the range. Highlight all the records in the database that are to be sorted and then press Enter.

   When you highlight the data range, make sure that you include all the fields (columns) in each record (row), not just the field that you want to sort on. At the same time, make sure that you do *not* include the row of field names at the top of the database in this cell selection. If you include them, 1-2-3 sorts them in with the other database records — not good!

2. Choose the **Primary-Key** command on the **/Data Sort** menu, position the cell pointer in one of the cells in the field (column) that you want the records sorted on in response to the Primary sort key: prompt, and press Enter. To sort the records in descending order, press Enter in response to the Sort order (A or D): (D is the default choice). To sort the records in ascending order, press A and then press Enter.

3. If the primary key field contains duplicates and you want to specify how these records should be sorted, choose the **S**econdary-Key command, position the cell pointer in a cell in the field to be used as the secondary key, and press Enter. To sort the records in descending order, press Enter again to choose D as the sort order. To sort the records in ascending order, press A, instead, and then press Enter.

4. After you define the sort keys, choose the **G**o command to sort the records in the Data range. If you see that you sorted the database on the wrong fields or in the wrong order, press the Alt-F4 (Undo) key to immediately restore the database records to their previous order.

Figure 8-4 shows the Sort Settings dialog box after you select the first and second keys for sorting the records in the Three Little Pigs client database in alphabetical order by last name and then first name. Figure 8-5 shows the database after sorting.

 Release 2.4 Wysiwyg users please note: You can use the Sort Ascending SmartIcon, the one with A above Z (located at the bottom of the first icon palette and also in the middle of the third icon palette), or the Sort Descending SmartIcon, the one with Z above A (located in the middle of the third icon palette), to sort records in the database either in ascending or descending order using the first field as the sorting key.

When you click on either of these SmartIcons, 1-2-3 displays a QuickSort dialog box that shows the data range to be sorted, the column letter of the sort key (which contains the first field), and the sort order (Ascending or Descending).

```
A3: (G) [W12] 'Bryant                                             MENU
Data-Range  Primary-Key  Secondary-Key  Reset  Go  Quit
Sort data and return to READY mode
          A                        Sort Settings                     F
1   Three Littl
2   Last Name                 Data range: [A3..K34········]      ZIP Code
3   Bryant                                                       78705
4   Gearing             ┌─Primary key─┐                          90069
5   Wolfe               │ Column:           ( ) Descending │     85251
6   Cupid               │ [A3..A3········]  (*) Ascending  │     83331
7   Gookin              └─────────────┘                          81824
8   Cinderella                                                   87557
9   Baum                ┌─Secondary key─┐                        65432
10  Harvey              │ Column:           ( ) Descending │     60080
11  Sunnybrook          │ [B3..B3········]  (*) Ascending  │     97210
12  White               └─────────────┘                          98063
13  Dragon                                                       00001
14  Gondor                                                       80342
15  Baggins             ┌───Press F2 (EDIT) to edit settings───┐ 04047
16  Andersen            └──────────────────────────────────────┘ 58764
17  Humperdinck Engelbert   6 Hansel+Gretel Tr  Gingerbread   MD 20815
18  Oakenshield Rex         Mines of Goblins    Everest       NJ 07639
19  Jacken      Jill        Up the Hill         Pail of Water OK 45678
20  Ridinghoode Crimson     232 Cottage Path    Wulfen        PA 15201
CLIENTS.WK1                                                  NUM
```

Figure 8-4: The Sort Settings dialog box after the Primary key and the Secondary key have been selected.

```
A3: [W12] 'Andersen                                              READY

        A            B              C                 D          E    F        ◄
 1  Three Little Pigs Building Supply -- Client List                           ►
 2   Last Name    First Name      Street           City        State ZIP Code  ▲
 3  Andersen      Christian   340 The Shadow     Scholar        MN   58764     ▼
 4  Andersen      Hans        341 The Shadow     Scholar        MN   58764     ?
 5  Appleseed     Johnny      6789 Fruitree Tr   Along The Way  SD   66017
 6  Baggins       Bingo       99 Hobbithole      Shire          ME   04047
 7  Baum          L. Frank    447 Toto Too Rd    Oz             KS   65432
 8  Brown         Charles     59 Flat Plains     Saltewater     UT   84001
 9  Bryant        Michael     326 Chef's Lane    Paris          TX   78705
10  Cassidy       Butch       Sundance Kidde     Hole In Wall   CO   80477
11  Cinderella    Poore       8 Lucky Maiden Way Oxford         TN   07557
12  Cupid         Eros        97 Mount Olympus   Greece         CT   03331
13  Dragon        Kai         2 Pleistocene Era  Ann's World    ID   00001
14  Eaters        Big         444 Big Pigs Court Dogtown        AZ   85257
15  Foliage       Red         49 Maple Syrup     Waffle         VT   05452
16  Franklin      Ben         1789 Constitution  Jefferson      WV   20178
17  Fudde         Elmer       8 Warner Way       Hollywood      FL   33461
18  Gearing       Shane       1 Gunfighter's End LaLa Land      CA   90069
19  Gondor        Aragorn     2956 Gandalf       Midearth       WY   80342
20  Gookin        Polly       4 Feathertop Hill  Hawthorne      MA   01824
CLIENTS.WK1                   UNDO                               NUM
```

Figure 8-5: The database sorted into alphabetical order by last name and first name.

To sort the database using these settings, press Enter or click on the OK button. To cancel the sorting procedure, press Tab and then Enter, or click on the Cancel button.

When You Care Enough to Select the Very Best

As mentioned previously, 1-2-3 provides you with several tools for finding and retrieving the information you need from a database. Before you can use these tools to locate information in a database, however, you need to set up a special cell range in the worksheet, outside of the database itself, called the *criteria range,* where you can specify the search criteria.

The criteria range consists of cells containing the selection criteria that are placed below copies of the appropriate field names. For example, to find all of the clients in Paris, Texas, in the Three Little Pigs client database, you enter **Paris** in the cell below the field name City and **TX** in the cell under the field name State. Next you define these cells as the criteria range with the **C**riteria command on the **/D**ata **Q**uery menu. (This menu is a sticky menu, just like the **/G**raph and **/P**rint **P**rinter menus.) Then, when you choose the **F**ind, **E**xtract, **U**nique, or **D**elete command on the **/D**ata **Q**uery menu, 1-2-3 uses the City equal to Paris and the State equal to TX as the criteria for locating, retrieving, or removing records from the database (depending upon which command you use).

To make it easier to perform multiple searches with different selection criteria, copy all the field names to a new section of the worksheet and place the criteria that you want to use under the appropriate field names. You just have to remember to select the cells in the range and choose the /Data Query Criteria command any time changes to the selection criteria alter the size and shape of the original criteria range.

When you place the criteria range in the worksheet with the database, position it in the columns to the right of the columns containing the database, instead of in the same columns in the rows below the database. That way, you can always add new records without having to continually relocate the criteria range, and you can modify the size and shape of the criteria range without affecting any of the records in the database.

Wildcards and smooth operators establish correct criteria

Entering selection criteria in a criteria range is a fairly straightforward process. When you want to locate records that contain a particular label or value, just place the label or value entry under the appropriate field name in the criteria range.

When you enter the search criteria for fields that contain labels, you can use the question mark (?) and asterisk (*) as wildcard characters, just as you can when you specify the search string for the /Range Search command. (See Chapter 5 for more information on using these wildcard characters with the Search feature).

In addition to these two wildcard characters, you can use the tilde (~) before a particular label to find all of the records that contain everything but that particular label. For example, if you want to select all of the records except those where the state is Texas, you enter ~**TX** in the cell under the one with the State field name in the criteria range. So, too, if you want all the records except the ones where the last name begins with the letter *T*, you enter ~**T*** in the cell under the one with the Last Name field name.

When you set up selection criteria, you can use the following operators to find records equal to, greater than, greater than or equal to, less than or equal to, less than, or not equal to a particular entry:

```
=, >, >=, <=, <, or <>
```

Table 8-1 presents examples of some of the ways that you can use these operators in selection criteria.

Table 8-1		Various Operators Used in Selection Criteria		
Operator	**Meaning**	**Example**	**What It Locates in the Database**
=	Equal to	ZIP Code ='031*	Records where the ZIP code begins with 031 as in 03102, 03154, and so on
>	Greater than	Gross Receipts>12500	Records where the Cash Receipts field contains a value greater than 12500
>=	Greater than or equal to	Anniversary +G3>=@DATE(92,1,1)	Records where the Anniversary field date is on or after January 1, 1992
<	Less than	Last Name '<c	Records where the name in the Last Name field begins with a letter before *C* (that is, begins with either *A* or *B*)
<=	Less than or equal to	Anniversary +G3<=@DATE(91,3,4)	Records where the Anniversary field date is on or before March 4, 1991
<>	Not equal to	State '<>"IN"	Records where the State field isn't IN (Indiana)

When you want to enter a selection criterion that begins with <, <=, or <> in a cell in the criteria range, you have to begin the criterion entry with a label prefix, such as the apostrophe. Otherwise, 1-2-3 goes into MENU mode because pressing < is an alternative to pressing / to display the 1-2-3 main menu.

Looking for the lady who lost her glass slipper

Unless you have changed the collating sequence to ASCII, 1-2-3 does not distinguish between uppercase and lowercase letters entered as label search criteria. (If you think you want to change the collating sequence, see "Choosing a new collating sequence" earlier in this chapter.) When the collating sequence is set to Numbers first (as it is automatically unless you've fooled with it) or Numbers last, 1-2-3 considers a record to be a match even when the case used in its field entry does not match the case used in the criteria range. For example, if you enter **Cinderella** as the label in the criteria range, 1-2-3 considers records that contain Cinderella, cinderella, or even CINDERELLA to be a match.

You do not need to use a label prefix when you enter a criterion that begins with =, >, or >= because these symbols automatically put the program into LABEL mode.

Both this and that or either/or

When you enter two or more criteria in the same row below their respective field names in the criteria range, 1-2-3 selects only those records that meet both of the selection criteria. This is referred to as an *AND condition* because this *and* that criteria have to be true to make a match.

Figure 8-6 is an example of a criteria range with just such an AND condition. Here 1-2-3 selects only those records where the state is New York *and* the gross receipts are greater than $10,000 because both the selection criteria NY and >10000 are placed in the same row of the criteria range (row 3) under their respective field names.

When you enter two or more criteria in different rows of the criteria range, 1-2-3 selects records that meet any one of the criteria. This is referred to as an *OR condition* because only one criterion has to be true to make a match.

Figure 8-7 is an example of a criteria range with an OR condition. Here 1-2-3 selects records where the State is either NY or CA because NY is entered in the second row (row 3) of the criteria range above CA in the third row (row 4).

When you create these kinds of conditions, you need to remember to redefine the criteria range with the /**D**ata **Q**uery **C**riteria command to include all the rows that contain criteria. If you forget to redefine the range before you perform a **F**ind, **E**xtract, or **D**elete operation, 1-2-3 uses only the criteria in the rows that were selected when you previously set up the criteria range.

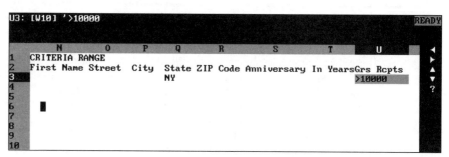

Figure 8-6: The use of two selection criteria in the same row creates an AND condition.

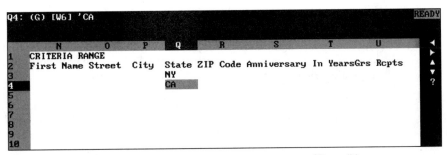

Figure 8-7: Using two selection criteria in different rows creates an OR condition.

Well within the criteria range

What if you want to find all the records in the database that fall within a range —
perhaps all the records where the gross receipts are between $10,000 and
$15,000, or where the ZIP code is between 02100 and 03555, or where the anni-
versary date is between January 15, 1990, and January 15, 1992? To enter these
types of selection criteria, you need to create a *criterion formula* that uses the
built-in *#AND#* *operator.* (The # signs on either side of the AND indicate to
1-2-3 that you are using a special operator.)

To get an idea of how you can use this #AND# operator to set up AND conditions
that define a range of matching entries, take a look at the formulas you create to
set up each of these selection criteria. To find all the records where the clients'
gross receipts are between $10,000 and $15,000, you enter the following criterion
formula under the field name `Grs Rcpts` in the criteria range:

```
+I3>=10000#AND#I3<=15000
```

Notice the reference to cell I3. This cell reference is used because the Grs Rcpts
field is located in column I and the first record is in row 3; cell I3 is the first gross
receipt field entry in the database. When you set up criterion formulas such as
this one, you always need to use the address of the cell in the database that
contains the very first field entry. This cell reference tells 1-2-3 what field to use
and what record to start with when it compares field entries against the result of
the criterion formula.

Notice also that you need to repeat the address of the cell with the first field
entry on both halves of the equation. In other words, you cannot use the following formula:

```
+I3>=10000#AND#<=15000
```

Although you have no trouble understanding that this formula means that the contents of cell I3 should be compared to see whether it's both greater than or equal to 10000 and less than or equal to 15000, 1-2-3 has no idea what to do. It has a panic attack, beeps at you, and goes into EDIT mode until you calm it down by repeating the cell reference after the #AND# operator.

A criterion formula such as +I3>=10000#AND#I3<=15000 is known as a *logical formula* because, instead of a new calculated result it returns either TRUE or FALSE as the answer (TRUE if the value in I3 falls between 10000 and 15000 or is either 10000 or 15000 on the nose; FALSE if it's any other value).

Of course, computers are never happy unless they can turn everything into a number, so instead of putting the word TRUE in the cell when the value in I3 does fall within the range and FALSE when it doesn't, 1-2-3 puts either 1 (for TRUE) or 0 (for FALSE) in the cell in the criteria range when you enter this criterion formula there.

Instead of looking at the 0 or 1 in the cell with the criterion formula, you might find it more enlightening to look at the formula itself. To display the formula instead of the result, select the cell, choose the /Range Format Text command, and press Enter. Don't forget that you can widen the column with the /Worksheet Column Set-Width command if you want to see more of the criterion formula displayed in its cell.

Okay, so that's the formula for the first condition. How about the second criterion formula for finding all the records where the ZIP code is between 02100 and 03555? You enter the following formula in the cell under the ZIP code field name in the criteria range:

```
+F3>='02100#AND#F3<='03555
```

Note the similarity of this formula to the first one. You use the cell address F3 this time because column F contains the ZIP code field and row 3 contains the first record. The only difference between this criterion formula and the preceding one is the use of the apostrophe label prefix before each value. The prefix, as you remember, keeps 1-2-3 from dropping the leading zero in the ZIP code.

The last sample #AND# condition is one for finding all the records where the anniversary date is between January 15, 1990, and January 15, 1992. For this condition, you enter the following formula in the cell under the Anniversary field name in the criteria range:

```
+G3>=@DATE(90,1,15)#AND#G3<=@DATE(92,1,15)
```

As has been the case several times before, because you're dealing with dates, you need to use the @DATE function to have 1-2-3 return the serial (star date) numbers. This formula uses the cell reference G3 because column G in the database contains the Anniversary field and row 3 contains the first record in the database.

Or else

Along with the #AND# operator, 1-2-3 has an *#OR# operator* that you can use to create a criterion formula with an OR condition (one that is considered to be matched as long as one or the other of the conditions on either side of the #OR# operator is found to be TRUE). You can use the #OR# operator to build a formula in a single cell of the criteria range that would normally require several stacked entries. For example, to find all the records where the state is Texas, California, or Idaho, you use the following criterion formula:

```
+E3="TX"#OR#E3="CA"#OR#E3="ID"
```

You enter the formula in the cell under the State field name in the criteria range, instead of entering **TX** in that cell, followed by **CA** in the one below, and **ID** in the one below that. Note that when the criterion formula specifies text that should match a cell entry with the equal sign (such as +E3="TX" or +J3="Yes"), you need to enclose the text in double quotation marks.

This requirement can be a tiny bit confusing. On the one hand, 1-2-3 doesn't accept the following criterion formula, which lacks quotes around the state abbreviations:

```
+E3=TX#OR#E3=CA#OR#E3=ID
```

On the other hand, it doesn't make you use quotes when you enter the same abbreviations in a column of cells in the criteria range. How come? Well, in the range, the abbreviations are all automatically entered in their cells as labels. Here you're dealing with a formula entered as a value.

You can also use the #OR# operator to create an OR condition which refers to different fields. For example, if you want to find all the records where the anniversary date is before April 15, 1988, or the gross receipts are greater than or equal to $25,000, you enter the following criterion formula:

```
+G3<=@DATE(88,4,15)#OR#I3>=25000
```

Note that you can put this formula in the cell under the Anniversary field name or in the one under Grs Rcpts in the criteria range. In fact, because the formula contains the cell references that indicate which database fields to search, this formula will work fine in any cell under any legitimate field name as long as it's part of the defined criteria range.

Find me some data

You choose the **Find** command on the **/Data Query** menu when you want to review, one at a time, the records in the database that match the selection criteria in the criteria range. Before you can use the Find command, however, you not only have to enter the selection criteria in the criteria range of the worksheet and then use the **Criteria** command on the /**Data Q**uery menu to define this range, but you also have to use the **I**nput command on this menu to define the location of the database. (The *input range* indicates where to search for matching records, just as the criteria range indicates the basis on which records are selected.) When you define the input range with the **I**nput command, be sure that you include the row of field names along with every record it contains.

After you define the input and criteria range with the **I**nput and **C**riteria commands on the /**Data Q**uery menu, you are ready to choose the **F**ind command. As soon as you choose this command, 1-2-3 highlights the first matching record in the database, and it goes into FIND mode.

> ✔ To see whether there are any more matching records and to move to the next matching record, press ↓ or click the scroll icon with the downward-pointing arrowhead.
>
> ✔ To move to the previous matching record, press ↑ or click on the scroll icon with the upward-pointing scroll arrowhead.
>
> ✔ To jump to the very first and last records in the database, respectively, use the Home and End keys.

When 1-2-3 highlights the last matching record in one direction or the other, or if none of the records matches the selection criteria, the program beeps at you when you press ↓ or ↑ or click on the corresponding scroll icon. When you finish viewing the matching records, press Esc or Enter to get out of FIND mode and return to MENU mode and the /**Data Q**uery menu. If you prefer to return to READY mode from FIND mode, press the F7 (Query) key.

Editing in the field

To edit a field in a record highlighted during a **F**ind operation, follow these steps:

1. Press → or ← or click on the corresponding scroll icon until you select the cell in the record that needs editing.

2. Press the F2 (Edit) key to return the cell's contents to the control panel and switch to EDIT mode.

3. Make deletions and insertions in the text as you normally do.

4. Press Enter to insert the edited contents into the current cell and return to FIND mode.

You can then advance to the next or previous matching record or press Esc or Enter to terminate the **F**ind operation. When you finish using the commands on the /**Data Q**uery menu, choose the **Q**uit command to get out of MENU mode and return to READY mode.

If you return to READY mode in order to change the selection criteria before you perform another **Find** operation, you can press the F7 (Query) key to perform the next **Find** operation. You don't have to choose the **/D**ata **Q**uery **F**ind command again. Note that the F7 (Query) key is kind of a chameleon key. If the last operation were an **Extract** operation, initiated with **/D**ata **Q**uery **E**xtract (see the following section), rather than a **Find** operation, initiated with **/D**ata **Q**uery **F**ind, pressing F7 would initiate another **Extract** operation, rather than another **Find** operation.

Extracts from a database

The **/D**ata **Q**uery **F**ind command is perfect for quickly locating a record or two for editing. For the times when you need to copy just the records that meet the selection criteria, however, you use the **Extract** command on the **/D**ata **Q**uery menu. Before you can extract records from a database, you need to set up and define an *output range,* in addition to the input and criteria ranges. The output range indicates where the records that match the selection criteria are to be copied.

When you set up the output range, you need to copy the field names for all the fields that you want copied.

✔ The field names that you put in the output range do not have to follow the order used in the database itself. For example, even when the Last Name field precedes the First Name field in the database, you can reverse this order and have the First Name field precede the Last Name field in the output range.

✔ You do not have to include all of the fields in the output range. For example, to create mailing labels for a client database, you include just the First Name, Last Name, Street, City, State, and ZIP code fields in the output range so that 1-2-3 copies only this information from the database.

After you enter the field names for the output range, you then use the **/D**ata **Q**uery **O**utput command to tell 1-2-3 where the range is. Before you perform an **Extract** operation using the selection criteria, you usually don't have any idea how many records will match and how large the range needs to be. You can leave the number of rows below the field names open by selecting just the cells with field names in response to the `Enter output range:` prompt. When the output range consists only of field names, 1-2-3 uses as many rows below these names as it needs to copy all the matching records from the database.

Be careful, however, that you don't have existing entries in the same columns in rows below the field names because 1-2-3 replaces any existing cell entries with the information extracted from the database. To avoid losing data during an **Extract** operation, locate the output range in an area of the worksheet where you know that you won't overwrite existing cell entries.

If you select the field names plus rows of blank cells when you set up the output range, you restrict the extraction to just the blank rows below the field names. Although selecting blank rows prevents 1-2-3 from overwriting existing entries in the rows below, you may not select enough blank rows to hold all of the matching records. When 1-2-3 fills the output range before it finishes copying all matching records, it beeps and displays an error message which indicates that there are too many records for the output range. You can't bail out at this point, so go ahead and press Esc or Enter to get out of ERROR mode. The program then fills the output range with whatever matching records it can cram in there. When it's done, you have to go back and increase the size of the output range and start all over again.

To initiate an **Extract** operation after you set up the selection criteria in the criteria range and define the current input, criteria, and output ranges, you choose the **/D**ata **Q**uery **E**xtract command. After 1-2-3 copies the matching records, you choose the **Q**uit command to return to READY mode so that you can check the output range in the worksheet. Remember that in READY mode, you can use the F7 (Query) key to perform another **Extract** operation after you edit the selection criteria (provided that you don't need to redefine the criteria with the **/D**ata **Q**uery **C**riteria command).

Figures 8-8 and 8-9 illustrate two typical **Extract** operations. In Figure 8-8, records matching both selection criteria (those records where the anniversary date is after June 1, 1986, *and* the gross receipts are greater than $15,000) in the criteria range are copied to the output range. Note that the output range uses only a few of the field names from the database, and they are in a different order than they are in the database.

```
S3: [W11] +G3>@DATE(86,6,1)                                            READY

        N         O       P       Q       R       S       T      U      ◄
1   CRITERIA RANGE                                                        ►
2   First NameStreet    City    State   ZIP Code AnniversaryIn YeaGrs Rcpts ▲
3                                                            1      >15000   ▼
4                                                                          ?
5   OUTPUT RANGE
6   First NameLast NameState   Grs RcptsAnniversary
7   Hans      Andersen    MN    $21,000 12/29/86
8   Bingo     Baggins     ME    $45,678 12/20/86
9   Eros      Cupid       CT    $78,655 11/13/86
10  Big       Eaters      AZ    $66,666 09/02/92
11  Ben       Franklin    WV    $34,400 10/21/87
12  Aragorn   Gondor      WY   $145,000 10/11/86
13  Rex       Oakenshie   NJ    $18,100 03/10/87
14  Crimson   Ridinghoo   PA    $18,900 05/27/87
15  George    Washingto   DC    $19,700 05/20/88
16  Snow      White       WA    $17,200 07/17/86
17
18
19
20
CLIENTS.WK1                    UNDO                           NUM
```

Figure 8-8: Records extracted with an AND condition.

```
Q4: (G) [W9] 'CA                                                    READY

      N         O          P         Q        R        S       T       U      ◄
 1 CRITERIA RANGE                                                              ►
 2 First NameStreet      City      State    ZIP Code AnniversaryIn YeaGrs Rcpts ▲
 3                                 MN                                          ▼
 4                                 CA                                          ?
 5 OUTPUT RANGE
 6 First NameLast NameState       Grs RcptsAnniversary
 7 Christian Andersen     MN       $12,000 12/29/86
 8 Hans      Andersen     MN       $21,000 12/29/86
 9 Elmer     Fudde        CA            $2 08/13/87
10 Shane     Gearing      CA       $12,180 03/04/81
11
12
13
14
15
16
17
18                                                    ■
19
20
CLIENTS.WK1                    UNDO                          NUM
```

Figure 8-9: Records extracted with an OR condition.

In Figure 8-9, records matching either selection criterion (those records where the State is MN *or* CA) in the criteria range are copied to the output range. Note that when you perform a second **Extract** operation using the same output range, 1-2-3 erases the records copied in the previous **Extract** operation before it copies the new matching records.

If you change the selection criteria and perform a subsequent **Extract** operation without changing the output range, 1-2-3 clears the existing contents of the output range before it copies the new information from the matching records. You can save the results of an **Extract** operation in one of two ways before you perform another one:

   ✔ Copy its contents to a new part of the same worksheet or to an entirely new worksheet (see the following section).

   ✔ Set up and define another output range for the new **Extract** operation in a different part of the worksheet where it can't affect the original results.

You can use the **/D**ata **Q**uery **R**eset command to clear the current input, criteria, and output ranges before you begin **F**ind and/or **E**xtract operations with a new database.

I need a worksheet of my own

You can easily save the results of an **Extract** operation in a new worksheet:

   1. Position the cell pointer in the first cell in the output range that you want to save in a separate file (the cell with the first field name if you want to copy the field names along with the extracted information).

2. Choose the **/File X**tract **V**alues command.

3. In response to the `Enter name of file to extract to:` prompt, enter a name for the new file and then press Enter.

4. In response to the `Enter extract range:` prompt, extend the range to highlight all the cells that you want to save in the new file and then press Enter to save the file.

When you open this new file with the **/File R**etrieve command, all the entries copied from the specified output range appear in the upper left corner of the worksheet, starting with cell A1.

Only the unique need apply

Normally, 1-2-3 copies any record (or part of a record) from the database that meets the selection criteria when you perform the **Extract** operation. You can, if you like, have the program extract only unique records into the output range by choosing the **/D**ata **Q**uery **U**nique command instead of **/D**ata **Q**uery **E**xtract.

The **/D**ata **Q**uery **U**nique command comes in handy when you need to know how many times a different response occurs in a database. For example, you can use it in the Three Little Pigs Building Supply client database to find out how many different states Boss Hog's company is servicing. To do this, you clear the criteria range of all selection criteria, restrict the output range to just the cell with the State field name with the **/D**ata **Q**uery **O**utput command, and then choose the **U**nique command.

1-2-3 then extracts all the unique state codes into the output range, ignoring any duplicates. You can then use the @COUNT function to count the number of states in the output range (see Chapter 12 for details), or you can count them yourself if you don't have anything better to do.

Deadly data deletions

You can use the **/D**ata **Q**uery **D**elete command to get rid of records in the database that you no longer need to keep. When you use this command, 1-2-3 removes all records in the database (as defined with the **/D**ata **Q**uery **I**nput command) that meet the selection criteria entered in the criteria range (as defined with the **/D**ata **Q**uery **C**riteria command). As part of the deletion process, 1-2-3 not only removes each matching record but also pulls the remaining database records up so that there are no gaps in the rows of the database.

Of course, deletions are always potentially dangerous (especially when you are using an automated process like the **/D**ata **Q**uery **D**elete command), so you have to protect yourself.

- Never ever use the /**D**ata **Q**uery **D**elete command on a database that you haven't saved.

- Never undertake such an operation with the Undo feature turned off (unless you just don't have enough memory to open the database file and use Undo at the same time).

- As a final precaution, perform a **F**ind operation with the /**D**ata **Q**uery **F**ind command to preview the records that will be destroyed when you later choose the **D**elete command. That way, you can tell if the selection criteria is hitting the right records before you take them out of commission. If it is selecting the wrong ones, you can modify the selection criteria and perform the **F**ind again. Then, once you're thoroughly satisfied that you're going to remove only records you really no longer need, you can go ahead with the /**D**ata **Q**uery **D**elete command.

When you choose this command, 1-2-3 does not delete the records right away. Instead, the program gives you a second chance to bail out of the deletion by displaying these menu options on the second line of the control panel:

```
Cancel  Delete
```

If you're the least bit unsure, choose **C**ancel or press Enter to cancel the deletion. Otherwise, choose the **D**elete command on this menu to finally remove all records matching the selection criteria. And they are outta there!

Chapter 9
Holy Macros!

● ●

In This Chapter

▶ Finding out what macros are and how you can use them

▶ Recording and playing back macros that you can use in your 1-2-3 worksheets

▶ Attaching the macros in a macro library worksheet to another worksheet

▶ Using the Macro Library Manager add-in to save macros in a special macro library file

● ●

*M*acros! Just the word is enough to make you want to head for the hills. Before you take off (or turn to the next chapter), however, try to replace your idea of this term as so much techno-babble with what macro really means: *macro instruction*. At the level of this book, a macro is nothing more than a way to record the keystrokes that you use to perform a particular task and have 1-2-3 play them back for you.

Using a macro to perform a routine task, such as entering a company name in a worksheet, saving and printing a worksheet, or entering and formatting a row of headings, has some definite advantages over doing the same tasks by hand.

✔ 1-2-3 can execute commands much faster than you can, no matter how good you are at the keyboard or how familiar you are with the program.

✔ 1-2-3 performs the task flawlessly each and every time because the macro always plays back keystrokes exactly as you recorded them. You just need to be sure that you record or enter them correctly.

✔ You can streamline the playback process by assigning a special name to your favorite macros that enables you to play the macros back by pressing Alt plus a letter of the alphabet, essentially reducing tasks that otherwise require quite a few steps to just two keystrokes.

Macro Mania

In its most basic form, a macro is simply a collection of keystrokes that you store in a worksheet so that you can replay them any time you need them. The keystrokes can consist of 1-2-3 commands or simple text and values or, as is most common, a combination of the two.

After you record or enter the macro keystrokes in a worksheet, you assign a range name to the first cell of the macro with the **/R**ange **N**ame **C**reate command. You can name macros in two different ways:

- ✔ You can use the backslash key (\) and a single letter between A and Z. To run such a backslash macro, you hold down the Alt key and type the letter that is assigned to the range name.

- ✔ You can use standard, descriptive range names (up to 15 characters in length). To run these macros with longer names, you press the Alt-F3 (Run) key and then type the range name or select it from the list of range names displayed on the last line of the control panel.

You can create one other backslash macro in addition to \A through \Z, and that is \0 (zero). If you name a macro \0, 1-2-3 runs the macro automatically the moment you retrieve the worksheet.

You enter the keystrokes for a macro in one of two ways:

- ✔ By setting up a special learn range in the worksheet and then manually performing the commands in the worksheet as 1-2-3 records the keystrokes in the range

- ✔ By typing the keystrokes into a range of the worksheet yourself

Note: The learn-range business wasn't introduced until Release 2.2, so if you're still using Release 2.0, you can create only backslash macros, which means that you're restricted to 26 macros per worksheet (\A through \Z). What's more, you have to type in all the macro keystrokes.

This chapter covers both methods of creating macros, starting with the learn range recording method — because it's the real no-brainer of the two. Much of the information in the description of recording a macro with the learn range method also applies to typing in the keystrokes, so don't skip over the learn range method if you're using Release 2.0.

Let the Record Show

When you use the learn range recording method, you first need to decide where to locate the learn range in the worksheet and how big to make it.

- ✔ A learn range is always a single column of the worksheet. When you run a macro, 1-2-3 plays it back by starting with the keystrokes in the first cell in the range and then by moving down the column row by row.

- ✔ A macro automatically stops running as soon as 1-2-3 encounters either a blank cell or a cell with some sort of value. As a result, you can't skip any cells, and you have to enter all macro instructions as labels. Otherwise, the whole business shuts down.

When you decide on the number of rows for the learn range, you need to figure out how many rows 1-2-3 needs for all the keystrokes you want to include in the macro. This is a hard call to make because you don't know how many cells 1-2-3 needs for the actions you're going to record until after you record them — and then it's too late. (Catch 22!)

If the learn range is too small for 1-2-3 to cram all the keystrokes into it, the program automatically turns off the Learn feature, thereby abruptly ending the recording session. It then displays a message telling you that the learn range is full and that no more stuff will go into it. When this happens, you have to en-large the learn range by increasing the number of rows and then you must re-record the macro.

When you decide exactly where in the worksheet to put the learn range, you need to find an out-of-the-way place with plenty of blank cells. You want to locate the range where it won't get in the way of other worksheet data or be harmed by any editing changes that you make.

Keep in mind that inserting a blank row that opens up a hole in a macro's range is just as detrimental to the macro's health as deleting a row of the range.

✔ If you locate the macro range in columns to the right of a table and later insert a blank row in the table which results in splitting up the macro's range, the macro will shut down prematurely the next time you run it. It will stop as soon as it reaches the new blank row in the middle of the macro range, instead of stopping at the row that follows the range.

✔ If you delete a row that affects the macro range, the macro will do weird things the next time you run it because the instructions in that row will be missing.

The safest place for macros, therefore, is in columns well to the right of the columns that contain the worksheet data, starting in rows well below the rows with worksheet data — in other words, catty-corner to the area containing the worksheet data. The only problem with this safe area is that it uses up more memory than locating the macro ranges in columns to the immediate right of the worksheet data or in the rows just below it.

The macro for today is...

The best way to get a feel for how easily you can record and play back a simple macro with the Learn feature is to try out some macros yourself. Just follow the steps for recording macros that can help you perform common worksheet tasks. The first macro enters and formats the current date in a cell of the worksheet, using the @NOW function.

The very first thing you need is a place in which to perform and record the keystrokes for the macro. For this macro, you want to open a new worksheet that will eventually become a library of useful macros. (Remember that you can use the /Worksheet Erase command if you need to clear the current worksheet and start a new one.) After you clear the screen, you're ready to define the learn range and record the macro as follows:

1. Choose the /Worksheet Learn Range command.

2. Position the cell pointer in cell C3, type a period to anchor the range, press ↓ until you've extended the range down to row 10, and press Enter.

   The range C3..C10 should provide more than enough cells for recording the few keystrokes in this first macro.

3. Press the Home key to move the cell pointer directly to cell A1, where you will enter and format the @NOW function.

   You cannot use any part of the learn range because the macro instructions for repeating the keystrokes need to go there.

4. Press the Alt-F5 (Learn) key to turn on LEARN mode.

   The LEARN indicator appears on the status line to let you know that from now on all your keystrokes will be recorded.

5. Type @NOW and press Enter to have 1-2-3 put the serial number (you know, the star date) for the current date in cell A1.

6. Type /RFD1 to choose the /Range Format Date 1 (DD-MMM-YY) command and press Enter to format the serial number with the first date format.

7. Type /WCS to choose the /Worksheet Column Set-Width command, press → once, and then press Enter to widen column A enough to display the formatted date.

8. Press the Alt-F5 (Learn) key again to turn off LEARN mode.

   The LEARN indicator disappears from the status line, indicating that 1-2-3 is no longer recording keystrokes, and the CALC indicator appears.

9. Press the F9 (Calc) key.

   As soon as you calculate the worksheet with the F9 (Calc) key to get rid of the CALC indicator, the keystrokes that you made in LEARN mode magically appear in the first cell (C3) of the learn range. The recorded keystrokes look like the ones in Figure 9-1.

Take a moment to examine the way 1-2-3 recorded the keystrokes in cell C3 of the learn range:

```
@now~/rfd1~/wcs{R}~
```

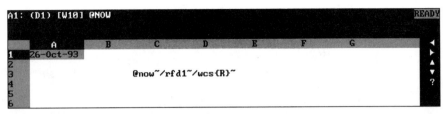

Figure 9-1: Recorded keystrokes in the first cell of the learn range.

It looks like some sort of weird shorthand, doesn't it? Actually, only a couple of notations are completely unfamiliar. Look at it one piece at a time. First, you have

```
@now~
```

You know, @NOW — the function that calculates the current date. (Note that 1-2-3 can't be bothered with capital letters when it records keystrokes.) The squiggly character, called a *tilde,* that follows @NOW represents pressing the Enter key. This little wiggle enters the @NOW function in the current cell.

After @now~, 1-2-3 recorded the following keystrokes:

```
/rfd1~
```

These keystrokes format the serial date number with the **/R**ange **F**ormat **D**ate **1** (DD-MMM-YY) command. The tilde at the end applies this date format to the single-cell default range (A1..A1 during the recording).

When you're recording 1-2-3 commands, you need to *type* the command letters for the entire command sequence. Choosing menu commands or scrolling or selecting cell ranges à la mouse simply doesn't work here because 1-2-3 can't record any mouse actions for a macro. It can record only keystrokes.

You could have selected the first date format by pressing Enter, instead of typing **1**, because this format choice is automatically highlighted as soon as you choose the **D**ate format menu. However, the keystrokes in the learn range would then be /rfd~~, rather than /rfd1~. If you look back over these keystrokes later and try to make out what the blazes this part of the macro is supposed to do, double squiggly marks following /rfd are even less explicit and harder to recall than a single one following /rfd1. You have to know the 1-2-3 menus pretty well to know what command was chosen with Enter.

Take my advice. Keep the number of mysterious tildes in a macro to a minimum. Limit pressing the Enter key to those situations where you must do so in order to complete a 1-2-3 command or action (for example, when you select the range to format with the Date 1 format).

The last part of the macro contains the following keystrokes:

```
/wcs{R}~
```

These keystrokes widen the column one character by choosing the **/W**orksheet **C**olumn **S**et-Width command, pressing → once to increase the column width to 10 characters, and then pressing Enter. As you have probably figured out, when you press → while you are in LEARN mode, 1-2-3 records this keystroke as {R}. Actually, {R} is an abbreviation for {RIGHT}, which is the other way you can indicate this keystroke. (To see how to represent other keys, such as ↑ and ↓, see Table 9-1 in "Making Macros the Old-Fashioned Way," later in this chapter.)

Keystrokes alone do not a macro make

You have to do more than just record or enter the keystrokes for a macro in a range of worksheet cells to make it a macro. You also have to name the first cell of the range with the **/R**ange **N**ame **C**reate command. (You have to name only the first cell because 1-2-3 is preprogrammed to read all the cells in rows below it as macro instructions until it encounters a blank cell or one with a value.)

When you name a macro, remember that if you want to be able to play it back by pressing Alt plus a single letter of the alphabet, you need to make it a backslash macro by naming the range with a \ followed by the letter you want to use. Otherwise, you just give a standard, descriptive name, observing the same guidelines you follow when you name any other cell range.

In the case of the date macro, you make it a backslash macro by giving it the name \T (for today's date) so that you can run it by simply pressing Alt-T. Here's how you name the date macro:

1. Move the cell pointer to cell C3.

2. Choose the **/R**ange **N**ame **C**reate command.

3. Type **\T** (be sure to type a backslash and not the forward slash you use to get the 1-2-3 menus) and press Enter.

4. Press Enter again to accept the default range C3..C3.

    Remember that you have to name only the first cell of a macro range, even when the macro instructions use several rows in the same column.

5. Move the cell pointer to cell B3 and type **'\T** to put the name of the macro next to the cell with its instructions.

    Make certain that you type the apostrophe label prefix before you type **\T,** or you will end up with *Ts* all across cell B3 rather than with the label \T.

Run, macro, run

After you name the macro, you are ready to test it. Before you unleash a new macro on a worksheet — especially one that does lots of potentially dangerous things to the worksheet, such as erasing cells or inserting new columns or rows — you need to save the worksheet. In the case of the new worksheet that contains the \T macro, you want to choose the /File Save command and then name the file MACROLIB.WK1 because it will become the macro library worksheet.

Even after you save the worksheet with the new macro, you may have to move the cell pointer to neutral territory before you actually run the macro. For example, if you try out the \T macro while the cell pointer is still in cell C3, which contains the macro instructions that you just named, 1-2-3 replaces the macro keystrokes with today's date — not exactly what you want to do. So move next door to cell B1, where you can't do any harm to the macro, yet you can still see that the macro does exactly what it's supposed to do.

After you move to cell B1, press Alt-T. You see a blur of activity on the control panel as 1-2-3 enters the current date, formats it with the first date format, and widens the column — all in a flash. After the dust settles, you see the same date in the top row of column B that you put in column A.

If the macro didn't perform as expected, you need to edit its contents:

1. Press the Alt-F4 (Undo) key to restore the worksheet to the condition it was in before the macro messed it up.

2. Put the cell pointer back in C3, press the F2 (Edit) key, check the macro instructions against the ones shown in Figure 9-1, and make any necessary changes.

   For heaven's sake, don't mess with the label prefix at the very beginning of the keystroke instructions! Remember, all macro instructions must be entered as labels at all times.

3. Press Enter.

Save the worksheet. Then put the cell pointer back in cell B1 and press Alt-T to test the revised date macro. This time, 1-2-3 plays back the keystrokes as you've edited them and, with any luck at all, you should end up with exactly what you want.

If you ever find that a new macro is running amok in the worksheet when you are playing it back, immediately press Ctrl-Break to shut down the macro prematurely. Because 1-2-3 goes into ERROR mode when you use this keystroke, you have to press Esc or Enter to return to READY mode.

The calendar maker

The second sample macro enters the three-letter abbreviations for the 12 months of the year across a single row of the worksheet. Then it centers the names in their cells. You'll use this macro much less frequently than the one that enters and formats the current date, so it does not need to be a backslash macro. Instead, you can give it a regular range name, *Month_Mac*. (If you're using Release 2.0, however, you need to make it a backslash macro, such as \M, and, of course, you need to type in the keystrokes.) To run a macro with a normal range name, you press the Alt-F3 (Run) key and then select the range name on the last line of the control panel.

As with the first macro, you first need to find a place in the worksheet where you can enter and format the names. To record this calendar macro, use new columns to the right of the first macro. Before you can start recording it, however, you need to define a new learn range as follows:

1. Choose the /**W**orksheet **L**earn **C**ancel command to clear the previous learn range.

2. Move the cell pointer to cell C5 (skip a row between macros), choose the /**W**orksheet **L**earn **R**ange command, and type a period to anchor the range. Press ↓ to extend the range to cell C11 (making the new learn range C5..C11) and then press Enter.

3. Position the cell pointer in cell E5 and then press the Alt-F5 (Learn) key to turn on LEARN mode.

4. Type **Jan** and then press →.

5. Type **Feb** and then press →. Continue in this manner, entering the rest of the months (**Mar Apr May Jun Jul Aug Sep Oct Nov Dec**) in succeeding columns to the right. When you enter **Dec** in cell P5, press Enter instead of →.

6. Choose the /**R**ange **L**abel **C**enter command, press End, ← to highlight the range with the names of the months, and then press Enter.

7. Press the Alt-F5 (Learn) key again to turn off LEARN mode.

Figure 9-2 shows the keystrokes entered into the learn range by 1-2-3 when you turn off LEARN mode. (Note that column C has been widened so that all the keystrokes appear in this column.)

Now you're ready to name the macro, save it as part of the worksheet, and test it out:

1. Position the cell pointer in cell C5 and then choose the /**R**ange **N**ame **C**reate command.

2. Type **Month_Mac** as the range name (use the underscore [Shift-hyphen] between the words), press Enter, and then press Enter again to accept the default range (C5..C5).

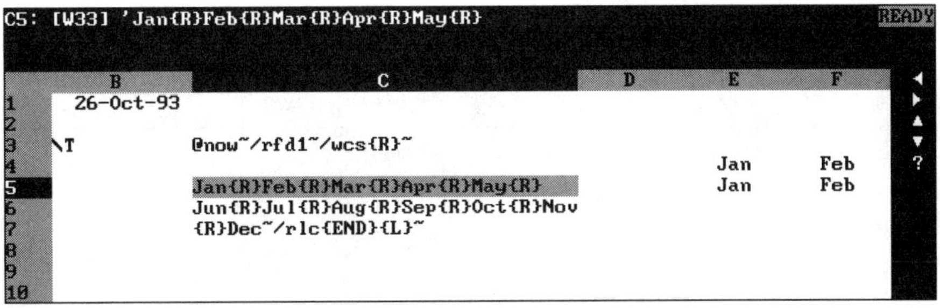

```
C5: [W33] 'Jan{R}Feb{R}Mar{R}Apr{R}May{R}                              READY
```

	B	C	D	E	F	
1	26-Oct-93					▶
2						▲
3	\T	@now~/rfd1~/wcs{R}~		Jan	Feb	▼
4				Jan	Feb	?
5		Jan{R}Feb{R}Mar{R}Apr{R}May{R}				
6		Jun{R}Jul{R}Aug{R}Sep{R}Oct{R}Nov				
7		{R}Dec~/rlc{END}{L}~				
8						
9						
10						

Figure 9-2: Recorded keystrokes for the calendar maker macro.

3. Move the cell pointer to cell B5 and enter the macro name, **Month_Mac,** in this cell.

4. Choose the **/F**ile **S**ave command, press Enter, and then choose the **R**eplace command to save the macro.

5. Move the cell pointer to cell E4 (just above Jan, centered below in E5), press the Alt-F3 (Run) key, and then press Enter (the Month-Mac range name should already be highlighted) to run the macro.

When the macro is finished running, the cell pointer is in cell P4, and the abbreviations for the months Jan through Dec are centered in their cells in row 4, mirroring those you just entered in row 5.

Making Macros the Old-Fashioned Way

In the olden days (the days, that is, of Release 1A and 2.0), before the advent of the Learn feature, when dinosaurs ruled the earth, creating 1-2-3 macros meant typing all the macro keystrokes yourself. When you type the macro instructions, you need to know how to represent special keys, such as those that move the cell pointer (the arrow keys, Tab, Home, and so on), as well as the 10 function keys. Table 9-1 lists the macro key names for all these keys. In looking over this table, note that all the key names, with the exception of the tilde for the Enter key, are enclosed in a pair of curly braces. You enter the curly braces by holding the Shift key as you press the [key or the] key.

Table 9-1	Macro Key Names
Key	*Macro Key Name*
Enter	~ (Tilde)
←	{LEFT} or {L}
→	{RIGHT} or {R}
↑	{UP} or {U}
↓	{DOWN} or {D}
Home	{HOME}
End	{END}
Tab or Ctrl-→	{BIGRIGHT}
Shift-Tab or Ctrl-←	{BIGLEFT}
PgUp	{PGUP}
PgDn	{PGDN}
← Backspace	{BACKSPACE} or {BS}
Del	{DELETE} or {DEL}
Ins	{INSERT} or {INS}
/ or < (for Slash menus)	/ or < or {MENU}
F1 (Help)	{HELP}
F2 (Edit)	{EDIT}
F3 (Name)	{NAME}
F4 (Abs)	{ABS}
F5 (GoTo)	{GOTO}
F6 (Window)	{WINDOW}
F7 (Query)	{QUERY}
F8 (Table)	{TABLE}
F9 (Calc)	{CALC}
F10 (Graph)	{GRAPH}
Alt-F7 (Add-in 1)	{APP1}
Alt-F8 (Add-in 2)	{APP2}
Alt-F9 (Add-in 3)	{APP3}
Alt-F10 (Add-in 4)	{APP4}

Sometimes you need to repeat a keystroke a set number of times in a macro. For example, you may want to move the cell pointer three columns to the left before you have the macro enter something in a worksheet. Instead of entering three separate {L} instructions, such as this:

```
{L}{L}{L}
```

you can just add the number of times that you want ← pressed inside the key name. It looks like this:

```
{L 3}
```

(Note that you need to have a space between the L and the 3.) When you enter the number of times to repeat a keystroke, you can use the address of a cell that contains the number of repetitions instead of entering the number directly. Suppose that you store in cell B2 the number of characters to be deleted from a cell entry after returning it to the control panel. You can then enter the following as part of a macro:

```
{EDIT}{BS B2}
```

That way, if B2 contains 4 when you run the macro, 1-2-3 removes the last four characters from the end of the entry by backspacing over them. (The entry is returned to the control panel with the {EDIT} instruction that works just like pressing the F2 [Edit] key.) If, however, cell B2 contains the number 2 at the time you run the macro, the macro deletes the last two characters, and so on. If cell B2 is empty, the {BS} keystroke is ignored (which is what you should do with any BS) because this is the same as entering **{BS 0}** in the macro.

- ✔ When you type the macro instructions yourself, you get to decide where to break them up. You can keep discrete commands on separate lines, which is not possible when you use the Learn feature to enter the keystrokes.

- ✔ Be sure to enter each new line as a label when you break up the macro instructions. You need to use the apostrophe label prefix if you're entering a line that begins with a slash command or a character that puts 1-2-3 into VALUE mode.

- ✔ Don't skip any rows and stay in the same column (and be careful when you come to Dinosaur Crossing signs).

- ✔ In the next column over, to the right of each macro instruction, enter a short comment that explains what the keystrokes on that line in the macro do. Documenting macros may initially strike you as a waste of time, but, in fact, these comments not only help you understand what's going on two months down the line when you look at the macro, but also help you verify that the macro does all you want it to do at the time that you're creating it.

To see how easy it is to create macros the old-fashioned way, try the instructions in the next section to create the last four macros without the Learn feature.

The worksheet saver

The next macro saves changes to the worksheet, replacing the cumbersome procedure of choosing /File Save, pressing Enter to accept the current filename, and then choosing the **R**eplace command. This macro reduces all of these keystrokes to Alt-S.

To create the macro, follow these steps:

1. Move the cell pointer to B9, type '\\S, and press → to enter the macro name in cell B9.

2. With the cell pointer in cell C9, type the keystrokes '/**FS~R.** (You need to start with an apostrophe so that you don't get handed a menu.) Then press → to enter the keystrokes to save the worksheet.

3. Document the purpose of the macro by entering the comment **Save worksheet changes** in cell D9. The macro worksheet looks like the one in Figure 9-3.

Now you're ready to name the macro. This time, because you've already entered the macro name in the cell to the immediate left of the one with the macro keystrokes, you can use the /**R**ange Name **L**abels **R**ight command to assign the label in cell B9 to cell C9 as follows:

1. Position the cell pointer in cell B9 (the cell that contains the label you want to assign as a range name).

2. Choose the /**R**ange Name **L**abels command.

3. Choose the **R**ight command to assign the label in current cell B9 to cell C9 to the immediate right; then press Enter to accept the default range B9..B9.

4. Save the new save macro and test it at the same time by pressing Alt-S.

```
D9: 'Save worksheet changes                                          READY

         A           B              C              D        E        F      ◄
1   26-Oct-93    26-Oct-93                                                   ►
2                                                                           ▲
3               \T            @now~/rfd1~/wcs{R}~                           ▼
4                                                             Jan      Feb   ?
5               Month_Mac     Jan{R}Feb{R}Mar{R}Apr{R}May{R   Jan      Feb
6                             Jun{R}Jul{R}Aug{R}Sep{R}Oct{R}Nov
7                             {R}Dec~/rlc{END}{L}~
8
9               \S            /fs~r          Save worksheet changes
10
11
12
```

Figure 9-3: Keystrokes for the worksheet saver macro.

The WAIT mode indicator appears very briefly as 1-2-3 saves the new macro as part of the MACROLIB.WK1 file. From now on, you can just use Alt-S anytime you need to save changes to this worksheet.

The column widener

The next macro enters the keystrokes for choosing the /**W**orksheet **C**olumn **S**et-Width command to widen the current column. Instead of entering a particular value, such as 12, for the column width (which would limit use of the macro to just those times when you want the column to be 12 characters wide), the column-widener macro will stop after it types /**wcs**. You can then press → or ← or type in a value before you press Enter to set the new column width.

To create this macro, which you will call \W, you take these steps:

1. Position the cell pointer in cell B11, type '**W,** and press →.

2. Type '/**WCS** in cell C11 and then press →.

3. Type the comment **Widen current column** in cell D11. The macro worksheet resembles the worksheet in Figure 9-4.

4. Position the cell pointer in cell B11, choose the /**R**ange Name **L**abels **R**ight command, and press Enter to accept the default range.

5. Press Alt-S to save the macro as part of the worksheet.

6. Press Alt-W and respond to the Enter column width: prompt on the control panel by increasing the width of column B to 11 and then pressing Enter.

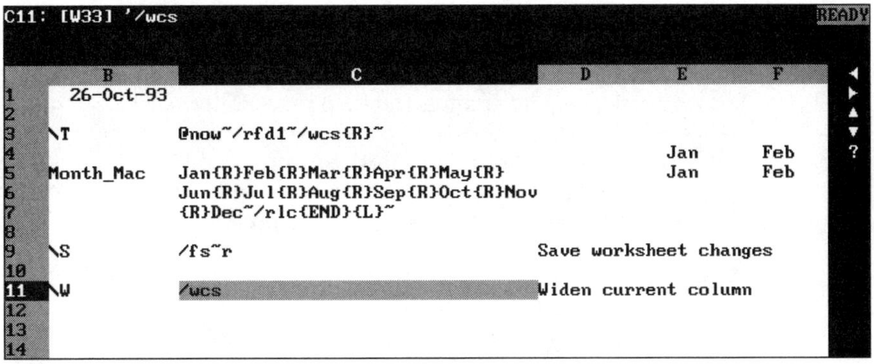

Figure 9-4: Keystrokes for the column-widener macro.

The date maker

No doubt about it, entering dates in a 1-2-3 worksheet with the @DATE function is a real drag. To make dealing with this function a heck of a lot easier, you can create a \D macro that starts the @DATE function and enters all the pertinent information while stopping in all the right places so that you can enter the year, month, and day.

To pause a macro, you enter {?} in the macro instructions. When 1-2-3 encounters a question mark enclosed in braces, it stops running the macro until you press Enter. Then it resumes the macro by running the instruction that immediately follows the {?} pause instruction. In the \D macro, you put this pause instruction in the places in the @DATE function where the three arguments belong. Follow these steps to create the macro:

1. Position the cell pointer in cell B13, type '**\D,** and press →.

2. Type '**@DATE({?},{?},{?})~** in cell C13 and then press →.

3. Type the comment **Enter @DATE, pause to get input** in cell D13.

4. Position the cell pointer in cell C14 (immediately below the macro instructions to enter @DATE).

5. Type '**/RFD4~** in cell C14 and then press →.

6. Type the comment **Format date w/ Long Int'l** in cell D14.

   A macro worksheet similar to the one shown in Figure 9-5 appears.

7. Position the cell pointer in cell B13 again, choose the **/R**ange Name Labels **R**ight command, and press Enter to accept the default range.

8. Press Alt-S to save the macro as part of the worksheet.

9. Move the cell pointer up to cell B1 (which contains the current date). Press Alt-D, type the last two digits of the year of your birth immediately after @DATE(, and then press Enter. Type the number of the month of your birth after the comma and then press Enter. Type the day of your birth after the second comma and then press Enter.

After you enter the day of your birth and press Enter, 1-2-3 completes the entry of the @DATE function and formats the date with the Long International Date format. (You can change the format if you prefer a different one.)

Unfortunately, having your birth date on the screen doesn't mean you'll get any extra presents, but at least you have simplified the process of putting dates into a worksheet. All you need to do now is press Alt-D and enter the three pieces of date information with the Enter key. Get out the balloons and celebrate!

```
D14: 'Format date w/ Long Int'l                                    READY

        B               C                    D      E      F     ◄
1     26-Oct-93                                                   ►
2                                                                 ▲
3    \T           @now~/rfd1~/wcs{R}~                             ▼
4                                                 Jan    Feb      ?
5    Month_Mac    Jan{R}Feb{R}Mar{R}Apr{R}May{R}  Jan    Feb
6                 Jun{R}Jul{R}Aug{R}Sep{R}Oct{R}Nov
7                 {R}Dec~/rlc{END}{L}~
8
9    \S           /fs~r                 Save worksheet changes
10
11   \W           /wcs                  Widen current column
12
13   \D           @date({?},{?},{?})~   Enter @date, pause to get input
14                /rfd4~                Format date w/ Long Int'l
15
16
17
18
19
20
MACROLIB.WK1                UNDO                                  ▌
```

Figure 9-5: Keystrokes for the date-maker macro.

The cell eraser

The last macro that you create here is especially helpful if you use an early version of 1-2-3 because it enables you to erase a single cell entry by pressing Alt-E, instead of having to choose the /**R**ange Erase command and then press Enter. Users of versions 2.3 and 2.4 already have an easy way to erase the current cell: just press Delete.

To create the cell eraser macro, you follow these steps:

1. Position the cell pointer in cell B16, type '**E,** and press →.

2. Type '/**RE~** in cell C16 and press →.

3. Type the comment **Erase the current cell** in cell D16. The macro worksheet resembles the one shown in Figure 9-6.

4. Position the cell pointer in cell B16, choose the /**R**ange Name Labels **R**ight command, and press Enter to accept the default range.

5. Press Alt-S to save the macro as part of the worksheet.

6. Press Home to position the cell pointer in cell A1, which holds the current date; then press Alt-E to wipe out that date. Press → to move to cell B1 and then do the Alt-E trick again, this time to get rid of the birth date that you entered with the \D macro.

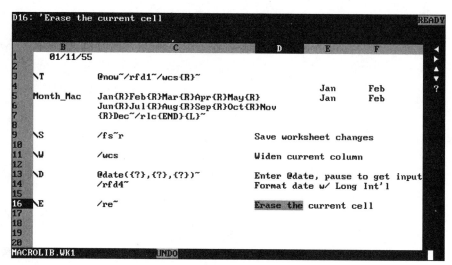

Figure 9-6: Keystrokes for the cell eraser macro.

Macro editing

What if you decide that instead of having the \E macro always delete the current cell, you want the macro to stop after it chooses the /Range Erase command so that you can decide how large a range to delete? In other words, if you want to delete just the current cell, you can simply press Enter, but if you want to erase a larger range, you can extend the range and then press Enter.

To make this editing change to the \E macro, you follow these steps:

1. Position the cell pointer in cell C16.

2. Press the F2 (Edit) key, press Backspace to get rid of the tilde, and press Enter.

3. Press Alt-S to save the change.

4. Test the revised \E macro by positioning the cell pointer in cell E4 (which contains the first of 12 months you entered earlier when you created the Month_Mac macro) and then pressing Alt-E. Press End, →, and then ↓ in response to the Enter range to erase: prompt. Then press Enter. Poof! The months are gone in a flash.

Support Your Local Macro Library

Assuming that you actually got off your duff and created the sample macros described in previous sections, you now have a nice library of macros that are useful whenever you start a new worksheet or need to do some serious editing of an existing worksheet. 1-2-3 provides two methods for making the macros stored in a macro library worksheet available when you are working on another worksheet:

- ✔ You can copy the macros into an out-of-the-way place in the new worksheet (as if you had created them in that worksheet).

- ✔ You can use the Macro Library Manager add-in to save the macros in a special macro library file that you load into the computer's memory. After you load the file into memory, you can use any of its macros in any worksheet.

Both methods have advantages, and you should know how to use both of them.

- ✔ Combining the macros with the worksheet you're building is your only option if you're using Release 2.0 of 1-2-3 because it doesn't include the Macro Library Manager add-in program.

- ✔ If you are using a later version of 1-2-3, you cannot use the add-in program when the computer doesn't have enough memory for you to run both 1-2-3 and the add-in.

- ✔ Using the Macro Library Manager add-in to create a special macro library file and then loading it in memory is the way to go if you can swing it. This method can save you a great deal of time when you're working with many different worksheet files: you only have to go through the rigmarole of loading the macro library file once, at the outset of your work session; then you can use the macros with any of the files you retrieve.

Combining and activating the macros in another worksheet

To copy the macros from a macro library worksheet into another worksheet, you use the /File Combine Copy command. You can use this command to copy a specific range in the worksheet or all the data in the worksheet. To make it easy to copy just the cells with macro information in the MACROLIB.WK1 file, you should assign a range name to these cells. As part of this process, you should finish documenting the macros that you created in LEARN mode:

1. In the macro library worksheet, add column headings in row 2. Enter the labels **Macro Name** in cell B2, **Macro Keystrokes** in cell C2, and **Comments** in cell D2.

2. Enter the comment **Enter current date in Lotus date format** in cell D3.

3. Enter the comment **Enter month, then move right** in cell D5.

4. Enter the comment **Center months in cells** in cell D6.

5. Position the cell pointer in cell B2 and then choose the **/R**ange Name Create command.

6. Type **MACROS** as the name in response to the `Enter name:` prompt, press Enter, extend the range over and down until you highlight the cell range B2..D16, and then press Enter again.

7. Press Alt-S to save changes to the MACROLIB.WK1 file.

Now that you've named the range with the macros in your macro library worksheet, you can copy just this cell range into any worksheet you want. To see how this works, copy this range into a new worksheet by taking these steps:

1. Choose the **/W**orksheet Erase **Y**es command to clear the screen and start a new worksheet.

2. Press Tab three times to move to column Y; then press PgDn three times to move to row 61. (This should move the macros enough out of the way so that you can enter and edit the worksheet data without doing the macros any harm.)

3. With the cell pointer in cell Y61, choose the **/F**ile Combine Copy Named/Specified-Range command.

4. Type **MACROS** and press Enter in response to the `Enter range name or address:` prompt.

5. Highlight MACROLIB.WK1 on the third line of the control panel and press Enter in response to the `Enter name of file to combine:` prompt.

You should now see the macros (names, instructions, comments, and all) in the range Y61..AA75 of the new worksheet. Before you can use these macros, you need to do just one more thing — reassign the range names to the macros. (Because the **/F**ile Combine Copy command can bring in only *data* from another file, the range names get left behind.) Fortunately, you can make short work of renaming the macros:

1. Position the cell pointer in cell Y2, which contains \T, the name for the first macro.

2. Choose the **/R**ange Name Labels **R**ight command, extend the range down until you've highlighted the cell range Y2..Y75 (including \E, the name for the last macro), and then press Enter.

3. Move the cell pointer to cell Z62, press Alt-W, and use this macro to widen the column of macro instructions to 20 (to make sure that the macros are working in the new worksheet).

That wasn't so bad, now, was it? Just don't forget to use the /**R**ange **N**ame **L**abels **R**ight command to reassign the range names to macros after you bring them into the new file with the /**F**ile **C**ombine **C**opy **N**amed/Specified-Range command. Then these macros, plus any you choose to add on your own, will always be at your fingertips!

Creating macro library files with the Macro Library Manager

If you use the Macro Library Manager add-in program to create macro library files and load them into memory so that the macros are available as you work, you need to load it each time you start 1-2-3. To load the Macro Library Manager add-in program, you take these steps:

1. Choose the /**A**dd-**I**n **A**ttach command, highlight the MACROMGR.ADN file on the third line of the control panel, and press Enter in response to the `Enter add-in to attach:` prompt.

2. Highlight the next available number (**7, 8, 9,** or **10**) and press Enter to assign the function key (Alt-F7, Alt-F8, Alt-F9, or Alt-F10) that you press to display the Macro Library Manager menu.

3. Choose the **Q**uit command on the /**A**dd-**I**n menu.

To speed things up, you can have 1-2-3 automatically load the Macro Library Manager and assign a function key to it each time you start 1-2-3. Follow these steps to have 1-2-3 load the Macro Library Manager automatically:

1. Choose the /**W**orksheet **G**lobal **D**efault **O**ther **A**dd-**I**n **S**et command.

2. Choose the next available setting number (**1** if you haven't set up any other Auto-attach add-ins).

3. Highlight MACROMGR.ADN on the third line of the control panel, and press Enter.

Then follow these steps to use a function key to display the Macro Library Manager menu:

1. Choose the next available key (**7, 8, 9,** or **10**) and press Enter.

2. Choose **Y**es when asked whether you want to invoke this add-in whenever you start 1-2-3.

3. Choose **Q**uit to return to the /**W**orksheet **G**lobal **D**efault menu.

4. Choose the **U**pdate and **Q**uit commands.

After you load the Macro Library Manager add-in, you can then use this program to save the macros you created in this chapter in a macro library file. (You can have as many different macro library files as you want.) To save the macros in your macro library worksheet in a macro library file, you follow these steps:

1. Retrieve the MACROLIB.WK1 file with the /**F**ile **R**etrieve command.

2. Press Alt plus the function key (such as Alt-F7 if you selected **7**) that you assigned to the Macro Library Manager program to display its command menu; then choose the **S**ave command from this menu.

3. Type **TOOLS** as the filename and press Enter in response to the `Enter name of macro library to save:` prompt. (1-2-3 automatically adds the extension MLB to the end of this filename to mark it as a special macro library file.)

4. Type **MACROS** and press Enter or press the F3 (Name) key, highlight the range name MACROS in the control panel, and press Enter in response to the `Enter macro library range:` prompt.

5. Choose **N**o when you are asked whether you want to lock the file with a password. (You can assign a password of up to 80 characters to a macro library file.) As soon as you choose **N**o, all the data in the range B2..D16 disappears from the macro library worksheet. (The Macro Library Manager doesn't fool around. Instead of just copying the macros into a new library file, it literally sucks them right out of the worksheet.)

6. Choose the /**W**orksheet **E**rase **Y**es command. When 1-2-3 beeps and tells you that the worksheet changes haven't been saved, go ahead and choose **Y**es again to clear the macro worksheet without saving the changes. I know, it's kind of scary, but it's okay. This time you want to retain the original disk version that still has all the macros in it.

After you create a macro library file, all that you have to do to use its macros is load the file from the Macro Manager Library menu. (Note that 1-2-3 automatically loads this file when you first save it.) In future work sessions in 1-2-3, after you load the Macro Library Manager add-in into memory and assign it to a function key, such as Alt-F7, you take these steps to load the TOOLS.MLB macro library file:

1. Press Alt-F7 (or whatever function key you assigned to the Macro Library Manager add-in) to display the menu and then choose the **L**oad command.

2. Highlight the TOOLS.MLB macro library file and press Enter in response to the `Enter name of macro library to load:` prompt.

3. Choose **Q**uit on the Macro Library Manager menu to return to READY mode.

After you load the TOOLS.MLB file in this way, you can use its macros in any of the worksheets you build or edit during a 1-2-3 work session.

If you want to skip the step of loading the macro library file into memory each time you want to use the file, give it the filename AUTOLOAD when you save it. Thereafter, whenever you load the MACROMGR.ADN file with the /Add-In Attach command, the Macro Library Manager add-in program will automatically load the library file named AUTOLOAD.MLB into memory as well, making all its macros immediately available.

Part V
Wysiwyging through 1-2-3

The 5th Wave   By Rich Tennant

THE SYSTEM CAME BUNDLED WITH A GRAPHICS BOARD, A SPREADSHEET, AND THE DEVELOPER'S OUT OF WORK NEPHEW.

The part in which...

You learn what a wonderful and welcome addition Wysiwyg is to the 1-2-3 program! Wysiwyg maybe a horrible name, but this part speaks to those of you who are fortunate enough to be using Release 2.3 or 2.4. You learn how to use this add-in program to brighten up the worksheet with different fonts, font enhancements like bold and italics, and different types of cell borders and shading. In addition, you learn how to use Wysiwyg to add graphs and other graphic images right into the worksheet as well as to print even better looking reports than are possible in 1-2-3.

Those of you using Release 2.4 learn how to really live the life of Reilly by using the Icons add-in program. This program adds all sorts of "smart" icons to 1-2-3 that perform a variety of useful tasks with a single, simple mouse click. You learn how to place and arrange your favorite SmartIcons on the custom palette to make them easier to get to, and, to become fully "iconized," you can assign your favorite macros to any of the twelve User Icons so that you can run the macros just by clicking their icons!

Chapter 10
Showing It Off in Graphic Detail

- -

In This Chapter

▶ Attaching the Wysiwyg add-in

▶ Modifying the worksheet display

▶ Changing column widths and row heights

▶ Formatting with font changes, attributes, lines, and shading

▶ Formatting cell ranges with styles

▶ Adding graphs to a worksheet

▶ Printing a worksheet

- -

*W*ysiwyg (which stands for *what you see is what you get* and is — don't laugh — pronounced *wizzy-wig*) is the name of the add-in program that magically transforms Release 2.3 or 2.4 of 1-2-3 from a rather dull, character-based program into an exciting graphical program. Wysiwyg gives you the advantage of having the on-screen version of the worksheet very close to the printed version (that's where the *what you see is what you get* comes in).

With this nifty little add-in program, you can take the otherwise bland worksheet display and spruce it up with such things as new colors, grid lines that set off the columns and rows, and shading that makes the frame appear sculpted. Even better, you can enhance plain worksheet entries by adding new fonts and font attributes (such as bold, italics, and underlining) to the text and various types of shading and borders to the cells.

Not only can you use Wysiwyg to give the worksheet display and worksheet data a new improved look, but you can also use the program to add graphs directly to the worksheet and to print 1-2-3 reports. By adding graphs to the worksheet and then printing the worksheet with Wysiwyg, you can avoid the use of the PrintGraph utility altogether. Also when you print reports with Wysiwyg, you have the benefit of a print preview feature that allows you to see how the report will be paged along with how all the neat graphical effects will look in print.

Attaching the Wysiwyg Add-In

If the Wysiwyg program files were transferred to the hard disk during the installation of 1-2-3, Wysiwyg is automatically loaded into the computer's memory each and every time you start 1-2-3. If you have no idea what went on when your copy of 1-2-3 was installed, you can find out whether Wysiwyg is attached to 1-2-3 simply by typing a colon (:). Just as the / activates the 1-2-3 command menus, the : activates the Wysiwyg menus. If the Wysiwyg add-in is attached, a menu of commands similar, although not identical, to the 1-2-3 command menus appears on the control panel and, more informatively, the program goes into WYSIWYG mode rather than into the normal MENU mode.

Mouse owners can use their computer pets to display the Wysiwyg menus. Just position the mouse pointer somewhere in the control panel, as you normally do to display the menus. If the 1-2-3 menus appear when you do this, click the right mouse button to switch to the Wysiwyg menus. When the Wysiwyg menus are displayed, choose commands by positioning the mouse pointer on the command and then clicking with the left mouse button, as you do with the 1-2-3 menus. Note that in Wysiwyg, the mouse pointer appears as an arrowhead pointing up and to the left instead of as a block (see Figure 10-1).

Suppose that you type a colon and the only thing that happens is that a colon is entered on the second line of the control panel. Well, then, you have some work to do because the Wysiwyg add-in is not attached to 1-2-3. Here's what you need to do to attach it:

1. Choose the /Add-In Attach command, highlight the WYSIWYG.ADN file on the third line of the control panel and press Enter in response to the `Enter add-in to attach:` prompt.

2. If you want to assign a function key to display the Wysiwyg menus (in addition to using the colon), highlight the next available number (**7**, **8**, **9**, or **10**) and press Enter to assign a function key (Alt-F7, Alt-F8, Alt-F9, or Alt-F10). If the colon key will do just fine, choose the **No-Key** command and press Enter.

3. After 1-2-3 loads Wysiwyg (indicated by the Wysiwyg Publishing and Presentation startup screen that briefly appears), choose the **Q**uit command on the /Add-In menu.

After you load the Wysiwyg add-in, you immediately see a small difference in the appearance of the screen: the column letters and row numbers are bordered by lines in the worksheet frame.

If 1-2-3 does not automatically load the Wysiwyg add-in each time you start 1-2-3, follow these steps to have it loaded automatically:

1. Choose the /**W**orksheet **G**lobal **D**efault **O**ther **A**dd-In **S**et command.

2. Choose the next available setting number (**1** if you haven't set up any other Auto-attach add-ins).

3. Highlight WYSIWYG.ADN on the third line of the control panel and press Enter.

4. If you want to be able to use a function key, as well as the colon, to display the Wysiwyg menus, choose the next available key (**7**, **8**, **9**, or **10**) and press Enter. Otherwise, press Enter to choose the default **N**o-Key command.

5. Choose **Y**es when the program asks whether you want to invoke this add-in whenever you start 1-2-3.

6. Choose **Q**uit to return to the /**W**orksheet **G**lobal **D**efault menu.

7. Choose the **U**pdate and **Q**uit commands.

Note that if you ever get into a situation where you need to free up some computer memory in order to cram more data into the worksheet, you can detach the Wysiwyg program. Send it packing by following these steps:

1. Choose the /**A**dd-In **D**etach command.

2. Choose WYSIWYG as the add-in to detach.

3. Press Enter.

4. Choose the **Q**uit command to leave the /**A**dd-In menu.

Detaching Wysiwyg is kind of like coming back to Kansas from OZ. The worksheet display and data suddenly lose all the beautiful colors and special attributes that they had when Wysiwyg was attached. You go back to working in a character-based mode where all the fonts look alike, the worksheet lacks any grid lines, and you no longer have control over any of the screen display.

When you save the worksheet with Wysiwyg attached, 1-2-3 saves all the formatting changes that you make with this add-in program in a separate file. The file uses the same main filename as the original worksheet, but it sports a FMT file extension instead of WK1. So, for example, if you're working on a worksheet named 93SALES.WK1 and you format it with Wysiwyg and then save these changes with the /**F**ile **S**ave command, 1-2-3 saves the Wysiwyg formatting changes in a file called 93SALES.FMT. All the data changes or changes made with the regular 1-2-3 menus are, of course, saved in the original 93SALES.WK1 file.

When you make copies of a worksheet that you've formatted with the Wysiwyg add-in program, don't forget to copy the FMT file along with the WK1 file. If, for example, you give a copy of your worksheet to a co-worker without the FMT file, all your fancy formatting will fail to materialize when she attaches Wysiwyg and then retrieves the worksheet file. To avoid this kind of formatting loss, always keep the WK1 and FMT versions of the file together on the same disk and in the same directory. After all, you want to share your OZ experience with someone besides Toto.

Putting the Worksheet on Display

Wysiwyg gives you control over how most of the screen elements are displayed, including the colors used to represent each part, the appearance of the frame with the column letters and row numbers, and the use of grid lines showing the borders of each column and row in the worksheet. In addition to making the background pretty, you can change how many worksheet rows are displayed on the screen and zoom in and out on the data.

Well, color my cursor

If you have a color monitor, you can redesign the color scheme in the worksheet, using a palette with these eight colors:

| Black | White | Red | Green | Dark-Blue | Cyan | Yellow | Magenta |

To change the colors, choose the :**D**isplay **C**olors command and then specify what element to modify on this menu:

| Background | Text | Unprot | Cell-Pointer | Grid | Frame | Neg | Lines | Shadow | Replace | Quit |

Then choose the color you want to use from the palette of eight colors.

The menu items change the worksheet as follows:

- ✔ **Background** changes the color of all the cells in the worksheet (that is, everything but the frame). Wysiwyg normally uses white for the background color.

- ✔ **Text** changes the color of the characters in the cell entry. Wysiwyg uses black for text.

- ✔ **Unprot** changes the color used to represent characters in cells that you have unprotected with the /**R**ange **U**nprot command. Wysiwyg normally represents text in unprotected cells with dark-blue.

- ✔ **Cell-Pointer** changes the color of the cell pointer, which is normally cyan, the same color as the frame.

- ✔ **Grid** changes the color of the grid lines when they are displayed with the :**D**isplay **O**ptions **G**rid command (see next section for details). Normally the grid lines are magenta in Wysiwyg.

- ✔ **Frame** changes the background color of the row containing the column letters and the column containing the row numbers at the top and left of the worksheet. Wysiwyg normally represents the worksheet frame in cyan.

- ✔ **Neg** changes the color of negative numbers in the worksheet, which are usually black like all the other text. (Red, of course, is the natural choice for this option.)

✔ Lines changes the color of cell borders applied to cell ranges with the :Format Lines command. Wysiwyg normally represents cells borders in black.

✔ Shadow changes the color used for the shading in a drop shadow that is added with the :Format Lines Shadow command. Wysiwyg normally shows this shading in black.

✔ Replace modifies the hue of a particular palette color by changing its palette setting number.

After you change the screen colors, you can save the new Wysiwyg color scheme by choosing the :Display Default Update command. If, on the other hand, you made such a garish mess out of the screen colors that you never want to see this color scheme again, you can restore the previous colors by choosing the :Display Default Restore command.

Grid lock

Normally, the part of the 1-2-3 worksheet that you can see on the screen is just a big white rectangle. In Wysiwyg, however, you can add grid lines that clearly demarcate the borders of the columns and rows. To display grid lines, choose the :Display Options Grid command and then choose Yes.

As noted earlier in the chapter, whenever you attach Wysiwyg, the worksheet frame appears with lines that define the borders of each column and row. (This frame is called an *enhanced frame.*) When you display the grid lines in the worksheet, the grid lines appear as extensions of these lines on the frame.

You can change how the frame appears with the :Display Options Frame command. When you choose this command, the following menu lists options for the frame's appearance:

```
1-2-3     Enhanced     Relief     Special     None
```

✔ 1-2-3 gets rid of the lines that separate the columns and rows, so the frame looks the way it does when Wysiwyg isn't running.

✔ Enhanced returns to the normal Wysiwyg frame with dividing lines.

✔ Relief adds shading, giving the frame sort of a 3-D sculpted look (see Figure 10-1).

✔ Special replaces column letters and row numbers with on-screen measurements. When you choose this command, you can choose from Characters to display the number of characters and lines per inch, Inches to display the frame in inches, Metric to display it in centimeters, or Points/Picas to display the frame in points.

✔ None suppresses the display of the frame, thus maximizing the number of cells that are displayed on the screen. Note that when you choose this option the only way to tell the address of the cell pointer is by looking at the reference listed at the top of the control panel.

Figure 10-1 shows how the worksheet looks after you display the grid lines and choose **R**elief on the **:D**isplay **O**ptions **F**rame menu.

Zoom in, zoom out

Wysiwyg's **:D**isplay **Z**oom command makes it a snap to enlarge or reduce the size of the cells in the worksheet. You can enlarge the cells up to 400 percent of the normal size or reduce them down to a scant 25 percent.

✔ Enlarging cells gives you an ant's eye view by making the cells and their data appear larger and displaying fewer columns and rows on the screen.

✔ Reducing cells gives you a bird's eye view by making the cells and their data appear smaller and displaying more columns and rows.

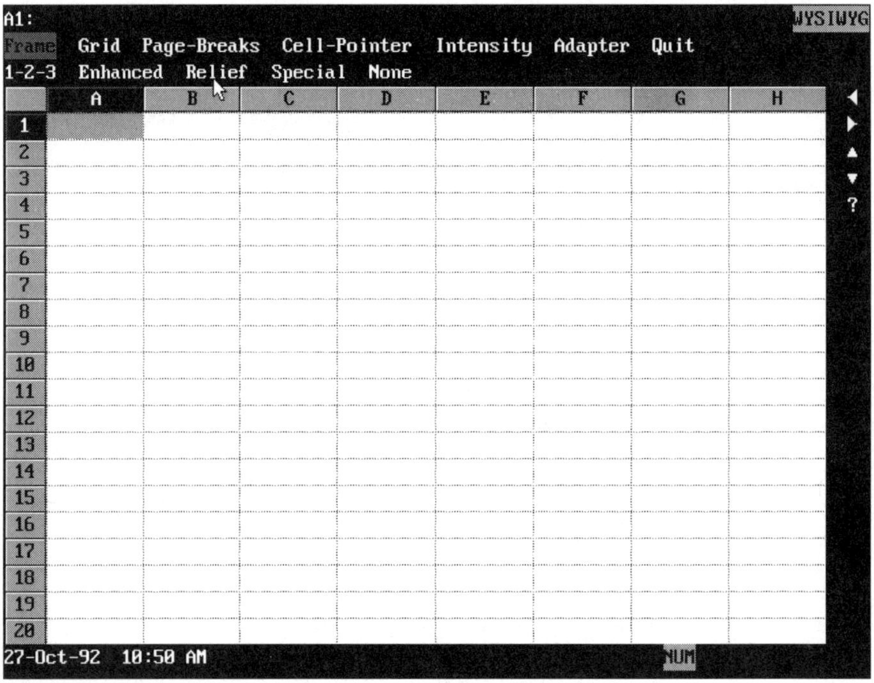

Figure 10-1: A worksheet with a relief frame and grid lines.

When you choose the :Display Zoom command, the following menu gives you a choice of size options:

    Tiny   Small   Normal   Large   Huge   Manual

▶ **Tiny** reduces the cells to 63% of the normal size (as shown in Figure 10-2).

▶ **Small** reduces the cells to 87% of the normal size.

▶ **Normal** restores the cells to the normal size.

▶ **Large** increases the cells to 125% of the normal size.

▶ **Huge** increases the cells to 150% of the normal size (as shown in Figure 10-3).

▶ **Manual** sets the cells to any percentage of normal size from a minimum of 25% to a maximum of 400%.

After you use one of these options to zoom in or out, Wysiwyg displays the percentage you've selected in the upper left corner of the frame. For example, in Figure 10-2, 63% appears in the upper left corner of the frame after you select the Tiny option, and, in Figure 10-3, 150% appears there after you select the Huge option.

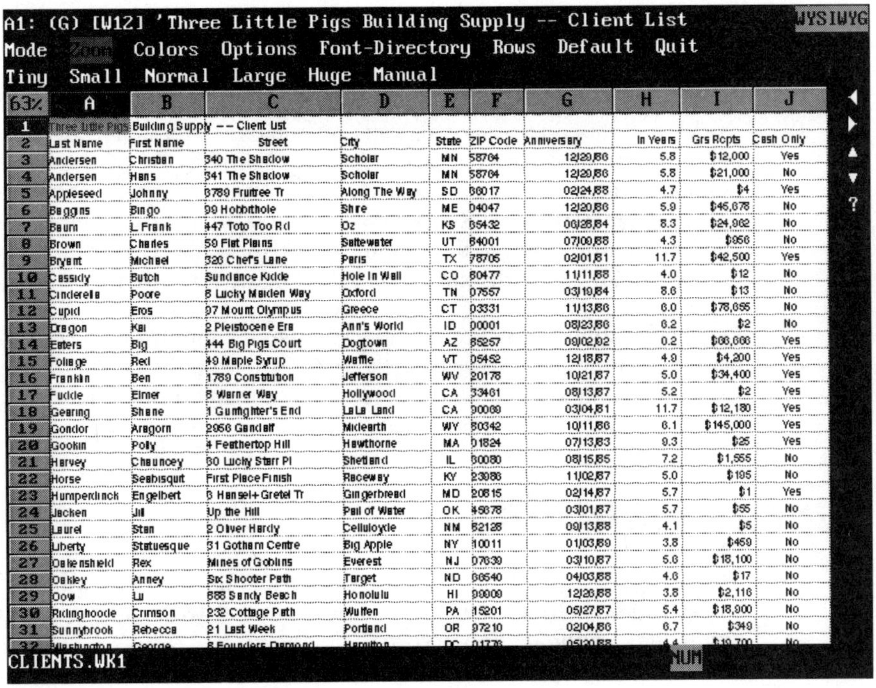

Figure 10-2: A worksheet displayed with the Tiny zoom option.

```
A1: (G) [W12] 'Three Little Pigs Building Supply -- Client List      WYSIWYG
Mode  Zoom   Colors  Options  Font-Directory  Rows  Default  Quit
Tiny  Small  Normal  Large   Huge   Manual
150%          A                 B                    C
   1 Three Little Pigs Building Supply -- Client List
   2 Last Name      First Name          Street         City
   3 Andersen       Christian     340 The Shadow       Schola
   4 Andersen       Hans          341 The Shadow       Schola
   5 Appleseed      Johnny        6789 Fruitree Tr     Along
   6 Baggins        Bingo         99 Hobbithole        Shire
   7 Baum           L. Frank      447 Toto Too Rd      Oz
   8 Brown          Charles       59 Flat Plains       Saltew
   9 Bryant         Michael       326 Chef's Lane      Paris
  10 Cassidy        Butch         Sundance Kidde       Hole In
  11 Cinderella     Poore         8 Lucky Maiden Way   Oxford
  12 Cupid          Eros          97 Mount Olympus     Greece
  13 Dragon         Kai           2 Pleistocene Era    Ann's
CLIENTS.WK1                                            NUM
```

Figure 10-3: A worksheet displayed with the **H**uge option.

Choosing the **:D**isplay **Z**oom command is not the only way to get more of the worksheet data on the screen. You also can use the **:D**isplay **R**ows command to set the number of rows that are displayed. Normally, Wysiwyg displays 20 rows of data on the screen at a time, just as the regular 1-2-3 worksheet does. After you choose the **:D**isplay **R**ows command, you can set the number of rows from a minimum of 16 rows to a maximum of 60 rows. Wysiwyg adjusts the size of the data as best it can to display the selected number of rows.

Figure 10-4 shows the Three Little Pigs Building Supply client list after you increase the number of rows from 20 to 34. Note that the entries appear somewhat squashed together in order to show so many rows at one time.

Fancy Formatting

The real power of Wysiwyg lies not so much in its ability to pretty up the worksheet screen as in its ability to pretty up the worksheet data. With the commands on the Wysiwyg **:F**ormat menu, you can transform the worksheet from its drab normal appearance, where all entries look exactly alike, to a much

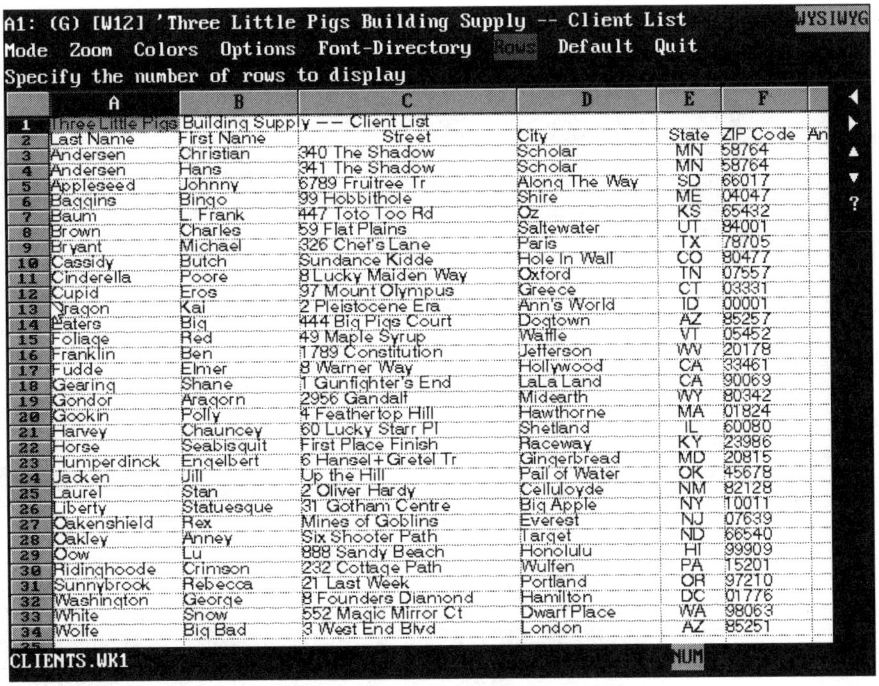

Figure 10-4: A worksheet displayed with the number of rows set to 34.

more dynamic look, where important data is emphasized through a combination of fonts, attributes, cell borders, and shading.

For a very *graphic* illustration of just this kind of transformation, compare the way the Three Little Pigs 1992 Sales worksheet appears in the normal text mode used by 1-2-3 with the way it looks in Wysiwyg's graphics mode after you format its data. Figure 10-5 shows the plain vanilla worksheet as it normally appears (and prints) in text mode in 1-2-3. Figure 10-6 shows the same worksheet as it appears (and prints) in Wysiwyg's graphics mode after you format its data with a combination of new fonts, font attributes, cell borders, and shading.

Tripping the light fontastic

When you install Wysiwyg, the Install program creates a series of different fonts using such typefaces as Bitstream Swiss (better known as Helvetica), Courier, Dutch (better known as Times Roman), and Dingbats (yes, Archie, Dingbats) in various point sizes. When you format cell entries with the Wysiwyg :Format Font command, you can choose from a set of eight of these different fonts (which are conveniently numbered **1** through **8** on the menu). Keep in mind

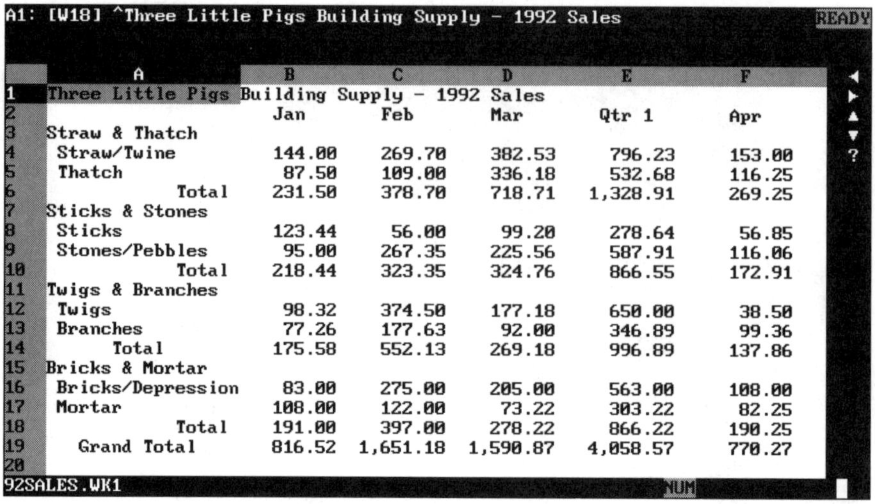

```
A1: [W18] ^Three Little Pigs Building Supply - 1992 Sales            READY

        A            B        C        D          E          F       ◄
1  Three Little Pigs Building Supply - 1992 Sales                    ►
2                     Jan      Feb      Mar        Qtr 1      Apr     ▲
3  Straw & Thatch                                                    ▼
4     Straw/Twine    144.00   269.70   382.53     796.23     153.00  ?
5     Thatch          87.50   109.00   336.18     532.68     116.25
6           Total    231.50   378.70   718.71   1,328.91     269.25
7  Sticks & Stones
8     Sticks         123.44    56.00    99.20     278.64      56.85
9     Stones/Pebbles  95.00   267.35   225.56     587.91     116.06
10          Total    218.44   323.35   324.76     866.55     172.91
11 Twigs & Branches
12    Twigs           98.32   374.50   177.18     650.00      38.50
13    Branches        77.26   177.63    92.00     346.89      99.36
14          Total    175.58   552.13   269.18     996.89     137.86
15 Bricks & Mortar
16    Bricks/Depression 83.00 275.00   205.00     563.00     108.00
17 Mortar            108.00   122.00    73.22     303.22      82.25
18          Total    191.00   397.00   278.22     866.22     190.25
19   Grand Total     816.52 1,651.18 1,590.87   4,058.57     770.27
20
92SALES.WK1                                                     NUM
```

Figure 10-5: The 1992 Sales worksheet as it appears in normal text mode on the 1-2-3 screen.

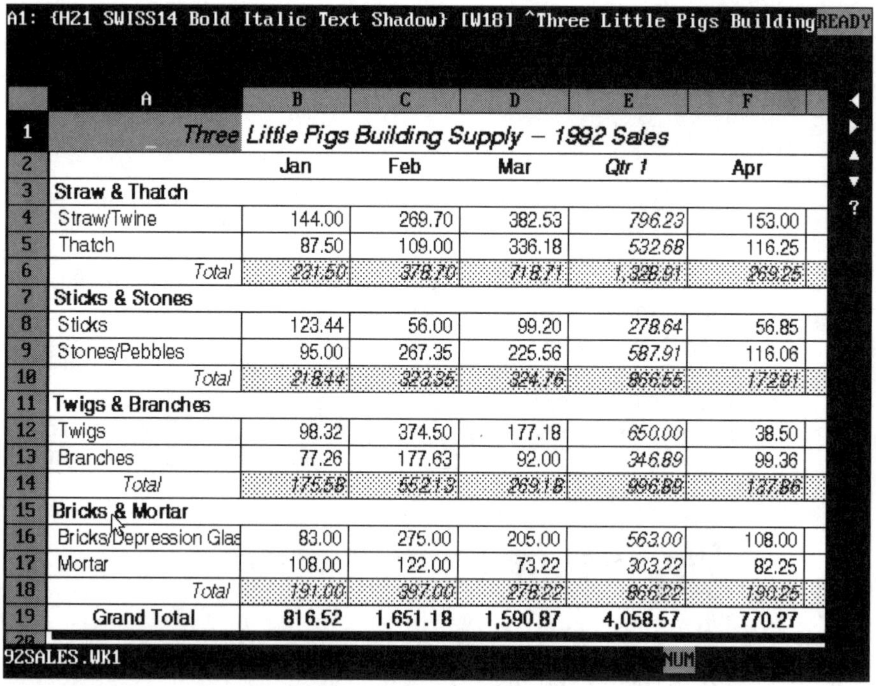

```
A1: {H21 SWISS14 Bold Italic Text Shadow} [W18] ^Three Little Pigs Building READY

          A          B        C        D          E          F       ◄
1        Three Little Pigs Building Supply - 1992 Sales              ►
2                     Jan      Feb      Mar        Qtr 1      Apr     ▲
3  Straw & Thatch                                                    ▼
4  Straw/Twine       144.00   269.70   382.53     796.23     153.00  ?
5  Thatch             87.50   109.00   336.18     532.68     116.25
6           Total    231.50   378.70   718.71   1,328.91     269.25
7  Sticks & Stones
8  Sticks            123.44    56.00    99.20     278.64      56.85
9  Stones/Pebbles     95.00   267.35   225.56     587.91     116.06
10          Total    218.44   323.35   324.76     866.55     172.91
11 Twigs & Branches
12 Twigs              98.32   374.50   177.18     650.00      38.50
13 Branches           77.26   177.63    92.00     346.89      99.36
14          Total    175.58   552.13   269.18     996.89     137.86
15 Bricks & Mortar
16 Bricks/Depression Glas 83.00 275.00 205.00     563.00     108.00
17 Mortar            108.00   122.00    73.22     303.22      82.25
18          Total    191.00   397.00   278.22     866.22     190.25
19   Grand Total     816.52 1,651.18 1,590.87   4,058.57     770.27
20
92SALES.WK1                                                     NUM
```

Figure 10-6: The 1992 Sales worksheet as it appears in Wysiwyg's graphics mode with formatting applied.

that the number 1 font in the set is the font that Wysiwyg automatically assigns to all the cells in the worksheet.

To choose a new font in the set and apply it to the text in a range of cells, you follow these steps:

1. Choose the **:Format Font** command.

2. Choose the number of the font you want to use from the menu on the control panel or in the Wysiwyg Font Selection dialog box.

3. Select the range to which you want to apply the font.

Wysiwyg indicates the font change for the current cell by listing its name enclosed in curly braces after the cell address on the first line of the control panel. For example, if you select Bitstream Swiss 14 Point as the new font in the current cell, you see the following listed after the cell address:

```
{SWISS14}
```

Figure 10-7 shows the **:Format Font** menu, as well as the Wysiwyg Font Selection dialog box that appears when you choose **:Format Font**.

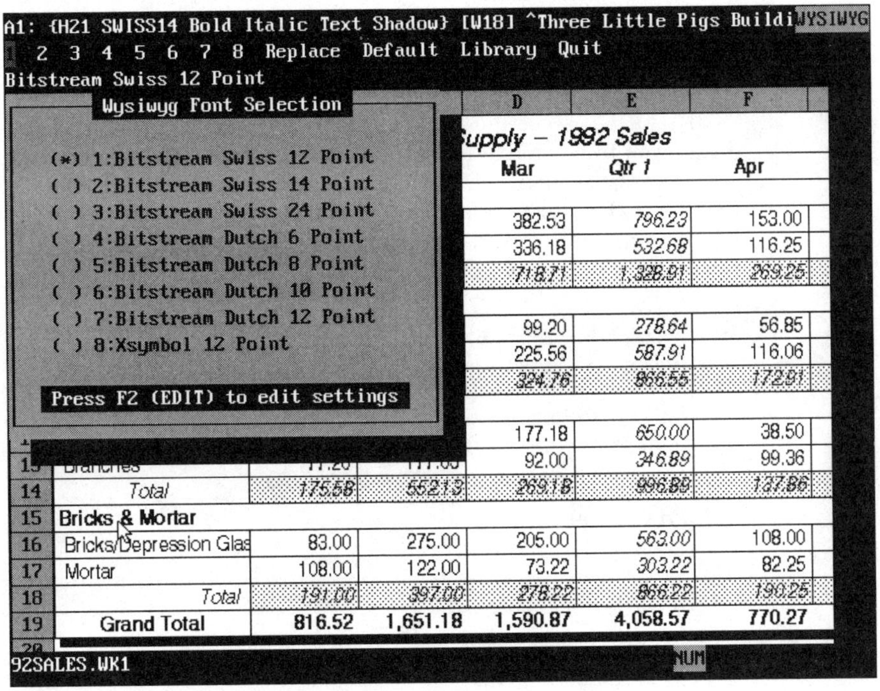

```
A1: {H21 SWISS14 Bold Italic Text Shadow} [W18] ^Three Little Pigs BuildiWYSIWYG
   2  3  4  5  6  7  8  Replace  Default  Library  Quit
Bitstream Swiss 12 Point
```

	Wysiwyg Font Selection	D	E	F
		Supply – 1992 Sales		
		Mar	Qtr 1	Apr
(*) 1:Bitstream Swiss 12 Point		382.53	796.23	153.00
( ) 2:Bitstream Swiss 14 Point		336.18	532.68	116.25
( ) 3:Bitstream Swiss 24 Point		718.71	1,328.91	269.25
( ) 4:Bitstream Dutch 6 Point				
( ) 5:Bitstream Dutch 8 Point		99.20	278.64	56.85
( ) 6:Bitstream Dutch 10 Point		225.56	587.91	116.06
( ) 7:Bitstream Dutch 12 Point		324.76	866.55	172.91
( ) 8:Xsymbol 12 Point				
		177.18	650.00	38.50
Press F2 (EDIT) to edit settings		92.00	346.89	99.36

13	Branches	77.20	111.05		
14	Total	175.58	552.13	269.18	996.89	137.86
15	Bricks & Mortar				
16	Bricks/Depression Glas	83.00	275.00	205.00	563.00	108.00
17	Mortar	108.00	122.00	73.22	303.22	82.25
18	Total	191.00	397.00	278.22	866.22	190.25
19	Grand Total	816.52	1,651.18	1,590.87	4,058.57	770.27

```
9ZSALES.WK1                                                    NUM
```

Figure 10-7: The Wysiwyg Font Selection dialog box.

If you're using Release 2.3 or 2.4, you can select the cell range with the F4 (Abs) key (position the cell pointer in the first cell of the range, press F4 [Abs] to anchor the range, use the cursor keys to move the cell pointer and highlight the range, and press Enter) or with the mouse before you choose the font on the :Format Font menu. You can use this nifty technique — selecting the range you want to format before you choose the formatting command — with the other commands on the :Format menu as well.

The fonts that 1-2-3 assigns to the font set shown in the Wysiwyg Font Selection dialog box are not carved in stone. You can change any of the default assignments by replacing it with another installed font. To replace a particular font in the current font set, you follow these steps:

1. Choose the :Format Font **R**eplace command.

2. Choose the number of the font you want to replace (**1** through **8**) and press Enter.

3. Choose the name of the typeface you want to use (such as **S**wiss, **D**utch, or **C**ourier) and press Enter.

4. Enter the type size in points (3 through 72) and press Enter.

That's all there is to it!

- ✔ If, after you change fonts, you decide that you want to restore the original set, choose the :Format Font **D**efault **R**estore command.

- ✔ If you want to make the changes to the font set permanent, choose the :Format Font **D**efault **U**pdate command.

If you want to be able to reuse a particular combination of fonts but maintain access to the original (default) font set, you can save the changes in a special font library file. When you have a font library file, you can replace the default font set simply by retrieving the font library. You don't have to go through the rigmarole of replacing individual fonts in the default set each time.

To save replacements to a font set in a font library file, follow these steps:

1. Choose the :Format Font **L**ibrary **S**ave command.

2. Enter the filename in response to the `Enter the name of the fontset library:` prompt. Wysiwyg automatically tacks on the extension AFS to any main filename that you enter.

3. Press Enter.

To have access to the fonts in a font library file so that you can use them in a worksheet, follow these steps:

1. Choose the **:Format Font Library R**etrieve command.

2. Highlight the name of the font library file in the control panel.

3. Press Enter.

As soon as you select the library file, its fonts replace those in the current font set, and you can use them by choosing the appropriate font number on the **:Format Font** menu (to restore the default font set, you choose the **:Format Font Default R**estore command).

Unless you have lots and lots of free computer memory lying around that you don't need for more important things (such as storing more worksheet data), keep the number of different fonts in a worksheet to a minimum. Wysiwyg fonts are real memory hogs! (No offense, Three Little Pigs.) Instead of changing the font, try using the bold and italics attributes when you need to differentiate and emphasize particular ranges in the worksheet.

May I be so bold?

Wysiwyg supports three different attributes that you can apply to the text in a cell range — bold, italics, and underlining. When you select one of these attributes, it is added to whatever font is currently assigned to the cells in the range you select.

Each attribute command, **B**old, **I**talics, and **U**nderline, on the **:Format** menu works the same way. After you choose the **B**old or **I**talics attribute command, you are given a choice between a **S**et command and a **C**lear command. When you choose **U**nderline, you can choose from four options: **S**ingle, **D**ouble, **W**ide, and **C**lear.

✔ When you want to add the attribute, choose the **S**et (or the type of underline) command and then designate the cell or cell range where you want to apply it.

✔ When you want to remove the attribute, choose the **C**lear command and then designate the cell or cell range to remove it from.

Note that when you use the **:Format U**nderline command, Wysiwyg underlines only the text in the cells in the specified range, not the cell borders. If you want to add an underline to cells in the range, you use the **:Format L**ines command. (See "On the borderline," later in this chapter, for details.)

Color me

The :Format Color command enables you to change either the color of the text in a specified cell range or the background color of the cells. You cannot, however, turn color on or off in a particular cell range, as you can the **Bold** and **Italics** attributes. When you choose the :Format Color command, the program presents you with the following choices:

Text	Background	Negative	Reverse	Quit

✔ To choose a new color for the text in a particular range, choose the **Text** command and then pick from the following options:

Normal	Red	Green	Dark-Blue	Cyan	Yellow	Magenta

Choose the **Normal** option when you want to return to the default color (black), or choose one of the other six color options. Then specify the cell range to which you want to apply the color.

✔ To change the fill color in a cell range, choose the **Background** command on the :Format Color menu and repeat the same process as for the **Text** command.

✔ If you want to display negative values in red, choose the **Negative** and **Red** commands and then specify the cell range.

✔ If you want to reverse the colors so that the text color becomes the background color and vice versa, choose the **Reverse** command and then specify the range. Figure 10-8 shows how this reverse effect looks in black and white. The :Format Color Reverse command has been applied to cell range B2..E2, which contains the table's column headings. Because the standard black text on a white background is used, the **Reverse** command creates the effect of a white text on a black background.

B2: {White / Black} [W12] ^January						READY

	A	B	C	D	E	F
1		*Three Little Pigs Building Supply — Quarter 1 1994 Sales*				
2		January	February	March	Q1 Total	
3	Straw & Thatch	421.35	602.00	733.03	$1,756.38	
4	Sticks & Stones	645.75	700.15	790.50	$2,136.40	
5	Bricks & Mortar	1,453.00	1,560.20	1,918.80	$4,932.00	
6	Total	$2,520.10	$2,862.35	$3,442.33	$8,824.78	
7						
8						

Figure 10-8: A worksheet with the :Format Color Reverse applied to the column headings.

Keep in mind that the colors you assign to cell ranges appear only on your color monitor unless you are also printing in Wysiwyg with a color printer. (See "Printing the Wysiwyg Way," later in this chapter, for information on how to print with this add-in.)

On the borderline

Grid lines displayed with the :Display Options Grid command are just guidelines to help you keep your place as you work. You can print them with the data or not, as you choose. To emphasize sections of the worksheet or parts of a particular table, you can add borderlines and/or shading to certain cell ranges. Unlike grid lines, which are not automatically printed with the worksheet data, borderlines added to ranges are always printed when these ranges are printed.

To add borderlines to a cell range, choose the :Format Lines command and then choose the appropriate option from this menu:

Outline   Left   Right   Top   Bottom   All   Double   Wide   Clear   Shadow

- ✔ Choose the **O**utline command when you want borderlines drawn around the outside edges of the *entire* cell range that you specify.

- ✔ To draw borderlines around one particular edge of the cell range, choose the appropriate direction (**L**eft, **R**ight, **T**op, or **B**ottom).

- ✔ To create borderlines around all four edges of each cell in the specified cell range, choose the **A**ll command.

- ✔ Normally, Wysiwyg draws the borderlines with a single line, but you also have the options of double lines or thick lines. To use a double line, choose the **D**ouble command on the :Format Lines menu and then designate where the double lines are to be drawn by choosing from these options before you specify the cell range:

    Outline   Left   Right   Top   Bottom   All

- ✔ To use a thick line, choose the **W**ide command on the :Format Lines menu and then specify which borders to apply to which cell range. Figure 10-9 shows the Three Little Pigs 1994 First Quarter sales table with a wide borderline at the top edge of the range B6..E6 and a double borderline at the bottom of the same range.

- ✔ When you want to add a *drop-shadow* effect to a range to make it appear three-dimensional, you can draw a thick borderline on just the bottom and right edges. Choose the :Format Lines Shadow Set command and then specify the range where you want the effect added. Figure 10-10 shows the same first quarter sales table with the addition of a drop shadow to cell range A1..E7.

> ✔ To get rid of borderlines, you must choose the **:Format Lines Clear** command and then specify which borders to remove before you select the cell or cell range that presently contains the lines. To remove a drop shadow, you choose the **:Format Lines Shadow Clear** command, instead, and then specify the range where it should be removed.

Just let me put my shades on

You also can add emphasis to particular sections of the worksheet or to one of its tables by shading them. To shade a range, you choose the **:Format Shade** command and then choose the type of shading:

```
Light    Dark    Solid    Clear
```

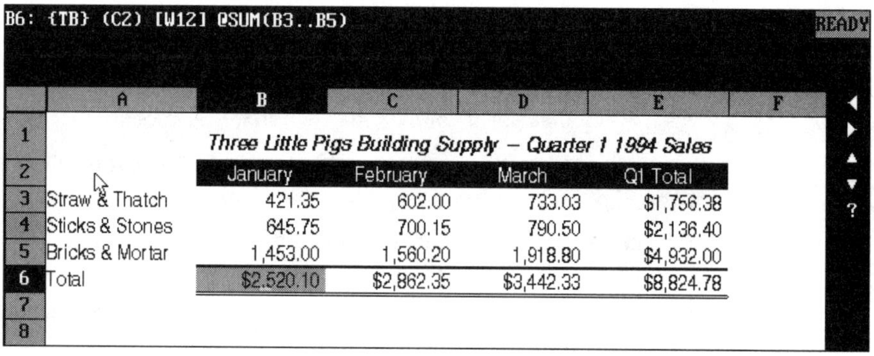

Figure 10-9: A worksheet with wide and double line cell borders in cell range B6..E6.

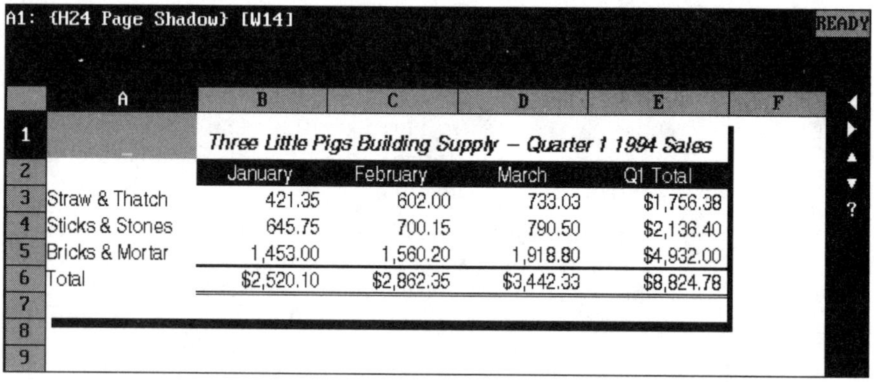

Figure 10-10: A worksheet with a drop shadow added to the entire table.

Next you specify the range to be shaded.

Shading is produced by almost all printers by adding patterns of dots to the specified area on the paper.

- ✔ Stick to either the **L**ight or **D**ark command when you are shading cell ranges with cell entries.

- ✔ If you use the **S**olid command on cell ranges that contain entries, you won't be able to see them anymore! Instead, reserve this command for adding extra bold borders to separate sections of the worksheet or to different parts of a table. To add such borders, first apply the solid shading to the part of a blank row or blank column that you want to use to divide the table and then narrow the column or row until the shading appears as a heavy border.

- ✔ To remove shading from cells, choose the **:**Format **S**hade **C**lear command and then specify the range that presently contains the shading.

You're just my style!

Named styles are Wysiwyg's way of bringing many different kinds of formatting, including a new font, various attributes, cell borderlines, and shading, all together under one roof. In Wysiwyg you can define up to eight different named styles that you can use in any worksheet. When you apply a named style to a cell range, all the formatting that is part of that style is applied to its cells.

Creating a named style is as easy as falling off a log:

1. Use the appropriate **:**Format commands to format one of the cell entries in the worksheet so that it uses all the formatting that you want to include in the new style.

2. Choose the **:**Named-Style **D**efine command.

3. Select the number (from **1** through **8**) of the style that you want to redefine. (When you start out, all eight styles are *Normal styles,* which restore a cell range to its rather bland default formatting. Believe me, one Normal is plenty.)

4. Move the cell pointer to the cell that contains the formatting you want in the new style and press Enter.

5. Replace the default style name Normal with a new name up to 6 characters long and press Enter.

6. Type a description of the style (up to 37 characters long) that will appear on the third line of the control panel when you highlight this style on the **:**Named-Style menu; then press Enter.

After you define styles in this manner, here's what you need to do to apply them to a range:

1. Position the cell pointer in the first cell of the range to be formatted.

2. Choose the :Named-Style command.

3. Choose the number of the style (**1** through **8**).

4. Extend the range to include all the cells to be formatted.

5. Press Enter.

Columns that fit like a glove

All this fancy Wysiwyg formatting can really play havoc with the column widths in a worksheet. (Surprisingly, many times the columns are too wide after you use the Wysiwyg fonts.) When you need to reset the width of a column or a range of columns, you can use either the good old /Worksheet Column Set-Width (or Column-Range) command in 1-2-3 or the :Worksheet Column Set-Width command in Wysiwyg. Unless you feel like doing some extra work, you'll probably want to use the menu that's active at the time you decide to modify the column width.

When you use the Wysiwyg version of the Set-Width command, Wysiwyg prompts you to select the range of columns to use. (If you want to set only the current column, you just press Enter.) After you define the range, you set the new column width by entering the number of characters (from 1 to 240) that you want to be able to fit in the column or by pressing → or ← and then pressing Enter.

If you're handy with the mouse, you can reset the width of a column by dragging the column's right border to the left to make it skinnier or to the right to make it fatter. How do you do this trick?

1. Position the mouse pointer on the right edge of the frame.

2. Hold down the left mouse button until the pointer changes from the normal arrowhead shape to a double-headed arrow.

3. Start dragging the border right or left.

    As you drag, Wysiwyg shows you the right border of the column as a grid line extending down the worksheet.

4. When this grid line is positioned where you want it, release the left mouse button to set the column width at that place.

Rambling rows

In the normal 1-2-3 worksheet, you don't need to change the height of the rows. In Wysiwyg, however, you need to be able to change the row height to accommodate changes in the font size (especially, when you use larger font sizes). The story with adjusting the height of rows in Wysiwyg is pretty much the same as adjusting columns, except that you do a lot less row adjusting than you do column adjusting. Wysiwyg automatically changes the height of a row to accommodate changes to its entries, such as a change to a larger font. Nevertheless, sometimes you want to adjust a row height manually to give it just a little bit more or a little bit less space.

To adjust the height of a row or range of rows with the keyboard, you follow these steps:

1. Position the cell pointer somewhere in the first row that you want to change.

2. Choose the :**W**orksheet **R**ow **S**et-Height command.

   Wysiwyg then prompts you to specify the range of rows to change.

3. Indicate the range or press Enter if you want to change only the current row.

4. Enter the new row height in points (between 1 and 255) or press ↑ or ↓ until the row (or row range) is the height you want.

5. Press Enter.

You mouse users can put your pets to work when you want to change the height of a row:

1. Position the mouse pointer on the bottom border of the frame for the row.

2. Hold down the left mouse button until the mouse pointer changes to a double-headed arrow pointing up and down.

3. Drag the mouse up to shorten the row or down to heighten the row.

4. When the row is the height you want it to be, release the left mouse button to set the new row height.

Getting Graphs into the Worksheet

With Wysiwyg, you can not only add 1-2-3 graphs directly to a range in the worksheet but also print them as part of the worksheet (see the next section for printing information). Wysiwyg makes those trips to the PrintGraph utility obsolete. When you add graphs to a worksheet, you can add either named graphs saved as part of the worksheet or graphs saved in separate PIC graphics files. (See Chapter 7 if you need a review of how to name 1-2-3 graphs and/or save them in separate graphics files.)

To add a 1-2-3 graph to a worksheet range requires only a few steps:

1. Position the cell pointer in the first cell of the range in the worksheet where you want to put the graph.

2. Choose the **:G**raph **A**dd command.

3. To add the current graph to the worksheet, choose the **C**urrent command (remember that you can always view the current graph in READY mode by pressing the F10 [Graph] key). To add a named graph that isn't the current one, choose the **N**amed command, highlight the graph name in the control panel, and press Enter. To add a graph saved in a graphics file in the PIC file format, choose the **P**IC command, choose the PIC file on the control panel, and press Enter.

4. Type a period to anchor the worksheet range to hold the graph, extend it as needed, and press Enter in response to the Enter the graphic display range: prompt.

When you press Enter, Wysiwyg draws the graph in the specified range. Note that if the cell range you specified as the graphic display range contains entries, the graph covers them up but does not wipe them out (as is usually the case when you enter new values in the same cells in 1-2-3). You can think of graphs (as well as any other graphics) that you add to the worksheet as floating on top of the worksheet itself, obscuring any data in the cells beneath the graph.

Figure 10-11 shows the first quarter 1994 sales worksheet for the Three Little Pigs Building Supply after you add the graph named Vert_Bar to the cell range A9..E19. Wysiwyg indicates the presence of the graph by including the following information after the cell address in the control panel:

```
{Page Graph VERT_BAR}
```

You see this indicator whenever you move the cell pointer into any cell in the graphic display range. If you add a graph saved in a PIC file, the name of the graphics file, rather than the name of the graph, appears in the curly braces.

If you find that the screen response becomes somewhat sluggish after you add a graph to the worksheet, you can temporarily hide the graph by choosing the **:G**raph **S**ettings **D**isplay **N**o command, selecting a cell in the graphic display range, and pressing Enter. Wysiwyg then replaces the graph with a shaded rectangle in the graphic display range, and the screen should speed up. Be sure to redisplay the graph in the worksheet with the **:G**raph **S**ettings **D**isplay **Y**es command, however, before you try to print this cell range.

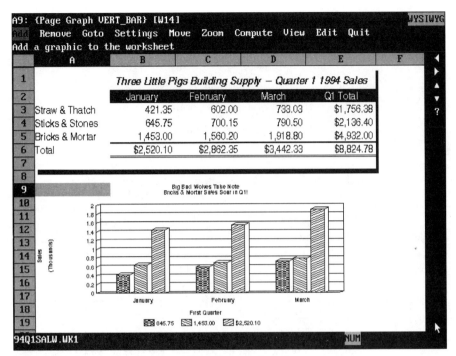

A9: {Page Graph VERT_BAR} [W14]

	A	B	C	D	E	F

Figure 10-11: A worksheet after the addition of a named graph.

Moving, resizing, replacing, or nixing a graph

After you add a graph to a cell range in the worksheet, you can't just move, resize, or delete it as you would with normal cell entries in a range. For example, if you want to move or change the size of a graph, you need to choose the Wysiwyg :**G**raph **S**ettings **R**ange command, instead of using the 1-2-3 /**M**ove command. The program then asks you to select the graph to resize. To select a graph, all you have to do is put the cell pointer in one of the cells of the graphic display range and press Enter. Wysiwyg then highlights the graphic display range so that you can move and/or resize the graph by redefining the cell range. Select the new cell range, press Enter, and, presto, Wysiwyg redraws the graph in the new range.

To replace one graph with another, follow these steps:

1. Choose the :**G**raph **S**ettings **G**raph command.

2. Select the graph to replace by positioning the cell pointer in one of the cells in its graphic display range and pressing Enter.

3. Select the type of graph (**C**urrent, **N**amed or **P**IC) and then, if applicable, its graph name or graphics filename.

4. Press Enter.

Removing a graph from a worksheet is even easier:

1. Choose the **:G**raph **R**emove command.

2. Select the graph to be removed.

3. Press Enter.

Note that if you placed the graph over some existing cell entries, they miraculously reappear as soon as you delete the graph that covered them.

You can use the **:G**raph **G**oto command to quickly select a graph in the worksheet. When you choose this command, Wysiwyg displays a list of all the graphs added to the worksheet. (The current graph is designated by `<CURRENT>`; all the others are listed by name.) Highlight the name of the graph you want to move to in this list and then press Enter. Wysiwyg moves the cell pointer to the first cell in the graphic display range specified for this graph.

Adding other graphics to the worksheet

Graphs aren't the only kind of graphics that you can add to the worksheet. Wysiwyg also reads graphics saved in the so-called Metafile graphics format, which uses the CGM file extension instead of PIC. This format is generated by other Lotus Development products, such as 1-2-3 for Windows and Freelance Plus.

Even if you don't own these programs, you have access to a number of Metafile graphics within Release 2.3 or 2.4 of 1-2-3. To add one of these graphics to a worksheet, follow these steps:

1. Choose the **:G**raph **A**dd **M**etafile command.

   Wysiwyg displays a list of all the Metafile graphics files (ending in the file extension CGM).

2. Highlight the name of the graphics file you want to use and press Enter.

3. Specify the cell range where you want the graphics image displayed and press Enter.

Figure 10-12 shows the first quarter 1994 sales worksheet for the Three Little Pigs Building Supply after you add the Metafile graphic image in FARM.CGM (what else for the Three Little Pigs?) to the cell range A1..A2 in the upper left corner of the sales table.

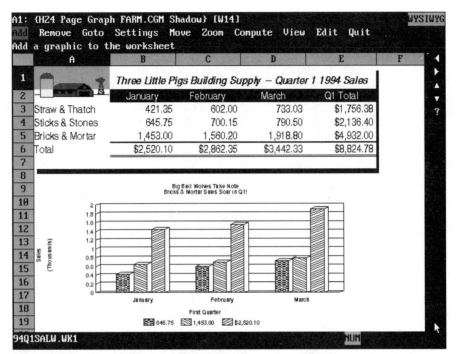

Figure 10-12: A worksheet with the farm graphic added in the upper left corner of the table.

 To preview a graph saved in a PIC graphics file or one of the images saved in a Metafile graphics file, follow these steps:

1. Choose the **:G**raph **V**iew command.

2. Choose the **P**IC or **M**etafile option.

3. Highlight the name of the graphics file you want to see.

4. Press Enter.

Wysiwyg then draws the graph or graphic image full screen. After you finish viewing the graphic, press any key to return to the **:G**raph menu.

Printing the Wysiwyg Way

To print all the wonderful enhancements that you add to the worksheet with Wysiwyg, you need to print the worksheet from this add-in program. If you print with the 1-2-3 **/P**rint **P**rinter command, the document loses all its great Wysiwyg

formatting. Fortunately, printing with Wysiwyg is very similar to printing with
1-2-3. If anything, printing is even easier because Wysiwyg gives you greater
control over the printout and you can preview the printout before you actually
start printing it. (Think of the reams of paper you'll save!)

To print with Wysiwyg, you use the :**P**rint command instead of the /**P**rint
Printer command. As soon as you choose this command, Wysiwyg shows you
all the current print settings in the Wysiwyg Print Settings dialog box, which is
shown below the :**P**rint menu in Figure 10-13. Before you can print using these
settings, you need to see a range listed in the Print Range text box (below the
Configuration settings on the left side).

If no print range has been set, define the range:

1. Choose the **R**ange **S**et command on the :**P**rint menu.

2. Move the cell pointer to the first cell, anchor the range with the period,
   extend the range to include all cells to be printed, and press Enter (just as
   you do when you specify a print range with the /**P**rint **P**rinter **R**ange command).

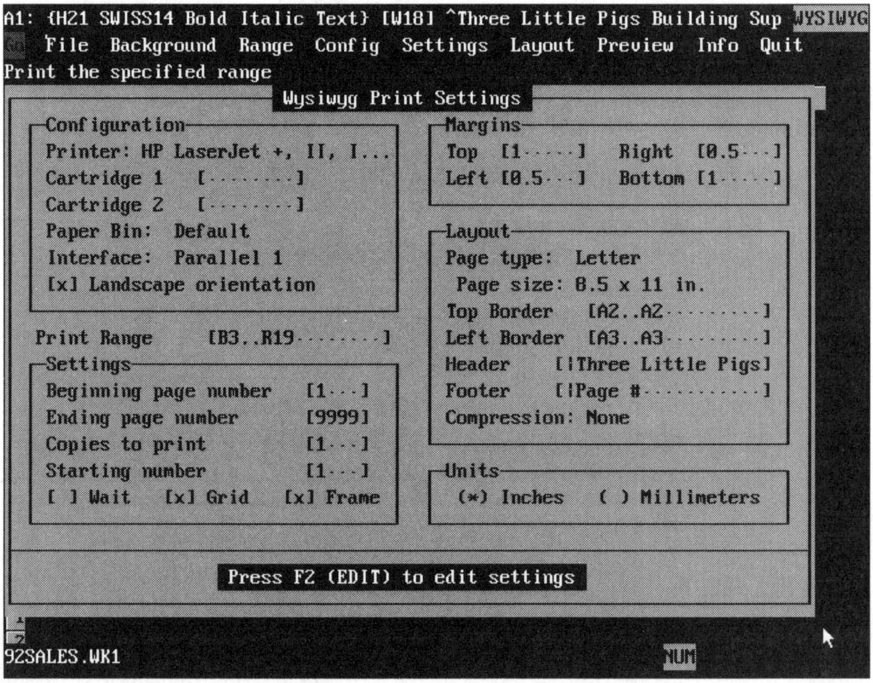

Figure 10-13: The :Print menu with the Wysiwyg Print Settings dialog box.

After you specify the print range (which now is listed in the Print Range text box), look over the other settings in the Wysiwyg Print Settings dialog box to make sure they're okay.

- ✔ If the print range includes a graph or other graphics images, be sure that the printer listed in the Printer text box in the Configuration section can print graphics. If you need to change printers, choose the **C**onfig **P**rinter command on the **:P**rint menu and then choose the appropriate printer in the Printer List dialog box.

- ✔ Wysiwyg can print reports in landscape orientation (horizontally, rather than vertically) with many printers. To print a report in landscape mode, choose the **C**onfig **O**rientation **L**andscape command on the **:P**rint menu or just select the **L**andscape orientation check box in the **C**onfiguration section of the Wysiwyg Print Settings dialog box.

In the **S**ettings section of this dialog box, you can specify such things as how many copies to print, the range of pages to be printed, and the starting number (which designates which page number to start with when you used the # symbol in your report header or footer).

- ✔ Choose the **W**ait check box if you need to feed the paper manually so that Wysiwyg will pause after printing each report page and prompt you to continue printing.

- ✔ Choose the **G**rid check box to print the grid lines as part of the report.

- ✔ Choose the **F**rame check box to print the frame with the column letters and row numbers on each page of the report.

- ✔ In the **M**argins section of the Wysiwyg Print Settings dialog box, you can adjust the margin settings for the top, left, right, or bottom margin by selecting the appropriate text box (**T**op, **L**eft, **R**ight, or **B**ottom) and entering the new value. Note that when you set new margins in Wysiwyg, you specify all margin settings in inches (assuming the **I**nches option button is selected in the **U**nits section instead of the **M**illimeters button), as measured from the edge of the paper. (This method is quite unlike setting margins in 1-2-3, where the left and right margins are set in characters from the left edge and the top and bottom margins are set in the number of lines from the top and bottom edges.)

- ✔ In the **L**ayout section of the dialog box, you can change the page size by selecting the **P**age type option and then selecting the desired size option button in the Page Type dialog box that appears.

- ✔ To set border rows and columns for a report, choose the **T**op Border and **L**eft Border options and specify the range of rows or columns in the accompanying text boxes. (Specifying these ranges is just like specifying the ranges for the border rows and columns for a report printed with 1-2-3, so you need to be sure that the print range doesn't include the cells in the border rows and columns.)

✔ To enter a header or footer for a report, choose the **Header** or **Footer** option and enter the text in the associated text box. (You can use the # symbol to print page numbers, the @ symbol to print the current date, and the | symbol to align the text of the header or footer, just as you do with 1-2-3 reports. See Chapter 6 for details.)

✔ The last option in the **Layout** section of the Wysiwyg Print Settings dialog box is called **Compression**. When you select this option, a Compression dialog box appears. You use this box to choose from **None**, **Manual**, and **Automatic** if the printer is capable of resizing the printing by set percentages. To set the percentage by which the printing should be compressed or expanded in the printout, choose the **Manual** option button and then choose the **Ratio** option in the Manual dialog box and enter the percentage between 1 and 1000 in its text box (100 is full size, which is the same as no compression, so a percentage below 100 compresses the type and a percentage above 100 expands the type). To have Wysiwyg automatically set the compression percentage so that the print range fits on one page, choose the **Automatic** option button in the Compression dialog box.

After you check all the print settings in the Wysiwyg Print Settings dialog box and change the ones that need modification, you are ready to preview the printout by choosing the **Preview** command on the **:P**rint menu. When you choose this command, Wysiwyg displays a full-screen view of the first page of the report as it will be printed, including any header or footer. The margin settings for the report are shown with dotted lines that form a rectangle. To see the next page of the report in Print Preview, press PgDn or Enter. (When you reach the last page, you can press either of these keys to return immediately to the **:P**rint menu.) If you want to review a previous page, press PgUp. If you want to return to the **:P**rint menu before you reach the last page of the report, press Esc.

Figure 10-14 shows the Print Preview screen with the first page of the Three Little Pigs Building Supply 1992 Sales Report (the report featured in Figures 6-4 and 6-5). Here, as you can see, the landscape orientation is selected and both the worksheet **G**rid and **F**rame options are being used.

When you are back in the **:P**rint menu, you can either adjust the settings as needed in the Wysiwyg Print Settings dialog box or, if everything is okay, you can print the report by choosing the **G**o command. (Wysiwyg has no **A**lign command. This add-in program can keep track of its place on the page without being told when to start counting lines.) After you choose **G**o, the **:P**rint menu disappears, and the program goes into WAIT mode as Wysiwyg sends the print range data to the printer. Wysiwyg keeps you informed of its progress in printing the report by displaying the percentage sent to the printer of each page that's being printed. When Wysiwyg finishes sending all of the last page included in the print job, the program automatically returns to READY mode so that you can resume working in 1-2-3 or in Wysiwyg.

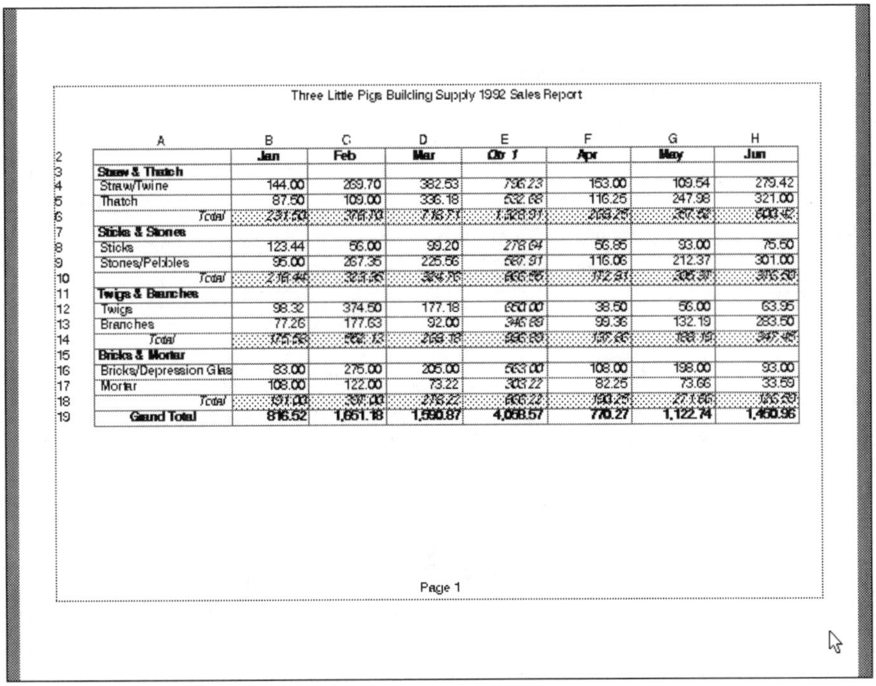

Three Little Pigs Building Supply 1992 Sales Report

	A	B	C	D	E	F	G	H
2		Jan	Feb	Mar	Qtr 1	Apr	May	Jun
3	Straw & Thatch							
4	Straw/Twine	144.00	269.70	382.53	796.23	153.00	109.54	279.42
5	Thatch	87.50	109.00	336.18	532.68	116.25	247.98	321.00
6	Total	231.50	378.70	718.71	1,328.91	269.25	357.52	600.42
7	Sticks & Stones							
8	Sticks	123.44	56.00	99.20	278.64	56.85	93.00	75.50
9	Stones/Pebbles	95.00	267.35	225.56	587.91	116.06	212.37	301.00
10	Total	218.44	323.35	324.76	866.55	172.91	305.37	376.50
11	Twigs & Branches							
12	Twigs	98.32	374.50	177.18	650.00	38.50	56.00	63.95
13	Branches	77.26	177.63	92.00	346.89	99.36	132.19	283.50
14	Total	175.58	552.13	269.18	996.89	137.86	188.19	347.45
15	Bricks & Mortar							
16	Bricks/Depression Glas	83.00	275.00	205.00	563.00	108.00	198.00	93.00
17	Mortar	108.00	122.00	73.22	303.22	82.25	73.66	33.59
18	Total	191.00	397.00	278.22	866.22	190.25	271.66	126.59
19	Grand Total	816.52	1,651.18	1,590.87	4,058.57	770.27	1,122.74	1,450.96

Page 1

Figure 10-14: A preview of how the first page of a report will look when it is printed.

If you need to stop the printing before Wysiwyg finishes sending all the pages to the printer, you press Ctrl-Break (just as you do in 1-2-3) and then press Esc to get out of ERROR mode and back to READY mode.

Chapter 11

Teaching Old SmartIcons
New Tricks

● ●

In This Chapter

▶ Displaying the SmartIcons with Wysiwyg

▶ Identifying what each SmartIcon does

▶ Modifying the custom palette

▶ Assigning macros to the User Icons

● ●

*T*he SmartIcons feature introduced in Release 2.4 of 1-2-3 is the latest and greatest way to choose commonly used 1-2-3 and Wysiwyg commands. Instead of having to work your way through the 1-2-3 / command menus or, even worse, through the Wysiwyg : command menus, you can choose a command by choosing the appropriate icon. If you are one of those people who has a "Honk if you love mice" bumper sticker, you can click on the appropriate icon. If you're not really all that keen on mice, you can press the function key you've assigned to the Icons add-in, use the arrow keys to select the icon, and then press Enter.

Before you can use the SmartIcons in Release 2.4 of 1-2-3, you need to attach the Icons add-in program. This program gives you access to up to 77 different icons that are organized into separate *palettes* (or sets of icons). When Wysiwyg is attached, the icons are arranged in seven palettes. When it is not attached or when you switch it to text mode with the **:D**isplay **M**ode **T**ext command, the icons are arranged in ten different palettes.

The individual icon palettes appear on the right side of the worksheet with their SmartIcons arranged in a single column. At the bottom of each palette, the number of the palette appears between two arrowheads, one facing right and the other facing left. To display the next or preceding icon palette in the series, you simply click on the right or left arrowhead or press the function key assigned to the Icons add-in and then press → or ←.

The first icon palette is known as the *custom icon palette* because it is the one icon palette you can customize by adding icons from the other palettes, deleting existing icons that you don't often use, and changing the arrangement of the SmartIcons on the palette. In addition to being able to modify the custom icon palette by creating new combinations of SmartIcons, you also can assign macros that you've created to the twelve User Icons located on the very last icon palette. (See Chapter 9 for details on creating macros that everyone can love.)

Attaching the Icons Add-In

Until you attach the Icons add-in program, all that you see on the right side of the worksheet are the scroll arrows and Help icon. Attaching the Icons add-in is no different from attaching any other add-in (such as Wysiwyg):

1. Choose the /**A**dd-In **A**ttach command, highlight the ICONS.ADN file on the third line of the control panel, and press Enter in response to the Enter add-in to attach: prompt.

2. If you want to assign a function key so that you can select SmartIcons with the keyboard, as well as with the mouse, highlight the next available number (**7, 8, 9,** or **10**) and press Enter to assign a function key (Alt-F7, Alt-F8, Alt-F9, or Alt-F10). If you plan to select the SmartIcons only with the mouse, choose the **No-Key** command and press Enter.

3. After 1-2-3 attaches the Icons add-in, you probably want to attach the Wysiwyg add-in if it is not already running. When you are ready to return to READY mode, choose the **Q**uit command on the /**A**dd-In menu.

When you return to READY mode, you see the custom icon palette (marked 1 between the arrows at the bottom), running down the right side of the worksheet. The appearance of this palette appears and the icons it contains depend on whether you are running Wysiwyg in graphics mode. When Wysiwyg is loaded and it is in graphics mode, the custom icon palette appears with the SmartIcons as shown in Figure 11-1. When Wysiwyg isn't attached, or when it is attached but you've switched to text mode with the :**D**isplay **M**ode **T**ext command, the custom icon palette appears with the icons as shown in Figure 11-2.

Suffice it to say, without Wysiwyg, the SmartIcons are not only rather crude but also fewer in number (only the first eight of the possible 16 are included). Some icons are so crude that they're not even icons; they're abbreviations, such as PRN for Print or PVU for Preview (or, uh, Prevu?). Also keep in mind that some of the SmartIcons work only when Wysiwyg is attached. For example, you can't use the icons that bold, italicize, or underline the text in a range when Wysiwyg isn't attached because these attributes are *only* available in Wysiwyg.

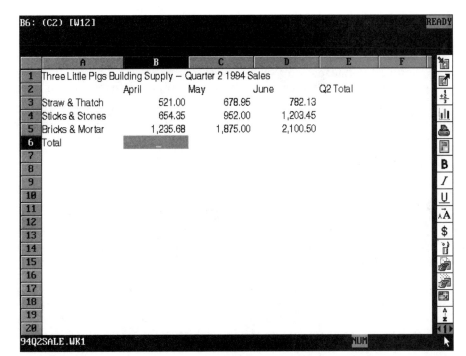

Figure 11-1: The custom icon palette as it appears in graphics mode.

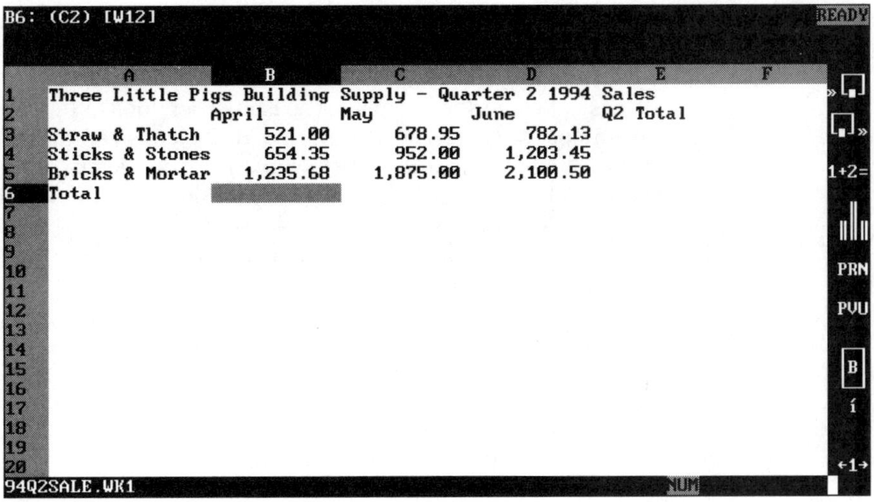

Figure 11-2: The custom icon palette as it appears in text mode or when Wysiwyg is not attached.

Therefore, if at all possible, you want to run Wysiwyg in graphics mode whenever you load the Icons add-in.

- ✔ If you're flush in memory, you probably want to have both these add-ins attached automatically whenever you start 1-2-3. (For details, refer to the tip in Chapter 10 on how to make Wysiwyg an auto-attach add-in.)

- ✔ If you get low on memory while you're working on a worksheet with both of these add-ins attached (you can tell because the MEM indicator flashes furiously), use the /**A**dd-In **D**etach command to free up needed memory by unloading one or both of the add-ins.

Picking the Right Icon for the Job

Before you can use the icons on the custom palette (or any other palette for that matter), you need to know what they do. Although the icons are supposed to be little pictures that immediately communicate their purpose the moment you see them, sometimes their purpose isn't all that clear until after someone explains what the picture represents. (It's like when someone explains the punch line of a joke, and then you finally get it and laugh.) At other times, their purpose doesn't seem to be represented by the picture at all — even after it has been explained to you. The picture is too simple, or too small, or the action is too complex, or you just can't see any relationship between the picture and the action.

As an example of really clear icons on the custom palette, look at the icons with **B**, *I*, and U̲ in the middle of the palette in Figure 11-1. I'll bet you had no trouble figuring out that you use these icons to bold, italicize, and underline text in a cell range. These icons show exactly what they do and are fairly self-explanatory.

Now, as a case of when some explanation is in order, look at the top two icons on the custom palette in Figure 11-1. Both of these icons contain pictures of floppy disks (oh, that's what they are!) with arrows. In the first icon, the arrow is pointing toward the center of the disk. In the second icon, the arrow is pointing away from the disk. The first icon saves the worksheet, a process when information is written onto the disk, so the arrow points to the center of the disk. The second icon retrieves a worksheet, a process whereby information is read from the disk into the computer's memory, so the arrow points away from the disk. The functions of these icons are very clear when you understand the pictures.

Finally, as an example of when icon representations just don't quite work, look at the two icons with the pointing hands near the bottom of the custom palette in Figure 11-1. The meaning of these little pictures is relatively unclear. In fact, even when you know what these icons do, you still don't know why these pictures were chosen or what the difference is (at least, I don't). The lower of the two hand icons (the one where it looks as if it's snowing in the background) is used to move a range of data to a new place in the worksheet. The icon above it (where the hand is kind of dematerializing) is used to copy a range of data in the worksheet. The actions are probably too complex to be pictured — or maybe I just don't get it!

All is not lost. You can display a brief description of what an icon does on the last line of the control panel by pressing the function key that you assigned to the Icons add-in and then pressing ↓ or ↑ until you select the icon on the palette. You can tell that an icon is selected because it has a flashing border (in graphics mode) or a standard highlight (in text mode).

Table 11-1 shows the icons on the custom palette and explains what they do.

✔ The first column shows the icons as they appear on the custom palette when you're in graphics mode and Wysiwyg is attached.

✔ The second column shows the icons as they appear when Wysiwyg is attached but you're in text mode or when Wysiwyg is not attached. (Keep in mind that the custom palette contains only the first eight icons under these circumstances.)

Table 11-1	Icons on the Custom Icon Palette	
Icon in Graphics Mode (Wysiwyg Is Attached)	**Icon in Text Mode (Wysiwyg Is Not Attached)**	**What the Icon Does**
	» ⌷	Saves a worksheet file
	⌷ »	Retrieves a worksheet file
	1+2=	Sums values in a selected cell range in empty cells below or to the right of the range; or, if the selected cell range is blank, sums the nearest range of values and places the sums in the empty range
	ılᵢlıı	Graphs the values in the selected cell range or the values in the area of the worksheet surrounding the cell pointer if no range is selected
	PRN	Prints the selected range, or, if no range is selected, the print range defined with the 1-2-3 **/P**rint **P**rinter **R**ange command or the Wysiwyg **:P**rint **R**ange **S**et command
	PVU	Displays the selected range in the Print Preview screen; if no range is selected, displays the print range defined with the 1-2-3 **/P**rint **P**rinter **R**ange command or the Wysiwyg **:P**rint **R**ange **S**et command (Wysiwyg must be attached)

(continued)

Table 11-1	Icons on the Custom Icon Palette *(continued)*	
Icon in Graphics Mode (Wysiwyg Is Attached)	**Icon in Text Mode (Wysiwyg Is Not Attached)**	**What the Icon Does**
B	B	Adds or removes bold typeface from the selected range (Wysiwyg must be attached)
I	*i*	Adds or removes italics from the selected range (Wysiwyg must be attached)
U	N/A	Adds or removes single underlining from the selected range (Wysiwyg must be attached)
A	N/A	Displays the data in the selected range in the next font in the current font library (Wysiwyg must be attached)
$	N/A	Formats the values in the selected range with the Currency number format with 2 decimal places
🗑	N/A	Erases the contents of the selected range
📋	N/A	Copies the selected range when you select the Copy To range
📋	N/A	Moves the selected range when you select the Move To range
📋	N/A	Copies the contents of the current cell to all the other cells in the selected range
A z	N/A	Sorts the database in ascending (A–Z) order, using the selected column as the sort key

Using SmartIcons in the Worksheet

Before you start learning how to customize the custom icon palette, it might be a good idea to learn how to use the icons it already contains. As a general rule, before you select the SmartIcon that you want to use, you select the cell range that you want to apply its action to.

✔ If you use the mouse, you select the range by dragging through all the cells.

✔ If you use the keyboard, you position the cell pointer in the first cell of the range, press the F4 (Abs) key to anchor the range on the current cell, use the cursor keys to move the cell pointer and highlight the range, and then press Enter.

After you select the range, you then select the SmartIcon that you want to use on the range.

- ✔ The easiest way to select the SmartIcon is to click on it with the mouse.

- ✔ If you're not into the mouse, or you don't even have one, or they make you stand on a chair and scream, you can select the SmartIcon with the keyboard. Just press the function key you assigned to the Icons add-in when you attached it, press ↓ or ↑ until the icon is selected (indicated by a flashing border around the icon in graphics mode or a standard highlight in text mode), and then press Enter.

SmartIcons make quick work of performing common tasks, such as summing columns and rows of values, copying a formula to a cell range, and formatting data. To get a feel for how easily you can perform these tasks, work through the steps that follow. The example for using the icons on the custom palette completes the Quarter 2 sales table shown in Figure 11-1 for the Three Little Pigs Building Supply. The first thing that you need to do is attach both the Wysiwyg and Icons add-in programs. Then you can proceed with the following steps:

1. To sum the columns of monthly sales figures and format them with the Currency format, as shown in Figure 11-3, select the cell range B6..D6, select the Sum icon (the one with the 1+2=3 picture), and then select the Currency Format icon (the one with the $).

2. To sum and format the row of sales of Straw & Thatch, put the cell pointer in cell E3, select the Sum icon, and then select the Currency icon.

3. To copy the @SUM formula in cell E3 to the cell range E4..E6, as shown in Figure 11-4, select the range E3..E6 and then select the Replicate icon. (The Replicate icon is the second-to-the-last icon, and it is a picture of a worksheet with a cell that is selected and an arrow pointing down to the right.)

4. Add bold and italics to the worksheet title in cell A1 by positioning the cell pointer in that cell and then selecting the Bold icon (the one with the B) and the Italics icon (the one below it with the I.)

Not bad, huh? With just a few clicks of the icons on the old custom palette, you've almost got the whole table finished. About the only things left to do might be to center the column headings in row 2, center the worksheet title over the table, and shade the monthly totals in the last row. You can fancy the table up even more by adding a drop shadow to the entire table. To do these things with SmartIcons, you have to switch to the second icon palette as follows:

1. Click on the arrowhead pointing to the right of the 1 at the bottom of the custom palette or activate the palette with the function key you assigned to the icons and press → to dial up the second icon palette.

2. Select the range of column headings B2..E2 and then select the Center icon (the one that's third from the bottom and has all the lines centered).

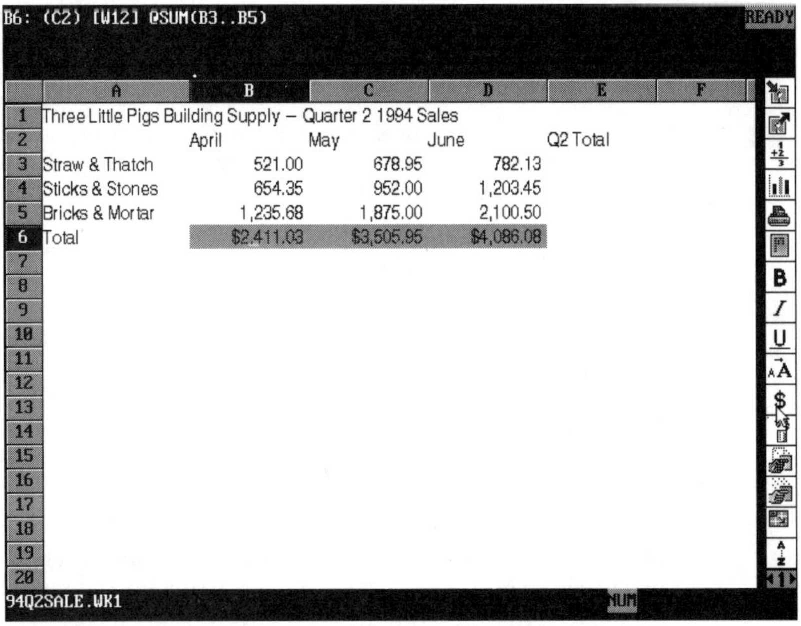

B6: (C2) [W12] @SUM(B3..B5)   READY

	A	B	C	D	E	F	
1	Three Little Pigs Building Supply — Quarter 2 1994 Sales						
2		April	May	June	Q2 Total		
3	Straw & Thatch	521.00	678.95	782.13			
4	Sticks & Stones	654.35	952.00	1,203.45			
5	Bricks & Mortar	1,235.68	1,875.00	2,100.50			
6	Total	$2,411.03	$3,505.95	$4,086.08			
7							
8							
9							
10							
11							
12							
13							
14							
15							
16							
17							
18							
19							
20							

94Q2SALE.WK1   NUM

Figure 11-3: The Quarter 2 sales table with formatted monthly totals.

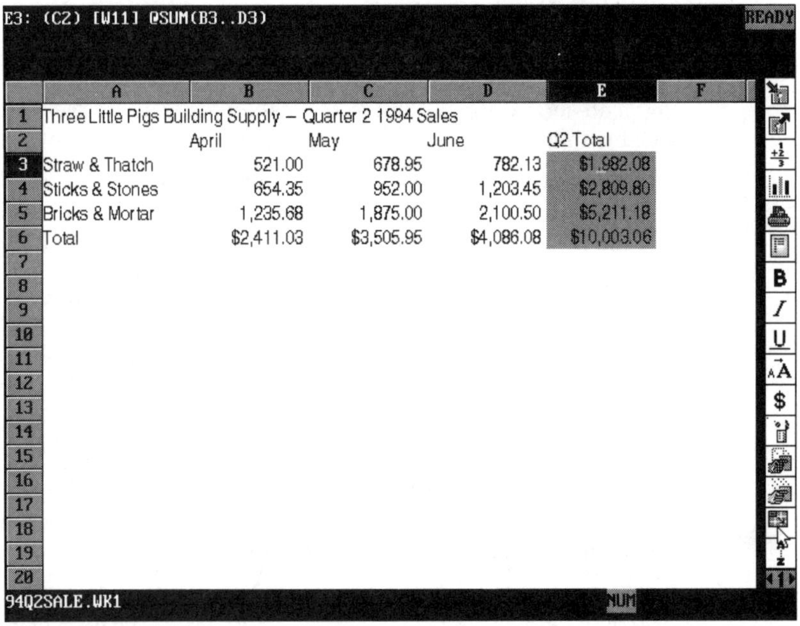

E3: (C2) [W11] @SUM(B3..D3)   READY

	A	B	C	D	E	F	
1	Three Little Pigs Building Supply — Quarter 2 1994 Sales						
2		April	May	June	Q2 Total		
3	Straw & Thatch	521.00	678.95	782.13	$1,982.08		
4	Sticks & Stones	654.35	952.00	1,203.45	$2,809.80		
5	Bricks & Mortar	1,235.68	1,875.00	2,100.50	$5,211.18		
6	Total	$2,411.03	$3,505.95	$4,086.08	$10,003.06		
7							
8							
9							
10							
11							
12							
13							
14							
15							
16							
17							
18							
19							
20							

94Q2SALE.WK1   NUM

Figure 11-4: The Quarter 2 sales table after the @SUM formula has been copied from cell E3 to the cell range E4..E6.

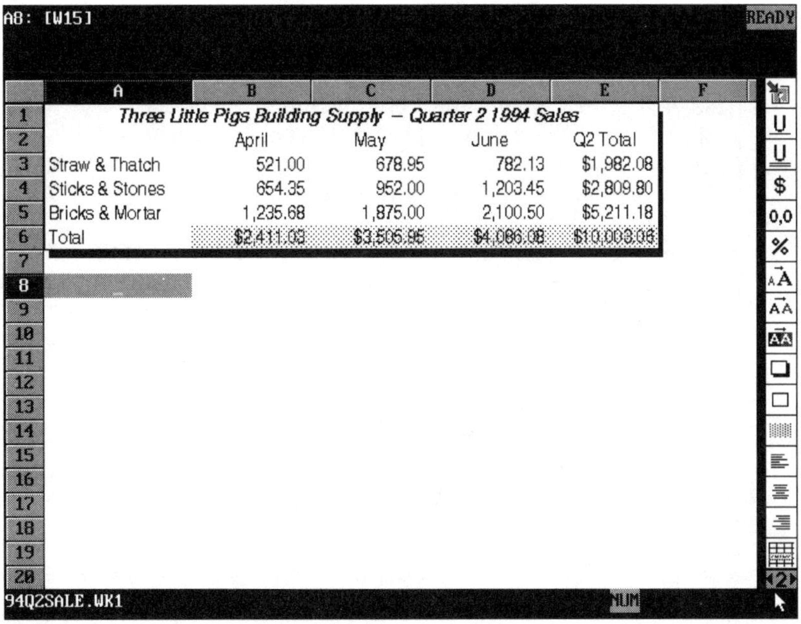

Figure 11-5: The completed Quarter 2 sales table.

3. Select the range of A1..E1 and then select the Center Text icon (the last one, with one row selected in a tiny worksheet grid) to center the title in A1 over the entire range.

4. Select the range of totals B6..E6 and then select the Shading icon (the one that's fifth from the bottom and shows a shaded rectangle composed of dots) to lightly shade the range.

5. Select the cell range A1..E6 and then select the Drop Shadow icon (the one that's seventh from the bottom and shows a rectangle with a drop shadow) to add a drop shadow to the table.

Figure 11-5 shows the results of this latest formatting. Nice work, huh? And, even better, quick work, because SmartIcons really make short work of these kinds of common worksheet tasks.

Musical SmartIcons

The custom icon palette contains a potpourri of SmartIcons taken from the other icon palettes. As you learn in the next section, you can copy icons from any of these palettes to the custom palette to make them more accessible.

When you are deciding which SmartIcons to include on the custom palette, you can use Table 11-2 to get a feel for the possibilities.

This table shows all the SmartIcons included in Release 2.4, arranged basically in the order in which they appear on the palettes when you're running Wysiwyg in graphics mode. (Note, however, that icons that are duplicated on different palettes are *not* duplicated in this table.)

The second column of Table 11-2 shows how the icons look without the Wysiwyg add-in. Remember that when you're running in text mode, the icons are arranged in much different palette arrangements (although they still perform the same function no matter what they look like or on which palette you find them).

You can move from palette to palette with the mouse or with the keyboard.

✔ To use the mouse, click on either the left-pointing or right-pointing arrow-head icon on either side of the number at the bottom of the palette until the palette you want is displayed.

✔ To use the keyboard, press the function key assigned to the Icons add-in and then press → or ← until the palette you want is displayed.

Table 11-2	**The SmartIcons**	
Icon in Graphics Mode (Wysiwyg Is Attached)	**Icon in Text Mode (Wysiwyg Is Not Attached)**	**What the Icon Does**
🖫	» ⌷	Saves a worksheet file
U̲	U̲	Adds or removes single underlining from the selected range (Wysiwyg must be attached)
U̲̲	U̳	Adds or removes double underlining from the selected range (Wysiwyg must be attached)
$	$	Formats the values in the selected range with the Currency number format with 2 decimal places
0,0	0,0	Formats the values in the selected range with the Comma number format with 0 decimal places
%	%	Formats the values in the selected range with the Percent number format with 2 decimal places
ᴀA̅	ᶻ→2	Displays the data in the selected range in the next font in the current font library (Wysiwyg must be attached)

(continued)

Table 11-2	The SmartIcons *(continued)*	
Icon in Graphics Mode (Wysiwyg Is Attached)	**Icon in Text Mode (Wysiwyg Is Not Attached)**	**What the Icon Does**
	FGRD	Displays the data in the selected range in the next available color (Wysiwyg must be attached)
	BGRD	Displays the background of the selected range in the next available color (Wysiwyg must be attached)
		Draws an outline and adds a drop shadow to the selected range or removes an existing drop shadow (Wysiwyg must be attached)
		Draws an outline around the selected range; cycles through all the outline choices: single, double, wide, or clear (Wysiwyg must be attached)
	###	Shades the selected range; cycles through shading: light, dark, solid, or clear (Wysiwyg must be attached)
	←L	Left-aligns labels in the selected range
	←C→	Centers labels in the selected range
	R→	Right-aligns labels in the selected range
	ALGN TEXT	Centers text across selected columns
	+ROW	Inserts one or more rows above the selected range
	+COL	Inserts one or more columns to the left of the selected range
	−ROW	Deletes the rows in the selected range
	−COL	Deletes the columns in the selected range
		Inserts a horizontal page break in the row with the cell pointer
		Inserts a vertical page break in the column with the cell pointer (Wysiwyg must be attached)
	A→Z	Sorts the database in ascending (A–Z) order, using the selected column as the sort key

(continued)

Table 11-2	The SmartIcons *(continued)*	
Icon in Graphics Mode (Wysiwyg Is Attached)	**Icon in Text Mode (Wysiwyg Is Not Attached)**	**What the Icon Does**
	Z→A	Sorts the database in descending (Z - A) order, using the selected column as the sort key
	FILL	Fills the selected range with a series of values, using the Start, Step, and Stop values assigned to /Data Fill (0, 1, and 8191 unless changed)
	CALC	Recalculates all formulas in the worksheet (the same as pressing the F9 [Calc] key)
	DATE	Inserts today's date in the current cell and formats it with the Long International format
	CRCL	Draws a circle around the selected range (Wysiwyg must be attached)
	ZOOM	Zooms the worksheet display by cycling through the zoom options: **T**iny, **S**mall, **N**ormal, **L**arge, and **H**uge (Wysiwyg must be attached)
	STEP	Turns on STEP mode to execute a macro one step at a time
	RUN	Runs the macro of your choice
	◄	Moves the cell pointer one cell to the left
	►	Moves the cell pointer one cell to the right
	▲	Moves the cell pointer one cell up
	▼	Moves the cell pointer one cell down
	?	Displays the 1-2-3 Main Help Index from READY mode
		Moves the cell pointer to cell A1, like pressing Home
		Moves the cell pointer to the last cell in the active area, like pressing End, Home

(continued)

Table 11-2	The SmartIcons *(continued)*	
Icon in Graphics Mode (Wysiwyg Is Attached)	***Icon in Text Mode (Wysiwyg Is Not Attached)***	***What the Icon Does***
	‖↓ =	Moves the cell pointer to the first occupied cell below in the same column that is either preceded or followed by a blank cell, like pressing End, ↓
	= ‖↑	Moves the cell pointer to the first occupied cell above in the same column that is either followed or preceded by a blank cell, like pressing End, ↑
	→ == =	Moves the cell pointer to the first occupied cell to the right in the same row that is either preceded or followed by a blank cell, like pressing End, →
	== == ←	Moves the cell pointer to the first occupied cell to the left in the same row that is either followed or preceded by a blank cell, like pressing End, ←
	GOTO	Enables you to select the address or cell range to move the cell pointer to, like pressing the F5 (GoTo) key
	FIND	Enables you to find or replace a text string in the worksheet, like choosing the /Range Search command
	UNDO	Undoes your latest goof-up, like pressing the Alt-F4 (Undo) key
	DEL	Erases the contents of the selected range, like choosing the /Range Erase command
	⌐▪⌐»	Retrieves a worksheet file
	1+2=	Sums values in a selected cell range in empty cells below or to the right of the range, or, if the selected cell range is blank, sums the nearest range of values and places the sums in the empty range
	‖‖‖	Graphs the values in the selected cell range or the values in the worksheet area surrounding the cell pointer if no range is selected

(continued)

Table 11-2	The SmartIcons *(continued)*	
Icon in Graphics Mode (Wysiwyg Is Attached)	**Icon in Text Mode (Wysiwyg Is Not Attached)**	**What the Icon Does**
	┤·₁ⅼₗⅼₗ	Adds the current graph to the selected range (Wysiwyg must be attached)
	VIEW GRPH	Displays the current graph, like pressing the F10 (Graph) key
	EDIT TEXT	Enables you to edit a selected text range right in the worksheet itself (Wysiwyg must be attached)
	PRN	Prints the selected range, or, if no range is selected, the print range defined with the 1-2-3 /Print Printer Range or the Wysiwyg :Print Range Set command
	PVU	Displays the selected range in the Print Preview screen, or, if no range is selected, the print range defined with the 1-2-3 /Print Printer Range or the Wysiwyg :Print Range Set command (Wysiwyg must be attached)
	COPY	Copies the selected range when you select the Copy To range
	MOVE	Moves the selected range when you select the Move To range
	COPY FRMT	Copies just the Wysiwyg formatting from the selected range to the new range that you specify
	REP DATA	Copies the contents of the current cell to all the other cells in the selected range
B	B	Adds or removes bold typeface from the selected range (Wysiwyg must be attached)
I	í	Adds or removes italics from the selected range (Wysiwyg must be attached)
N	N	Clears all Wysiwyg formatting from the selected range and restores the default font (Wysiwyg must be attached)

(continued)

Table 11-2	The SmartIcons *(continued)*	
Icon in Graphics Mode (Wysiwyg Is Attached)	**Icon in Text Mode (Wysiwyg Is Not Attached)**	**What the Icon Does**
		Adds an icon to the custom icon palette
		Removes an icon from the custom icon palette
		Enables you to move an icon to a new position in the custom icon palette
		Enables you to assign macros to the twelve User Icons, U1 through U12

A custom palette made to order

You use the SmartIcons called Add Icon, Delete Icon, and Move Icon to make changes to the custom icon palette. These icons are located on icon palette 6 when you're running the program in graphics mode or on icon palette 9 when you're running it in text mode. In either case, they're on the second-to-last palette.

To add a new icon to the custom palette, you follow these steps:

1. Select the Add Icon SmartIcon (the one at the top with the + sign) on the second-to-the-last icon palette.

2. Move to the icon palette that contains the SmartIcon you want to add to the custom palette.

3. Select the SmartIcon you want to add.

   1-2-3 adds the icon you selected to the very bottom of the custom palette (but does not remove the icon from the original palette).

If the palette is full because you haven't removed any icons from it, 1-2-3 automatically removes the last icon and replaces it with the new one. Then the program returns to the palette with the Add Icon SmartIcon. To see the addition, you need to move to the custom palette.

Figure 11-6 shows the custom palette after the addition of the Zoom icon (from the third icon palette). Note that 1-2-3 has added this Zoom icon to the bottom of the custom palette, while at the same time removing the Sort Ascending icon to make room for it.

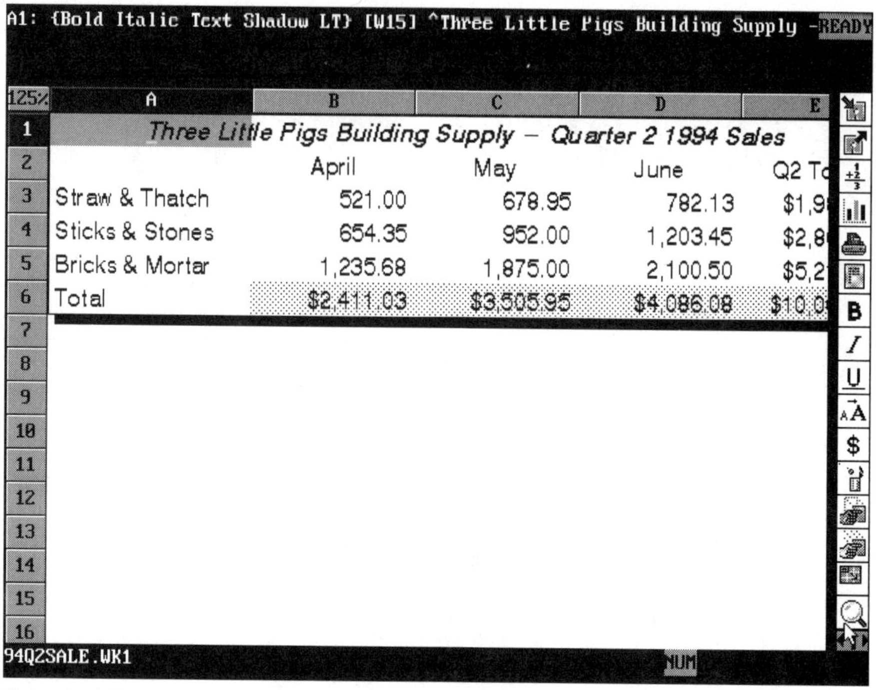

Figure 11-6: The custom palette after the addition of the Zoom icon.

To remove an icon from the custom palette, you take these steps:

1. Select the Delete Icon SmartIcon (the one second from the top with the
   – sign) on the second-to-the-last icon palette.

   1-2-3 automatically displays the custom palette.

2. Select the SmartIcon that you want to get rid of on the custom palette.

As soon as you select the icon to remove from the custom palette, 1-2-3 immediately returns to the palette with the Delete Icon SmartIcon. To confirm the
deletion, you must then move back to the custom palette.

Figure 11-7 shows the custom palette after you remove the Underline icon. This
SmartIcon used to appear between the Italics icon and the Select-Next-Font icon
on this palette.

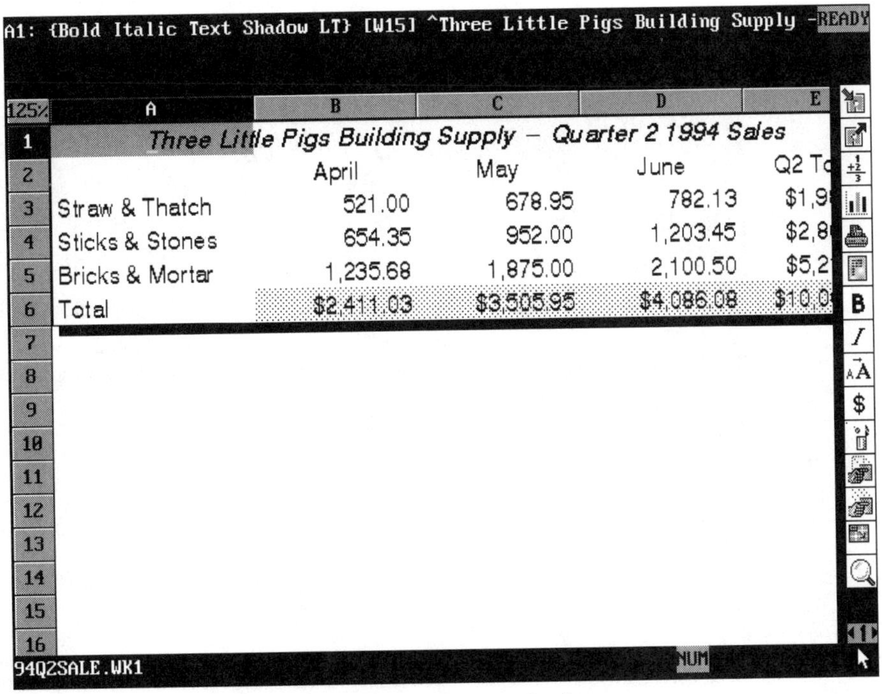

Figure 11-7: The custom palette after removing the Underline icon.

To move an icon to a new position on the custom palette, follow these steps:

1. Select the Move Icon SmartIcon (the one third from the top that shows an icon being moved from the bottom to the top of a palette) on the second-to-the-last icon palette.

   1-2-3 automatically displays the custom palette.

2. Select the SmartIcon that you want to move on the custom palette. 1-2-3 replaces the icon you select with a blank, shaded square.

3. Select the SmartIcon that is at the position on the palette where you want the icon you just selected to appear.

   1-2-3 inserts the icon at the position you selected, while at the same time repositioning the other icons on the palette as needed to make room for it.

Figure 11-8 shows the custom icon palette after the Zoom icon (which was added to the very bottom of the palette in Figure 11-6) is moved so that it appears above the Print icon.

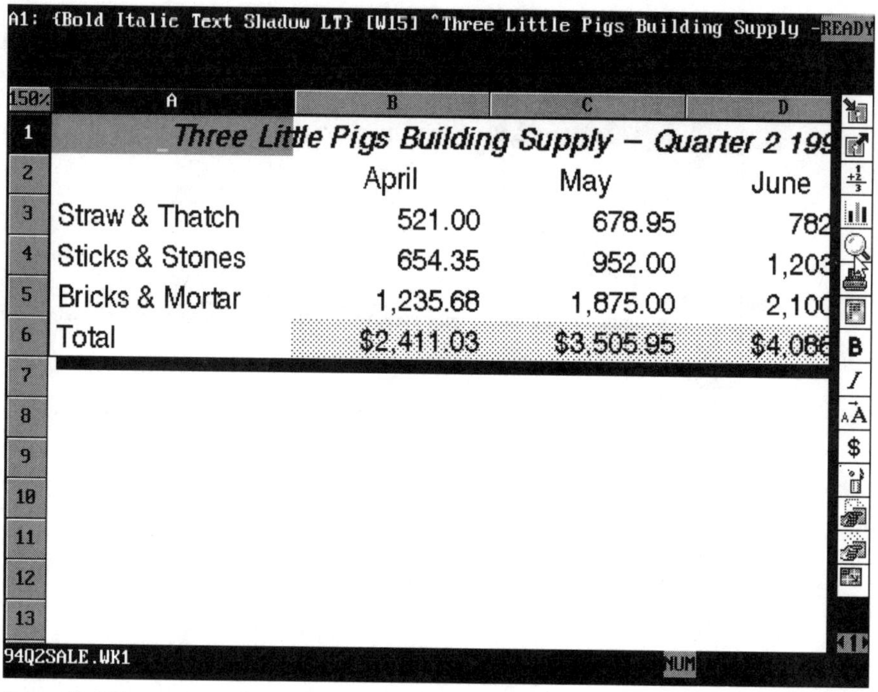

Figure 11-8: The custom palette after moving the Zoom icon above the Print icon.

Assigning macros to the User Icons

By assigning a macro to one of the twelve User Icons, you ensure that you have immediate access to that macro in whatever worksheet you're working on when the Icons add-in is attached. The steps for attaching a macro are very straightforward (assuming that the Icons add-in is already attached):

1. Retrieve the worksheet that contains the macro that you want to assign to one of the user icons.

   For example, to assign one of the macros in macro library worksheet to a User Icon, use the /**File R**etrieve command to open the MACROLIB.WK1 file.

2. Select the cell range that contains the macro keystrokes.

   For example, to assign the Month_Mac macro that enters the names of the 12 months as column headings, select the cell range C5..C7. (Note that you select all the cells with macro keystrokes, not just the first one, as you do when you are naming the macro.)

3. Select the User Icon SmartIcon (the last one, with the U and the picture of a pencil) on the second-to-the-last icon palette.

   1-2-3 displays the User Icon Descriptions dialog box shown in Figure 11-9.

4. Select the option button for the number of the next available User Icon (U1 through U12) in the **S**elect Icon section and then select the **A**ssign Macro to the Icon command button.

1-2-3 displays a User-Defined Icon dialog box similar to the one shown in Figure 11-10. The range of macro instructions that you selected in the worksheet appears in the **S**ource range text box of this dialog box.

5. Select the **G**et Macro from Sheet command button to the right of the Source range text box.

1-2-3 copies the instructions from the source range into the Macro **T**ext text box.

6. Select the Icon **D**escription option and then enter a description of the macro's function (up to 37 characters long) in this text box.

7. Select the OK command button.

1-2-3 returns to the User Icon Descriptions dialog box, where the icon description you just entered appears next to the User Icon number.

8. Select the OK command button in the User Icon Descriptions dialog box to return to the worksheet in READY mode.

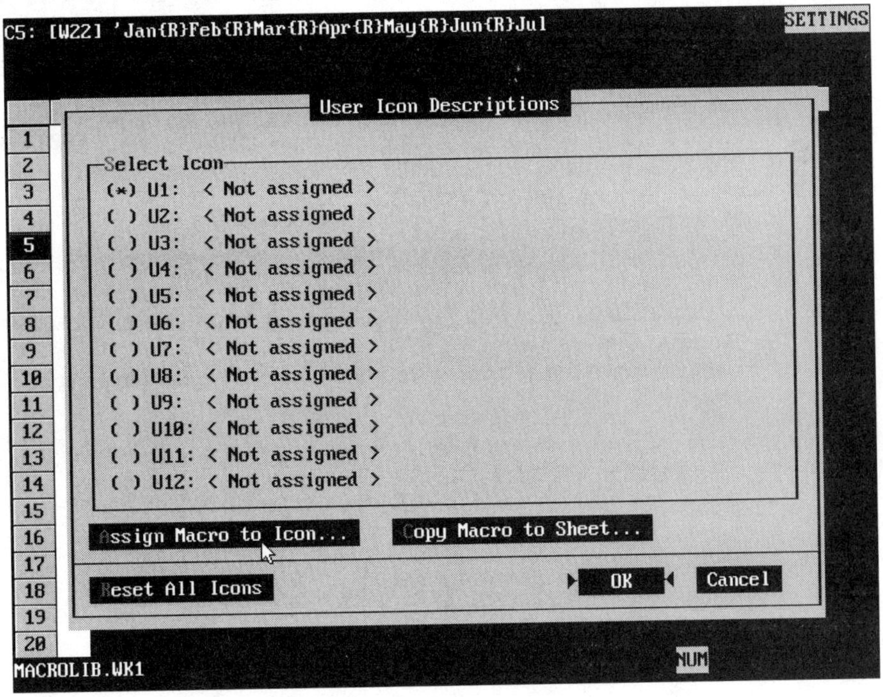

Figure 11-9: The User Icon Descriptions dialog box.

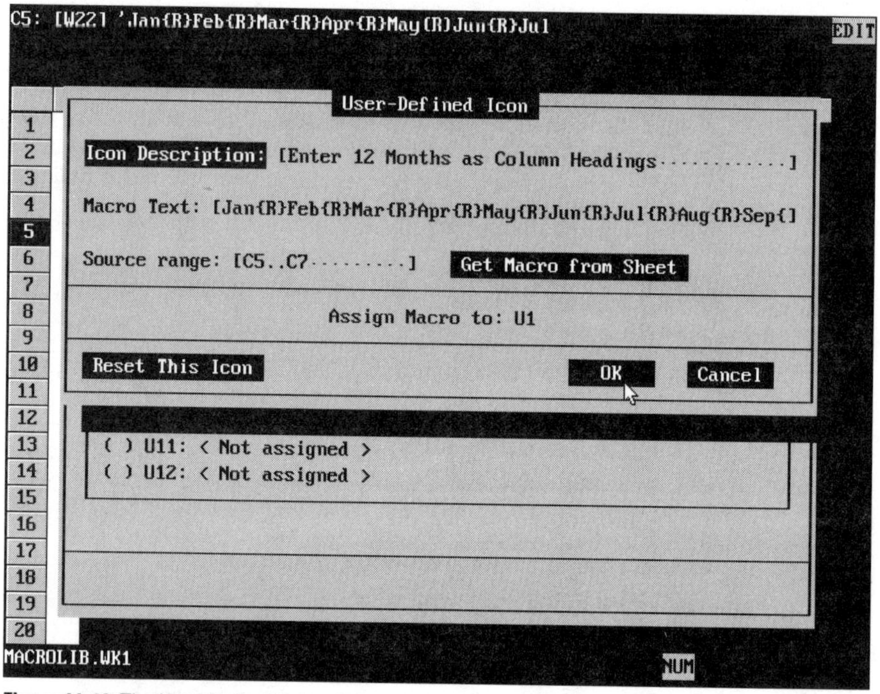

```
C5: [W22] 'Jan{R}Feb{R}Mar{R}Apr{R}May{R}Jun{R}Jul                         EDIT
```

1	

┌─────────────── User-Defined Icon ───────────────┐

Icon Description: [Enter 12 Months as Column Headings··········]

Macro Text: [Jan{R}Feb{R}Mar{R}Apr{R}May{R}Jun{R}Jul{R}Aug{R}Sep{]

Source range: [C5..C7·········]   **Get Macro from Sheet**

Assign Macro to: U1

Reset This Icon   **OK**   **Cancel**

( ) U11: < Not assigned >
( ) U12: < Not assigned >

MACROLIB.WK1   NUM

Figure 11-10: The User-Defined Icon dialog box.

After you assign a macro to one of the User Icons, you can run the macro by simply selecting its User Icon on the User Icon palette — icon palette 7 in graphics mode or icon palette 10 in text mode.

If you want to, you can even add the User Icon with your macro to the custom palette and select it from there. Figure 11-11 illustrates this situation. Here you see a worksheet after you select the U1 User Icon to insert the names of the months as column headings for a new worksheet. Note that this User Icon has been added to the bottom of the custom icon palette to make it readily accessible.

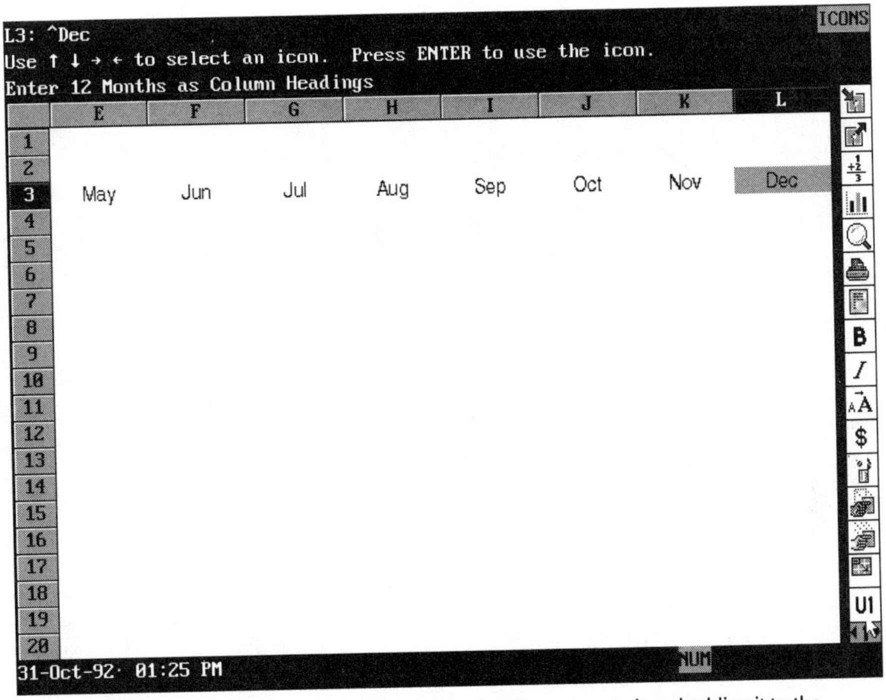

Figure 11-11: User Icon U1 after assigning the Month_Mac macro to it and adding it to the custom palette.

Part VI

1-2-3 Function Reference (for Real People)

The part in which...

You learn that this Part is not just for the @functionally illiterate. This is the place where you find out how to perform some very interesting tricks with a variety of handy @functions. You learn how to use the most common functions, including @SUM, @AVG (for average), @MAX, and @MIN.

You learn how to use more advanced (well, specialized, then) @functions, including the financial functions @PV and @PMT, the text functions @PROPER, @UPPER, and @LOWER, the special lookup functions @VLOOKUP and @HLOOKUP, as well as the logical function @IF. When you finish this part, you will be fully @functional!

Chapter 12
I Love Everyday Functions

*A*rguably, if formulas are going to become your life, you need to get pretty intimate with the built-in worksheet functions. Functions perform specific predefined calculations based on the type of information (*arguments*) you supply. To use a 1-2-3 function, all you have to know is where the @ symbol is on the keyboard and what arguments the function takes (remember all 1-2-3 functions begin with @). You can't argue with that!

This chapter summarizes the more common, everyday functions you will use. You won't be surprised that the bulk of these functions are statistical — bean counting is what this worksheet stuff is about.

To @SUM It Up

You're already familiar with the @SUM function from Chapter 2. Being the most commonly used function in the world of spreadsheets, it's only fitting that this Function Reference start with a brief discussion of the ways you can use @SUM. If you look in your 1-2-3 *@Functions and Macros Guide,* you'll see the format of the @SUM function as

```
@SUM(list)
```

Typically, arguments (the text between the pair of parentheses) of any @function are shown in italics, signifying that they are *variables*. In place of the *list* argument in the preceding @SUM function, then, you can substitute such things as the cell reference **B5,** the value **100,** or even a simple calculation like **100*B5.**

Any argument shown in italics in the 1-2-3 *@Functions and Macros Guide* is *required* to get the function to work at all. In the @SUM function, you must substitute something for the *list* argument. This list can be a series of numbers or a series of cells, cell ranges, or even range names that contain the values to be summed (like, added).

Suppose that you need to find the grand total of the values in three different columns of your worksheet, in the ranges of C3..C15, G3..G19, and H2..H25. To do this calculation, use the @SUM function formula

```
@SUM(C3..C15,G3..G19,H2..H25)
```

in the cell where you want the total (of all the numbers in all these cells) to appear.

When you create @SUM formulas like this one, just don't forget to separate each number, cell, cell range, or range name in the *list* argument with a comma.

1-2-3 allows you to select the individual cell ranges with the mouse or with the keyboard (*pointing*) so that you don't have to type the address of the cell range in the formula (unless it makes you feel better).

I'm Just an @AVERAGE Guy

The @AVG (for Average) function calculates what's technically known as the *arithmetic mean.* The @AVERAGE function follows the same form as the @SUM function

```
@AVG(list)
```

1-2-3 calculates the average by adding up all the values specified by the number arguments (what you substitute for *list*), counting the number of values, and dividing the summed total by the result of the value count (just like you were taught in grade school math class).

The only catch with using the @AVG function is how 1-2-3 counts (or miscounts, depending on how you look at it) the number of entries when it calculates the values. The easiest way to explain this little quirk is by way of the following illustration:

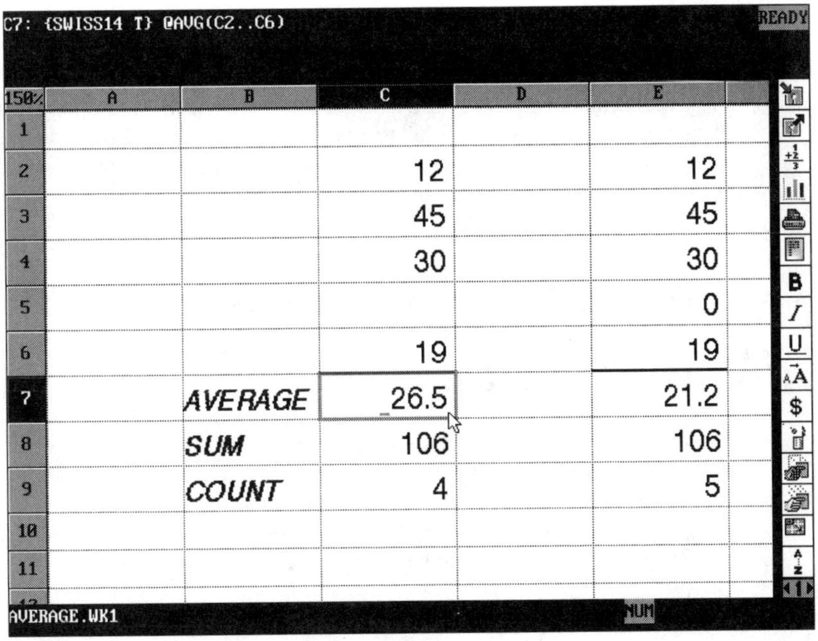

Figure 12-1: Averaging, summing, and counting two ranges that are identical, except for a zero.

Figure 12-1 shows two ranges of figures in separate columns that are identical to each other except that the fourth cell in the first range (C5) is empty and the fourth cell in the second range (E5) has a 0 in it. Although the addition of the zero to the second range makes no difference in the *sum* of these two ranges, it does change the *count* (zeros in cells are counted; blank cells are not counted). 1-2-3 calculates a different average for the two "identical" ranges. What a difference a zero makes!

Don't @COUNT Me Out

The @COUNT function is very useful when you are dealing with a really large cell range and you need to know how many items the range contains. You might, for example, use @COUNT to get an accurate count of the number of records in a database. When you use the @COUNT function, however, keep in mind that blank cells in a range you use as an argument can affect the outcome. (Remember this effect in the @AVG function.)

Just keep in mind that if you designate a range that has blank cells, the @COUNT function will *not* include the blank cells in the tally. So when you count records in a database, you need to make sure that you don't skew the result by selecting a field that is missing a lot of entries — 1-2-3 will count fewer records than you actually have because it will fail to count the records that are missing entries in that particular field. Always choose a field that has an entry in each and every record and select its cell range as the @COUNT argument.

Get the @MAXIMUM for the @MINIMUM Effort

The @MAX function returns the highest value; the @MIN function returns the lowest one. Like @COUNT, these two functions are most useful when you are dealing with a large range of values (especially when they haven't been sorted), and you need to quickly find out which value is highest or lowest. The @MAX and @MIN functions take the same argument series as the @SUM or @AVG functions.

@ROUND It Off

In Chapter 3, I made a great big deal about how formatting values in a worksheet affects only the on-screen display, not how the values are stored in the cell. Back there, I recommended using the @ROUND function to instruct 1-2-3 to round off all the values to the number of decimal places allowed by their number formats. The @ROUND function has two arguments that you enter according to the following pattern:

```
@ROUND(x,n)
```

The first argument, *x*, tells 1-2-3 the value (or its cell reference) you want rounded. The second argument, *n*, indicates the number of decimal places you want in the rounded number — you have the following options:

✔ To round a value to a specific number of decimal places, enter a positive value that represents the number of decimal places to the right of the decimal point (up to 15) for the *n* argument.

✔ To round a decimal value to the nearest whole number (*integer*), enter **0** as the *n* argument.

✔ To round off a whole number, enter a negative value that represents the number of places to round to the left of the decimal point (down to –5) for the *n* argument.

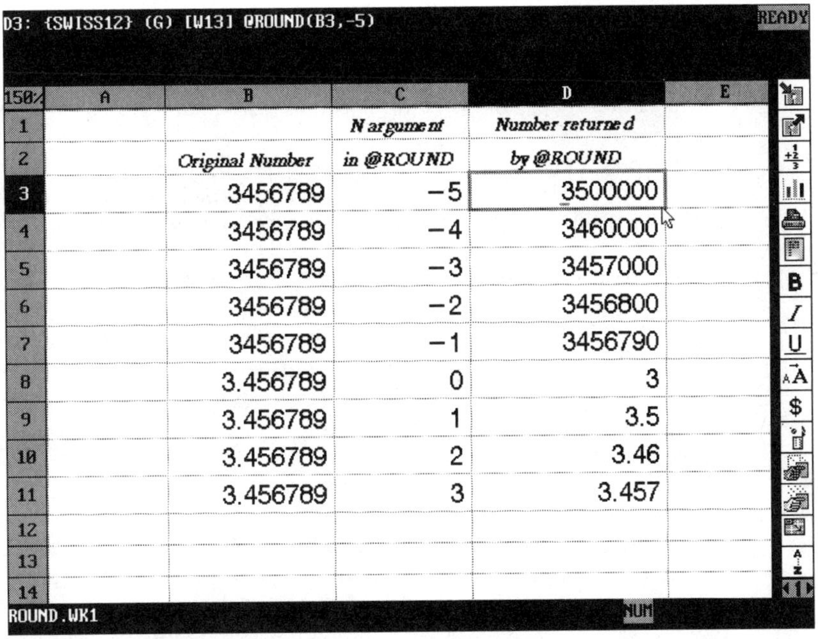

```
D3: {SWISS12} (G) [W13] @ROUND(B3,-5)                          READY
```

150%	A	B	C	D	E
1			*N argument*	*Number returned*	
2		*Original Number*	*in @ROUND*	*by @ROUND*	
3		3456789	−5	3500000	
4		3456789	−4	3460000	
5		3456789	−3	3457000	
6		3456789	−2	3456800	
7		3456789	−1	3456790	
8		3.456789	0	3	
9		3.456789	1	3.5	
10		3.456789	2	3.46	
11		3.456789	3	3.457	
12					
13					
14					

```
ROUND.WK1                                            NUM
```

Figure 12-2: Using @ROUND to round off a range of values.

Figure 12-2 illustrates the effect that changing the *n* argument has on the result when you round two values, one a large whole number with seven digits and the other a small decimal value with six decimal places.

It's @NOW or Never

The last function you're going to learn in this chapter is the @NOW date function that returns the current date and time to the worksheet. Because this function gets its date and time information directly from your computer's clock/calendar, it doesn't require any arguments; you simply enter

```
@NOW
```

in a cell when you want to stamp the worksheet with the current date and/or time.

When you first enter this function, 1-2-3 enters both the date and the time in the cell with the date serial number ahead of the time fraction. After that it's up to you to select a date or time number format that displays one or the other in the cell.

Suppose that today's date were September 3, 1993, and you entered the @NOW function in a cell exactly at 3:45 p.m. The value

```
34215.65625
```

would appear in the worksheet. The value 34215 represents the date serial number for September 3, 1993, while the fraction 0.65625 represents the time fraction for 3:45 p.m. (that is, this time's portion of an entire 24-hour period).

After entering the current date serial and time fraction with the @NOW function, you must choose one of the date or time number formats. If you aren't concerned with the time and only want the date, choose the /Range Format Date command. Then choose one of the five date formats and apply it to the cell with @NOW. On the other hand, if you don't care about the date and only want to see the time in the cell, choose the /Range Format Date Time command. Then choose one of the four time formats and apply it to the cell with @NOW.

When you use the @NOW function, keep in mind that 1-2-3 enters the date and time in a *dynamic function* so that each time the program recalculates the worksheet, it updates the date and time. To test this out, enter the @NOW function in the blank cell of your worksheet, widen the column to about 20 with the /Worksheet Column Set-Width command, wait a minute or more, and then press the F9 (Calc) key. When 1-2-3 recalculates the worksheet, the program updates the time in the cell with the @NOW function, adding a minute to it.

Automatic updating is useful when you have formulas that you need to keep up-to-date (or up-to-the-minute as the case may be). For example, you can use the @NOW function to calculate the age of equipment purchases by subtracting the date of purchase from the current date. This operation gives you the number of days; divide by 365.25 if you want to convert this figure into years. Every time you open the worksheet that contains these formulas, 1-2-3 updates the results, advancing the ages by the number of days that elapsed between that work session and the preceding time you worked with the document.

But what if you don't want the date or time to change? What if your purpose is to record forever in the worksheet the date you made a sale or a purchase. In this case, you must freeze the date/time entry made with the @NOW function so that it is never again subject to being updated. To freeze the entry, position the cell pointer in the cell with the @NOW function, press F2 to bring the @NOW to the second line of the control panel, press F9 to calculate @NOW and return the date serial number and time fraction to the control panel, and then press Enter to replace @NOW in the cell with its calculated date/time value.

Chapter 13
Functions for the More Adventurous

● ●

In This Chapter

▶ Using financial functions, such as @PV and @PMT

▶ Using string functions, such as @PROPER

▶ Using special functions, such as @HLOOKUP and @VLOOKUP

▶ Using logical functions, such as @IF

● ●

*B*eyond the realm of run-of-the-mill functions, such as @SUM, @AVG, and @NOW, lies a whole world of specialized worksheet functions. This chapter introduces a few of the financial, string, special, and logical functions. Although some functions are full of arguments that look like so much gobbledygook at first glance, you don't have to be a spreadsheet guru to comprehend and use any of them. Believe me, you're ready for the functions that are presented here, even given your limited experience with formulas and functions.

When you are learning a more complex function, you need to concentrate mainly on what type of arguments it uses, what order the arguments follow in the function, which arguments are required, and which arguments are optional. Mastering the few functions covered in this chapter and learning how their calculations can help you create more effective worksheets will put you in great shape for learning any of the other functions on your own.

Financial Highs and Lows

1-2-3, as you'd expect of any good spreadsheet program, offers many sophisticated *financial functions*. This section covers just two of the most common financial functions, the @PV (Present Value) and @PMT (Payment) functions.

You use the @PV function to calculate the current worth of a series of future payments (the very definition of the *present value*). You can use this function to determine whether the return on a particular investment is a sound one, considering the initial cost to you. The @PV function follows this pattern:

```
@PV(payments,interest,term)
```

✔ The *payments argument* is the payment made each period.

✔ The *interest argument* is the interest rate per period.

✔ The *term argument* is the total number of payment periods.

When you use financial functions, such as @PV, @PMT, and @FV, you first need to be sure that you're dealing with a true *annuity,* which in normal English just means an investment where all the payments are the same and are made at regular intervals (such as monthly, quarterly, or yearly). The best example of an annuity is a fixed-rate mortgage, where you pay a set amount each month for a continuous fixed period. An adjustable-rate mortgage, however, where the interest rate is adjusted annually or semi-annually, is a not a true annuity.

The most common mistake in working with annuity functions is not expressing the *interest argument* in the same time units as the *term argument.* Be sure that the interest is in either decimal or percentage format (.10 or 10%).

Most interest rates are quoted as annual rates, but most payment periods are monthly. In this case, you need to divide the annual interest rate by 12. Likewise, if you make payments on the annuity on a monthly basis but the worksheet gives the term in years (as in 30 for a standard 30-year mortgage), you need to convert this value into equivalent monthly periods by multiplying it by 12.

Figure 13-1 shows an example of using the @PV function to determine the advisability of an annuity by comparing its present value against the initial cash outlay. Here you are evaluating the present value of an annuity that will pay $150.00 at the end of each month for the next 10 years. The example assumes that the initial investment is $10,000 and that the money paid out by the annuity will earn an annual rate of interest of 7 percent. The @PV function calculates the present value for this annuity at $12,918.95. And because you're required to invest only $10,000, this is not at all a bad deal.

The @PMT function is another commonly used annuity function. It uses almost the same arguments as the @PV function, except that instead of a *payments argument* (which is what the function finds), it requires a *principal* (the amount you borrow) *argument*:

```
@PMT(principal,interest,term)
```

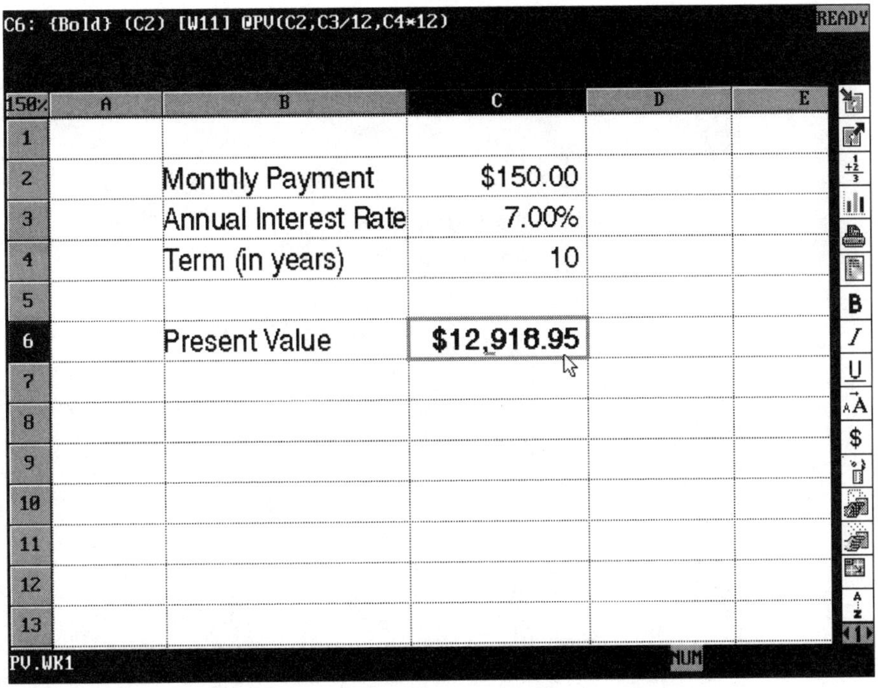

```
C6: {Bold} (C2) [W11] @PV(C2,C3/12,C4*12)                           READY
```

150%	A	B	C	D	E
1					
2		Monthly Payment	$150.00		
3		Annual Interest Rate	7.00%		
4		Term (in years)	10		
5					
6		Present Value	**$12,918.95**		
7					
8					
9					
10					
11					
12					
13					

```
PV.WK1                                                          NUM
```

Figure 13-1: Using the @PV function to determine the present value of an annuity.

The @PMT function is most often used to calculate loan payments.

- ✔ Enter the amount of the loan as the *principal argument.*

- ✔ Enter the interest rate as the *interest argument.*

- ✔ Enter the period of the loan as the *term argument.*

Again, make sure that the *interest* and *term arguments* are expressed in the same time units (monthly interest and number of monthly payments, if you want to calculate the amount of the *monthly* payment), and that the interest is in either decimal or percentage format.

Figure 13-2 shows an example of using the @PMT function to calculate a monthly mortgage payment. Here the amount of the loan is $375,000, the annual interest is 7.25 percent, and the period is the standard 30 years. Note that to calculate the monthly mortgage payment, you divide the annual interest in cell C3 by 12 and multiply the period in years in cell C4 by 12.

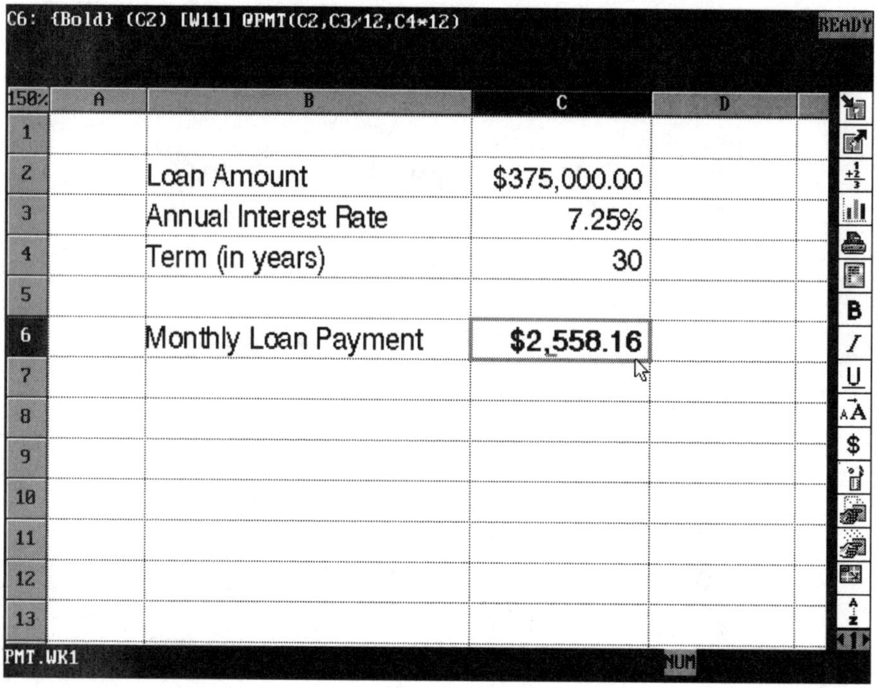

```
C6: {Bold} (C2) [W11] @PMT(C2,C3/12,C4*12)                          READY
```

	A	B	C	D	
1					
2		Loan Amount	$375,000.00		
3		Annual Interest Rate	7.25%		
4		Term (in years)	30		
5					
6		Monthly Loan Payment	$2,558.16		
7					
8					
9					
10					
11					
12					
13					

```
PMT.WK1                                                            NUM
```

Figure 13-2: Using the @PMT function to calculate a loan payment.

Don't String Me Up!

You may be a bit surprised to learn that you can construct formulas for performing various operations on *text* because you normally associate calculations in the worksheet with numbers. Well, believe it or not, 1-2-3 includes a wide variety of functions, called *string functions,* that work exclusively with text arguments. Admittedly, you may not find many uses for string functions unless you routinely take information into worksheets from other sources (such as Dow Jones and other on-line services) where you don't have any control over how the information is formatted.

For example, you may find that the text that you take into the worksheet is in all-uppercase or all-lowercase letters. (When you purchase lists on disk, the text is often in all-uppercase letters.) Instead of wasting time retyping the information with the correct capitalization (for mailing labels, for example), you can use the @PROPER function to convert the text.

Figure 13-3 illustrates how you can use the @PROPER function to convert a list of names entered in all-uppercase letters to proper capitalization. You begin by entering the following formula in cell B2:

```
@PROPER(A2)
```

Then you use the /Copy command to copy this formula to the cell range B3..B12. The @PROPER function capitalizes all the entries correctly, with the exception of Pooh'S Corner, where the function mistakenly capitalizes the *S* that follows the apostrophe. (The @PROPER function uppercases the first letter of each word as well as any letter that does not follow another letter.) You need to edit this particular entry in the control panel.

After you use the @PROPER function, you need to convert the formulas with the @PROPER functions to their calculated values (labels, in this case) if you want to do any more processing to the entries. Suppose that you want to sort the entries. If you don't convert the formulas to values, 1-2-3 will sort the *formulas*. For example, it will sort @PROPER(A2) in cell B2, instead of the label H. Andersen.

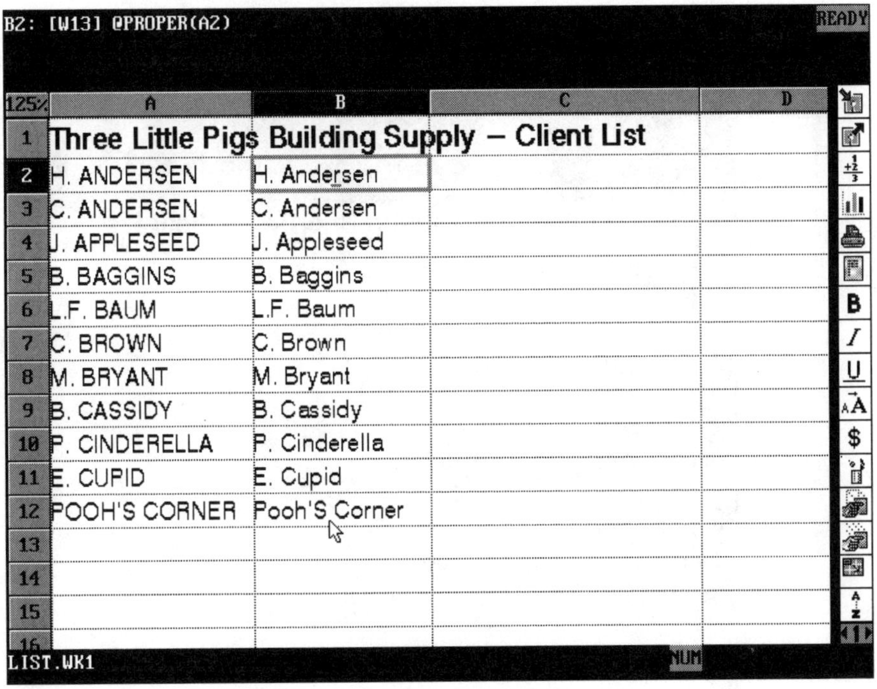

B2: [W13] @PROPER(A2)				READY
125%	A	B	C	D
1	Three Little Pigs Building Supply — Client List			
2	H. ANDERSEN	H. Andersen		
3	C. ANDERSEN	C. Andersen		
4	J. APPLESEED	J. Appleseed		
5	B. BAGGINS	B. Baggins		
6	L.F. BAUM	L.F. Baum		
7	C. BROWN	C. Brown		
8	M. BRYANT	M. Bryant		
9	B. CASSIDY	B. Cassidy		
10	P. CINDERELLA	P. Cinderella		
11	E. CUPID	E. Cupid		
12	POOH'S CORNER	Pooh'S Corner		
13				
14				
15				
16				
LIST.WK1			NUM	

Figure 13-3: Using the @PROPER function to edit capitalization.

To convert @PROPER formulas to the text they return, you use the **/R**ange Value command, which automatically converts all formulas to their calculated values when it copies them. To convert the formulas in the sample worksheet, follow these steps:

1. Choose **/R**ange Value.

2. Select the range B2..B12, which contains the @PROPER functions, in response to the Convert what: prompt.

3. Select cell A2 in response to the To where: prompt.

1-2-3 replaces the original range in all-uppercase letters with the properly capitalized text by copying the values in the range B2..B12 over the original entries in the range A2..A12. (Remember that 1-2-3 always replaces existing entries with new entries.)

Figure 13-4 shows the results of copying the values to the cell range A2..A12. Note that the contents of cell A2 on the top line of the control panel is 'H. Andersen, just as if you had typed it, rather than calculating it with a 1-2-3 function. After you copy the values to the range A2..A12, you can delete the formulas in the cell range B2..B12 with the **/R**ange **E**rase command and then edit the Pooh'S Corner entry in cell A12 before you save the worksheet.

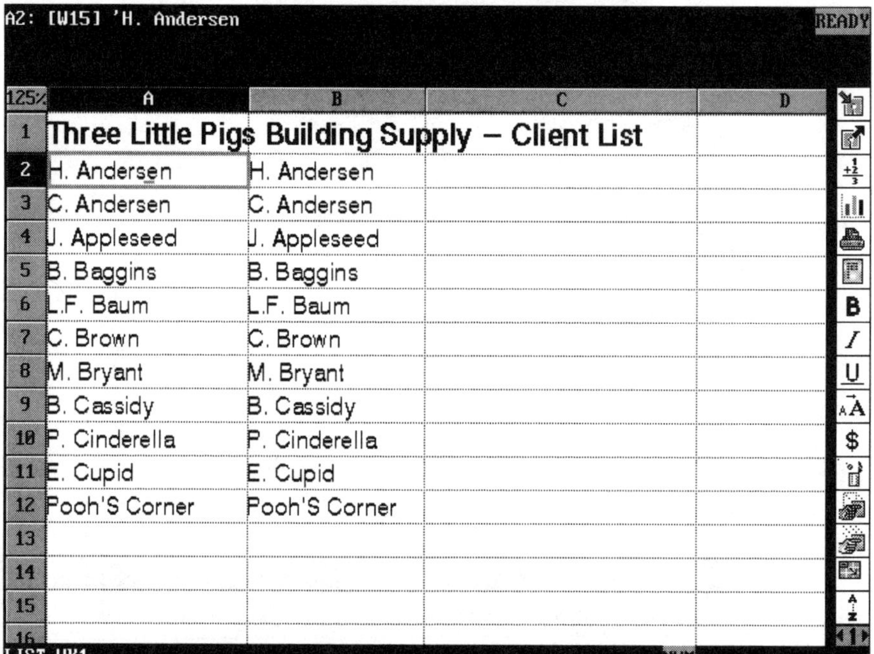

A2: [W15] 'H. Andersen				READY
125%	A	B	C	D
1	Three Little Pigs Building Supply – Client List			
2	H. Andersen	H. Andersen		
3	C. Andersen	C. Andersen		
4	J. Appleseed	J. Appleseed		
5	B. Baggins	B. Baggins		
6	L.F. Baum	L.F. Baum		
7	C. Brown	C. Brown		
8	M. Bryant	M. Bryant		
9	B. Cassidy	B. Cassidy		
10	P. Cinderella	P. Cinderella		
11	E. Cupid	E. Cupid		
12	Pooh'S Corner	Pooh'S Corner		
13				
14				
15				
16				
LIST.WK1			NUM	

Figure 13-4: Using **/R**ange **V**alue command to convert the formulas with the @PROPER function to labels.

In addition to the @PROPER function, 1-2-3 includes an @UPPER function and a @LOWER function.

✔ You use the @UPPER function to convert all the letters in a label entered into a cell to all-uppercase letters.

✔ You use the @LOWER function to convert all the letters in a label entered into a cell to all-lowercase letters.

✔ You need to convert the @UPPER or @LOWER formulas to their resulting labels if you want to perform further text-based operations, such as searching or sorting these cells.

Hey, Look Me Over!

The *special functions* category offers you a rather mixed bag of tricks. Some of the functions in this category return various kinds of information about where you are in a worksheet. (Computer whizzes primarily use these functions to keep track of the current position when they are running complex macros to process worksheet data. You don't need to worry about those functions just yet.)

The special functions category also includes lookup functions that have more practical uses for the average spreadsheet user. These functions can return particular information from a series or table of data in a worksheet. They can, for example, help the Second Little Pig find out the cost of 15 pounds of twigs.

The most common of these lookup functions are @VLOOKUP (for vertical lookup) and @HLOOKUP (for horizontal lookup). Both of these functions look up a particular value or text entry in a table and then return related information from the table. They differ in the way they do their work.

✔ The @VLOOKUP function moves vertically down the rows of the lookup table, hunting for matching information in the first column of the table.

✔ The @HLOOKUP function moves horizontally across the columns of the lookup table, hunting for matching information in the top row of the table.

To get an idea of how handy these lookup functions can be, consider how the Second Little Pig can use the @VLOOKUP function to return specific information to a worksheet. Figure 13-5 shows a simple vertical *lookup table* that relates the description and cost of various items, which are sold by the Three Little Pigs Building Supply company, to an item number. When you set up a vertical lookup table, such as the one shown in this figure, you always make sure that you place the information that you use to look up other information in the first (leftmost) column. In this case, because the Second Little Pig wants to be able to look up the description and cost of an item by its item code, he enters the item codes in the first column.

```
K1: {Bold} (G) [W8] ^Item #                                          READY
```

	K	L	M	N	O	P	Q	R	
1	Item #	Description	Cost						
2	3P1	sm. bunch wolfbane	1.00						
3	3P10	1lb. straw – loose	3.75						
4	3P11	5" steel nose ring	3.00						
5	3P12	1lb. herbal mud add.	4.50						
6	3P13	1 lb. thatch	8.00						
7	3P14	2 lb. thatch bundle	12.00						
8	3P15	10 plastic grommets	2.50						
9	3P16	5 yds. sand	16.00						
10	3P17	90 lb. bag piggy portland	12.00						
11	3P2	lg. bunch wolfbane	2.00						
12	3P3	10 roof sticks	3.50						
13	3P4	saw	24.25						
14	3P5	gloves	6.00						
15	3P6	trowel	2.00						
16	3P7	1 lb. sm. wall stones	0.50						
17	3P8	15 lb. twigs	6.00						
18	3P9	2 lb. bricks	4.00						
19									
20									

```
ITEMS.WK1                                                      NUM
```

Figure 13-5: The lookup table with the description and cost of items arranged by item number.

After you enter all the information in a lookup table, you then need to sort its data in ascending order, using the first column of the lookup table as the sorting key (see Chapter 8 for a complete rundown on sorting with the /Data Sort command; if you have the SmartIcons, see Chapter 11). Note in Figure 13-5 that the Second Little Pig has sorted the table in ascending order by item number. (At first glance, this table looks out of order because the information for item 3P10 immediately follows the information for item 3P1, instead of following the information for item 3P2 as you might expect. Because these item numbers mix text and numbers and are, therefore, entered as labels, rather than as numbers, 1-2-3 does not sort them according to the values they contain.)

After you create and sort the information in a vertical lookup table, you can use the @VLOOKUP function to return any of its information. The arguments for this function are as follows:

```
@VLOOKUP(x,range,column-offset)
```

The *x argument* in this example is the cell in the worksheet that contains the item number that the Second Little Pig wants to look up in the table shown in Figure 13-5.

The _range argument_ is the cell range that contains the lookup table data itself (excluding column headings). In this example, the cell range is K2..M18. However, to make things simpler, the Second Little Pig gave this cell range the name COST_TABLE, which he can use as the range argument instead of using the actual cell references.

The _column-offset argument_ indicates the column in the lookup table which contains the information that you want the @VLOOKUP function to return. To come up with the column-offset argument, you simply count (from left to right) to the column that contains the information you want returned and then you subtract 1 from this number (because the first column is always the lookup column). If, for example, the Second Little Pig wants to use the @VLOOKUP function to return the description of an item when he enters the item number, he enters **1** as the column-offset argument (because the descriptions are in the second column of the lookup table, and 2 – 1 = 1). If he wants to return the cost of the item, he enters **2** as the column-offset argument (because the cost is in the third column, and 3 – 1 = 2).

Figure 13-6 illustrates the use of the @VLOOKUP function to return both the description and the cost of an item by entering just the item code. Cell B3 contains the formula

```
@VLOOKUP(A3,$COST_TABLE,1)
```

This formula looks up the item code number that Mr. Pig entered in cell A3 (item code 3P8 in Figure 13-6) in the first column of the lookup table, which is named COST_TABLE (cell range K2..M18). To look up the item code number, it moves vertically down the rows. When 1-2-3 locates this item number in the lookup table, the @VLOOKUP function returns the description entered in the next column over in that row (15 lb. twigs for item number 3P8) to cell B3, the one containing the @VLOOKUP function.

The cost of the item is returned to cell C3 from the lookup table with a very similar formula that also uses the @VLOOKUP function:

```
@VLOOKUP(A3,$COST_TABLE,2)
```

The only difference between this formula in cell C3 and the formula in cell B3 is that this formula uses 2 as the column-offset argument, and, therefore, this formula returns the cost (6.00 for item number 3P8) because the cost column is two rows to the right of the lookup column with the item numbers.

By copying the formulas entered in cells B3 and C3 down their columns, Mr. Pig can continue to use the lookup table to find the description and cost for whatever item code he enters in column A. Note that the $ in front of the range name COST_TABLE converts the cell addresses in this named range to absolute values (as if the Second Little Pig had entered $K$2..$M$18) to prevent 1-2-3 from adjusting these references as he copies these formulas down the columns. (Each formula looks up information in the same table.)

```
B3: (G) [W19] @VLOOKUP(A3,$COST_TABLE,1)                          READY
```

	A	B	C		K	L	M
1	Three Little Pigs Building Supply			1	Item #	Description	Cost
2	*Item No.*	*Description*	*Cost*	2	3P1	sm. bunch wolfbane	1.00
3	3P8	15 lb. twigs _	$6.00	3	3P10	1lb. straw – loose	3.75
4				4	3P11	5" steel nose ring	3.00
5				5	3P12	1lb. herbal mud add.	4.50
6				6	3P13	1 lb. thatch	8.00
7				7	3P14	2 lb. thatch bundle	12.00
8				8	3P15	10 plastic grommets	2.50
9				9	3P16	5 yds. sand	16.00
10				10	3P17	90 lb. bag piggy portland	12.00
11				11	3P2	lg. bunch wolfbane	2.00
12				12	3P3	10 roof sticks	3.50
13				13	3P4	saw	24.25
14				14	3P5	gloves	6.00
15				15	3P6	trowel	2.00
16				16	3P7	1 lb. sm. wall stones	0.50
17				17	3P8	15 lb. twigs	6.00
18				18	3P9	2 lb. bricks	4.00
19				19			
20				20			

```
ITEMS.WK1                                              NUM
```

Figure 13-6: Using the @VLOOKUP function to return the description and cost of an item from the lookup table.

Logically Speaking

The *logical functions* are a rather small group that is noted primarily for black or white answers. Logical functions, you see, can return only one of two possible results: TRUE or FALSE. The most common and powerful of the logical functions is the @IF function. This function is particularly powerful because it can test for a particular condition in the worksheet and then use one value if the condition is true and another value if the condition is false.

To run a test with the @IF function in this way, you use the following arguments:

```
@IF(condition,x,y)
```

The *condition argument* can be any expression that, when evaluated, returns a TRUE or FALSE response.

✔ To indicate what value should be used when the *condition argument* is TRUE, you enter the *x argument* immediately after the *condition argument*.

✔ To indicate what value should be used when the *condition argument* is FALSE, you enter the *y argument* immediately after the *x argument*.

For example, you can test whether a value in one cell is greater than or equal to 0. Then if the value is greater than 0, copy that value, but if it isn't, enter the label, *You're in the Hole!* in the cell. Use this formula:

```
@IF(B2>=0,B2,"You're in the Hole!")
```

In this example, the @IF condition returns TRUE when B2 contains 0 or any larger value and returns FALSE when the value in this cell is anything less than 0. (Note: You might not want to use this label at the office!)

As another example, you can have 1-2-3 put the value 100 in the cell when B2 contains a value greater than or equal to 1000 and 50 in the cell when it is less than 1000. Enter this formula:

```
@IF(B2>=1000,100,50)
```

Alternatively, if you want 1-2-3 to put 10 percent of the value in B2 in the cell when B2 contains a value greater than or equal to 1000 and 5 percent of the value when the value is less than 1000, you enter this formula:

```
@IF(B2>=1000,B2*10%,B2*5%)
```

Although you usually want to have an @IF function enter or calculate a particular value depending upon whether the condition argument returns TRUE or FALSE, you also can have the @IF function enter alternative text, depending on the outcome. You do this by entering the different text alternatives as the x and y arguments of the @IF function. Suppose that you want 1-2-3 to enter the text *A grand or better* in the cell when B2 contains a value greater than or equal to 1000, but enter the text *Less than a grand* when B2 contains any lesser value. You enter the following formula:

```
@IF(B2>=1000,"A grand or better","Less than a grand")
```

Note that when you use text as the x and y arguments, you need to enclose the text in a pair of double quotation marks.

Figure 13-7 illustrates a typical use for the @IF function. Here Polly Pig is using the @IF function to calculate the price of a particular item, based on what it costs. If the item costs $5 or more, the markup is 75 percent. If the item costs less than $5, the markup is only 50 percent.

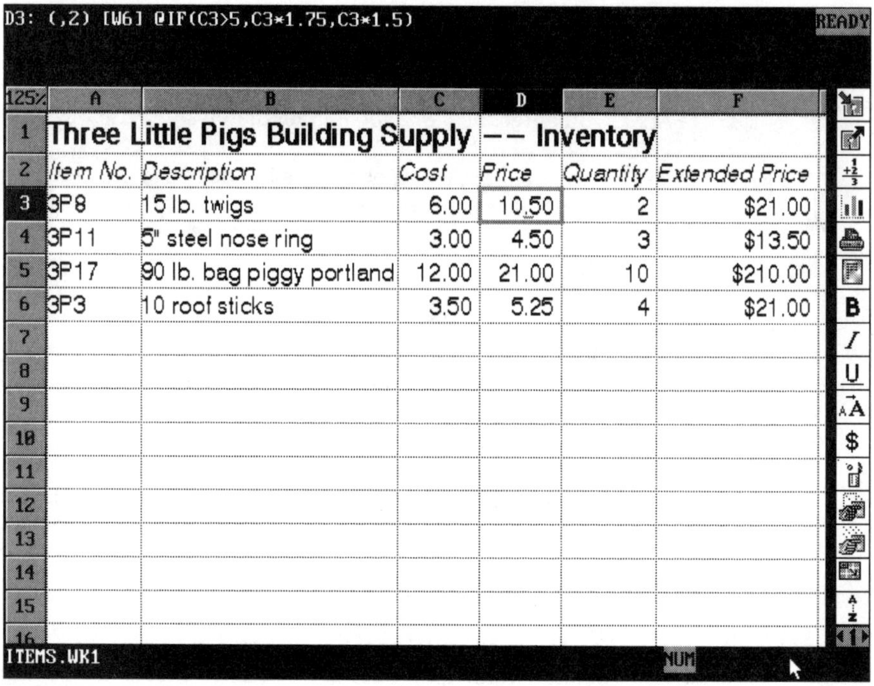

```
D3: (,2) [W6] @IF(C3>5,C3*1.75,C3*1.5)                          READY
```

125%	A	B	C	D	E	F	
1	Three Little Pigs Building Supply		-- Inventory				
2	Item No.	Description	Cost	Price	Quantity	Extended Price	
3	3P8	15 lb. twigs	6.00	10.50	2	$21.00	
4	3P11	5" steel nose ring	3.00	4.50	3	$13.50	
5	3P17	90 lb. bag piggy portland	12.00	21.00	10	$210.00	
6	3P3	10 roof sticks	3.50	5.25	4	$21.00	
7							
8							
9							
10							
11							
12							
13							
14							
15							
16							

```
ITEMS.WK1                                              NUM
```

Figure 13-7: Using the @IF function to determine the price of an item.

The formula for determining which markup percentage to use in calculating the
price is entered in cell D3:

```
@IF(C3>5,C3*1.75,C3*1.5)
```

In this formula, the condition argument, $C3>5$, tests whether the price entered
in cell C3 is greater than $5. If the value is greater than $5, 1-2-3 uses the x argument, $C3*1.75$ (1.75 because the price is the total cost plus a markup of 75
percent of that cost), and returns this calculated value to cell D3. If the value is
less than $5, 1-2-3 uses the y argument, $C3*1.50$ (total cost plus a markup of 50
percent of that cost), and returns this calculated value to cell D3. (In this particular example, the @IF function calculates the price in cell D3 according to the
x argument because the cost in cell C3 is 6.00.)

After Polly creates this @IF formula in cell D3, she can then copy it down column D to calculate the prices for the other items that she entered in this
worksheet based solely on the cost. In Figure 13-7, she has copied the formula
down to cell D6. There the @IF function sets the price according to the y argument because the cost in cell C6 is only 3.50.

Part VII
The Part of Tens

The 5th Wave   By Rich Tennant

GRIATENNANT

*Green Computing

Solar-powered Monitor

Recycled keyboard

SAVE OZONE

Wind-driven disk drive

Biodegradable mouse

* Comes bundled with Lettus 1·2·3 spreadsheet.

The part in which...

You get a taste of what it's like to perform a little creative accounting in 1-2-3 so that you always arrive at the same preconceived result, in this case, the number 10. Part VI is brought to you by the number 10.

As you would expect, each of the four chapters (I know, there should be ten) in Part VI (which should rightfully be Part X) contains ten key points (and don't think this didn't take some doing) that you can refer to as needed.

✔ Chapter 14 contains the 10 basic skills you use all the time in 1-2-3 (this may be all the information you really need, in which case, you won't have to waste time reading the rest of the boring chapters, giving you lots of time to spend with the cartoons).

✔ Chapter 15 contains the 10 Commandments of 1-2-3 (which were revealed to me in the parking lot at the end of a particularly grueling all-day Beginning 1-2-3 class).

✔ Chapter 16 contains the 10 "gotchas," those stupid little things in 1-2-3 that always seem to screw you up when you're new to the program.

✔ Chapter 17 contains 10 hints, which, if followed, are bound to make working with 1-2-3 much more productive and a heckuva lot more fun!

Chapter 14
Ten Beginner Basics

*I*f the ten basics listed here are all you ever master in 1-2-3, you'll still be light years ahead of your competition. When all is said and done, this list of 10 represents the skills essential to creating, preserving, and outputting worksheets with 1-2-3:

1. To start 1-2-3 from DOS, you type **123** and press Enter.

   To start 1-2-3 from the Lotus Access Menu, you type **lotus** and press Enter.

   If you get an error message telling you that your command was bogus, you're not in the right directory. Try changing to the directory with the 1-2-3 program files by typing **cd\123** (warning: this directory might be called something other than \123, like \123r23 or \123r24).

2. Before you can make a new entry in a cell, you must move the cell pointer to that cell, and the program must be in READY mode.

   1-2-3 accepts each cell entry either as a label or as a value. A label can be all text or a combination of text and numbers. A value can be a number or a formula that 1-2-3 can calculate. 1-2-3 determines the kind of entry by evaluating the first character you type and then going either into LABEL or VALUE mode. To enter a label that 1-2-3 would otherwise enter as a value, you precede it with a label prefix — the apostrophe (') if you want it left aligned, the circumflex (^) if you want it centered, or the quotation mark (") if you want it right aligned.

3. To enter a formula in a cell, you build the formula with the arithmetic operators + (for addition), – (for subtraction), * (for multiplication), / (for division), or ^ (for raising a value to a power), or you use one of the built-in functions.

   When entering a formula that begins with a reference to a cell address, remember to start the formula with a plus sign (+) to place 1-2-3 in VALUE mode.

   When entering a function, remember to start the function with the at symbol (@), separate each argument of the function with a comma, and enclose the list of arguments in a closed paired of parentheses. (A few functions, such as @NOW that don't require any arguments, don't use any parentheses.)

4. To change the alignment of labels after you've entered them, you choose the /**R**ange **L**abel command; choose the **L**eft, **C**enter, or **R**ight command; select the cell range; and press Enter.

   To format values after you've entered them, you choose /**R**ange **F**ormat followed by the particular format option you want to apply, select the cell range to be formatted, and press Enter.

5. To name a file when saving it the first time, you choose the /**F**ile **S**ave command and then type a new filename of up to eight characters (with no spaces). Don't bother to enter a filename extension; 1-2-3 will automatically add the extension *WK1* to whatever filename you enter.

   To save the worksheet in a directory different from the current one, you can either choose the /**F**ile **D**irectory command to change the current directory before you save the file, or type the complete pathname as part of the new filename.

6. To open a worksheet file so that you can edit or print it, you use the /**F**ile **R**etrieve command, select the filename on the third line of the control panel, and press Enter. (To switch to a full-screen listing of files in the current directory, press the F3 (Name) key.)

   If the file you want to work with is not in the current directory, you use the /**F**ile **D**irectory command to change the current directory before you choose the /**F**ile **R**etrieve command.

7. To edit the contents of a cell, move the cell pointer to that cell and press the F2 (Edit) key to return the cell's contents to the second line of the control panel. Use the arrow keys to move the cursor to the place in the text that needs to be changed and either delete or insert new characters. Press Enter to update the cell in the worksheet with your changes.

8. To print the data in your worksheet, you first need to define the cell range you want to print by choosing the /**P**rint **P**rinter **R**ange command and then selecting the cell range. (Be sure to include in the range any columns that contain spilled-over parts of labels from cells to the left.)

   After you select the print range, make sure that your printer is turned on and loaded with paper, and, if necessary, make sure that the print head is properly aligned with the top of the first page. Then choose the **A**lign and **G**o commands on the /**P**rint **P**rinter menu to start the printing.

   When the printing stops, choose the **P**age command on the /**P**rint **P**rinter menu to advance the printer to the top of the next form and eject the last page of the report.

9. To erase the worksheet screen so that you can begin work on a new worksheet, you choose the /**W**orksheet **E**rase **Y**es command.

   If you've made changes that you haven't saved in the worksheet currently on-screen, 1-2-3 beeps and displays a warning. To clear the screen without bothering to save the changes, you choose the **Y**es option. To return to the current worksheet so that you can save your changes before you clear the screen, choose the **N**o option.

Remember that the /Worksheet Erase command only deletes the version of the worksheet on-screen. To delete a worksheet on disk, you use the /File Erase command.

10. To quit 1-2-3 when you've finished your work session, you choose the /Quit Yes command.

If you've made changes that you haven't saved in the worksheet currently on-screen, 1-2-3 beeps and displays a warning. To quit 1-2-3 without saving these changes, you choose the Yes option. To return to the current worksheet so that you can save your changes before you quit the program, choose the No option.

After you quit 1-2-3, the DOS prompt (if you started the program with the **123** startup command) or the Lotus Access Menu (if you started the program with the **lotus** startup command) appears.

Chapter 15
Ten 1-2-3 Commandments

*I*n 1-2-3, just as in life itself, there are certain *shall's* and *shall not's* that, if followed *religiously*, make working with the program just *heavenly*. With this *doctrine* in mind, you should consider these 1-2-3 *Ten Commandments* as written in *stone*:

1. Thou shalt not spread wide thy data in thy worksheet, but rather thou shalt gather together thy tables of data and avoid skipping columns and rows unnecessarily so that thou mightest conserve the memory of thy computer.

2. Thou shalt not save thy worksheets in the same directory as that which containeth thy 1-2-3 program files.

3. Thou shalt save the changes to all thy worksheets with reverential regularity.

4. Thou shalt not enter, neither shalt thou copy nor move an entry into a cell which containeth already data, lest thou wishest to replace the data that existeth there already with that which thou bringest in.

5. Thou shalt enter all dates in thy worksheet as values with the @DATE function (and not as labels), thence thou shalt straightway format the results with thy **/R**ange Format **D**ate command.

6. Thou shalt not fall into temptation to useth the spacebar instead of the **/R**ange **E**rase command to eraseth the contents of a single cell.

7. Thou shalt enable the Undo feature and useth it immediately after thou committest any kind of transgression in thy worksheet.

8. Thou shalt not insert nor shalt thou delete columns or rows in the worksheet unless that thou first explorest those columns or rows in parts distant of thy worksheet and confirmest that no data there shall thereby be erased or otherwise displaced.

9. Thou shalt not start printing thy worksheet with the **G**o command except that thou hast first selected the **A**lign command on the **/P**rint **P**rinter menu.

10. Thou shalt always advance the paper in thy printer with the **L**ine or **P**age command on the **/P**rint **P**rinter menu rather than with thy hands, lest 1-2-3 messeth up the page breaks in thy printout, for verily I sayeth unto you that this shall surely come to pass.

Chapter 16
Ten Things That Always Get You

Although many of the workings of 1-2-3 are crystal clear from the get-go, the program does exhibit a few idiosyncrasies (all right, a bunch of them) that tend routinely to mess up new users. To help reduce your frustration level with 1-2-3 (hey, after all, it's only a spreadsheet), you need to get a handle on at least these ten things that tend to screw up, confuse, and otherwise play havoc with your efforts:

1. Certain entries start with a character (like a number) that put 1-2-3 into VALUE mode but then use characters (like letters) that the program won't accept in a value. As a result, 1-2-3 goes into EDIT mode as soon as you try to enter this mixture in the cell.

   Keep in mind that when making this kind of entry — like *123 Elm Street* — you must start the entry with one of the label prefixes (apostrophe) to get the program to accept your input.

2. In most (not all) 1-2-3 commands that use cell ranges, the program automatically anchors the range on the current cell. If you don't have the cell pointer in the correct cell when you choose the command, you must remember to press the Esc key before you move the pointer to the correct cell.

   If you fail to press Esc, 1-2-3 highlights all the cells you move through and adds them to the current range. After you unanchor the range and move the cell pointer to the correct cell, you can reanchor the range on that cell by typing the period.

3. When copying a single formula to a range of cells in the same column or row, you can too easily end up with no copies. This result occurs when you specify the same cell range in response to both the Copy what: and To where: prompts.

   Just remember to position the cell pointer in the cell that contains the formula you want to copy and then remember to press the Enter key right after you choose /Copy in response to the Copy what: prompt. Then anchor the range with the period key, move the cell pointer to extend the range so that it includes all the blank cells where the copies are to be made, and press Enter in response to the To where: prompt.

4. Selecting a range by using the keyboard: when you press the F4 (Abs) key before you choose your 1-2-3 or Wysiwyg command or select a SmartIcon, remember to press the Enter key after you highlight the cell range and before you choose your command.

If you don't press Enter, you will either end up replacing the range address with a / or : when you try to activate the menus or, in the case of the SmartIcons, nothing will happen to the selected range!

5. Certain /File commands like /File Save and /File Directory, to name a couple, expect you type in a filename or pathname or both on the second line of the control panel. Apparently, however, they don't provide you any place to do so. In the area where you would expect to enter the filename and pathname information after the prompt on the second line, you find the current pathname either by itself or terminating in *.wk1.

Although there doesn't seem to be any place to put the new information, you just have to make a leap of faith and start typing the filename and/or directory path you want to enter. As soon as you type your first character, 1-2-3 clears all or part of the information on the second line, giving you plenty of room in which to complete your entry.

6. When you use the /File Save command to save changes to a worksheet that's already been named, you just need to press Enter to save the changes with the current filename and pathname. Then when confronted with the Cancel, Replace, or Backup options, you must choose either Replace or Backup to instruct 1-2-3 to actually write the changes on the disk.

You choose the Cancel option only when you meant to change the name and/or the location of the updated worksheet file before you pressed Enter. Normally you choose the Replace option instead of Backup; save Backup for when you want the program to preserve a copy of the file, without the changes, using the same filename but with the BAK extension instead of WK1.

7. When creating more than one graph for your worksheet, be sure to name the first graph with the /Graph Name Create command before you start building the second one. If you do not use this naming rule, you won't be able to recall and display the first graph without having to re-create it. When naming a graph, you observe the same rules as when naming a range (up to 15 characters long with no spaces, and so on).

After you name the graph with this command, quit the /Graph menu and use /File Save to save the named graph as part of your worksheet file. To display a named graph and make it current (so that you can make changes to it or edit it), you choose the /Graph Name Use command and then select the name on the control panel.

8. Before you can print a graph with the PrintGraph program, remember that you must make it current and then save it as a special PIC file with the /Graph Save command. To identify the current graph, press the F10 (Graph) key or choose the /Graph View command. To make another graph current, choose the /Graph Name Use command and then choose its name on the third line of the control panel.

When saving the graph as a PIC file, observe the same file-naming rules as when saving a worksheet (up to 8 characters long with no spaces, and so on). If you are using the Wysiwyg add-in, remember that you can add either named graphs or graphs saved in PIC files to the worksheet with the **:G**raph **A**dd command. After you specify that the cell range that contains the graph is the print range (by using the **R**ange command on the **:P**rint menu), you can print the graphs with the **:P**rint **G**o command.

9. Your report may require that you specify a range of rows and/or columns that contain column and row headings as print borders so that you can identify the data on each page. When you use the **/P**rint **P**rinter **O**ptions **B**orders or **:P**rint **L**ayout **B**orders command, be sure that the print range you specify with either the **/P**rint **P**rinter **R**ange command or the **:P**rint **R**ange command excludes those rows and columns.

   If you don't exclude those rows and columns from the print range, the program will print border information twice on the first page of your report — as part of the borders and as part of the print range.

10. When sorting the records in a database with the **/D**ata **S**ort command, be sure that you do *not* include the first row of field names with the other records in the range you specify by using the **D**ata-**R**ange command. Otherwise, 1-2-3 will rearrange this row of information among the other records it sorts.

    However, when searching for records of a database with the Find, Extract, Unique, or **D**elete commands on the **/D**ata **Q**uery menu, be sure that you *do* include the first row of field names along with the other records in the range you specify with the **I**nput command. Otherwise, 1-2-3 will not have the foggiest notion to which of the fields in the database it should apply your selection criteria in the criteria range.

Chapter 17
Ten Tricks for Working
Faster and Smarter

*I*t's painful to see people wasting their time doing things the hard way when you know full well there are easier, more efficient methods in the software for getting the work done. Therefore, throughout this book I've chosen to teach you the most direct and productive methods for working in 1-2-3. Here, you'll find ten of the more important tricks that you should be using to make your work both more proficient and enjoyable:

1. If the end of the workday comes and you're not finished constructing your worksheet, place the cell pointer in the cell where you need to pick up work on the next day. Then save your worksheet; 1-2-3 saves the cell pointer's position as part of the file.

   When you open the worksheet the next day, the cell pointer will appear in the cell where you need to continue work (rather than cell A1) and you can get right to it!

2. If your worksheet gets so big that 1-2-3 slows down to a crawl every time you enter or edit information in a cell, it's time to turn off automatic recalculation by using the **/W**orksheet **G**lobal **R**ecalculation **M**anual command.

   Just remember that after you switch to manual recalculation, you must press the F9 (Calc) key to update the formulas in the worksheet before you save or print the file. You press F9 to ensure that the saved or printed worksheet contains the most up-to-date and correct information.

3. When working with a large worksheet that contains lots of tables of data spread all over the place, take the time to give each table a descriptive name by using the **/R**ange **N**ame **C**reate command. Then you can locate any table that needs editing right away, just by giving the range name after pressing the F5 (GoTo) key. Remember that you can also specify a particular table of data as the range to print by providing its range name after you choose the **/P**rint **P**rinter **R**ange command.

4. When using 1-2-3 or Wysiwyg commands that present you with a long list of names on the third line of the control panel (as happens when you choose the **/File Retrieve** or **/Graph Name Use** or **:Graph Add Named** command), remember that you can use the F3 (Name) key to switch to a full-screen listing. The full-screen list shows the names in as many columns as necessary for the length of the list. Often, it's easier to find a particular name in full-screen listing rather than in a long scrolling line, especially when you're dealing with many, many names.

Also remember that you can combine the F3 (Name) key with the F5 (GoTo) key to help you select the range you want in your worksheet. When you press F5 and then press F3, 1-2-3 displays all the range names on the third line of the control panel. (If you want to switch to a full-screen display, you need to press F3 a second time.) Then instead of typing the range name in response to the `Enter address to go to:` prompt, you can just select it in the list by highlighting it and pressing Enter.

5. If you start running low on computer memory (indicated by the flashing of the MEM indicator) and you still have more data to get in the worksheet, first try to free up enough memory to finish your data by turning off the Undo feature. Turn off Undo by using the **/Worksheet Global Default Other Undo Disable** command. Thereafter, be sure to save the worksheet often, especially before you make any major adjustments to the existing data.

If turning off Undo still doesn't free up enough memory, try dumping all the range names defined in the worksheet by using the **/Range Name Reset** command. If that still doesn't give you enough free memory to finish your data entry, you probably need to split up the data into more than one worksheet (or get your boss to buy more memory for your computer!).

6. When you need to compare distant parts of the same worksheet, remember that you can split the worksheet into two separate windows by using the **/Worksheet Window** command. Then you can scroll the different parts into view in each window. When the areas you're comparing use more columns than rows, use the **Horizontal** command to split the screen at a particular row. When the areas take up more rows than columns, use the **Vertical** command to split the screen at a particular column.

While the screen is split, you use the F6 (Window) key to move the cell pointer from window to window. Normally, 1-2-3 synchronizes scrolling in the direction of the split (horizontally with **Horizontal** windows, vertically with **Vertical** windows). If you find that this type of synchronization prevents you from displaying both areas in the worksheet on-screen at the same time, choose the **/Worksheet Window Unsync** command and then try scrolling the different parts into view.

7. When you're working with a table of data that uses more columns or rows than fit in one screen view, remember that you can use the **/Worksheet Titles** command to freeze the table's column and/or row headings on-screen. With frozen headings, you can always tell what you're dealing with as you scroll new columns and rows into view.

To freeze rows of column headings, place the cell pointer somewhere in the row right below the last row you want to freeze and choose the Horizontal command on the /Worksheet Titles menu.

To freeze columns of row headings, place the cell pointer somewhere in the column immediately to the right of the last column you want to freeze and choose the **Vertical** command on the /Worksheet Titles menu.

To freeze both rows and columns of headings, place the cell pointer in the intersecting cell of the row right below that last row to be frozen and the column immediately to the right of the last column to be frozen; then choose the **Both** command on the /Worksheet Titles menu.

8. When you want to include information, such as a report title, today's date, or the current page number on each page of a printout, put it in a header or footer by using the /Print Printer Options Header or Footer command (a header when you want it to appear at the top of each page or a footer when you want it to appear at the bottom of each page).

   When you want to print information that identifies data, such as rows or columns at the top and left edge of a worksheet table, define these columns and rows as borders by using the /Print Printer Options Borders command. The borders will then print on each page of your document.

9. Use Wysiwyg, whenever possible, to print any reports that need to run the long way on the page or that need to be compressed so that the entire print range fits on a single page.

   Remember that before you can use Wysiwyg to print a report, you must select the cell range to be printed by using the :Print Range command after you attach the Wysiwyg add-in program. Also keep in mind that when you print with Wysiwyg, you can add the cell grid lines or the worksheet frame to any printout simply by selecting the Grid or Frame command followed by the Yes option on the :Print Settings menu.

10. Don't forget about using macros to automate repetitive tasks and boost your productivity. You can record the keystrokes you use to perform a particular worksheet task (the kind of task you find yourself doing over and over again) and then use the macro instead of the individual keystrokes each time you need to perform the task. You can end up saving bunches of valuable time.

    Not only do macros perform tasks faster than you can, they also ensure that the routine goes exactly the same way each and every time the task is performed. This advantage can significantly cut down on the number of errors in a worksheet, thus reducing the time you spend in checking the worksheet and making you even more productive!

Glossary

. . . .

absolute cell reference

A cell reference that 1-2-3 cannot automatically adjust. If you're about to copy a formula and you want to prevent 1-2-3 from adjusting one or more of the cell references (the program has a tendency to change the column and row reference in copies), make the cell references absolute. Absolute cell references are indicated by a dollar sign (yes, a $) in front of the column letter and the row number — $K$11, for example. You can convert a relative reference to an absolute reference with the F4 key. See also **relative cell reference.**

arguments

Not what you have with your boss but rather the values that you give to a worksheet function to compute. Arguments are enclosed in parentheses and separated from one another by commas. See also **function.**

borders

The types of lines the 1-2-3 add-in program called Wysiwyg can draw around the edges of each cell or the outside edge of a bunch of cells. Wysiwyg offers a wide variety of different line styles and colors for this purpose. See also **Wysiwyg.**

cell

The basic building block of plant and animal life and also of the 1-2-3 worksheet. The worksheet cell is a block formed by the intersections of a column and a row in the sheet. Cells store all worksheet data. Each cell is identified by the letter of its column and the number of its row. See also **cell reference.**

cell pointer

The highlight that indicates which cell in the worksheet is selected. You must move the cell pointer to a particular cell before you can enter or edit information in that cell.

cell range

A bunch of cells that are right next to each other. To select a range of cells with the keyboard, you type a period to anchor the range on the current cell and then press the arrow keys or other keys that move the cell pointer to highlight the range. To select a cell range with the mouse, you simply point at the beginning of the range, click the mouse button, and drag through the cells. See also **drag.**

cell reference

The location of a cell in the worksheet; also known as the *cell address.* The cell reference consists of the column letter followed by the row number. For example, B3 indicates the cell in the second column and third row of the worksheet. When you place the cell pointer in a cell, 1-2-3 displays its cell reference in the control panel. See also **relative cell reference** and **absolute cell reference.**

check box

The box that turns an option on or off in a dialog box. If the check box contains an X (sorry, not a check mark), the option is turned on. If the check box is blank, the option is turned off. The nice thing about check boxes is that you can select more than one of the multiple options presented as a group.

click

The simplest mouse technique. You press and immediately release the mouse button. See also *drag.*

command button

A dialog-box button that initiates an action. A command button with an ellipsis (. . .) opens another dialog box or window. Frequently, after you choose options in the dialog box, you choose the OK or Cancel command button.

control panel

The first three lines of the 1-2-3 screen that contain the information about the current cell and the program mode. The control panel also displays the menus and command prompts. See also *mode indicator.*

criteria range

A special area you set up for a database worksheet that indicates what information 1-2-3 is to locate for you in the database.

cursor

The blinking underline that indicates your current location in the text in the control panel. The cursor shows you where the next character you type will appear or where the next one you delete will disappear!

database

A tool for organizing, managing, and retrieving large amounts of information. You create a database right on a worksheet. The first row of the database contains column headings called *field names,* which identify each

item of information you are tracking (like First Name, Last Name, City, and the like). Below the field names, you enter the information you want to store for each field (column) of each record. See also *field* and *record.*

default

(Don't be alarmed; we're not talking blame here.) A setting, value, or response that 1-2-3 automatically provides unless you choose something else. You can change and rearrange many defaults with the /**W**orksheet **G**lobal **D**efault commands.

dialog box

A box containing various options that appears when you select certain 1-2-3 commands in Release 2.3 and 2.4 of the program. The choices in a dialog box are presented in groups of buttons and boxes. (Oh, boy!) A dialog box can also display warnings and messages. See also *check box, command button, option button,* and *text box.*

drag

(Has nothing to do with your job.) A mouse technique for selecting a range of cells. You place the cell pointer in the first cell and then press and hold down the left mouse button as you move the pointer through the cells in the range. As you drag, 1-2-3 highlights the cells. When the entire range is highlighted, release the left mouse button. See also *cell range* and *mouse pointer.*

error value

A value, ERR, that 1-2-3 displays in a cell when it cannot calculate the formula for that cell. Error values have the nasty habit of spreading to all worksheet formulas that refer, either directly or indirectly, to the cell that first returns this ERR thing!

field

A column in a 1-2-3 database that tracks just one type of item (like a city, state, ZIP code, and so on). See also **database.**

file

The place on disk where you store the information you generate in 1-2-3. To save the information in your worksheet with the /File Save command, you must name the file in accordance with the horrid DOS naming conventions. To retrieve a document with the /File Retrieve command so that you can do more work on it or print it, you have to remember the name you gave the document.

font

Shapes for characters. A typeface. Fonts have a point size and typeface as in Bitstream Swiss 12 point. You can pick and choose new fonts for displaying information in your 1-2-3 worksheet when you are running the Wysiwyg add-in with the :Format Font command. See also **Wysiwyg.**

footer

Information you specify to be printed in the bottom margin of each page of a printed report. See also **header.**

formula

(Ready for some math anxiety?) A sequence of values, cell references, names, functions, or operators that is contained in a cell and produces a new value from existing values — in other words, a mathematical expression. Formulas in 1-2-3 normally begin with the plus sign (+).

function

(Let's see, I know what disfunction is. . .) Simplifies and shortens lengthy calculations. Functions have built-in formulas that use a series of values called arguments to perform the specified operations and return the results. All functions in 1-2-3 begin with the at symbol (@). See also **arguments.**

graph

A pictorial representation of values stored in a worksheet. Graphs you create can be viewed in 1-2-3 but must be printed with a separate PrintGraph program unless you are running Wysiwyg. Wysiwyg enables you to add graphs right in the worksheet and print them as well. See also **Wysiwyg.**

header

Information you specify to be printed in the top margin of each page of a printed report. See also **footer.**

label

One of the two types of data you can store in a cell. A label consists of text or a combination of text and values preceded by a *label prefix* that determines how the label is aligned. If your entry begins with a letter, punctuation mark, or space, 1-2-3 adds the apostrophe label prefix for you. Type your own label prefix to force a value into a cell as a label. See also **value.**

label prefix

An initial character that indicates how the characters that follow it are aligned in the cell. The apostrophe (') is the default label prefix that left aligns the label. The circumflex (^) centers the label. The quotation mark (") right aligns the label. The backslash (\) repeats the label across the entire cell.

macro

A sequence of recorded keystrokes that perform frequently used, repetitive tasks and calculations. At the touch of a couple keystrokes, 1-2-3 can play back the steps in the macro much faster than is humanly possible.

menu

A horizontal list of commands that appears on the second line of the control panel. You can apply a command to the current cell, cell range, or worksheet. To activate the 1-2-3 command menus, you press slash (/). To activate the Wysiwyg command menus, you press colon (:). To choose a menu item, type its first letter. Using the mouse, you display the menus by positioning the mouse pointer anywhere in the control panel; you choose a command by clicking on it (click the left mouse button). To switch back and forth between the 1-2-3 and Wysiwyg menus when one of them is displayed, you click the right mouse button. See also **Wysiwyg.**

mode indicator

The indicator on the right side of the first line of the control panel that keeps you informed of the current state of the program. The default mode is READY, which allows you to move the cell pointer to a new cell and enter information in the worksheet.

mouse pointer

The indicator of your position on-screen as you move the mouse on your desk. Normally in 1-2-3, when Wysiwyg is not attached, the mouse pointer appears as a rectangular block-type shape. When you attach Wysiwyg, the mouse pointer assumes the shape of an arrowhead pointing up to the left. See also **click, drag,** and **Wysiwyg.**

option button

The button that chooses among dialog box items which contain mutually exclusive options. You can choose only one of the item's options at a time. When you choose an option button, 1-2-3 places an asterisk inside the pair of parentheses in front of the option name (*).

pointing

The method of selecting a cell or cell range to automatically record the cell reference(s) in a formula you are entering in the control panel.

record

A single row in a database that defines one entity (like an employee, a client, or a sales transaction). See also **database.**

relative cell reference

The normal cell reference (like A2) that is automatically adjusted when you copy formulas that refer to the cell. Row references are adjusted when you copy up or down; column references are adjusted when you copy to the left or right. See also **absolute cell reference** and **cell reference.**

SmartIcon

A small button with a picture (icon) that represents the action initiated when you click on the button. When you attach the Icons add-in program, SmartIcons are organized into palettes that appear in a single column on the right side of the worksheet. To switch to a new palette of SmartIcons, you simply click on the arrow to the left or right of the palette number at the bottom of the current palette, or you press the function keys assigned to the Icons add-in and then press the ← or → keys. You can choose an icon on the current palette with the keyboard by pressing the ↑ or ↓ key until the icon is highlighted and then pressing Enter.

spreadsheet

A type of computer program that enables you to develop and perform all sorts of calculations between the text and values stored in a document. Most spreadsheet programs like 1-2-3 also include graphing and database capabilities. Spreadsheet is commonly used as an alternate term for worksheet — so, see also *worksheet.*

status line

The last line of the 1-2-3 screen that displays the current date and time, or the name of the current file on the left and various status indicators on the right. These status indicators tell you when certain keys or modes are engaged, such as CAPS or NUM when you press the Caps Lock or Num Lock keys or UNDO when the Undo feature is active.

text box

The area in a dialog box where you type a new selection or edit the current one. Text boxes in 1-2-3 dialog boxes appear as square brackets containing dots that represent blank spaces you can fill in. A text box follows the name of the text box option.

value

One of two types of entries you can make in a worksheet. A value consists of numbers or a formula that is calculated. A value always begins with one of the following characters:

$$0\ 1\ 2\ 3\ 4\ 5\ 6\ 7\ 8\ 9 + -, (\ @\ \#\ \$$$

See also *label.*

worksheet

Also called a *spreadsheet;* the primary document for recording, analyzing, and calculating data. The 1-2-3 worksheet is organized in a series of 256 columns and 8,192 rows, making for a heck of a lot of cells!

Wysiwyg

(What-You-See-Is-What-You-Get; pronounced whizzy-wig). A 1-2-3 add-in program that, when attached, gives the program a whole new graphical look. It displays, among other things, fonts and font attributes, cell borders, and shading as they will print and enables you to incorporate 1-2-3 graphs and other compatible graphic images right in the worksheet. Wysiwyg also includes a host of printing commands that give you a great deal of control over printed reports.

Index

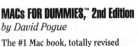

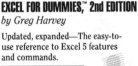

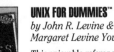

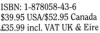

IDG BOOKS

Order Form

Order Center: (800) 762-2974 (8 a.m.-5 p.m., PST, weekdays) or (415) 312-0650

For Fastest Service: Photocopy This Order Form and FAX it to: (415) 358-1260

Quantity	ISBN	Title	Price	Total

Shipping & Handling Charges

Subtotal	U.S.	Canada & International	International Air Mail
Up to $20.00	Add $3.00	Add $4.00	Add $10.00
$20.01-40.00	$4.00	$5.00	$20.00
$40.01-60.00	$5.00	$6.00	$25.00
$60.01-80.00	$6.00	$8.00	$35.00
Over $80.00	$7.00	$10.00	$50.00

In U.S. and Canada, shipping is UPS ground or equivalent.
For Rush shipping call (800) 762-2974.

Subtotal _____

CA residents add
applicable sales tax _____

IN and MA residents add
5% sales tax _____

IL residents add
6.25% sales tax _____

RI residents add
7% sales tax _____

Shipping _____

Total _____

Ship to:

Name _____

Company _____

Address _____

City/State/Zip_____

Daytime Phone _____

Payment: ❑ Check to IDG Books (US Funds Only) ❑ Visa ❑ Mastercard ❑ American Express

Card# _____ Exp._____ Signature_____

Please send this order form to: IDG Books, 155 Bovet Road, Suite 310, San Mateo, CA 94402.

Allow up to 3 weeks for delivery. Thank you!

IDG BOOKS WORLDWIDE REGISTRATION CARD

RETURN THIS REGISTRATION CARD FOR FREE CATALOG

Title of this book: 1-2-3 For Dummies

My overall rating of this book: ❑ Very good [1] ❑ Good [2] ❑ Satisfactory [3] ❑ Fair [4] ❑ Poor [5]

How I first heard about this book:

❑ Found in bookstore; name: [6] _____

❑ Book review: [7]

❑ Advertisement: [8]

❑ Catalog: [9]

❑ Word of mouth; heard about book from friend, co-worker, etc.: [10]

❑ Other: [11]

What I liked most about this book:

_____

_____

What I would change, add, delete, etc., in future editions of this book:

_____

_____

Other comments:

_____

_____

Number of computer books I purchase in a year: ❑ 1 [12] ❑ 2-5 [13] ❑ 6-10 [14] ❑ More than 10 [15]

I would characterize my computer skills as: ❑ Beginner [16] ❑ Intermediate [17] ❑ Advanced [18] ❑ Professional [19]

I use ❑ DOS [20] ❑ Windows [21] ❑ OS/2 [22] ❑ Unix [23] ❑ Macintosh [24] ❑ Other: [25]_____
(please specify)

I would be interested in new books on the following subjects:
(please check all that apply, and use the spaces provided to identify specific software)

❑ Word processing: [26]

❑ Spreadsheets: [27]

❑ Data bases: [28]

❑ Desktop publishing: [29]

❑ File Utilities: [30]

❑ Money management: [31]

❑ Networking: [32]

❑ Programming languages: [33]

❑ Other: [34]

I use a PC at (please check all that apply): ❑ home [35] ❑ work [36] ❑ school [37] ❑ other: [38] _____

The disks I prefer to use are ❑ 5.25 [39] ❑ 3.5 [40] ❑ other: [41]_____

I have a CD ROM: ❑ yes [42] ❑ no [43]

I plan to buy or upgrade computer hardware this year: ❑ yes [44] ❑ no [45]

I plan to buy or upgrade computer software this year: ❑ yes [46] ❑ no [47]

Name: _____ Business title: [48] _____ Type of Business: [49] _____

Address (❑ home [50] ❑ work [51] /Company name: _____)

Street/Suite# _____

City [52] /State [53] /Zipcode [54] : _____ Country [55] _____

❑ **I liked this book!** You may quote me by name in future
IDG Books Worldwide promotional materials.

My daytime phone number is _____

IDG BOOKS

THE WORLD OF
COMPUTER
KNOWLEDGE

❏ # YES!

Please keep me informed about IDG's World of Computer Knowledge.
Send me the latest IDG Books catalog.